Googled

Ken Auletta, one of the pre-eminent US-based business journalists of the past thirty years, has written the Annals of Communications column for *The New Yorker* since 1992. He is the author of ten books, including four US bestsellers: *Three Blind Mice: How the TV Networks Lost Their Way*; *Greed and Glory on Wall Street: The Fall of the House of Lehman* and *World War 3.0: Microsoft and Its Enemies*. He lives in Manhattan with his wife, the agent Amanda Urban.

ALSO BY KEN AULETTA:

Googled

THE END OF THE WORLD AS WE KNOW IT

BY KEN AULETTA

Published by Virgin Books 2010

2 4 6 8 10 9 7 5 3 1

Copyright © Ken Auletta 2009

Ken Auletta has asserted his right under the Copyright, Designs
and Patents Act 1988 to be identified as the author of this work.

First published in the USA in 2009 by The Penguin Press,
a member of Penguin Group (USA) Inc.

First published in Great Britain in 2010 by
Virgin Books
Random House, 20 Vauxhall Bridge Road,
London SW1V 2SA

www.virginbooks.com
www.rbooks.co.uk

Addresses for companies within The Random House Group Limited can be found at:
www.randomhouse.co.uk/offices.htm

The Random House Group Limited Reg. No. 954009

A CIP catalogue record for this book
is available from the British Library

Trade paperback ISBN 9780753522660

The Random House Group Limited supports The Forest Stewardship Council [FSC], the
leading international forest certification organisation. All our titles that are printed on
Greenpeace-approved FSC-certified paper carry the FSC logo.
Our paper procurement policy can be found at www.rbooks.co.uk/environment

Mixed Sources
Product group from well-managed
forests and other controlled sources
www.fsc.org Cert no. TT-COC-2139
© 1996 Forest Stewardship Council

Designed by Nicole Laroche

Printed and bound in Great Britain by
CPI Mackays, Chatham ME5 8TD

For Kate and Mike

CONTENTS

PART THREE

Google Versus the Bears

PART FOUR

Googled

The world has been Googled. We don't search for information, we "Google" it. Type a question in the Google search box, as do more than 70 percent of all searchers worldwide, and in about a half second answers appear. Want to find an episode of *Charlie Rose* you missed, or a funny video made by some guy of his three-year-old daughter's brilliant ninety-second synopsis of *Star Wars: Episode IV*? Google's YouTube, with ninety million unique visitors in March 2009—two-thirds of all Web video traffic—has it. Want to place an online ad? Google's DoubleClick is the foremost digital advertising services company. Google's advertising revenues—more than twenty billion dollars a year—account for 40 percent of all the advertising dollars spent online. In turn, Google pumps ad dollars into tens of thousands of Web sites, bringing both traffic and commerce to them. Want to read a newspaper or magazine story from anywhere in the world? Google News aggregates twenty-five thousand news sites daily. Looking for an out-of-print book or a scholarly journal? Google is seeking to make almost every book ever published available in digitized form. Schools in impoverished nations that are without textbooks can now retrieve knowledge for free. "The Internet," said Google's chief economist, Hal Varian, "makes information available. Google makes information accessible."

Google's uncorporate slogan—"Don't be evil"—appeals to Americans who embrace underdogs like Apple that stand up to giants like Microsoft. Google's is one of the world's most trusted corporate brands. Among traditional media companies—from newspapers and magazines to book publishers, television, Hollywood studios, advertising agencies, telephone companies, and Microsoft—no company inspires more awe, or more fear.

There are sound reasons for traditional media to fear Google. Today, Google's software initiatives encroach on every media industry, from telephone to television to advertising to newspapers to magazines to book publishers to Hollywood studios to digital companies like Microsoft, Amazon, Apple, or eBay. For companies built on owning and selling or distributing that information, Google can be perceived as the new "Evil Empire."

Google is run by engineers, and engineers are people who ask why: Why must we do things the way they've always been done? Why shouldn't all the books ever published be digitized? Why shouldn't we be able to read any newspaper or magazine online? Why can't we watch television for free on our computers? Why can't we make copies of our music or DVDs and share them with friends? Why can't advertising be targeted and sold without paying fat fees to the media middleman? Why can't we make phone calls more cheaply? Google's leaders are not cold businessmen; they are cold engineers. They are scientists, always seeking new answers. They seek a construct, a formula, an algorithm that both graphs and predicts behavior. They naïvely believe that most mysteries, including the mysteries of human behavior, are unlocked with data. Of course, Wall Street's faith in such mathematical models for derivatives helped cripple the American economy.

Naïveté and passion make a potent mix; combine the two with power and you have an extraordinary force, one that can effect great change for good or for ill. Google fervently believes it has a mission. "Our goal is to change the world," Google's CEO, Eric Schmidt, told me. Making money, he continued, "is a technology to pay for it."

I came away from two and a half years of reporting on Google believing that its leaders genuinely want to make the world a better place. But they are in business to make money. Making money is not a dirty goal; nor is it a philanthropic activity. Any company with Google's power needs to be scrutinized. I also came away impatient with companies that spend too much time whining about Google and too little time devising an offense. Most old media companies were inexcusably slow to wake to the digital disruption.

In 2007, Eric Schmidt told me that one day Google could become a hundred-billion-dollar media company—more than twice the size of Time Warner, the Walt Disney Company, or News Corporation, the world's three largest media conglomerates. That Google might achieve this goal in less than a generation, in a time when copyright and privacy practices are being upended, when newspapers are declaring bankruptcy and in-depth journalism is endangered, when the profit margins of book publishers are squeezed along with their commitment to serious authors, when broadcast television networks dilute their programming with less expensive reality shows and unscripted fare, when cable news networks talk more than they listen, when the definitions of *community* and *privacy* are being redefined, and the way citizens read and process information is being altered, and when most traditional media models are being reconfigured by digital companies like Google—all this means that it's important to put Google under the microscope.

Brilliant engineers are at the core of the success of a company like Google. Drill down, as this book attempts to, and you'll see that engineering is a potent tool to deliver worthwhile efficiencies, and disruption as well. Google takes seriously its motto, "Don't be evil." But because we're dealing with humans not algorithms, intent sometimes matters less than effect. A company that questions everything and believes in acting without asking for permission has succeeded like few companies before. Unlike most technologies that disrupted existing business—the printed book that replaced scrolls, the telephone that replaced the telegraph, the automobile that replaced the horse and buggy, the airplane that supplanted cruise ships, the computer that supplanted typewriters—Google

search produces not a tangible product but something abstract: knowledge. This makes Google both less and more vulnerable to challenge.
Less because Google's prodigious Mount Everest of data is unrivaled.
More because Google depends for its continued success on users and
governments that trust it will not abuse this knowledge. Whether one
applauds or fears this eleven-year-old company, there is no question that
Google demands our attention.

PART ONE

Different Planets

CHAPTER ONE

Messing with the Magic

With his suit and tie and closely cropped gray hair, Mel Karmazin stood out as he crossed the Google campus in Mountain View, California, passing people in baggy T-shirts holding their laptops before them like waiters' trays. On this sunny June day in 2003, Google was nearly five years old, and Karmazin was among the first major executives from the old media to visit its headquarters. As the President of Viacom, he represented the world's then fourth-largest media company—the owner of the CBS network, of TV and radio stations, Paramount Studios, MTV and its sister cable networks, Simon & Schuster publishers, and an outdoor advertising concern, among other holdings. Short and pugnacious, Karmazin was by his own admission "always paranoid" about competitors. Two of Viacom's biggest competitors, AOL and Time Warner, had merged to forge the world's largest media conglomerate, and Karmazin was on the prowl for new business partners.

The son of a Queens cab driver, Karmazin, then fifty-nine, had begun his career at age seventeen selling radio advertising. He was said to be so pushy that advertisers capitulated just so he would leave their offices. He became a master salesman who did not play golf or tennis or tolerate long books, and whose idea of fun was pitching advertisers and Wall Street. He was an old-fashioned, show-me-the-money guy, and he was skeptical of Silicon Valley companies that boasted of their traffic and page views, but were mum about their balance sheets. At the time of his visit, Google was a private company, and he had no way of knowing whether it was making or losing money, or even how many employees it had. The actual financial figures—the January before Karmazin's visit Google's private books revealed 2002 revenues of $439.5 million and a profit of $99.6 million— would be unimposing figures to a man accustomed to dealing in billions. Nevertheless, a trusted associate, an Allen & Company investment banker, Nancy B. Peretsman, had convinced Karmazin that Google was a wave maker. She joined him and Viacom's then chief financial officer, Richard J. Bressler, on the trip.

Karmazin's destination that day was Building 21 at 2400 Bayshore Parkway, offices Google had acquired from the giant computer and software vendor Sun Microsystems. The two-story building shaded by trees was called the Googleplex, home to the company's engineers and separate from the building housing Google's finance and sales staff. Just outside the conference room on the second floor the visitors paused before a twenty-one-inch CRT monitor resting on a small table, which displayed a rotating three-dimensional globe flashing with bursts of colored light, each burst representing millions of Google searches being conducted all over the world. The screen was dark only in places like central Africa and Siberia, where the lack of electricity precluded searches. A second monitor showed samples of the search queries being conducted around the globe at that moment. "You realized the power of it," said Bressler. "And at the same time, you walked into this ratty conference room."

Waiting to greet them in the cramped Yellow Room was Google cofounder Larry Page, then thirty. With jet-black eyebrows, short black hair pushed down on his forehead, a permanent five-o'clock shadow, dark eyes that often remain fixed on the floor, and wearing a dark T-shirt and jeans, he seemed strange to Karmazin, as he does to many who meet him for the

first time. He was stonily silent. Sitting next to Page was Google CEO
Eric Schmidt, whose shirt and tie, frameless glasses, and relatively old
age—he was then forty-eight—were more welcoming. "Eric looked like
me," said Karmazin. Google's cofounder, Sergey Brin, born the same year
as Page, arrived late and out of breath in a T-shirt, gym shorts, and on
Rollerblades.

Karmazin began the meeting with what he thought was a joke: "Don't
worry, guys, I'm not here to buy you!" Over the next several hours, the
three computer scientists and the mogul sat in mismatched chairs on a tan
and soiled shaggy carpet, discussing their respective businesses. Schmidt
and Brin did most of the talking, and they spent as much time speaking of
Google's culture—engineers who always worked in teams and were given
a sense of freedom, three free and healthy meals a day, free massages, hair-
cuts, and medical attention—as about technology.

As they adjourned for lunch, Karmazin, walking past offices crowded
with engineers and dodging colored physio balls used for stretching or as
chairs for staff meetings, saw the evidence. Lunch was served in the employee café—six white Formica tables surrounded by metal folding chairs—
where free buffet meals were dispensed daily by Charlie Ayers, whom the
Google founders proudly introduced as the former chef for the Grateful
Dead. To Karmazin, a corporate belt-tightener who had endeared himself
to Wall Street by selling the Picassos off the walls of CBS headquarters, the
perks seemed extravagant. Google's corporate mission statement proclaims
an aim "to organize the world's information and make it universally accessible and useful." It quickly became apparent that Sergey Brin and Larry
Page saw themselves as missionaries. Karmazin's only corporate mission is
to make money.

Schmidt and Brin explained that Google was a digital Switzerland, a
"neutral" search engine that favored no content company and no advertisers. Their search results were "objective," based on secret algorithms, and
no one could bribe his way to the top of a search. They explained how
search worked. The speed of each search—now averaging about a half
second to answer each query—relied on an elaborate infrastructure.
Google in 2002 had scanned or indexed 3.1 billion Web pages, about 80

percent of what was then the World Wide Web. These pages were stored in a giant database and indexed by subject. Google software distributed each query among many hundreds of thousands of PCs and servers that are stacked in data centers and which work in tandem, simultaneously collecting different document links. The search is accelerated because Google stores on its servers three copies of its previous searches. Thus, Google does not have to scan the entire Web each time the same question is asked.

When a question is typed into the Google search box, the task is to divine the searcher's intention: when you wrote "Jobs" in the query box, did you mean *employment* or *Steve Jobs*? The query may produce thousands of links, but the promise of Google—what Google considers its secret sauce—is that the ones that appear near the top of the search results will be more relevant to you. The company's algorithms not only rank those links that generate the most traffic, and therefore are presumed to be more reliable, they also assign a slightly higher qualitative ranking to more reliable sources—like, for instance, a *New York Times* story. By mapping how many people click on a link, or found it interesting enough to link to, Google determines whether the link is "relevant" and assigns it a value. This quantified value is known as PageRank, after Larry Page.

All this was interesting enough, but where the Google executives really got Karmazin's attention was when they described the company's advertising business, which accounted for almost all its revenues. Google offered to advertisers a program called AdWords, which allowed potential advertisers to bid to place small text ads next to the results for key search words. Nike and Adidas might, for example, vie for ad space adjacent to keywords such as *sneakers* or *basketball*. All auctions for ads are run online, through an automated system. The highest bidder gets to place a small text ad appearing at the top of a gray box to the right of the search results; up to ten lower bidders win ad space below the coveted top listing. The minimum bid per keyword is set by Google. A commonly searched word or phrase like *eBay* or *JetBlue* might cost only a penny or two, while a more esoteric phrase like *helicopter parts* might fetch fifty dollars per click. In a second advertising program, AdSense, Google served as a matchmaker, marrying advertisers with Web destinations. If Intel wanted to advertise on technology blogs or a hotel in London wanted to promote itself on travel sites, Google put them together via a similar automated system. In both auctions, there were no ad reps, no negotiations, no relationships. Unlike the ads Karmazin and traditional media had sold for more than a century based on the estimated number of people reading a newspaper or watching a program (called CPMs, or cost per thousand viewers), Google's system (CPC, or cost per click) ensured that advertisers were charged only when the user clicked on an ad.

It was Google's ambition, Schmidt and Page and Brin liked to say, to provide an answer to the adman's legendary line "I know half of my advertising works, I just don't know which half." To help them sort through the digital clicks, Google and other new media companies relied on what are called cookies, software files that reside on a user's browser and keep track of their activities online: search questions asked, Web pages visited, time spent on each Web page, advertisements clicked on, items purchased. Because of these cookies, Google's searches improve with use, as they become more familiar with the kind of information the user seeks. Although the cookie doesn't identify the user by name or address, it does assemble data advertisers crave and couldn't get from traditional media companies like Karmazin's.

And unlike traditional analog media companies, which can't measure the effectiveness of their advertising, Google offered each advertiser a free tool: Google Analytics, which allowed the advertiser to track day by day, hour by hour, the number of clicks and sales, the traffic produced by the keywords chosen, the conversion rate from click to sale—in sum, the overall effectiveness of an ad.

Thus, the several hundred million daily searches Google performed in 2003 (today the number is 3 billion) provided a tantalizing trove of data. Google helped advertisers target consumers not just by age, sex, income, profession, or zip code, but by personal preferences for leisure time activities, frequently visited locations, product preferences, news preferences, etcetera. Google took much of the guessing out of advertising. "Our business is highly measurable," Schmidt said. "We know that if you spend X dollars on ads, you'll get Y dollars in revenues per industry, per customer."

Karmazin was aghast. Most of the American media—television, radio, newspapers, magazines—depended for their existence on a long-entrenched advertising model. In the old method, at which Karmazin excelled, the ad sales force depended on emotion and mystery, not metrics. "You buy a commercial in the Super Bowl, you're going to pay two and one-half million dollars for the spot," Karmazin said. "I have no idea if it's going to work. You pay your money, you take your chances." To turn this lucrative system over to a mechanized auction posed a serious threat. "I want a sales person in the process, taking that buyer out for drinks, getting an order they shouldn't have gotten." What would happen if advertisers expected measured results from the $3 million spent for each thirty-second ad for NBC's 2009 Super Bowl, or for the approximately $60 billion spent on television advertising in the United States each year? Or the estimated $172 billion spent in the United States on advertising, and the additional $227 billion spent on marketing, including public relations, direct mail, telemarketing, and sales promotions? "That's the worst kind of business model in the world," he said—the worst, that is, if you're an old-school ad man. "You don't want to have people know what works. When you know what works or not, you tend to charge less money than when you have this aura and you're selling this mystique." For sixty years, network television sold much of its advertising in an "up-front" each spring and summer after the new fall shows were announced. Even as audiences were declining, executives created a cattle-stampede mentality by convincing advertisers they'd get shut out of the hit shows if they didn't buy early. Karmazin and the networks continued to charge ever-steeper rates because, he said, "advertisers don't know what works and what doesn't. That's a great model."

The Google executives were equally appalled. They thought Karmazin's method manipulated emotions and cheated advertisers; just as egregiously, it wasn't measurable and was therefore inefficient. They were convinced they could engineer a better system.

By then, Karmazin knew there was little he and Google could do for each other. "I was selling twenty-five billion dollars of advertising," he said. "Did I want someone to know what worked and what didn't?" Like the aging Falstaff, he had "heard the chimes at midnight." Karmazin trained his eyes on his Google hosts, his hands folded on the table, his cuff links gleaming, and protested, only half in jest, "You're fucking with the magic!"

DAYS LATER, that line was still echoing in the halls of the Googleplex. Every Friday afternoon, Google employees assemble for what they call TGIF. They nibble on snacks and drink beer or soft drinks and sit in a semicircle as Schmidt and the company founders make surprisingly candid disclosures—about the latest financial results, visitors who've come that week, deals pending—and answer employee questions. Marissa Mayer, who joined the company in 1999 as an engineer and is today vice president, search products & user experience, remembered the meeting vividly. Schmidt, flanked by Page and Brin, said, "Mel Karmazin, the head of Viacom, came and found us interesting. They really don't know what to think of us. We really don't know what to think of them."

"The choice quote that characterizes the whole meeting," Brin chimed in, "was when the head of Viacom said, 'You're fucking with the magic!'" For Googlers, as they often refer to themselves, Karmazin's deference to tradition was anathema; they questioned *everything*. Mayer said the Google founders always asked, "Why does this have to be the way it is? Why can't you 'fuck with the magic?'"

Since Google's birth in 1998, as Schmidt acknowledges, Google has set out systematically to attack the magic. "If Google makes the market more efficient, that's a good thing," he said. Unlike Karmazin, Google engineers don't make *gut* decisions. They have no way to quantify relationships or judgment. They value efficiency more than experience. They require facts, beta testing, mathematical logic. Google fervently believes it is shaping a new and better media world by making the process of buying advertising more rational and transparent. In its view, the company serves consumers by offering advertising as information. It invites advertisers to bid for the best price, and invites media companies to slim their sales forces and automate part of their advertising and to reach into what author Chris Anderson dubbed "the long tail," in this case to those potential clients who rarely advertised but would if it was targeted and cheap to do so. Google also invites users to freely search newspapers, books, and magazines in what it sees as both free promotion and an opportunity for publications to sell advertising off this traffic. It invites television networks and movie studios to use YouTube, which Google acquired in 2006, as both a promotional trampoline and as a new online distribution system for their products. It invites advertisers to use DoubleClick, the digital advertising service company they acquired in 2007, for their online ads.

Still, Page told me, he does not see Google as a content company. Google's computers can "aggregate content; we can process it, rank it, we can do lots of things that are valuable. We can build systems that let lots of people create content themselves. That's really where our leverage is." That leverage, inevitably, makes it easier for audiences to migrate away from old media. This will cause some distress, but satisfying everyone, including traditional media companies, is not Google's goal, he said; serving users is. "You don't want to do the wrong things in a way that is causing real damage to the world or to people. But you also need to make progress, and that's not always going to make everybody happy." Armed with this conviction, Page and Google's engineers have made many media companies very unhappy indeed.

It wouldn't happen all at once. In the early days of the new century, few old media companies had yet lapsed into panic mode. Newspapers saw their circulation and ad revenues slipping. From a peak daily newspaper circulation of sixty-three million in 1984, circulation slid an average of 1 percent each year until 2004, when the drop became more precipitous. Publishers did speak of moving aggressively to create digital newsrooms, and in the nineties the Tribune Company and Knight Ridder, among others, made digital investments. But the chains that owned most newspapers were predominantly interested in getting bigger in order to gain more leverage. There was little urgency to move to the Web; online newspapers were usually stepchildren of print editions, not allowed to break stories or employ their own separate staff, not allowed to look or feel much different from a print newspaper.

Network television viewing had similarly been eroding. On a typical night in 1976, 92 percent of all viewers were watching CBS, NBC, or ABC;

today, those networks (along with Fox) attract about 46 percent of viewers. The networks responded to the decline by cutting costs, buying local TV stations and cable properties, producing and syndicating more of their own shows, and—like the movie studios—putting their faith in hits like NBC's *Seinfeld,* to save them.

The media buzzwords were *convergence* and *synergy.* The common credo was that the advantage accrued to vertically integrated corporate giants—to Viacom, AOL Time Warner, News Corporation, Disney, Gannett, Tribune—those able to control every step in the process from an idea to its manufacture to its distribution. The synergies would come not from partnering with other companies but from owning content and the means to distribute it. With that in mind, media companies pushed to blur the borders between traditional industries: broadcast networks acquired cable networks; telephone companies acquired cable distribution companies; cable system owners invested in content companies and telephone services; Hollywood studios bought broadcast networks along with music and game and book companies; newspapers bought local cable and radio.

Advertising agencies were also convinced size equaled leverage, so they acquired one another, consolidated their media-buying services, and purchased public relations and direct mail and marketing firms, aware that marketing and public relations spending was double the money spent on traditional advertising. Four giant worldwide firms now insisted on being called marketing companies.

Meanwhile, music companies, rather than marketing singles as they once did, continued to push the sale of entire albums; as Napster and its clones delighted young fans by offering free digital downloads of their music, they refused to make a deal, choosing instead to prosecute not just Napster but its users—the music companies' own customers.

For their part, movie executives continued to spend profligately and were distracted by piracy in China. Like music executives, they often blamed their flattening sales on the failure to come up with a hit like *Titanic* or on outside mischief. They believed content was King. Cable and telephone companies swallowed their smaller peers and vied to expand their broadband wires, convinced that he who controlled distribution was King. Book publishers merged while sales sputtered and bookstores closed, dwarfed by chains like Barnes & Noble. Publishers resisted electronic books, as a decade earlier they had resisted CD-ROMs.

Old media companies were trapped in the "the innovator's dilemma," what Clayton M. Christensen described in his book of that name, as well-managed companies that, confronted by new technologies or new business models, floundered by fiercely defending their existing business models and not changing fast enough. Christensen described how Xerox became defensive about its large, high-volume copying centers and missed the market for desktop photocopy machines, and how IBM was late to move from its lucrative large mainframe computer business and delayed entering the minicomputer business, and how Sears, Roebuck and Co. pioneered chain stores and catalogue sales but was eclipsed by discount retailing.

Old media faced excruciating choices. "Your choices suck," Karmazin said. "Either you keep your head in the sand and say, 'No, no, I'm only going to make my content available on my network.' Or you listen to your employees, who say 'Why don't we go on the Internet?' And then you go on the Internet and see yourself more fragmented and you see yourself not able to charge as much for your advertising because your audience is down." The money generated by the Internet, and its promotional value, does not compensate for this loss. "There are no easy answers."

Defensiveness mixed with fear fueled resistance to change. In a 1994 speech to the National Press Club in Washington, Viacom chairman Sumner Redstone proclaimed, "I will believe in the 500-channel world only when I see it. . . ." The Web, he said, was just another "distribution technology," more "a road to fantasyland" than a game changer. He envisioned that traditional media—movies, television, books, all content—would remain "King," concluding: "To me it seems apparent that the Information Superhighway, at least to the extent that it is defined in extravagant and esoteric applications, is a long way coming if it comes at all."

In 1995, Craig Newmark launched craigslist.org, a Web site where people could post apartments for rent, job openings, services for hire, products for sale, dating invitations. In retrospect, it seems clear that this posed a threat to newspaper classified sections, which produced about a third of their ad revenue. But newspapers usually saw craigslist as a quaint Web bulletin board. Vinod Khosla, a founder of Sun Microsystems and later a thriving Silicon Valley venture capitalist, once told *Vanity Fair* of a meeting he convened in 1996 with nine of the ten major American newspaper companies, including the New York Times, Washington Post, and Gannett. To save their classified business from the Internet, Khosla urged them to join New Century Network to sell advertising on the Web. His advice was rejected. "They couldn't convince themselves that a Google, a Yahoo, or an eBay . . . could ever replace classified advertising." Newspaper classified advertising plummeted from nearly eighteen billion dollars in 2005 to about nine billion dollars in 2008.

Like Google's founders, Newmark was an engineer who devised a really cool free service. Drowning newspapers was not Newmark's intent; creating a more efficient system for consumers was, as it was Google's. Newmark likens the digital revolution to "a tsunami, which when you're in the ocean is only a foot high but when it hits shore it's bigger." Vastly bigger.

TRADITIONAL MEDIA COMPANIES did not see themselves as potentially superfluous middlemen. They fervently believed relationships mattered—with advertisers, with Hollywood talent, with writers. They believed in professional storytellers, not amateurs producing "user-generated" content. They tended to believe most digital devices were too complicated, too unfriendly to consumers. They clung to a conviction that people prefered to lean back rather than lean forward to be entertained, to relax on a couch rather than sit upright at a desk. They believed few of their customers would read a newspaper, magazine, or book online or on a handheld device. It was too hard on the eyes, screens were too small, desktop computers were not portable. They believed consumers would gravitate toward their bundled services, pleased to receive a single bill for a variety of offerings. They knew Google had bested many of the search firm pioneers—Excite, AltaVista, Inktomi, Infoseek, GoTo, Lycos. But to most old media executives, Google was an exotic search service with puny text ads and a cute corporate motto.

They were wrong about how a new generation interacted with their electronic devices. And they were wrong about Google. Technology moved fast, and was no friend to entrenched media companies. Only a dozen years before Karmazin's 2003 visit, there was no World Wide Web, no DVDs, no satellite TV, no mobile phones or PDAs, no Tivos or DVRs, no digital cameras, no iPods, no PlayStation or Wii games, no blogs. By May 2009, Nielsen reported that 230 million Americans had Internet access, 93 percent had high-speed access (broadband) and digital cable service, and 228 million used a mobile phone. Advertising dollars for newspapers, broadcast television, and radio were receding. In 2008, more Americans got their national and international news from the Internet than from any other medium save television, according to a national survey by the Pew Research Center. More choices meant a shrinking mass audience. The number one network television program in the 1988–1989 season was *The Cosby Show*, which was watched by 41 percent of all households owning television sets; twenty years later, the top show was *American Idol*, and it reached just one-fifth of those watching television.

Information and entertainment were rapidly democratizing, as technology empowered consumers not just to unearth any fact from a Google search but to copy and share it, to access a variety of opinions, to watch television on their own schedule, to program their own music, publish their own blogs, shop online, carry portable devices untethered to a wire, bypass the post office or the Yellow Pages, communicate instantly with an associate or a loved one. By April 2009, an estimated 1.6 billion people worldwide connected to the Internet, less than one-quarter of whom were located in North America.

While digital companies burgeoned, between 2000 and 2007 traditional media companies lost 167,600 jobs, or one out of every 6. Newspapers, which traditionally claimed nearly a quarter of the just under two hundred billion dollars spent on advertising in the United States, by 2007 were watching their share of ads plunge below 20 percent, and this number was projected to soon fall to 15 percent or lower. These shifts do not lead to the conclusion embraced by many in Silicon Valley that the digital age is the most liberating and meaningful period of technological change the world has yet experienced. Even if one were to discount fire, the wheel, Gutenberg's printing press, or the combustion engine, what about Mr. Edison? Without electricity, there would be no Internet, no computers, no wireless devices, no subways, not to mention no lightbulbs, no air-conditioning, no telephone, radio, or television. But what *does* set this era apart from others is velocity. It took telephones seventy-one years to penetrate 50 percent of American homes, electricity fifty-two years, and TV three decades. The Internet reached more than 50 percent of Americans in a mere decade; DVD penetration was faster, taking just seven years. Facebook built up a community of two hundred million users in just five years. Because the digital realm is made up of bits, it does not run out of supplies or have space constraints.

Events were moving so rapidly that even the smartest people were guessing, and often guessing wrong. In the nineties, Rupert Murdoch, among others, was convinced his News Corporation could grow by acquiring more local TV stations; Bill Gates of Microsoft asserted that the Internet would kill television networks, which it didn't; Time Warner mistakenly bet that television, not the Internet, would be the preferred interactive medium; telephone companies rushed to acquire cable companies, only later to sell them; investors clamored to bet on companies that later faded, such as Excite, Netscape, Wang Laboratories, Commodore, Lycos. Israeli entrepreneur Yossi Vardi, whose company was behind the invention of instant messaging, compiled a chart of thirty-four technology stocks that were ranked as premier growth stocks in 1980. By 1999, only one, Intel, was a consistent growth company, while twenty-three had drowned and the others were treading water.

Meanwhile, as traditional media was slicing employees, Google in early 2008 was receiving 1 million job applications per year, adding 150 employees per week, and employing nearly 20,000. After the company went public in 2004, its ledger sheet astonished the media. Its revenues, which were $3.2 billion in 2004, zoomed to $16.6 billion in 2007; in that same span, its net profits climbed from $399 million to over $3 billion. Defying a worldwide recession, its 2008 profits were $4.2 billion and its revenues rose to $21.8 billion (97 percent of it from advertising).

Google had become a juggernaut; it now produced two-thirds of all Internet searches in the United States and nearly 70 percent worldwide. Its index contained one trillion Web pages in 2008, and according to Brin, every four hours Google indexed the equivalent of the entire Library of Congress. In early 2009, users were clicking on and off billions of pages per day and receiving tens of billions of daily advertising impressions. Google's wingspan was also getting wider. In 2006, it acquired YouTube, the largest user-generated video Web site, with an estimated twenty-five million unique daily visitors in November of that year. In 2007, it acquired DoubleClick, the foremost digital marketing company; that year, DoubleClick posted seventeen billion display ads daily. Google now hogged 40 percent of both the twenty-three billion dollars spent to advertise online in the United States, and the fifty-four billion dollars worldwide online advertising. Google's ad revenues in 2008 matched the combined advertising revenues of the five broadcast networks (CBS, NBC, ABC, Fox, and the CW). By 2011, Web advertising in the United States was expected to climb to sixty billion dollars, or 13 percent of all ad dollars. This meant more dollars siphoned from traditional media, with the largest slice probably going to Google. And Google had started initiatives to sell advertising for television, radio, and newspapers, which could boost its market share. Google also introduced other services: Gmail, Google News, Google Earth, Google Maps, Google Video, Picasa for sharing digital photographs, Google Books to search every book ever published, Orkut, a social network site, or additional "cloud computing" applications such as Desktop or Docs.

By 2008, Mel Karmazin was no longer alone in questioning Google's intentions. Nor were those intentions obscure. In the disclosure documents it filed with the SEC in 2008, Google declared, "We began as a technology company, and have evolved into a software, technology, internet, advertising and media company all rolled into one." When Google adds mobile phones and a full menu of software applications to its cloud computing, and if it figures out a way to monetize YouTube, Eric Schmidt told me, he thinks it is conceivable that Google can become the first media company to generate one hundred billion dollars in revenues. It irritated media executives to hear Schmidt say, "We are in the advertising business," yet hear

Google employees constantly say they were on a quest to bring information to the masses, as if they toiled for a nonprofit that awarded no bonuses.

Marc Andreessen, thirty-eight, who transformed the Internet into a mass medium by helping invent what became the Netscape browser when he was a student and who is today a successful Internet entrepreneur seeking to build his third billion-dollar-plus company, is suspicious of Google's intentions: "Their game plan is to do everything. Google is Andy Kaufman. The whole thing with Andy Kaufman is you could never tell when he was joking. Google comes out with a straight face and said, 'We're just going to be a search engine. We're not going to be doing any of this other stuff'"—competing with advertising agencies, with telephone companies by getting into the cell phone business, with Hollywood, with publishers, with newspapers. "But I am quite sure they're joking."

THERE IS A DISCONNECT between the way Google is often perceived and the way it perceives itself. "I sometimes feel like I live on another planet and speak a different language from traditional media companies," Eric Schmidt said. And in a sense, Google does live on a separate planet. When it moved to its first Mountain View campus in August 1999, the move reflected the determination of its two young founders to keep employees focused inward. The current Googleplex in Mountain View is a collection of two- and three-story buildings with outdoor tables and park benches shaded by trees, a vegetable garden, and walkways pulsing with people and bicycles. Employees enjoy free meals and luxurious snacks (at a cost to Google of about seventy million dollars per year), and are offered bicycles to travel between buildings containing massage rooms and gyms staffed with trainers. Employees eat at large cafeteria tables, take breaks in lounges with pool tables and espresso machines. No need to leave campus for a car wash or oil change; they're available on Thursdays. Also available are barbers, dry cleaners, day care, dog care, dentists, and five physicians to dispense free physicals and medical care. Comfortable, Wi-Fi-equipped, biodiesel commuter buses transport employees to and from campus from as far away as San Francisco, and they run from early morning to late at night. No need to buy laptop computers; employees choose their own for free. Maternity leave consists of five months off at full salary, and new dads can take seven weeks off at full pay.

Most employees are alloted a day a week, or 20 percent of their time, to work on projects they feel passionate about. This has produced more than a few of Google's technological breakthroughs. Just as important, it conveys a sense of freedom. "It's a way of assuring people that they are scientists and artists," said Indian-born engineer Krishna Bharat, who used his 20 percent time to invent Google News. It's also a way to encourage engineers to push the envelope, to assume that their mission is to disrupt traditional ways of doing things.

There is at Google a utopian spirit not unlike that found at Burning Man, the annual anarchic-animistic retreat in Nevada's Black Rock Desert that culminates in the burning in effigy of a giant wood and desert brush "man." It does not go unnoticed by their friends that Brin and Page have been regular attendees at this weeklong retreat in August, whose Woodstock-like spirit is captured in Burning Man's ten stated principles, which include a devotion "to acts of gift giving"; creating "social environments that are unmediated by commercial sponsorships, transactions, or advertising"; and "a radically participatory ethic" that can lead to "transformative change." "Google is a cross between a start-up and graduate school," said Peter Norvig, Google's director of research, who joined the company in 2001 and wears bright Hawaiian shirts and sneakers with laces left untied. "Formal rules don't matter. There's still a loose feel. The disadvantage of being a start-up is the fear that you will run out of money. There is stress. Google is more like graduate school in that you don't have that stress. You expect one day that the guys in suits will take over. That hasn't happened." The engineers remain in charge. Google aims to be nonhierarchical. Stacy Savides Sullivan, who joined the company in December 1999 and said she was its fiftieth employee, is Google's chief cultural officer. She described the culture as "flat," and said her mission is to ensure that it stays that way. The reason the founders "smashed together" employees—making them share offices and work in teams on projects—is to "create a company everyone wants to work at," to impose a team culture. She described her task this

way: "My role is to help facilitate and orchestrate the culture." It is no accident, many Googlers believe, that in 2007 and 2008 *Fortune* magazine
christened Google the best U.S. company to work for.

Google is both egalitarian and elitist. Salaries are modest, and there are
no executive dining rooms. The two founders and CEO Schmidt (all now
billionaires) have insisted on being paid $1 a year and have declined stock
option grants since 2004; they were each paid bonuses of $1,700 in 2007
and declined bonuses altogether in 2008. The top salary of $450,000 was
paid equally to the other members of the executive committee, who in most
cases received bonuses equal to 150 percent of their salary. Most employees
are invited to share the riches. Google projected that stock option grants
to employees in 2008 would total $1.1 billion. These grants confer million-
aire status on many Googlers. Google's approach to users is also egalitarian, from its reliance on "the wisdom of crowds" approach to search results
to its demonstrated faith in "open source" systems.

It is a close-knit culture. Google is not egalitarian about sharing information with outsiders. Ask just about any Googler basic questions—How
many searches does Google perform each day? How many of its employees
are non-Americans? What is the starting salary of engineers?—and you'll
receive a robotic, "We don't disclose those numbers for competitive reasons." Google has deliberately set out to build a team culture composed of
elite performers, and an inevitable consequence is that it can be an opaque
and insular culture.

Google's hiring practices are certainly elitist. On the first day of work
at Google, new employees attend an all-day orientation session at which
they are told how few of the more than one million yearly applicants were
hired at Google. They are reassured that more applicants are accepted by
Harvard (about 7 percent) than are hired by Google (about 1 percent). The
screening process relies on measurable things, like grades and SAT scores.

The applicants most scrutinized are the engineers and technical employees, who make up half of Google's work force. "It's an engineering-driven
and -focused culture," said a former Google executive who did not wish to
be identified. "The founders don't value marketing"—or most nonengi-
neering disciplines. Larry Page is aggressively disdainful of marketing and

public relations. In early 2008, Page instructed Google's public relations department, which consisted of 130 people, that he would only give them a total of eight hours of his time that year for press conferences, speeches, or interviews.

The thirst to quantify everything drove several visual designers to quit Google in early 2009. Douglas Bowman, who was hired as Google's first visual designer in May 2006, wrote a blog explaining why he left. "When a company is filled with engineers, it turns to engineering to solve problems," he wrote. Google wanted to test market every color, every design. Unlike Apple, Google was more concerned with functionality than taste, elegance. Management, said Bowman, pushed to "reduce each decision to a simple logic problem. Remove all subjectivity and just look at the data. . . . And that data eventually becomes a crutch for every decision, paralyzing the company and preventing it from making any daring design decisions."

Google honors its engineers as creators, treating them the way the legendary management consultant Peter Drucker suggested a half century ago that companies should treat "knowledge workers," said Hal R. Varian, Google's chief economist. But an engineering-dominated culture has drawbacks. "In some ways, they have not done enough to communicate what they are doing internally or externally," said Paul Buchheit, Google's twenty-third employee, the one who coined their "Don't be evil" motto and who left with three other Googlers to launch a social network, FriendFeed, in 2006. "Part of the culture is not to communicate. That's what we did when we started Gmail. We put it out without an announcement." In beta testing new products, Google does get feedback from users. But something else is at work here as well. Engineers are rarely accomplished communicators. Google is a culture dominated by a belief in science, in data, and facts, not instinct or perception or opinion. This reflects not just a disdain for public relations, but also a whiff of arrogance.

Whether the employee is an engineer, a manager, or a marketer, a belief in the company's virtue is central to the Google culture. From day one, Google forfeited advertising revenues by refusing to run ads on its home page and by refusing to allow advertisers—as competitors like GoTo did—to pay to get their products ranked higher in search results. Google could run more ads than it does, but instead discards ads that don't attract clicks or are not deemed "relevant" to users as information. At the core of the Google value system, said engineer Matt Cutts, is the belief that the user experience matters most, and if the user experience is simple, and fast, and uncluttered with ads, and if Google makes no attempt to steer users to its own sites, a bond of trust will form. "We maintain a church/state wall" between the information a Google search provides and advertising, said Larry Page, who likened what Google does to how newspapers strive to keep the influence of advertisers away from the reporting of news because "there is an inherent conflict between the two."

Google won friends among users by being free; it won friends among advertisers by charging only if users clicked on the text ad; it won friends among news readers with Google News, which is both free and until early 2009 was ad-free; it won friends among Web sites and small businesses by generating advertising dollars and new customers. From its second auction program, AdSense, Google said it pockets 20 percent of the revenues, giving the rest to these Web sites, or what Google calls its business partners. (Actually, said several of those partners, Google also charges 10 percent of "overhead" costs, so partners net about two-thirds.) Google, in 2008, provided a total of over five billion dollars to its hundreds of thousands of "partners." Little wonder, then, that Google was often seen as a savior by those dependent on the Web. Jason Calacanis, who cofounded Weblogs, Inc., a company that publishes blogs, said AdSense generated in 2008 a total of four thousand dollars a day in advertising income for his bloggers.

Google does its part to address global warming. It places on its roofs the largest installation of solar photovoltaic panels of any corporate campus in the United States, generating sufficient electricity to power one thousand homes. It has solar-powered stations in its outdoor parking lots to charge its fleet of hybrid cars, and offers subsidies (five thousand dollars at first and now three thousand) to any employee who purchases a hybrid that gets at least forty-five miles per gallon (one thousand employees have received this subsidy). The company earmarks 1 percent of its profits to its philanthropic arm, the Google Foundation. CEO Schmidt sometimes lapses into speaking of Google as a "moral force," as if its purpose were to save the world, not make money.

Al Gore, who has served as a consultant and adviser to Google since soon after he left the White House in 2001, likes to talk of Google's "great values." He told me he believes these values are spreading to other companies. Those who attribute Google's success to its algorithms or "the law of increasing returns," he said, fail to fully appreciate "the extent to which Google's superior talent recruitment stems from its unusual empowerment of employees and the attention they pay to the quality of the employee experience at Google." The best engineering schools produce a few near geniuses each year, and the reason he said Google is "getting more than their fair share of the most talented" is that they target them. "I've called college seniors for them," he said, adding, "It's not only in the recruiting and retention of the higher-quality employees. It also has to do with their alignment with community values, with trying to make the world a better place. People unlock a higher fraction of their creative potential when they feel that what they're doing is about more than making a buck, or more than enhancing the business scorecard and building the value of the company. When they think that what they're doing is something that makes the world a better place, I don't think that's just touchy-feely stuff."

THE REST OF THE world, particularly the media part of it, doesn't always have a "touchy-feely" view of the company. Google has been sued by Viacom for allegedly allowing YouTube to pirate its television programs, by publishers and the Authors Guild for digitizing their books without permission, and came close to being sued by the Associated Press for linking to its stories without paying compensation. Newspapers and magazines are alarmed that Google News and Google search link to their content and don't pay for it. Hollywood frets that YouTube enlarges its own audience and diminishes theirs. Advertising companies are alarmed that Google and DoubleClick retain so much information that their advertising clients might turn to Google to purchase their online advertising, and maybe design their ads. Telephone companies are alarmed that Google is pushing into their mobile phone business. All feared Google would devise a navigation system for their media akin to what search was for the Web, and thus would be poised to become the traffic cop for all media.

Schmidt said he, Brin, and Page often ask themselves: "How can you grow big without doing evil?" He believes Google has become a lightning rod, particularly for old media. "In our society bigness is often associated with bad," he said. "There is no question that a company with the ambitions of Google will generate controversy, will have people upset with us. The question is: Where does it come from? Is it coming from a competitor? Is it coming from a business whose business model is being endangered by the Internet? Or is it because we're behaving badly?"

Schmidt believes the hostility comes from threatened competitors who scapegoat Google. "When you have a technology that is as engrossing as the Internet, you're going to have winners and losers," he said. "I'm not trying to sound arrogant. I'm trying to sound rational about it. The Internet allows people to consume media in a different way. They're going to do it." Schmidt acknowledged that, in his own naivete, Google has probably fanned paranoia. "Google is run by three computer scientists," he said. "We're going to make all the mistakes computer scientists running a company would make. But one of the mistakes we're not going to make is the mistake that nonscientists make. We're going to make mistakes based on facts and data and analysis."

Schmidt's summation understates the mistakes Google will make, and has made, because its computer scientists live on their own planet and often harbor disdain for the way others think. Terry Winograd, who was Larry Page's graduate school mentor at Stanford, and who still serves as an engineering consultant to Google, recounted a discussion at a TGIF he attended where an employee raised the question of one day splitting Google's stock and asserted that a stock purchased at, say, four hundred dollars a share that was now selling at forty dollars per share because it had been split, would be perceived as not a good thing for employees because the perception would be that their stock was worth less. Page erupted, "It's stupid. If you own ten shares at forty dollars and one share at four hundred dollars, it's the same thing! You just need to know how to divide."

This is "logically true," said Winograd. "But there is an emotional issue here. He felt that those who disagreed were not thinking logically, were being stupid."

Logic, however, is not always universal. The planet is occupied by humans, who often make decisions under the guise of a logic that others deem stupid. Great leaders have the empathy to factor this wisdom into their deliberations. They know Robert Louis Stevenson understood a broader truth when he wrote: "No man lives in the external truth among salts and acids, but in the warm, phantomagoric chamber of his brain, with all the painted windows and storied wall." That Larry Page and Sergey Brin—and many Google employees—are brilliant is a conclusion cemented by the tale of Google's rise. Whether they are also wise is not as clear-cut.

PART TWO

The Google Story

CHAPTER TWO

Starting in a Garage

n early 1998, Bill Gates couldn't envision what was to come. Microsoft was at the apex of its power, with revenues that would reach $14.5 billion by year's end, with ever-rising profits, a soaring stock valuation, more than twenty-seven thousand employees, and a market share of computer operating systems that encompassed more than 90 percent of all desk and laptop PCs. The government had not yet sued it for monopolistic practices, or convinced two federal courts that Bill Gates's company was guilty. At the time, Microsoft was so flush that it had flirted with investing in Hollywood, having already dispatched its chief technology officer and dealmaker, Nathan P. Myhrvold, to spend an anthropological week with DreamWorks cofounder Jeffrey Katzenberg.

It was in that confident time that I visited Gates in his office on the sprawling Microsoft campus in Redmond, Washington, in 1998. In the course of our interview, I asked him to describe his competitive nightmare: "What challenge do you most fear?" He rocked gently back and forth, sipping from a can of Diet Coke, and silently pondered the question. When he finally spoke he did not recite the usual litany of prominent foes: Netscape, Sun Microsystems, Oracle, Apple. Nor did he cite the federal government. Instead, he said, "I fear someone in a garage who is devising something completely new." He had no idea where the garage might be—or even what country it might be in—nor could he guess the nature of the new technology. He just knew that innovation was usually the enemy of established companies.

As it happens, in 1998, in a Silicon Valley garage, Bill Gates's nightmare came alive courtesy of Larry Page and Sergey Brin. Page and Brin had met three years before, at orientation for incoming Stanford graduate students. They had much in common. Their fathers were college professors and their mothers worked in science; both were born in 1973 and raised in homes where issues were rigorously debated; both attended Montessori elementary schools, where they were granted freedom to study what they wished, and as public high school students they were besotted by computers; both were pursuing Ph.D.'s in computer science. They shared what John Battelle described as "a reflexive belief that whatever the status quo is, it's wrong and there must be a better solution"; both, as Mark Malseed observed, had a "penchant for pushing boundaries—without asking for permission . . ."

SERGEY MIKHAILOVICH BRIN'S PATH to Stanford started in Moscow, where he was born into a family steeped in science. His grandfather was a math professor; his great-grandmother had left the Soviet Union to study microbiology at the University of Chicago; his parents, Michael and Eugenia, were mathematicians. There were obstacles to their pursuit of science, though. Despite Michael's Ph.D., anti-Semitism impeded his career: at Moscow State University he was not permitted to study his preferred subject, astrophysics, because it fell into the same department as nuclear research, and Jews were deemed too untrustworthy to enter that field. Eugenia Brin, a civil engineer, was more welcome in the renowned research lab of the Soviet Oil and Gas Institute, but she, too, felt constraints. "We were quite poor," recalled Sergey, describing a three-hundred- to four-hundred-square-foot Moscow flat he shared with his parents and his grandmother, an English teacher. "My parents, both of them, went through periods of hardship. My life, in comparison, has been easy."

In 1977, Michael Brin attended an international conference in Europe, and when he returned home he insisted that the family must apply for visas to escape the USSR. When he submitted an application the following year, though, he was abruptly fired. Warned of retribution, Eugenia quit her job. They eked out a life doing temporary work, schooling four-year-old Sergey at home. It wasn't until two years later that their exit visas were granted. With assistance from the Hebrew Immigrant Aid Society, they immigrated to America, leaving most of their possessions behind.

They rented a cinder-block house in a multiracial, working-class suburb near the University of Maryland. As in Moscow, they were poor, relying on the support of local Russian Jews. "My parents sort of lived in the dining room," Sergey remembers. "There was no wall between the dining room and the kitchen. They used that as their bedroom." Eventually, Michael became a professor of mathematics at the University of Maryland, where he specializes in Riemannian geometry; Eugenia Brin became a scientist at NASA's Goddard Space Flight Center. They had a second son, Sam, fourteen years Sergey's junior.

Sergey enrolled in the local Montessori school where classes were comprised of students in a three-year age range. Typical of Montessori programs, the school adapted itself to the child. "It's not like somebody is telling you what to do," Sergey said. "You have to plot your own path." Because he initially spoke little English, he retreated into math puzzles, science projects, and maps. For his ninth birthday, his parents gave Sergey a Commodore 64 computer, a seminal gift for a man who now gleefully describes himself as a nerd. Some years later, when a friend got an early Macintosh computer, they began to devise artificial intelligence programs and software to simulate gravity.

Sergey's prowess at math was encouraged by his father, a stern tutor, who sometimes graded student papers with the salutation "My sincere condolences." Family meals featured intense discussions. Sergey was not much interested in listening to music or watching TV. Nor was he an avid reader of books, though he was engrossed by the life of Richard P. Feynman, a winner of the Nobel Prize in Physics who "not only made big contributions in his field," Sergey once said, but wanted to be "a Leonardo, an artist" as well as a scientist. "I found that pretty inspiring." Although he says he "probably had more nerdy interests than most of my peers," his heroes— Feynman at a young age, Steve Jobs and Warren Buffett later—suggest the breadth of his ambition.

He was also a rebellious child. When he was thirteen, his parents took him to visit the Soviet Union and he threw pebbles at Soviet policemen, causing a scene that his parents defused only by pledging to the irate authorities that he would be severely punished at home. Sergey is still very emotional about autocratic governments and anti-Semitism. But even though he was raised as a Jew and attended Hebrew school for a few years, he was nonpracticing, did not have a bar mitzvah, and was put off by traditional Jewish celebrations, which he once told an Israeli reporter he "associated with getting lots of gifts and money, and I was never comfortable with that." When he was married on an island in the Bahamas in May of 2007 to Anne Wojcicki, cofounder of 23andMe, a genetics research company, the couple stood in bathing suits under a chuppah, the traditional Jewish wedding canopy, but no rabbi officiated.

Then, as now, he was uncomfortable with introspection. Asked by the same Israeli reporter if it was a coincidence that his wife was Jewish, he said, "I believe there are lots of nice non-Jewish girls out there. My wife is, I guess, half Jewish."

So was it a coincidence, the reporter pressed, that his wife was half Jewish?

"That wasn't a concern for me," he responded. "I don't know, maybe it was for her."

I once asked him, "What part of your success do you trace to qualities in your parents?"

"It's hard to say," he answered.

After much coaxing, he added, "A certain love for science and learning and the beautiful mathematical things I have been able to put into practice is part of my upbringing."

He attended Eleanor Roosevelt High School in Baltimore, a public school where muscles counted more than brains. This setting didn't diminish Sergey's cocky swagger, though, and he blitzed through in three years, gathering enough college credits there to allow him to also graduate from the University of Maryland in three years. Although he was just nineteen, Sergey flourished at college, where he was a math and computer science major and was treated by the faculty as a peer. "I was a pretty advanced student," he said.

After graduation, he received a National Science Foundation scholarship to study computer science at Stanford, where he believed he was "better prepared" than classmates. His special interest, data mining, was a relatively new field in which computers are used to extract and analyze information from enormous fields of data. He expected to get a Ph.D. and maybe become a professor. As at Montessori, he worked at his own pace. His father once told authors David Vise and Mark Malseed for their book, *The Google Story*, "I asked him if he was taking any advanced courses one semester. He said, 'Yes, advanced swimming.'" Craig Silverstein, a fellow data-mining student who would become Google's first employee, remembers that Sergey rarely studied, yet "he passed all his tests in the first year, and didn't take any in the second year. Already he had this reputation as a kind of genius." Brin recalled taking eight comprehensive tests: "When I first tried, I passed all seven. The one I thought I was best at, I didn't pass. I went to the prof and debated the answers. I wound up talking him into it. So I passed all eight. I think I was the only one."

Brin was athletic but uninterested in team sports; he lost himself instead in gymnastics, swimming, Rollerblading, and biking. Still, Brin was more outgoing than many self-described geeks and enjoyed playing practical jokes. He also took on extra projects that aroused his interest; a typical project was the numbering system for the rooms in the Computer Science Building (donated by Bill Gates, who would become a nemesis). In the building, each room was identified with a four-digit code, which Brin felt did not convey the most useful information to the building's tenants. "We were offended at having four-digit numbers when you don't have ten thousand rooms," he said. Along with computer science professor Vaughan Pratt, he set out to devise a better system, one that would enable someone leaving a given room to calculate the distance to his destination. "We came up with a sensible three-digit numbering system. It was quite elegant. Most buildings are numbered in a really stupid way. The architect or somebody sits down with the blueprint and they collate across and they number things. It looks great to them when they are looking at the blueprint. When you're actually walking around, it makes no sense at all. The Gates building is fairly simple. I just had the numbers roll around the building. Even numbers were exterior, odd numbers were interior. . . . The second digit told you how far around the building you had to go. It was very intuitive, if I may say so myself."

THE SERGEY BRIN WHO was obsessed with efficiency would find a soul mate in Larry Page. Larry was born in Lansing, Michigan, where his father, Dr. Carl Victor Page, was a professor of computer science and artificial intelligence at Michigan State. His mother, Gloria Page, had a master's degree in computer science; she taught at the university before becoming a database consultant. With Larry and his older brother, Carl, the Pages lived comfortably in a middle-class neighborhood. By age seven, Larry was proficient on the Exidy Sorcerer computer his dad had brought home, and this ignited his interest in technology, as did the technical magazines and electrical engineering assignments his father also brought home, and his brother Carl's skill at taking things apart. Larry's family, like Sergey's, welcomed argumentative challenges. The Pages were readers, and Larry fondly remembers vacations to Oregon when they'd take an empty suitcase to fill it with books from the renowned Powell's Books, in Portland. Unlike Sergey, however, he was conspicuously quiet, and had a bad case of acne. He was a loner, someone who as an adult friends would describe as shy and strangers would describe as asocial. He chose not to follow his mother's faith, Judaism, but like his father chose not to embrace a religion. Perhaps this was but one reflection of an unsettled home; his parents divorced when he was eight, and his father married a colleague at Michigan State. Carl, nine years older, left home after high school to get a computer science degree.

He later was a founder of eGroups.com, an Internet company sold to Yahoo in 2000 for about four hundred million dollars.

Just as Sergey was fascinated by Richard Feynman, Larry was inspired at age twelve by a biography of Nikola Tesla, whose pioneering work led to the development of electricity, power grids, X-rays, and wireless communication. Tesla was an extraordinary but unsung scientist, an Edison without the fame or wealth and who, despite his discoveries, died bitter and destitute. Page told me he learned from Tesla that "you can invent the world's greatest things, but if you just invent them it doesn't accomplish that much. . . . I found it very sad. You can imagine if he were slightly more skilled in business, or with people, he'd have gotten a lot more done." Brilliant ideas alone would not suffice. Timing and follow-through, and raising resources, really mattered.

"I realized I wanted to invent things, but I also wanted to change the world," Page once said. He became convinced that in order to effect scientific change he needed to start a business. Inventing things, he once said, "wasn't any good; you really had to get them out into the world and have people use them to have any effect. So probably from when I was 12, I knew I was going to start a company eventually." When he thought about the kind of company he wanted, Larry told me, he thought of his grandfather, an assembly-line worker in the Chevrolet plant in Flint, Michigan, who during sit-down strikes fearfully carried a heavy iron pipe wrapped in leather as protection from what he described as strike-breaking "goons." Happy employees, Larry came to believe, are more productive.

The rival for Larry's attention was music. He had begun playing the saxophone as a child, and he played with considerable skill. After finishing his first year at East Lansing High School, Larry was among the talented musicians chosen to attend summer sessions at the prestigious Interlochen Arts Academy in Northern Michigan. But the lure of engineering soon triumphed over music. Like his father, mother, and brother, Larry enrolled at the University of Michigan. He didn't have much choice. "My dad actually said to me when I was deciding what school to go to, 'We'll pay for any school you want to go to—as long as it's Michigan,'" he once said.

With his short dark hair and stark black eyebrows and 5 o'clock shadow, he looked like Italian tenor Andrea Bocelli, but his high-pitched voice made him sound like Kermit the Frog. He remained an introvert while studying engineering at the university. Nevertheless, he imagined that one day he might start a company, and insisted on taking business courses. He also stood out; a brilliant student, he served as president of Eta Kappa Nu, a national honor society for electrical and computer engineering students. Preoccupied with finding more efficient ways to do things, he led a still nascent effort to build a monorail that would replace forty buses to connect the North and the Central Campus. He attended a leadership training program at the university, where he encountered a slogan he would often repeat as an adult: "Have a healthy disregard for the impossible."

For his graduate studies, he had his heart set on Stanford, a university where even the names of the buildings attest to the men whose careers were spawned there: William R. Hewlett, David Packard, Jerry Yang, James Clark. Yet for all of his ambition and achievements, he feared he was not up to the task. "I kept complaining to my friends that I was going to get sent home on the bus," he once told Michigan's alumni magazine. "It didn't quite happen that way."

THE STANFORD CAMPUS, designed by Frederick Law Olmstead, is spread over eight thousand acres. Like the Google campus that Page and Brin would one day build, Stanford offers free bus service, plentiful food, a bucolic setting, and shared spaces where students can collaborate. By the time Larry arrived in 1995, Sergey had been there two years; he was on the orientation team that welcomed Larry to campus. Sergey, as was his wont, immediately began needling Larry with questions. "We argued a lot," recalled Brin, mostly about local zoning and city planning. The field didn't particularly interest Brin, but arguing did. "We ended up talking a lot." The other students were content to tour San Francisco; Larry and Sergey were curious about other things. Even today, their idea of a relaxing time is to attend the annual Consumer Electronics Show and ask questions about the cool new technologies on display, or quiz astronauts about space flight.

Larry found an academic mentor in Terry A. Winograd, a computer science professor who had won a National Science Foundation grant to explore the future of online information. Larry bolted upright one night from a dream, he said many years later when describing how he suddenly had a vision for search. "I was thinking: What if we could download the whole Web, and just keep the links. . . . I grabbed a pen and started writing!" He told Professor Winograd, "It would take a couple of weeks to download the Web." Winograd nodded, he said, "fully aware it would take much longer but wise enough to not tell me." Larry downloaded the entire link structure of the Web, not quite knowing what he'd do with it. He realized that links weren't organic; they were the result of conscious effort. In a sense, users were voting for the best links when they chose to visit a site, or when they included a link on their own site. He had a bold idea to craft a different kind of search engine that would use these links to catalogue not just an island of the Web but the entire ocean.

His new friend Sergey was intrigued. He had been working with computer science professor Rajeev Motwani on data mining for the Web, still a nascent field in which one had to collect links, print them out, and study the printout to derive answers. The audacity of Larry's effort appealed to him. The math problems—how to count not just the original page links but the links affixed to the links—were the kind of challenge he tackled with gusto. "It was," Brin said, understatedly, "an interesting source of data." Sergey signed on, and the two became inseparable; when speaking of them, colleagues began to roll their names together, *LarryandSergey*.

The two were working at the dawn of the digital age. In 1993, two years before Brin and Page met, a mere fifteen million people in fifty countries used the Internet, and there were just over one hundred Web sites. The Mosaic browser had just been introduced, and Linus Torvalds empowered a community of software hackers to produce the open-source operating system called Linux. But the digital world was moving at breakneck speed, with the Internet doubling in size every year. In 1995, just two years later,

Yahoo was born, and its major online competitor, AOL, had nearly five million subscribers; the Mosaic browser had been renamed Netscape Navigator the prior year, and did for the Internet what Lewis and Clark did to open the West.

Mighty Microsoft was late to spot the menace Netscape and the Internet posed to its packaged software business. Microsoft's misreading of the Internet threat is conveyed in a sixteen-page November 15, 1994, memo to Bill Gates from Myhrvold deriding the "hype" surrounding the Internet, and asserting—just as dismissively as Sumner Redstone was that same year in his speech to the National Press Club—that it was just a distribution platform dominated by "hobbyists." Although Myhrvold presciently warned of the advent of a Web browser, Microsoft was slow to comprehend the impact of the Netscape browser, which liberated consumers from behind the walls AOL and other portals erected, allowing them to surf the Web. When Microsoft finally reacted, it was not tentative. Bill Gates galvanized his troops with a May 1995 memo, "The Internet Tidal Wave," warning of this disruptive technology.

The year 1995 was also when a Morgan Stanley analyst named Mary Meeker teamed up with a fellow analyst, Chris DePuy, to author *The Internet Report,* a thick volume that heralded a brave new world. "In this report," they wrote on page one, "we attempt to describe what may be one of the hottest new markets to develop in years—the growth of PC-based communications and the Internet." They said the "market for Internet-related products and services appears to be growing" faster than such early media start-ups as printing, telephones, movies, radio, recorded music, television. With a multiplying base of about 150 million PC users, they predicted e-mail "should become pervasive," and the Internet would serve as "an information distribution vehicle" for companies, slashing costs, birthing new competitors—"the next Microsofts, Ciscos, Oracles, and Compaqs. . . ."

The report was viral. The press heralded it. Companies downloaded more than a hundred thousand copies from Morgan Stanley's Web site. HarperCollins published it as a book. Within days, Meeker received an e-mail from someone who lived at Three Lighthouse Road in New

Zealand—to thank her. "He had a dial-up Web connection and he was able to connect to me from a remote location," she recalled. "This was the power of the Internet. That was a magical moment, for it represented what the report was about." *Barron's* would dub Meeker "Queen of the Internet." Wireless communications were exploding, and that year Americans spent twenty-two billion dollars on wireless services, as telephone companies and others vied to buy spectrum space that would speed the digital revolution.

Also that year, Nathan Myhrvold wrote a memo to Bill Gates in which he drew a distinction between incremental changes (like CD-ROMs or computers that double in speed every year) and "revolutionary" sea changes. He predicted computers that would be connected to networks, opening markets for e-commerce, information services, and video on demand; a "shift from a products business to a service business" that will allow services to be downloaded rather than sold in packages, opening the possibility that software companies like Microsoft would be able to charge per transaction; and new multimedia platforms that would permit the transmission of CD-quality audio and crisp video pictures. He also predicted there would be a radical change as we "move to an intelligent operating system," an intelligent agent or navigator that would free consumers to locate what they want on their PC or the Web.

It was at places like Stanford and in classes like Terry Winograd's that these systems might be designed. To tug his computer science students down from their theoretical heights and ground them in a sense of "how things work and an understanding of the user," Winograd assigned them to read Donald A. Norman's *The Design of Everyday Things*. The thesis of Norman's book is that those who design things—from video recorders to computers to impossible-to-open plastic packages—typically don't design from the vantage point of consumers. Thus they make products that are overly complicated and confusing. This, he wrote, is "the paradox of technology: added functionality generally comes along at the price of added complexity."

This idea became an obsession of Larry's. Years later, he called it a "seminal" book, and remembered being amazed when he first read it "that

people are so focused on outside things and are not focused on the functionality of things." (It still drives him mad to stay in a hotel and not be
able to figure out how to turn the lights off "in less than three minutes.")
The book, he said, strengthened the attitude he brought to designing the
Google search engine, which was the opposite approach from existing
search engines like AltaVista. If you did a search for *university* on AltaVista,
it heaved at you every text that contained the word *university*, without
ranking value or assessing whether people were actually using the links.
Doing the same search, Google relied on the collective intelligence of its
users and returned with the top ten universities. Thinking that "your customer or users are always right, and your goal is to build systems that work
for them in a natural way, is a good attitude to have," Page said. "You can
replace the system. You can't replace the user."

Page and Brin wanted to build an efficient search engine, one that didn't
waste users' time. Efficient use of time was paramount for them. Neither
Page nor Brin eagerly read novels or went to many movies or concerts, and
they disdained games like golf that took too long to play. Once, during the
early days of Google, *Time* magazine had arranged to photograph Sergey
in a white lab coat. When the photo shoot ran over the allotted time,
Sergey abruptly called out, "Red alert," and simply walked away without
explanation.

Page and Brin together, it was said, were "two swords sharpening each
other." They were not breathtakingly more brilliant than their peers, said
Winograd, observing that brilliance is commonplace among top Stanford
engineering students. What was unusual about them, he said, was their
boldness. "Page and Brin's breakthrough," writes Battelle in *The Search*,
his book on the history of search, "was to create an algorithm—dubbed
PageRank after Larry—that manages to take into account the number of
links into a particular site, and the number of links into each of the linking
sites." Instead of relying only on keywords as earlier search engines had,
PageRank did a link analysis, counting the sites that were most frequently
visited by users and jumping them to the top of the search results. They
believed this "wisdom of crowds" approach was a more objective way of
measuring which Web pages were most vital. The goal was to get better

answers to search queries. They understood one big thing: They were establishing a formula that would harness the growth of their search engine to the growth of the Web. What they needed was massive computing power to conduct lightning-fast searches, and huge servers to store the millions of indexed Web pages.

In 1996, Larry Page's father, a polio victim as a child, died of pneumonia. He was only fifty-eight. Bereft, Page threw himself into his project. To crawl and index the Web required enormous amounts of Stanford's computer system, and Page and Brin were not shy about using it. Together, he and Brin harassed the computer science department to grant them extra resources. Terry Winograd, who worked on the project, recalled that "they had more of a feel of teenage kids than most graduate students—'Don't tell me what to do!'" Professor Rajeev Motwani, who also worked on the project, said, "They didn't have this false respect for authority. They were challenging me all the time. They had no compunction in saying to me, 'You're full of crap!'" He recalled, "The fondest memory I have of Sergey is of him walking into my office when I was sitting at my desk and he would say, 'Bastard!' That was the kind of thing he would do. Larry was sitting outside. It was a joke. But behind the joke was that he wanted something from me: more computer time."

Once, Winograd said, they snuck onto the loading dock where new Stanford computers were delivered and "borrowed" them to expand their computing power. Page and Brin brought a cart to transport the crates. Some years later, Page confessed that their embryonic search engine in 1997 hogged so much computer capacity that "we caused the whole Stanford network to go down."

The new search engine, at first called BackRub, was an object of some secrecy. Spurred by Page's obsession with Tesla, who unwittingly gave away his inventions by sharing them with others, Page and Brin zealously guarded the algorithms that created PageRank. But as Ph.D. candidates, they were expected to present their work, so to satisfy Stanford's academic requirements they agreed to deliver a paper in January 1998. At the time it wasn't clear whether they wanted to be entrepreneurs or academics. "We almost didn't start Google," Page said. "We wanted to finish school," as their

fathers had. Page remembered the words of Stanford professor Jeffrey Ullman, who urged them to leave the university: "You guys can always come
back and finish your Ph.D.'s if you don't succeed." This argument ultimately proved persuasive, but not before the paper was delivered.

The database they discussed consisted of 24 million Web pages; a typical search took one to ten seconds. They chose the name Google to replace
BackRub because, they said, "it is a common spelling of googol, or 10^{100}
and fits well with our goal of building very large-scale search engines."
(Actually, they wanted to name it Googol but that domain name was taken.
They also thought of The Whatbox, Brin said a few years later, but "we
decided that Whatbox sounded like Wetbox, which sounded like some sort
of porn site.") Their paper stated that their search technology offered "two
important features that help it produce high precision results. First, it
makes use of the link structure of the Web to calculate a quality ranking
for each web page. This ranking is called PageRank. . . . Second, Google
utilizes" links—518 million hyperlinks at the time—to make maps that
"allow rapid calculation of a web page's 'PageRank.'" They presented
some calculations to describe how they approximated "a page's importance or quality."

Page and Brin's paper was attempting to advance a belief that both their
fathers had passed on to them: artificial intelligence (AI) was the next scientific frontier. The search engine would supplement the limited human
brain. "Brin and Page," Nicholas Carr would write years later, "are expressing a desire that has long been a hallmark of the mathematicians and
computer scientists who have devoted themselves to the creation of artificial intelligence." They were following the lead of René Descartes, the
French philosopher/mathematician who four centuries ago argued that
"the body is always a hindrance to the mind in its thinking," and mathematical formulas were the preferred route to "pure understanding."

Their paper derided search engines that had become "commercial" and
"advertising oriented," and offered an example of how "the advertising
business model" did not correspond "to providing quality search to users."
Suppose, they wrote, a user did a search for *cellular phones* and the top
result was a report on how the use of cell phones was a dangerous distrac-

tion while driving. Although this search result might be judged highly important by their PageRank algorithm, it would be likely to provoke protests from cell phone advertisers. Thus, they concluded, "we expect that advertising funded search engines will be inherently biased towards the advertisers and away from the needs of the consumers."

The search system they proposed—shaped around teams of engineers who shared information, beta tested everything, and treated users, not advertisers, as kings—was in turn shaped by the Stanford and Web culture of the time. "They were," observed Harvard Law professor Lawrence Lessig, an author and intellectual guru to a generation of Webheads, "part of an engineering tribe that defined itself as the anti-Microsoft. What it meant to be on the other side was to develop the exact opposite intuitions. Microsoft's approach was: 'You're going to live by my rules.' The opposite is: 'No, I'm going to build it and you're free to use it however you want. I'm just going to empower you to do what you want.' It's the Unix philosophy: Give me a little pile of code and you can plug it into anything you want. That was Stanford in the nineties." It was the Netscape philosophy too, for the same January 1998 month Page and Brin presented their paper, the company that grew out of the browser invented by Marc Andreessen announced that it was revealing the source code to its browser; the new open-source browser would later be named Mozilla.

The presentation was a hit among the "tribe," the professors and graduate students in the audience. Page and Brin had solved a problem for Internet users, said Motwani, who thought: "This is going to change the way the Internet is used!" The word of mouth was electric. Motwani was certain Internet companies would jockey to purchase the technology, and soon after, Brin said, the two partners began speaking to various Silicon Valley companies. Yet all passed on possibly acquiring Google. Even new media companies, it appears, were slow to peer over the horizon.

IN 1998, the year Google was incorporated, utopianism radiated from Silicon Valley and across the Web. Nicholas Negroponte, the founding director of MIT's Media Lab, published a book, *Being Digital,* proclaiming that the Web would usher in a new generation "free of many of the old prejudices. . . . Digital technology can be a natural force drawing people into greater world harmony." The Internet promised freedom from subscriptions and rental charges, and from the crass and misleading advertising dominating television. Digital companies giddily extolled their "traffic" and "page views" and "market valuations," ignoring their sparse revenues and nonexistent profits. "New media" executives marched to conferences attended by "old media" and gleefully insulted them: "You guys don't get it!" they'd say. "Open up. Share your content. Dump your expensive printing presses. Use the Internet as a promotional platform and your business will grow." But how to make money? No one knew.

Greed was also in the air, provoked by dreams of untold riches. Business students flocked to Silicon Valley. Optimism was the drug of choice. Page and Brin opened Google's first office in the living room of the two-bedroom graduate housing unit in Escondido Village that Sergey shared with a roommate. The Google computers and server were stored in the living room of Larry's graduate residence. Their machines placed a serious strain on the limited electrical supply, and they learned to break into the basement of Larry's building to reset the circuit breaker. "Fortunately, I had taken up lock picking so I could get us into there," recalled Brin. He had read a book written for the very purpose: *The MIT Guide to Lock Picking.*

Page and Brin had definite ideas and were not easily swayed. They "thought it was sleazy," Motwani said, to allow Web sites to pay to appear near the top of searches, as other search engines permitted. They were determined to build a computer system that would never lack capacity, as the one at Stanford sometimes did. To build user trust they wanted a simple, functional home page without advertising or pictures; they wanted to serve users by getting them off the Google site as quickly as possible and on to their destination. Page and Brin wouldn't spend a penny to market Google. Anyway, they didn't have a penny; they had just about maxed out their three credit cards. They believed in word-of-mouth advertising: they had the best search engine, and they were sure word would spread.

Their first employee, Craig Silverstein, joined them in Sergey's living room in 1998. Silverstein, who today is the company's director of technology, had the foresight, he laughs, to "negotiate the lowest salary. Instead I said, 'I'll take stock.'" It was phantom stock, and what the founders needed was real capital. That winter, a Stanford computer science professor, Jeffrey Ullman, introduced them to Ram Shriram, a well-connected angel investor in the Valley. After making his fortune at Netscape Communications, Shriram had recently launched Junglee.com, an online product search site. Larry and Sergey instinctively liked and felt comfortable with the Indian-born Shriram, an affable, unpompous man who asks pointed questions with the finesse of a politician. They wanted to demonstrate their search engine and Shriram suggested "a blind test" in which he picked a keyword and searched it on Google and three other search engines. Shriram was impressed with the speed and relevance of the results. But he told them, "I'm not sure there is room for another search engine." He offered to introduce them to InfoSeek, Yahoo, and Excite, and suggested they sell the technology. Larry and Sergey were still ambivalent; they wanted to build a great search engine themselves. But months later, in May, Shriram remembers, they called again and said they had completed the meetings he recommended. He assumed they had been rejected, but reluctantly agreed to meet.

Larry and Sergey drove to Junglee's offices in Sunnyvale and described each of their visits, the most interesting of which was with the founders of Yahoo, Jerry Yang and David Filo. Yahoo was a thriving company that attracted visitors with a broad menu of content encompassing finance, news, and other services. Yang and Filo, they reported, were impressed with their search engine. Very impressed, actually; their concern was that it was too good. Yahoo was a public company, and the more relevant the results of a search were, the fewer page views users would experience before leaving Yahoo. Instead of ten pages, they might see just a couple, and that would deflate the number of page views Yahoo sold advertisers.

"That was for me the *aha* moment," said Shriram. "For the first time, I saw this as something disruptive." Companies like Yahoo and Excite were more interested in being portals than in improving search, leaving an opening for Larry and Sergey. They were still piggybacking on the Stanford system, and they told Shriram that their search engine consumed so much computer capacity that the university wanted them to stop. They needed money.

Shriram offered to make an initial investment and help them incorporate. He also helped them work out a licensing agreement with Stanford so the university would benefit if their two graduate students were successful. On September 7, 1998, the day Google officially incorporated, he wrote out a check for just over $250,000, one of four of this size the founders received. The first was signed by Sun Microsystems cofounder and then Cisco executive Andy Bechtolsheim, who wrote his in August. He had been introduced to Page and Brin by Stanford computer science professor David Cheriton, who became the third initial investor. At the time, Shriram was in the process of selling Junglee to Amazon.com, and in August would start spending most of the week in Seattle as vice president, business development, at Amazon. This link produced the secret fourth investor, Amazon founder Jeffrey Bezos. One day Bezos asked Shriram what was interesting in the Valley. When he touted Google, Bezos asked Shriram to arrange a meeting with Larry and Sergey. "I just fell in love with Larry and Sergey," Bezos recalled; he wrote his check in November. His enthusiasm was ignited less by the idea, and "certainly not by the business plan. There was no business plan. They had a vision. It was a customer-focused point of view." In September, Shriram was asked to join Page and Brin as one of three Google directors, a seat he continues to hold on a board that now consists of ten members.

For $1,700 a month, the just-formed company sublet new office space: the two-car Menlo Park garage and two downstairs spare rooms of an 1,800-square-foot house in Menlo Park. The owners were friends: Susan Wojcicki, an engineer at Intel, and her husband Dennis Troper, a product manager at a tech company. The newly constituted Google had found its way to them because Sergey had dated Susan's roommate at Stanford Business School. The house was not located in the upscale sections of Menlo Park, near the Sand Hill Road offices made famous by the venture capitalists whose offices are there, or in nearby Atherton, where many of these venture capitalists live and in 2008 an acre of land could sell for $3 million. Rather, it was on a dreary flag lot at 232 Santa Margarita Avenue.

A concrete driveway led up to the garage, where a whiteboard had been attached with the legend, "Google Worldwide Headquarters." Inside were three tables, three chairs, a dirty turquoise shag carpet, a tiny refrigerator, an old washer and dryer, and a Ping-Pong table that was kept folded because there wasn't space to leave it open. They kept the garage door open for ventilation, and used a bathroom on the first floor of the house. Their desks were old pine doors that straddled sawhorses. On Monday mornings, Shriram met with Page and Brin in the cramped bedroom they used as an office, before flying to Amazon for the week. Days, nights, and weekends, Page and Brin and Silverstein lived and worked there, often leaving well after midnight in Silverstein's ancient Porsche. "He'd start it and it would backfire five times—*rat-tat-tat-tat-tat*," Brin said. "It sounded like a machine gun going off. We started pushing his car out onto the street before we'd start it."

Although it was still in beta testing in the early fall of 1998, Google was getting ten thousand search queries daily. "I was really getting excited about Google," said Shriram. The founders were getting excited too. "Larry said, 'We'll be at the doorstep of information,'" Susan Wojcicki recalled. Brin told her the company "was going to be worth billions of dollars." That was also what they told visitors from search and portal companies who came to Wojcicki's living room to discuss the possibility of acquiring Google. Even though the founders had no interest in selling, Wojcicki recalls that they'd propose an outrageous price, knowing it would deflect suitors. They also used the house for their first press interview, with a correspondent from the German magazine *Stern*, in which they displayed a combination of grandiosity and zeal. Search really "does have a potential to really change things forever," Brin said. It can "play a really important role in people's lives, determining what information they get to look at," said Page, adding, "and that's an important thing to do for the world." Although Google had scant income, Page and Brin believed that if they built Google, people would come.

CHAPTER THREE

Buzz but Few Dollars

(1999–2000)

n early 1999, Google didn't look like a company that would one day menace Microsoft. Aside from the one million dollars received from its four initial investors, and small amounts collected in the past half year from a handful of other angel investors like Ron Conway, Brin and Page had just a few sources of income: a twenty-thousand-dollar-per-month contract to provide specialized search results to Red Hat, a North Carolina consulting firm that advised companies using Linux and other open-source software, and the licensing of its search to several Web sites. Google had indexed only about 10 percent of the Web, and relied on a relatively primitive computer system to process search traffic that would explode from ten thousand to as many as five hundred thousand daily, each of which took three to four seconds to fetch results. To grow, Page and Brin knew their search engine had to "scale": it had to crawl the entire Web, which would require vast computing power.

The first priority was recruiting engineers. By the end of 1998, a total of six Google employees were crammed into the garage and two small bedrooms. They'd need more room if they were going to expand. So in early 1999 they relocated to a five-thousand-square-foot second-floor space over a bicycle store in downtown Palo Alto, where they balanced more pine doors on sawhorses to make desks and began hiring engineers to fill them. The result was "a graduate-student Disneyland," Michael Specter wrote in *The New Yorker* in 2000, stocked with hockey sticks, Rollerblades, granola, PowerBars, "urns of coffee, and coolers of fruit juice to drive anybody through to 4 A.M.—which is not an unusual time to find people in the office." Even then massages were part of the Google culture; there was a sign advertising that the service was available in the conference room—when the room was not being used for work. A green Ping-Pong table served as their conference table, and that was where, in April 1999, they interviewed Marissa Mayer, then completing a computer science degree from Stanford. It was the peak of the Internet bubble, and the cream of graduating engineers like Mayer had their pick of jobs. Mayer is a brilliant engineer and a proud computer nerd, but with her porcelain skin and lustrous blond hair she seems far from the stereotype—until one hears her jarring high-pitched giggle and tries to follow her words, which gush so rapidly that they collide. Brin, aware of her interest in using math to solve puzzles like how to make a Web site user-friendly, quizzed her for more than an hour. "Larry said nothing the entire time. At the end of the interview I asked, 'Do you speak?'"

She fit right in, and was invited back the next day to be interviewed separately by three engineers, who put her through the equivalent of a Ph.D. oral exam. Before making her an offer, Brin posed to his colleagues what has become known around Google as the airplane test. How would you feel, he asked, if you were stuck next to this person on a plane for several hours? Any candidate who failed this test was unlikely to be a good collaborator or team member. Mayer passed the test and became one of Google's first twenty employees. (Because she was hired before completing school, Mayer is only certain she was between the fifteenth and twentieth employee.) Like all new employees, she was granted stock options that would one day make her wealthy, in her case enough to own a five-million-dollar penthouse apartment at the Four Seasons Hotel in San Francisco, filled with Andy Warhol and Roy Lichtenstein paintings, and a large, three-level Cape Cod house in Palo Alto.

Google now had a team of engineers but no idea how to attract new investors. Ram Shriram recalled telling Brin, "We need a business plan," to which Brin replied, "What's a business plan?" Weeks earlier, Salar Kamangar, a biology major at Stanford who was taking a fifth year to study economics, had volunteered to work for free. With Shriram as a tutor, he was drafted to draw up the business plan. Kamangar, employee number 8, prepared, he said, "a binder on what other companies were doing in search and what was different about Google." Page and Brin were pleased, and asked him to develop a PowerPoint presentation to show potential investors that Shriram and Bechtolsheim were introducing them to. The founders also asked Kamangar to attend these meetings, but first needed to give him a title. They decided, he said, on "senior strategist." In their first business plan, Google had a sketchy idea that they'd make money by charging companies for advanced search results and by getting digital advertising companies like DoubleClick to sell online ads of some kind. The revenue plan wasn't very impressive, but the search engine was. Users were multiplying. Secrecy was the watchword. While Google search was still small, he knew it was much larger than competitors anticipated: "We were in stealth mode," Kamangar said. "If first Yahoo and then Microsoft knew that our number of searches was so much larger, they would be more aggressive." Repeatedly, Page explained his mania for secrecy by invoking the example of Tesla.

Google had to sell the venture capitalists (VCs), but they also had to build a sales force to secure revenues, and for this task they required an experienced senior strategist and salesman. Netscape had just been acquired by AOL, and Shriram knew that Omid Kordestani, the Iranian-born vice president of business development at Netscape, was ready to move on. He orchestrated a meeting between Kordestani and the founders. On paper, Kordestani was a perfect fit for vice president of sales and business development. He held an MBA from Stanford's business school, an undergraduate degree in electrical engineering, and the natural enthusiasm and agreeable personality of a salesman. But first he had to endure a free-for-all

Ping-Pong table grilling by the founders and the engineers. Brin opened the interrogation by saying, "I've never interviewed a business person before." From that inauspicious beginning, Kordestani remembers, "They drilled me for five hours." At the end, no job offer was tendered. The founders had an aversion to business executives, stereotyping them as bureaucrats, not entrepreneurs, and they wanted reference checks. They asked the angel investor who wrote their first check, Andy Bechtolsheim, to make some calls.

"It was a very thoughtful process," Kordestani said, perhaps euphemistically; the eventual job offer was followed by two weekends of intense negotiations in February 1999 with the founders and then with David Drummond, Google's outside counsel at the powerhouse Valley firm of Wilson Sonsini Goodrich & Rosati. (That the hiring process was so laborious would provide good preparation for Drummond; he himself would undergo a milder version of it in 2002, when he was hired as Google's chief legal officer and vice president of corporate development.) Drummond remembers how in the early days of Google, Page and Brin would visit Wilson Sonsini's offices and minutely inspect every legal document, asking him to explain each detail. Kordestani was finally hired, and received a hefty 2 percent of the phantom stock, more than any Google employee aside from the founders and Eric Schmidt, who joined in 2001; when Google's stock soared, Kordestani was a paper billionaire.

The hiring process at Google in some ways paralleled the algorithmic approach to search. Although the founders applied the airplane test, that criteria was less important than the premium they placed on SAT scores and on grades and degrees from the best colleges. Real-world experience counted less than objective measurements. The thought that an entire human being could be judged by objective criteria was preposterous. It was a reminder of the tunnel vision Brin and Page—like so many young entrepreneurs—brought to their work. One reason they succeed is that they refuse to be diverted from their goal. But aside from the business books Page read before he started Google, he and Brin were relatively narrow in scope, without a 360-degree view of the world.

The hiring process did have its light moments. David Krane was working in public relations at a software company when he heard about Google. He was taken with the quirky sensibility he found when he clicked on the "About Google" button on their Web site. The son of a nuclear physicist, Krane once harbored hopes of becoming a musician. He was enamored of technology and was a rarity among PR people in that he could explain the difference between PQA (palm query application software, which allowed Web material to be seen on a handheld device) and HTML (hypertext markup language, the dominant Web language). A friend passed his résumé to Google's then vice president of corporate communications, Cindy McCaffrey, who was hired in July 1999 as employee number 26. She interviewed him, as did countless other executives over the next four and a half months. Finally, separate interviews were arranged with Page and Brin, both of whom found public relations and marketing a form of hucksterism. It was no surprise that the first question Brin asked was, "Explain something technical to me? Topic of your choice."

Ideas rushed to Krane's brain, and he made a surprising choice. He explained how to make a reed for a clarinet, how to file and test and tweak it so the musical tone was clear and warm.

Brin listened, then quickly moved on to his second question: "Have you ever heard of Slashdot?"

Slashdot was a technology news site that encouraged user-generated comments, a pioneer of what came to be known as blogging. Krane smiled and pulled from his pocket a geeky badge of honor: a Palm 7, which permitted a wireless Internet connection to one of his favorite sites, Slashdot .com. "I thought," said Krane, "I had aced the interview!"

Brin shook hands and left, and Page entered. "He greeted me in a very reserved way. He asked me the equivalent of a tell-me-about-yourself icebreaker question." Krane waltzed through his life, his interests, his passion for Google. "I wasn't getting any kind of signal back from Larry. It was like talking to a stone wall." He thought, "I'm sinking!"

Desperate, he began to talk about music, and his musical training. He completed maybe three sentences when Page excitedly interrupted, "That's where I know you!"

Krane was mystified.

"That's where I know you! I was at Interlochen too, that same summer! And I also played saxophone!" They swapped memories of the three months at Interlochen Arts Camp. "We figured out that we sat next to each other. Larry was in my left ear in the same jazz band. I played tenor sax and he played alto sax. We were both joined by acne, big glasses, and blue corduroy pants and light blue polyester short-sleeved shirts with a big butterfly collar, the Interlochen uniform." Days later, Krane was hired on as employee number 84. Today he is Google's director of global communications and public affairs.

As the business took shape, the founders thought more and more about aesthetics. They wanted a home page that was both playful and uncluttered, so they hired a Stanford design teacher named Ruth Kedar. Her instructions, she recalled, were clear: "Google wanted to create a unique logo that would clearly differentiate them from the other search players at the time. . . . These other players were commercial portals first, and search engines second. Google wanted to convey that it was a search provider first and foremost. . . . Google as a brand should repudiate all things corporate, conventional or complacent." The design was meant "to look almost non-designed, the reading effortless. The colors evoke memories of child play."

Years later, Page and Brin demonstrated their playful irreverence. It was April 1, and the white space on the Google home page suddenly carried a line under the search box: "A Cool World: Enjoy a rosier future as a Virgle Pioneer." When the link was opened, an invitation appeared to sign up for an "Adventure of Many Lifetimes." The invitation read: "Earth has issues, and it's time humanity got started on a Plan B. So, starting in 2014, Virgin founder Richard Branson and Google co-founders Larry Page and Sergey Brin will be leading hundreds of users on one of the grandest adventures in human history: Project Virgle, the first permanent human colony on Mars." The site described the alleged deprivations, including low broadband rates and physical hardships and potential death. It was an April Fools' joke.

The home page design, and a few glowing mentions about its search prowess in media like *PC Magazine,* generated some buzz about Google in the Valley. Ron Conway, the angel investor, recalled a reception attended by Shawn Fanning, the founder of Napster, who had become a poster boy for the digital revolution. Brin and Page were unknowns and Conway remembers them approaching Fanning and saying, "What does it feel like to be on the cover of all those magazines?"

"You guys have a really cool search product," responded Fanning. "You'll be more famous than I am!"

Danny Sullivan, a former reporter who left newspapers in 1996 to publish a Web newsletter called *Search Engine Watch* (now called *Search Engine Land*), and who is the closest approximation to an umpire in the search world, remembers the early buzz about Google. The initial search engines—AltaVista, Highbot, Lycos, Excite, Infoseek, GoTo, Yahoo—were more interested in becoming "sticky portals" that trapped users on their sites, which diluted their focus on search. And when they performed a search, they were not impartial, allowing advertisers to buy their way to the top of the search results. Google, by contrast, "was really dedicated to search," and refused to allow advertisers to distort the "science" of their search results.

Despite their young age—they were twenty-six—and the tight focus of their education, Brin and Page had extraordinary clarity about what search users might want. They rejected the conventional wisdom embraced by AOL and Yahoo and Microsoft's MSN to create portals and try to keep users in their walled garden with an array of content. They believed the right approach was to get users out of Google and to their search destination quickly. They rejected advertisers who wanted to place banner ads alongside search results, because the banners slowed results, were not intrinsic to search, and were a distraction. In the late nineties, when pop-up ads were the dominant way to advertise on the Web, the founders had the Google tool bar block them. They declined to place ads on their most valuable piece of real estate, the uncluttered opening Google page containing the search box.

Brin and Page resisted ads because they shared an allergy then common among Webheads and many folks who attended Burning Man: that advertising was like a rude stranger interrupting a conversation to sell you something you neither wanted nor needed. "These guys were opposed to advertising because they had a purist view of the world," said Shriram. Like some Burning Man attendees, Page and Brin were—no other word will do—odd. Barry Diller, the CEO of the InterActiveCorp, a diverse collection of such e-commerce sites as Expedia and Ticketmaster, recalled visiting Page and Brin in the early days of Google. As they talked, Diller was disconcerted to see that Page did not lift his head from his PDA device; and Brin arrived late, on Rollerblades. "It's one thing if you're in a room with twenty people and someone is using their PDA," Diller recalled. "I said to Larry, 'Is this boring?'"

"No. I'm interested. I always do this," said Page.

"Well, you can't do this," said Diller. "Choose."

"I'll do this," said Page matter-of-factly, not lifting his eyes from his handheld device.

"So I talked to Sergey. I left thinking that more than most people they were wildly self-possessed."

The founders may not have had a clue how to make money at Google, but they were clear that their mission was to build a great search engine and offer this search for free. Susan Wojcicki, the engineer who rented her garage to the founders and became employee number 18 and who later introduced her sister, Anne, to Brin, said the founders "were on a mission to build the best search engine," and "early on understood that what mattered were users." Their initial mission statement declared that they aimed "to organize the world's information and make it universally acceptable." This mission on its face was not as crassly commercial as Microsoft's. Bill Gates's quest was to put "a computer in every home and on every desk." Each computer sold increased Microsoft's dominance over the software market for the PC. Google's missionary zeal, coupled with the fact that its search was free, cloaked its lust to also build a profit-making machine.

Building the machine, however, required capital. Relying mostly on original angel investors Shriram and Bechtolsheim for business advice, the founders decided early on to seek funding from more than one venture capital firm, so as not to rely on a single source of funds, and to assure their independence by selling no more than one-quarter of the company. They set out to recruit two of the most prominent VC firms in the Valley, Kleiner Perkins Caufield & Byers, whose senior partner John Doerr was a trained engineer who had helped fund such start-ups as Amazon, Netscape, and AOL, and Sequoia Capital, where Oxford-educated former *Time* magazine reporter Michael Moritz was a partner and an early backer of Yahoo and PayPal. Doerr remembers the meeting vividly. They met in the conference room next to his glassed office on Sand Hill Road. Page and Brin made a brief PowerPoint presentation to establish the most telling facts: by the end of 1998 they had indexed twenty-six million Web pages and were now doing half a million searches a day. Doerr was impressed. Instead of a long-winded explanation of their mission, Page and Brin made a high-concept pitch consisting of eight words: "We deliver the world's information in one click."

"I asked Page," Doerr recalled, "'how big will Google's business be?'"

"Ten billion," he said.

"Surely you mean market cap?" asked Doerr.

"No, revenue," answered Page. He did not volunteer that they had no plausible revenue plan; instead he expressed faith that they would find a way to monetize their exploding search traffic. Pulling out a laptop, they demonstrated how much faster and more relevant a Google search was than those of other search engines.

"I almost fell out of my chair!" Doerr said. It was "one of the most extraordinary conversations I ever had in my life. I knew in that first meeting I wanted to invest in this business." Page and Brin were similar to other founders he had funded—young men who had dropped out of school, who spoke quickly and were consumed by their work—but Doerr was struck by what he calls their audacity and singular focus. Doerr had been an investor in Excite, an early search engine, and had seen how the company lost focus as it chased becoming a portal. Moritz, too, was sold on Page and Brin's "devotion to their dream. They were on a mission. We've learned over the years to pay close attention" to this kind of clarity. Besides, he added, "Their product was better."

The plan was for Doerr and Moritz to sign a contract certifying that the two firms valued Google at $100 million and would invest a total of $25 million. There were some hitches, though. Each VC wanted to do the deal alone, but Page and Brin would not budge, insisting they do it together or not at all. And Doerr and Moritz were worried that Page (the CEO and chief financial officer) and Brin (the president and chairman of the board of directors) had between them roughly zero management experience; they wanted the founders to recruit professional managers. After protracted discussions, they finally reached a verbal agreement. "The understanding when we invested was that a CEO would, among others, be hired over time," Moritz said. The founders would ignore this understanding, which later created some friction. They hit one other speed bump. While the parties were haggling, recalled Shriram, Brin phoned him and said he had met with another venture capital firm, one Shriram had earlier recommended. The VC told Brin that Google was worth $150 million, substantially more than the current estimate. "Should we do it?" Brin asked. Should they dump Doerr and Moritz in favor of the higher valuation?

"You're already committed," Shriram told Brin.

Nevertheless, Shriram recalled later with a smile, "Sergey mentioned this to Doerr and Moritz and it speeded up the process!" Brin, he said, is no Boy Scout, but rather a sly, dexterous deal maker: "I think of him as Kobe Bryant, a game changer."

ON JUNE 7, 1999, Google issued its first press release announcing that Kleiner Perkins and Sequoia had invested twenty-five million dollars in Google. They also held their first press conference, in a small room in the Gates building at Stanford. Page and Brin, wearing white tennis shirts with the Google logo, sat at a Formica table flanked by Doerr, Shriram, and Moritz. Andy Bechtolsheim, Rajeev Motwani, and Terry Winograd sat in the audience with five reporters. As the journalists looked on, the founders gave a lengthy explanation of the technicalities of PageRank, their methods for indexing the Web and devising algorithms, their notions of "latency" and "scale," and just about anything else they could think of.

At last a reporter asked the obvious question: How does Google plan to make money?

"Our goal," Brin said, "is to maximize the search experience, not to maximize the revenues from search."

At what appeared to be the conclusion of the press conference, Brin rose with a broadly smiling Page beside him and said, "If you want to ask more questions, fine." He invited the reporters to stay and take a Google shirt and share refreshments. Unlike today, where their press appearances are not frequent and are treated, certainly by Page, as occasions to be endured, a home video of the press conference suggests that the two of them would happily have lingered all day.

Google's next business breakthrough came later that same month. Omid Kordestani negotiated a deal with Netscape and its new corporate owner, AOL, to designate Google as the default search engine for the popular Netscape browser. The deal boosted Google searches to more than three million per day. "That was pretty exciting," said Brin. "That was a big deal for us." It was a major endorsement of Google. It was also a major test, bringing in huge numbers of searchers. "We got overwhelmed with traffic. It was our first big search engine crisis," remembers Craig Silverstein. "We shut off Google.com that day to everyone but Netscape—till we could buy more computers!" They were burdened by another traffic jam, remembers senior software engineer Matt Cutts. When he joined the company in 1999, among his first tasks was to figure out how to block pornography searches, which accounted for one of every four queries. His solution was to assign a lesser weight in the Google algorithm to the words commonly used in porn searches, or for Google's engineers to misspell the keywords in the Google index so the porn was difficult to retrieve. First he had to figure out the pertinent words. He spent hours poring over porn documents. Then his wife came up with the idea of baking cookies and awarding one "porn cookie" to each engineer who discovered a salacious keyword. Porn search traffic plummeted.

By the summer of 1999, Google was flush with cash and had outgrown the five-thousand-square-foot Palo Alto office, where forty employees now knocked knees when sitting at their desks. They needed to move, so Susan Wojcicki called in a real estate agent, who suggested the founders clear their schedules to visit possible sites. The founders thought this was a waste of their time. They knew what they wanted: to re-create the feel of the Stanford campus. Wojcicki remembers their saying to the agent, "Why don't you go look at buildings and take some pictures and bring them back to us?"

In August, Google leased part of a two-story building rimmed by trees on Bayshore Boulevard in bucolic Mountain View. Initially, they rented the second floor but quickly expanded to the first, then to another building next door. It had obvious attractions: it was barely a ten-mile bike ride north to Stanford University, and in the distance to the west, the Santa Cruz Mountains formed a visible border. But unlike Palo Alto, where employees could walk to lunch, a meal in Mountain View required driving. The offices quickly became littered with pizza boxes and Chinese-food containers. The founders decided they'd need a chef. They'd select one in the same way fraternities and sororities at Stanford did: by having a Chef Audition Week. One chef, Charlie Ayers, "blew everyone away" with his array of "gourmet comfort food—like spaghetti and meatballs," said Marissa Mayer. (It helped that Ayers was the former chef for the Grateful Dead.) He was hired in November to supervise the preparation of favorites like pizza and hamburgers, and also what he called big-ass barbecues, as well as vegetarian stir-fry, salads with lush tomatoes and fresh vegetables, carved turkey, fiery chili, lamb chops, steak, and generous slabs of sushi, to which he affixed an attractive New Age explanation: "The fat found in fish helps make the cell membranes round the brain more elastic and more able to absorb nutrients easily."

In addition to free food, the founders signed off on an abundance of other amenities that made venture capitalists uneasy. "I think they were a little bit perturbed to see the front-page stories in the San Jose *Mercury News* that we were hiring a chef and a masseuse," Brin concedes. "But I think the actual economic and productivity outcome of this they grew pretty quickly to accept. They just didn't think we should be known for that [profligacy]." He explained how he and Page approach free food and employee benefits: "A lot of it is common sense, a combination of common sense and questioning rituals." Generous benefits help recruit and retain employees, he said. Compelling employees to drive for meals, and find parking "would be a real productivity sink . . . and they'd probably not eat healthy food." Besides, he added, waiting in line to pay would waste more time.

For all its intensity, Google could be a playful place to work. The first place in the Valley Al Gore visited after he left the vice presidency in January 2001 was Google. He had championed the Internet while serving in Congress and as vice president. His first meeting with Brin, Page, and Kordestani in February 2001 went smoothly, he said. "I liked them and they asked me to help them out and, initially, to join their board," which he declined because he wasn't sure whether he'd again seek the presidency. Instead, he said, "They asked me to be—the phrase they used was, 'a virtual board member.'"

Al and Tipper Gore went on a long European vacation. They returned later in the spring, and newspapers carried pictures of the full beard he had grown. "When I went back to Google, Larry and Sergey and Omid—there weren't that many of them—all ten of them had false beards on. It was hilarious!"

Google was growing into an informal, open place. At around 4:30 p.m. each Friday, employees now gather in the largest open space on campus, Charlie's Café in Building 40, for TGIF. Refreshments—nachos, mini-hamburgers, pretzels, beer, soft drinks—are available. Employees sit on chairs arranged in a semicircle, with employees at other Google locations around the world on video conference. Brin and Page stand on a small raised platform to share corporate news and to answer questions from thousands of employees. New employees hired that week sit up front, wearing Noogler beanies with propellers on top. Loud music blasts from speakers. The affectionate bond between the two founders is displayed every time they make a presentation together or at these weekly Friday appearances. On stage, Brin is funnier, and tends to dominate, yet in the dozens of times I've watched them together, I've never noticed a hint of exasperation from Page, who is an intense person but nevertheless laughs easily at Brin's jokes.

At the first TGIF I attended, in October 2007, Brin appeared wearing what looked like a green pilot's jacket and Page wore a black one. They were in jeans and sneakers, and took turns talking—introducing the Nooglers; telling of some deals Google had made the past week; showing a video clip of former Alaska senator Mike Gravel, who was a stealth candidate for president, as he gave a speech on campus in which he described his visit as comparable to "an intellectual orgasm." Brin cracked, "We'll use that as a recruiting tool!" They fielded questions from employees. And they had a surprise guest calling in from an airplane. The guest was competing with static, and didn't sound like himself, but managed to say hello.

"I heard that you won something today," Brin said.

Up on the large screen behind them appeared a picture of Al Gore, who on this day had won the Nobel Peace Prize for his work on behalf of the environment, an award that was featured in the morning papers and dominated the news.

"We all feel grateful to you," Brin said.

"Thank you, Sergey. And to you and Larry and Eric and the entire team. One of the fun things in my life is to be part of the extended Google family."

A roar of applause cascaded from the balcony and throughout the café, and soon Gore was gone.

"He sounded a little like Stephen Hawking," joked Page.

The hand of an engineer who spends too many hours in front of a computer screen shot up. "Larry and Sergey," he asked. "Which prize?"

The personalities of the founders permeate the company. Doerr described Sergey as the "more exuberant" of the two. "Sergey is more creative, more experimental than Larry is." One longtime Google executive decribes him as a ham. "I love Sergey," the executive adds. "He's an exhibitionist. He needs more attention than Larry does." Brin does most of the talking, and joking, at Friday TGIF gatherings. In the early days of Google, when they took the entire staff camping for a weekend, everyone had a canoe partner, except Brin. "He said, 'It doesn't matter. I'll swim.'" Wearing a lime-green Speedo swimsuit, he jumped into the lake, becoming the center of attention. One cannot imagine Larry Page agreeing to appear on the game show *To Tell the Truth*, as Brin did in March 2001. The question posed was "Who is the real Google guru?" Each of the three contestants wore a Google T-shirt, and after questioning them, the four celebrity panelists unanimously guessed that the real guru was panelist number 3, who turned out to be a professional bowler. Only 22 percent of the audience guessed that Brin was the guru. But when it came time to stand and identify the real guru, Brin histrionically pretended to stand, then sat, then rose to shocked audience applause, reciprocating with a slight but delighted smile.

Despite the playfulness, few would describe the founders as ideal mediators. They are often too brusque and intimidating for that role. "Larry can be a little raw, but never unkind," said Megan Smith, vice president of new business development. A part of the rawness is due to the fact that they are geeks, more comfortable staring at a computer screen than schmoozing, and too zealously impatient to waste time.

Page is more reclusive, and odder. He was once asked at a dinner, according to a dinner guest, "What's the most important thing the government should be doing?"

"Colonize Mars!" Page said.

Most of the dinner guests nodded as if he had said something profound.

Page can be almost monklike. He ruthlessly guards his time, and can treat those who ask him to make a speech or meet reporters as if they were thieves trying to steal his time. A longtime Google employee describes Page this way: "Larry is like a wall. He analyzes everything. He asks, 'Is this the most efficient way to do this?' You're always on trial with Larry. He always pushes you."

While Brin is more approachable than Page, he, too, can be awkward around strangers. His wife Anne Wojcicki's company, 23andMe, was feted at a fashionable cocktail party in September 2008 that was cohosted by

Diane von Furstenberg and her husband, Barry Diller, Wendi and Rupert
Murdoch, and Georgina Chapman and her husband, Harvey Weinstein.
The event was held at Diller's Frank Gehry–designed IAC headquarters in
Manhattan. Brin appeared wearing a dark crewneck sweater and gray
Crocs. He and Google are investors in her company and he is openly proud
of her work. But she had to quietly beseech him to stay. He did, but hid
behind his oversized Canon camera, moving about the vast room or retreat-
ing to a corner, always snapping pictures.

THE YEAR 2000 BEGAN with two bangs. The first was that Google entered
the new year averaging seven million searches a day, a massive jump from
half a million at the beginning of 1999. The second was the sudden crash
of technology stocks. Between March and October, the NASDAQ Com-
posite Index, which lists most tech and Internet companies, fell 78 percent.
Yahoo's stock at one point plunged from $119 a share to $4. As a private
company, Google was both spared and offered opportunities. "As in any
successful venture, there's a lot of luck," said Hal Varian. "One of the great
things from Google's point of view was the dot-com collapse in 2000. A lot
of talent became available." Google cherry-picked some good engineers.

But the company was burning through its cash. While Google's revenues
would total $19.1 million in 2000, its losses would be $14.7 million, more
than double those of the previous year. And they'd had "zero discussion"
about any kind of Google advertising until late 1999, recalled Salar Kamangar, who crafted Google's first business plan and became vice president
of product management. The founders feared ads would slow searches.
They still believed Google could outsource monetization to ad firms like
DoubleClick, or sell their search services to corporations. Page and Brin
were relying on their faith that a way would be found to make money. This
faith produced more friction with their two major investors, but Page and
Brin were undeterred.

In *The Search*, John Battelle describes an encounter around this time
between Page and Brin and Bill Gross, the founder of the GoTo search
engine. Gross had come up with an idea: he was convinced advertisers or

Web sites would pay more for certain keywords if they could pay on a cost-per-click (CPC) basis, meaning they paid only if the user showed enough interest in a given ad to click on their link and perhaps make a purchase. The price for the keyword and the placement of the ad would be set in an online auction process. By mid-1999, GoTo had a network of eight thousand advertisers, with some paying by the click and others paying a fee to appear at the top of the search results. Gross approached Page and Brin to propose that the two companies merge, reports Battelle, but "Brin and Page turned a cold shoulder to Gross's overture. The reason given: Google would never be associated with . . . a company that mixed paid advertising with organic results." (Gross later changed his company's name, GoTo, to Overture, and in 2002 would sue Google for allegedly stealing its cost-per-click model.)

Meanwhile, Google decided to offer its search to other Web sites and to share any revenues. It was a way to extend its reach, and to be paid for the use of its search engine. The most significant deal, signed in June 2000, established Google as Yahoo's official search engine. Google paid dearly for the privilege, granting Yahoo a warrant to acquire 3.7 million shares of Google when it was issued. And few users knew they were conducting a Google search, because Yahoo wouldn't allow Google's branded search box on its page. For Google, the deal was another milestone. Its search traffic doubled to fourteen million on the first day of the partnership.

While most experts by the end of 2000 thought Google had the best search engine, this claim was conjectural. What was indisputable was that Google was now the most-visited search engine on the Web, with one hundred million daily search queries and a worldwide market share of about 40 percent. Yahoo had given Google a boost, but "it was really about the quality of the search," said *Search Engine Land* editor Danny Sullivan. "People were coming to Google because they heard about it." The rapid growth would provide Google a vital and at the time overlooked asset. More searches generated more data for Google about users, which led to better searches, which would eventually lead to more ad dollars.

The question of how to monetize search by turning traffic and data into cash remained unanswered. Unlike AOL, Google didn't have subscription revenues. And unlike portals such as Yahoo, it didn't have content sites on which to place banner or display advertising. In October 2000, Google introduced its first advertising program, called AdWords. It was a small beta test, available to 350 advertisers who paid for a selection of search keywords that allowed the advertiser's small text ads to appear on the side of the search results. It was a self-service program. Companies gave Google their keywords and went online to retrieve data on the number of times users typed their keywords into the search box. The effort was clunky, and grew very slowly.

Although AdWords was a new media advertising effort, it borrowed an old media CPM (cost-per-thousand) model. Much in the way that a television network might know that millions of viewers were exposed to a thirty-second spot, but not whether they actually watched it or made a purchase because of it, advertisers paid based soley on the number of times their ad appeared. There was a link to the advertiser allowing users to learn more about a product, though Google did not get paid if the user clicked through. The program was also limited in that Google could not easily syndicate AdWords to partners because GoTo had already tied up other search engines, making Google less attractive to advertisers. In addition, prominent advertisers were not inclined to place their dollars on search keywords. Giving credence to something that seemed so puny was alien to the brand advertising they were accustomed to. Because Page and Brin insisted that all advertising be relevant to the keywords, Google only allowed ads to appear in 15 percent of all searches, which meant that Google was forgoing advertising dollars if the ads were not judged "relevant." Page and Brin liked to boast that Google could move on a dime, but their company was moving ever so gingerly to embrace advertising.

They were moving too gingerly for Doerr and Moritz, who admit they were frustrated by Google's mounting losses. In the eyes of investors, the issues of monetization and management were twined. Good managers would impose the discipline every profit maker requires. "The understanding when we invested was that a CEO, among others, would be hired over time," said Moritz. The venture capitalists finally persuaded Page and Brin to hire a headhunter to find a CEO, but the young founders were resistant, fearful that "a suit" would subvert the Google culture. They met with about fifteen candidates, all accomplished executives who were invited to attend TGIF, to share meals with the founders in the cafeteria, to sit in on staff meetings. Brin went heli-skiing with one prospective CEO who boasted that he was an expert at the sport. (He wasn't.) "They thought everyone they had talked to was a clown," Paul Buchheit said. "The candidates didn't understand technology." Omid Kordestani said Page and Brin "knew in their gut that they wanted a fellow intellectual."

The VCs feared the founders would find an excuse to reject every candidate, which was true. Marissa Mayer said she believes the CEO search was so protracted in part because "they were not convinced it needed to happen." Mayer knew Page and Brin's thinking. She was a central member of the engineering team. And she and Page were dating, as they would for about three years. Like most company founders, they believed they could better manage their baby, better ensure the implementation of their vision, better preserve the culture. Asked if the founders resisted, Moritz now responds like a State Department official: "They resisted hiring ordinary people, and that's a wonderful tribute to them. One of the many lessons I learned from the Google investment is the importance of hiring spectacular people. Sometimes it frustrated us, but they were spot-on."

Moritz, however, did not feel that way at the end of 2000. "All of us on the board, in particular John and Mike, felt we needed someone who had been there, done that. You can call it adult supervision," said Ram Shriram. Caught between the VCs and the founders, his "job was to keep the two sides talking," he said, describing his role as that of "a coach." Some at Google even feared a VC coup. "The VCs figured, 'Once we get a CEO in there we'd get control,'" said one early Googler.

Doerr and Moritz arranged for Page and Brin to meet with the founders of other Valley companies, such as Intel, Intuit, and Apple, to talk about management issues. "We like Steve Jobs!" Page and Brin chorused, to the annoyance of the VCs and, eventually, to the consternation of other Google executives. One new hire that year, Tim Armstrong, the president of advertising and commerce, said, "It was chaos when I got to Google." Executives were needed to manage the brilliant engineers and help set priorities, he said. Under pressure internally and externally, the founders interviewed two computer scientists who met their standards, said Marissa Mayer. One was from New York, the other from the Valley. Both were offered the job, she said. But the New Yorker did not want to relocate his family, and the other thought he was on the CEO fast track at Intel. Both declined the offer.

By the end of 2000, Google had indexed one billion Web pages. But no CEO had been hired, nor had any professional managers, and there was still no clear path to making money. Google had built it, the traffic came, but the revenue had not followed. The venture capitalists worried that Page and Brin were humoring them—and maybe leading Google astray.

CHAPTER FOUR

Prepping the Google Rocket

(2001-2002)

While Google's venture capitalists fretted that Page and Brin were spinning their wheels and that the company cried out for professional management, the Internet was growing and changing at warp speed. January 2001 brought two innovations that profoundly disrupted the existing order. Steve Jobs launched Apple's iTunes application, and within seven years, iPod owners had purchased and downloaded five billion songs. Already reeling from piracy, the big four music companies felt compelled to allow individual songs to be sold at a price Apple chose (ninety-nine cents), inevitably undermining the sale of entire CDs, the centerpiece of their business model. That same January, Jimmy Wales and Larry Sanger launched Wikipedia. Within seven years this nonprofit effort would contain ten million entries in 253 languages, changing the way people gathered information. Wikipedia and iTunes were reminders, as if any were needed, that we had entered the dawn of a new digital democracy that granted more power to individuals.

Page and Brin were convinced that Google would become an even more profound disrupter of the existing order. Their philosophy, Page told a class at Stanford, can be distilled into two words: *Don't settle*. He defended the exhaustive process of hiring at Google, and finding managers who respected and nurtured Google's engineer-is-king culture. But there were too many kings. It wasn't until January 2001 that Google finally hired its first vice president of engineering operations, Wayne Rosing, who had held a series of senior management positions at Apple, Sun Microsystems, and the Digital Equipment Corporation. The process was laborious, but eventually Rosing was hired. That was "the real turning point," said employee number 1, Craig Silverstein. "He brought a professionalism to management we had not had before." When he stepped into the chaos at Google, a shocked Rosing found that one senior engineer "had 130 direct reports." Instead of doing what most companies did by relying on financial management software made by companies such as Intuit, Page and Brin had insisted that Google engineers invent a new system.

DOERR WAS EAGER to find a CEO for Google, and thought his friend Eric Schmidt might be a perfect fit. Because Schmidt held a Ph.D. in computer science—making him the rare professional manager who could speak the language of engineers—and did not have an oversized ego, Doerr assumed he could work with the founders. At the time, Schmidt was the chairman and CEO of Novell, a computer networking and software company then in the midst of a merger with Cambridge Technology. He wasn't thrilled with the job; the commute from his home in the Valley to Novell's headquarters in Provo, Utah, was arduous, and Novell was underperforming. One night, Doerr and Schmidt were chatting at a cocktail party. Doerr asked Schmidt what his plans were, and Schmidt said he hadn't thought deeply about it.

"I think you should look at Google," Doerr said.

"I can't imagine that Google would be worth much," said Schmidt.

"I think you should have a talk with Larry and Sergey," said Doerr.

As it happened, he already had. During the process of vetting Wayne Rosing, Brin had called Schmidt, a former colleague of Rosing's at Sun, for an opinion. The call lasted forty-five minutes and ended with Brin inviting Schmidt to visit Google.

Schmidt visited Google in December 2000. He knew Building 21 well, for he had worked there when it was Sun's headquarters. In the office Page and Brin shared, he found two desks, a sofa, and the same lava lamps Sun had had on display. In contrast to the carefully groomed Schmidt, Page and Brin seemed to use their fingers rather than a comb to tidy their dark hair; Page's shorter hair is pulled down and clings to his forehead, while Brin's wavy locks are pushed back and one sideburn is longer and slants more sharply than the other. To his surprise, Schmidt saw his bio projected on the wall above the couch. There was little foreplay. "They started going at it," Schmidt recalled. "They said I was mistaken in my business strategy with regard to proxy caches, a method Novell was using at the time to try to speed up Internet connections. Their thesis was that there was so much bandwidth coming down that such proxy caches were a bad business and would be unnecessary. I, of course, disagreed, and disagreed violently. This was a forty-five-minute meeting that went on for an hour and a half. I could not get them to accept the brilliance of my argument. They started from the data they saw at Google, and peppered me with questions. I hadn't had that good an argument in all my years at Novell." Page and Brin were also pleased. They appreciated Schmidt's technical prowess, and he passed the airplane test when he revealed that he, too, was a regular attendee at Burning Man. How much of a suit could he be?

Schmidt was born April 27, 1955, in Falls Church, Virginia, and like Page and Brin was raised in an academic family. Wilson Schmidt, his father, was a professor of international economics at Johns Hopkins and worked for a time in Richard Nixon's Treasury Department; Eleanor, his mother, received a master's degree in psychology but stayed home to look after Eric and two brothers. Eric attended public schools, where he got hooked on time-share computers, which in those prehistoric days still relied on punch cards. Another solo-sports enthusiast, he earned eight high school letters as a distance runner. After graduating, he was accepted at Princeton as an architecture major, but switched to electrical engineering because, he said, "I lacked creativity." He became adept at programming. "All of us never slept at night because computers were faster at night," he said. He worked summers at Bell Labs, where he was skilled enough to write a software program called Lex, a code that facilitated the writing of text. He received an electrical engineering B.S. from Princeton in 1979 and an M.S. and a Ph.D. in 1982 from the University of California, Berkeley. Graduate school summers were spent working at Xerox PARC, the famed lab that hosted the creation of computer work stations, that forged the technology that became the mouse, laser printers, and the Ethernet. After completing Berkeley, he joined the research staff in the Computer Science Lab at PARC, where he worked alongside such software pioneers as Bill Joy (who became one of four founders of Sun Microsystems) and Charles Simonyi (who would oversee the development of Microsoft Word and Excel).

His first corporate job was at Sun, which he joined in 1983. Over the next fourteen years, Schmidt would demonstrate a repertoire of talents: as a manager who hired and supervised ten thousand engineers, as a scientist who nurtured the innovative programming language Java, and as Sun's chief technical officer. He left in 1997 to become CEO of Novell. By his own admission, he failed to do proper due diligence before he took the job. "When you grow up in a company that is well run, it's hard to imagine a company not well run," he said. Novell was not well run. When he arrived, Novell had a $14,600,000 shortfall to declare in its quarterly report, and executives there proposed they tap their reserves to cloak it. Schmidt chose to report the shortfall, and Novell's stock took a dive. Chapter 11 was a real possibility. "Getting near bankruptcy is a pretty good experience for being a tough CEO," said Schmidt. Looking back on his tenure at Novell, Schmidt candidly said, "I did an undistinguished job."

Still, his skills and temperament were attractive to Page and Brin. More conversations ensued, and in February of 2001 they offered him the CEO job. Schmidt could not accept until the Novell merger was completed; it was in March that he was named chairman of Google. He assumed the title of CEO in August, and Page was named president, products, and Brin president, technology. According to SEC documents Google filed when it went public, Schmidt was paid a salary of $250,000 and an annual performance bonus. He was granted 14,331,708 shares of class B common stock at a price of 30 cents per share, and 426,892 Series C preferred stock at a purchase price of $2.34. LarryandSergey had a partner.

THE APPOINTMENT WAS GREETED with some skepticism. Schmidt's critics said he was barely escaping from Novell. They sneered at the Mercedes he drove, the suits and ties he wore. They wondered whether he had the right skill set. "No one from his previous jobs," said one industry insider who knows him well, "would say that Eric was an inspirational leader, a great speaker or salesman, a take-charge leader like Paul Otellini of Intel, Carol Bartz of Autodesk, or John Chambers of Cisco." Skepticism about Schmidt was reinforced by the management structure announced by Google. Although Schmidt was named CEO, there was an unusual division of power. He, Brin, and Page would work as a team, and if there was a difference between the two founders over routine decisions, Schmidt would act as the tiebreaker. "We agreed that on any major decision, the three of us must agree," he said.

When Schmidt arrived full time at Google there was some hissing that he was a stooge. "Eric doesn't have a huge ego," venture capitalist and former *Fortune* columnist Stewart Alsop told *GQ*. "He's willing to suffer the myriad small indignities of being a pet CEO." Reminded of this disparagement, Schmidt declined to take the bait and after a pause said, "I think it's inappropriate for me to comment on myself. . . . Self-reporting is always suspect." His low-key demeanor; monotone voice; and round, frameless professorial glasses were interpreted by some as signs of timidity. But over time, detractors came to appreciate his competence and maturity. His modesty also won converts. Instead of wearing his customary suits, Schmidt soon donned the Google uniform: khakis and a white or black golf shirt with the Google logo. He was building trust. Schmidt was assigned a small office containing two desks, but before he arrived an engineer looking for a place to park spotted the empty office and moved in. According to Rajeev Motwani, who continued to advise his Stanford protégés, when Schmidt arrived he assessed the situation and quietly took the second desk. "They became office mates. Can you imagine a company where an engineer can move into the CEO's office? That tells you a lot about Eric, and about the company. He understood the company's DNA, which is that what you do defines your importance."

While Schmidt did not believe he had come to Google to fix a company that was broken, he knew its management systems were dysfunctional. He also knew he needed to go slowly in changing them. He saw that Page and Brin wanted to stay focused on technology and products, and had an aversion to intrusive bureaucrats. Schmidt set out to convince the founders and the engineers that good managers would liberate the engineers, reduce bureaucracy, provide an audited financial system that would better allocate resources and provide more *transparency*, a word the founders often invoked. "He found a way to bring the discipline of running a company but not lose the magic," said Omid Kordestani.

Deftly, Schmidt shed old practices. The weekly free-for-all meeting of about a dozen executives, recalled Craig Silverstein, "had outgrown its usefulness. Yet it was hard to disinvite people." So Schmidt simply said the meeting was too unwieldy and canceled it. Because he did not substitute another meeting, "no one felt excluded," Silverstein said. Only later did Schmidt establish his own weekly management meeting.

There was an adjustment period, particularly for Schmidt, to get used to his two unusual partners. "Larry is shy, thoughtful, detailed, a linear thinker," he said. "Sergey is loud, crazy, brilliant, insightful. Their personalities are so different. When I first came here I didn't think Larry could talk, because Sergey did all the talking." An unofficial part of Schmidt's mission was to police the wildest ideas of the founders.

On one occasion, Brin proposed to Schmidt, "We should run a hedge fund."

"Sergey, among your many ideas, this is the worst," Schmidt said.

"No, we can do it better because we have so much information."

Schmidt explained the legal complications, and said he talked him out of it.

And Page, for all his mania about efficiency, could be obsessive. A foot-

note buried at the back of Battelle's book on search provides an illustration. He writes of seeking an interview with Page and receiving this weird
counterproposal:

> In exchange for sitting down with me, Page wanted the right to review
> every mention of Google, Page, or Brin in my book, then respond in
> footnotes. Such a deal would have been nearly impossible to realize, and
> would have required untold hours of work on Page's part. Page and I
> negotiated for weeks over his proposal. . . . In the end, Page relented.

Like the founders', Schmidt's background was fairly narrow. He was an
engineer, with management experience. He had little experience working
with advertisers or media companies, which would soon become apparent.
But what he did have was maturity and an even temperament. It was said,
sometimes by Schmidt himself, that he was brought in to supply "adult
supervision." He was the friendly, wise man with a touch of gray in his
neatly parted sandy hair. Eventually, Schmidt became Google's facilitator,
or "catcher," as he likes to describe his role. "I catch whatever the problem
is." (When I later asked the decidedly non-sports-loving Brin if this description was accurate, he said, "I don't know what a catcher does.") The
more serious answer, Schmidt added, is that he facilitates decisions that
need to be made, establishing management systems, meeting with financial
analysts and reporters, serving as Google's chief link to industry and government. To the founders these were odious tasks, but increasingly important ones. He focused Google on outside technological dangers. "He made
us better understand competition in the technology space," said Marissa
Mayer. Google once thought its competition came from search engines like
AltaVista or Overture. "Eric said, 'If we're successful, Microsoft is going
to jump in [to search].' Larry and Sergey and I were surprised."

What could a late entrant like Microsoft do to impede Google? Schmidt,
having spent much of his career in opposition to Microsoft, and having
supported the government's antitrust prosecution of the software giant,
explained how Microsoft could use its dominant Internet Explorer browser

or Windows operating system, on which search engines depended, to cripple Google. Discussions like this, said Mayer, helped persuade Google to build its own applications and, eventually, its own browser, to ensure its independence.

Schmidt also helped focus Google internally. When he discovered that nearly half of Google's searches were coming from outside America, yet there was no concerted effort to sell ads against these searches, he seized the opportunity. He prodded Omid Kordestani to travel overseas, jokingly saying, "I'll call you Monday morning at the United terminal and tell you what plane to get on." Kordestani gained so much weight from eating fast food while on the road that when he returned from his successful trips abroad he would touch his belly and laugh, "Body by United!" Among Schmidt's signal accomplishments, said Paul Buchheit, was that he kept Page and Brin "focused" and "kept things on track." Often at meetings, he said, Page and Brin would suddenly change the topic at whim. "Eric would say, 'No, we need to come to an understanding right now.'"

Soon after Schmidt's arrival, the troika was romanced by Yahoo's new CEO, Terry S. Semel, who had come to a Web business after twenty-four years as co-chairman and co-CEO of Warner Bros. Semel came to Yahoo at a time when Internet stocks had plunged; Yahoo's stock had fallen from a market value peak of $127 billion to $12.6 billion. His arrival aroused the righteous anger of many in the Valley, who were suspicious of "outsiders." He was dismissed as a representative of old media, as a troglodyte, a Hollywood suit. But the old media warhorse knew how to calm an anxious company, handing out backslaps, compliments. He was a self-proclaimed content guy, and wanted Yahoo to create more of its own, not just license the content of others. And he wanted to sell more ads. He brought in a former ABC network executive, Lloyd Braun, to oversee new content, and an experienced sales team led by Wenda Harris Millard. "Terry brought two things," said Bobby Kotick, now the CEO of the game company Activision Blizzard, who served on the Yahoo board. Semel was "genetically predisposed to making money," and if he was presented with one hundred ideas, he could spot the one or two that would make money. "He brought that. And he just brought the maturity and wisdom that comes from experience. He asked the simple question: 'How do we make money?'"

Semel had huge gaps in his knowledge of the digital world and of Yahoo. He was shocked to learn that Yahoo had lost ninety-eight million dollars the year he arrived. Ron Conway recalled a dinner with Semel on his first day at Yahoo. He said, "Semel did not know Yahoo owned part of Google" in the form of the warrants it banked when it signed its search engine contract with Google. An avid deal maker, Semel became intrigued by Google, particularly after Jerry Yang and David Filo, Yahoo's founders, urged him, he recalled, to "go meet these guys."

Semel joined Page, Brin, and Schmidt for dinner in the Google cafeteria. Semel began the discussion: "Help me with something. We're your biggest customer in the world, right? We both know what we pay you for the whole world is less than ten million dollars, right?"

"Yes," they concurred.

"So what's your business?" Semel asked. "You don't really have a business."

"We love what we do," Page and Brin responded.

"Maybe we should buy your company?" said Semel, who thought it was enough of a business to throw out a billion-dollar purchase price tag.

"No, no. We don't really want to sell our company."

Semel walked away convinced "one hundred percent they did not want to sell." He also walked away with assurances from Schmidt that Google was working on "their own technology" to monetize search. Later that year, when Overture approached Yahoo with their patented monetization technology and offered Yahoo a revenue guarantee, Semel signed a contract for Overture to sell its ads. Google was upset, but Semel said that in the first full year, Overture generated two hundred million dollars of advertising revenues. By 2003, Overture separately approached Yahoo and Microsoft with an offer to be acquired. Microsoft declined to bid. (They later reversed course and started up their own search engine.) In the end, Semel acquired two search engines, Overture and Inktomi, and Yahoo dropped its search license agreement with Google. (It was beginning to become clear what a colossal blunder it had been for Yahoo to farm out search in order to focus on building its portal traffic, relegating Yahoo to a weak second place in search. By buying Overture, Yahoo also inherited its April 2002 patent infringement lawsuit against Google.)

Google was growing fast, and the founders worried they'd divide into cliques and lose their cohesive culture. Stacy Sullivan, who had been hired in 1999 as the first employee in human resources, and Joan Braddi, Omid Kordestani's trusted deputy, were asked to assemble a disparate group of early Googlers to devise a coherent mission statement of core principles the company could embrace. Twelve employees gathered in the café, each from a different department. The discussion went in circles for several hours, with Sullivan dutifully writing clichés on a whiteboard. Some wanted the group to enunciate a set of rules: Don't mistreat people; Don't be late; Don't lose user focus; Play hard but keep the puck down. The engineers in the room weren't interested in codified dos and don'ts because they reeked of corporate America and offended their sense of efficiency. They also took too long to read. After hours of exasperating discussion, Paul Buchheit blurted, "All of these things can be covered by just saying *'Don't be evil.'*"

Within a day, engineer Amit Patel, Google employee number 7, wrote the slogan in impeccable handwriting on whiteboards all over Google's offices. The slogan became viral. When opposing an idea at internal meetings, Googlers would proclaim, "That could be evil." The slogan became Google's rallying cry, a way to distinguish itself from other corporations and Microsoft in particular, a way to harness the goodwill Google enjoyed as a free service bringing the world's information to everyone's fingertips. To former Intel chairman and CEO Andy Grove, the slogan was too vague to define a boundary, and smacked of self-righteousness. "Do you think Hitler thought he was evil?" Grove said he thought at the time. "It's too vague, too self-serving, self-defining. 'I'm not evil, therefore I'm not evil.'"

Eric Schmidt was happy with the slogan, though, and happy with what he was accomplishing at Google. Years later, he sat on one of three canvas-backed directors chairs jammed into the closet-sized conference room dubbed "the directors room" that is next to his office in Building 42. The view from a narrow vertical window overlooked a Google parking lot; the white brick wall to his left held a whiteboard containing mathematical formulas; to his right were several framed newspaper clippings, including one headlined "The Grown-Up at Google." He admitted to feeling that he had grown as an executive since his days at Novell. "Most people who worked with me ten years ago," Schmidt said, "would have said, 'He's smart, a nice guy, but he can't lead.' What is the distinction between then and now? Toughness."

Back in 2001, his "toughness" was circumscribed. He did not issue orders to the founders, he had to persuade, to prioritize his concerns, and pick his battles. There were palpable tensions—the founders would sometimes loudly explode in meetings that the company was becoming bureaucratic, and Schmidt knew he was the target. These were three strangers working together, and the founders were uncomfortably ceding some management control over their invention, their baby. Schmidt knew the founders did not blame each other. There was rarely a hint of tension between Page and Brin—"In all the years I've worked with them," said John Doerr, who is a Google director, "I've never seen them get angry with each other." But it was not unusual, said another early investor, to witness emotional outbursts by the founders aimed at others, and to see these outbursts fielded and defused by the calm, self-effacing Schmidt. The go-slow, relaxed way that Schmidt approached the founders or changed the management meetings or eventually chased a squatter from his office was at times exasperating to others. While describing Schmidt as "the unsung hero" of Google, Shriram admits, "He had a slow start." The founders at first, he said, "challenged everything," and openly wondered: "Could they trust his judgment?" Meanwhile, the VCs were pushing for a revenue plan. And Moritz was skeptical that Schmidt was the right man to bully it through Google.

Schmidt needed help to lower the emotional temperature, and to upgrade Google's management. That help came in the form of Bill Campbell, then sixty-one, a barrel-chested man known throughout Silicon Valley as "the coach." At one time Columbia University's head football coach, Campbell had also been a senior executive at Apple and a CEO of several

Valley companies, including the Go Corporation and Intuit, the now-thriving online software company that provides financial services to individuals and small businesses and where he worked side by side with the founder. John Doerr knew that Campbell felt an obligation to give back to a Silicon Valley that had made him rich enough to own his own Gulfstream IV. His discretion is legendary, and part of his allure. Aside from a profile in the magazine of his alma mater, the only other time he has ever been profiled was in a superb 2008 *Fortune* magazine piece by Jennifer Reingold titled, "The Secret Coach." His many friends offered tributes but Campbell would not sit for an interview. A Google search retrieves very few Campbell press mentions.

Doerr served on Campbell's Intuit board, and had called on him to mentor young leaders of Valley companies. Regularly, Campbell would join fifteen or so of Doerr's dot-com CEO clients over dinner. The sessions are dubbed Camp Campbell, "and I'm not allowed to attend," said Doerr, who described Campbell "as one of my two best friends." In late summer of 2001, Doerr reached out to his friend to help Schmidt and the founders. "I felt it was an opportunity worth Bill's time," he said. "Eric had not been CEO on a scale Google would become. Larry and Sergey and Eric needed to be coached."

In the Valley, Coach Campbell is a magnet for friends old and new. Still the chairman of Intuit, he is also the colead outside director at Apple, and one of Steve Jobs's few confidants. On weekends and evenings, when big college or professional football and basketball games are televised, Campbell can often be found with a group of buddies in downtown Palo Alto's Old Pro sports bar, a Stanford student hangout he owns. He'll have a table in the middle of the pub piled high with hamburgers, French fries, pizzas, and his preferred drink, Bud Lite. Just under six feet tall, Campbell is easily spotted, and not just by the Kennedyesque thatch of gray hair that sprawls across his forehead: he's the guy in constant motion, moving about the room dispensing high fives, fist pumps, hugs, and baseball caps. He sports an oversized Columbia 1962 ring and weighs just three or four pounds more than he did as a college linebacker. At the Old Pro, he's garrulous. Outside, he's allergic to interviews with reporters, and even with friends he sequesters conversations he has with other intimates. His discretion is well known, and part of his allure.

In a rare 2007 interview with two McKinsey & Co's partners for the *McKinsey Quarterly*, Campbell said something that is music to engineers at places like Google: "empowered engineers are the single most important thing that you can have in a company." He was talking about a tech company, and he went on to say that to foster innovation "you've got to be careful that you don't make engineers beholden to product-marketing people. For me, growth is the goal, and growth comes through having innovation. Innovation comes through having great engineers, not great product-marketing guys." He also said that smart tech executives should spend entire days "doing nothing but reviewing projects. A whole day, with the whole management team, so that we can clean up those projects, clean out the ones that aren't going to be good, and take the bodies that are recovered and put them on the projects that look like they have the best prospects."

Explaining Campbell's role as a bridge builder at Google, Moritz said, "Bill's contribution has been to take the emotion out of decisions. He's more objective. He's seen as a neutral source and a fair man." The objectivity was needed, he explained, because: "You had two founders who were in their twenties and Eric was twenty years older, and you had to make that relationship work between people who did not know each other. It was natural that the founders would be suspicious. There were bumps at the beginning that Bill helped smooth over." The biggest bumps, another Google insider said, were not between Schmidt and the founders, but with two venture capitalists on the board, Doerr and Moritz: "Eric had a busybody board. The impression the board had was that Larry and Sergey were not focused. When they got Eric in, now they wanted to micromanage him." They wanted Schmidt to push harder to monetize search. Doerr and Moritz "were both impatient," said Shriram, who had served as a bridge between the founders and the board and gratefully handed this role to Campbell.

"I would sit with Larry and Sergey and try to figure out the things they more or less wanted from Eric," recalled Campbell. Then he'd sit with Schmidt. He performed this particular function for three years, until 2005. Looking back over the life of Google, these sessions where Campbell performed as both a psychologist and a coach loom especially large. The company could have imploded. On Campbell's shoulders rested a complex problem. He had to earn the trust of the founders, Schmidt, the board, and Google executives. He had to help put management systems in place, recruit executives, suggest financial controls and the structure of board and management meetings.

One would expect an ex-football coach to be an in-your-face, blustery, and threatening personality. And Campbell sounds like he would be, for he has a deep, hoarse voice that seems the product of yelling all day. But he is self-effacing, quick with a quip, more listener than talker. Schmidt likens Campbell's ability to listen to that of a shrink, adding, "When he walks into a room, everyone smiles. I've never seen that." But he also said that "shrinks are seen as passive," which is why he believes the "coach" appellation is more accurate. "A coach says, 'Let's go!'"

Campbell laughs when told that some refer to him as Google's shrink and offers this modest explanation of his role: "Sometimes when you are in a big and complex organization, your behavior is noted. And if your behavior is sometimes out of line, sometimes it's me that will say, 'Move it a little bit in this direction or that direction. Not much.' Shrink would not be the right description. It's more coaching people into the right direction."

It did not take long for Campbell to win over Schmidt and the founders. "Bill took me under his wing," said Schmidt, who refers to him as "my consiglieri." Campbell is so valuable at Google, Page said, because "he has the unique ability to be a warm person, one that everyone can relate to, but also has the experience of actually running a company." Brin smiles when asked about Campbell and speaks of his "especially high EQ," emotional intelligence. A principal criticism of Brin and Page is that they, like many of their engineers, lack EQ. Did *he*, I asked, think they lacked EQ? "We are ranked far below Bill Campbell," Brin conceded.

Two Campbell ideas embraced by the troika were an executive management meeting with their direct reports and Campbell that consumes several hours every Monday, and project review meetings with engineers that occupy much of Tuesday, Wednesday, and Friday afternoons. Campbell regularly holds one-on-one sessions with other senior executives to offer evaluations, mediate management disputes, hold hands. In other companies, Brin said, politics become excessive when you get to be large. "One of the reasons we've been able to avoid politics is Bill Campbell. When issues arise, he's willing to intercede." One day I'd scheduled an interview first with Brin and then Campbell. But Brin had arrived late and we backed into Campbell's allotted time. We were in the small conference room a few doors from Brin's office in Building 43 and Campbell ambled in for his scheduled interview. Brin smiled and instantly rose from his chair and the two men hugged.

Campbell participates in the Monday executive management meeting, discusses the agenda that Schmidt sends out to participants specifying the decisions they need to discuss at the meeting. He acts as envoy, visiting YouTube headquarters with some frequency in the first half of 2008 to find ways to generate revenues from the popular video site and improve communications between the two companies. Campbell is the only outside person ever welcomed into Google's inner sanctums. In addition to executive meetings, he attends board meetings. "He's closer to us than the board," said David Krane, director of global communications and public affairs. "Eric said management is a marathon, not a sprint. It's stressful," Page said. "Bill plays an important role of keeping us all healthy and interacting."

Why does he volunteer to spend approximately two full days a week on the Google campus? "This is family for me," he said, a catch in his voice. "These are people I love dearly. I've been doing this since late 2001. I probably get as much out of this as everybody gets out of me. The joy of participating at a company that is at the leading edge of anything going on in the personal technology space. It's centered here. There's innovation daily. They think about changing the world." He refuses to be paid more than a dollar a year; in 2007, his compensation was increased when he was given a reserved parking space on a campus where spaces are usually filled by 10 a.m. Brin said he and Page had to insist on compensating Campbell with Google stock options. The fact that Campbell plays such an atypical role at Google suggests that in addition to coach or shrink he can also be described as a babysitter. The fact that Google needs one is a reminder of its youth.

To better understand Bill Campbell, Jr., roll the reel back to Homestead, Pennsylvania, the small steel town near Pittsburgh where he was born on August 31, 1940. His mother, Virginia Marie Dauria, was a homemaker while his father, William V. Campbell, worked the night shift in the steel mill and taught high school physical education. He became the basketball coach at Duquesne University, where he was a close friend of the football coach Aldo T. "Buff" Donelli, then the principal of the local high school and finally the school superintendent of the district. Bill's mom stayed home to raise him and his younger brother, Jim, who went on to become an All-American wide receiver at the Naval Academy. Bill was an honor student at the public high school, and though he weighed only 175 pounds, he was voted All Western Pennsylvania as an offensive guard and linebacker. What was his football talent? "Speed. And I would *hit* ya!" he said with a laugh. "When colleges came around, I couldn't understand why guys who weren't as good as I was were going to Penn State and Pittsburgh. It pissed me off. So I got recruited by the Ivy schools."

Bill chose Columbia, where Buff Donelli, who had gone from Duquesne to Boston University, had just replaced Lou Little, the Columbia football team's longtime coach. Bill received a scholarship and played middle linebacker on defense and offensive guard. He went on to star and captain the 1961 Columbia team that tied Harvard for its first, and only, Ivy League football championship. He hurt his knee that year, which ended his playing career and earned him a 4-F draft deferment. When he graduated in 1962 with a degree in economics, he decided to stay at Columbia to get a master's degree so that he could stay involved with football. He was studying economics, but "I wanted to be a coach," he said. Donelli appointed him assistant freshman football coach, and he doubled as a resident adviser. His second year, he scaled back graduate studies to part-time in order to serve as the offensive and defensive end coach on the varsity football team.

His career goal was to become a head coach. "My dad was a coach," he said. "There was nobody I admired more than my dad and Buff Donelli. These were the two role models I had. I wanted to be Buff Donelli. I wanted to be Bill Campbell, Sr. My dad was so respected in town. He had been the coach, the superintendent. He just had this way about him. He could unite anybody."

Bill had a summer job after his second year as a coach at Columbia and eagerly anticipated year three, starting in September 1964. But he received a notice from his Pennsylvania draft board to report for a physical. Expecting to again be declared 4-F, he was surprised when he passed. He was even more surprised that "they took me in the service that same day." He was swiftly dispatched by train to Fort Knox and never got back to collect his belongings at Columbia. For the next two years he was an army private stationed at U.S. bases, landing at Fort Gordon, Georgia, where he ran the athletic program and was both the assistant football coach and the quarterback.

After being discharged from the army, Campbell returned to Columbia as the coach of the freshman football team, and studied for a master's degree in education. The next year, he became Donelli's offensive line coach and thought he was on his way to head coach—until Donelli chose to retire. The new coach brought in his own assistant coaches, and Campbell was out of a job. He found a new job as linebacker coach at Boston College, where he stayed six years, rising to defensive coordinator. He returned often to New York, where he met his future wife, Roberta Spagnola, a Columbia University dean, on a blind date. When Columbia called in 1974 and asked him to return as head coach, Campbell jumped at the chance. He and Roberta married in 1976, and would have a son and a daughter.

Over his six years at Columbia, Campbell had a record of twelve victories, forty-one defeats, and one tie. He blames his losing record on his devotion to the players as men rather than as athletes. He was a nurturer. "I really felt like I committed to these kids. My view was more father counselor and adviser . . . . I wanted these guys to achieve. I wanted them to go to work for Procter and Gamble or IBM, if that's what they wanted. I took great pride in getting summer internships for them at Merrill Lynch and Salomon Brothers. I was more engaged with them. I often think that had I been less worried about that and more dispassionate about playing, maybe I would have been better." If he had to do it over, though, he says, "I wouldn't change. I couldn't change."

After leaving Columbia, he became a sales and marketing executive at J. Walter Thompson, where he stayed until Eastman Kodak, a client, recruited him to be its director of marketing. Then, in 1983, John Sculley, recently appointed the CEO of Apple, heard about Campbell from a relative and began courting him for the job of vice president of marketing. He clinched the sale by demonstrating for Campbell the revolutionary Macintosh computer, which Apple would introduce in 1984. "It would be pretty unusual today to hire a football coach to be your VP of sales," Sculley later told a reporter. "But what I was looking for was someone who could help develop Apple into an organization." Campbell took over sales as well as marketing just months after he joined Apple, and set about firing the consultants and most of a sales force that "wore polyester pants and gold chains." He said he replaced them with recent college graduates, half of them women, and all hungry to succeed. "What I learned from coaching," he said, "is that if your guys are not as big and fast as the other guys, you're fucked!"

Campbell's boldness appealed to the ever-rebellious Steve Jobs. The two men bonded. By 1984, said Campbell, "Sculley and Jobs were going at each other already." Although Jobs had recruited Sculley to bring professional management to Apple, he came to think he was more interested in marketing, including marketing himself, than in Apple products; Sculley believed Jobs wanted an acolyte, not a CEO. Nevertheless, Campbell earned the rare distinction of being able to both befriend Jobs and command Sculley's respect. Before Sculley succeeded in pushing Jobs out of Apple in 1985, Campbell warned him it would be a huge mistake. Tensions flared between Campbell and Sculley, and in 1987 Campbell was put in charge of Apple's Claris software division, with the intention of spinning it off as a private company with Campbell at the helm. But with Claris thriving, Sculley changed his mind. Campbell left rather than remain as a division head under Sculley.

At the recommendation of John Doerr, the Go Corporation hired Campbell as their CEO. The company was an early pioneer in pen computing—too early, it seemed, and when the market didn't respond, Campbell unloaded the Go Corporation on AT&T, in 1993. He next became CEO of Intuit when Doerr suggested to founder Scott Cook that Campbell would be a great partner. Four years later, he moved up to chairman of the board. On the eve of Steve Jobs's return to Apple in 1997, he asked Campbell to join his board.

Today Campbell serves as a mentor to some of the Valley's most successful entrepreneurs, from Marc Andreessen to Steve Jobs, whom he walks and talks with most weekends in Palo Alto, where they are neighbors. He estimates that he spends about 10 percent of his time on Apple business, about 35 percent on Intuit business, an equal amount at Google, about 10 percent as chairman of the board of Columbia University, and the remainder on assorted activities. He said he has donated his Google stock to the foundation he established to make charitable gifts to his hometown, among others. He donated money to his Homestead high school for a new stadium, scholarships in his father's name for student athletes, a new gym named for his brother, who died of lung cancer in 2006, and Apple computers for the school. In the fall, he coaches sandlot football for eighth-graders from St. Joseph's School of the Sacred Heart in Atherton, California; in the spring, he coaches the eighth-grade girls in what's called powder puff football.

He doesn't have a lot of enemies. Marc Andreessen said of Campbell, "He's been incredibly important in the Valley. Business is changing so quickly," and less experienced entrepreneurs turn to Campbell for guidance. "Bill has been a model mentor. When he's not in the room, he's still there because people ask, 'What would Bill say?'"

IN SCHMIDT AND CAMPBELL, Google had executives who could work with the founders and mentors the whole organization to work together.

Now it needed to recruit senior executives. With an assist from Campbell, one of Schmidt's initial targets was Sheryl Sandberg, who had just concluded her service as chief of staff to treasury secretary Lawrence Summers. The Clinton administration was winding down, and Sandberg, who was just thirty-one, was much in demand.

Sandberg has short dark hair, an angular face that is softened by a bright smile, and an engaging manner that makes strangers feel comfortable. She was the first of three children born to Adele and Joel Sandberg, she then a professor of English and other languages, he an ophthalmologist. The Sandbergs moved to Miami from Washington, D.C., when Sheryl was three, and although Sheryl was considered the smartest student in her public high school, she wasn't a bookworm; from childhood, she has been popular. For college, she left Florida and went to Harvard and in her junior year there took a course from Lawrence Summers, then the rising star of the economics faculty. At the end of the semester he invited his five best students to lunch at the Harvard Faculty Club and offered to serve as their senior thesis adviser. Sandberg accepted Summers's offer—"He changed my life," she said—and went on to win the John H. Williams Prize as the top graduating student in economics. When Summers was appointed chief economist at the World Bank, he brought her in as his special assistant.

Sandberg had a particular interest in health care, and in the early nineties went for a time with a team to India to work to alleviate leprosy and AIDS. Shaken by the poverty and suffering she witnessed, she vowed that she "was only going to do things that were good for the world." She wanted to work in nonprofits or government but felt she required a broader education. She stayed at the World Bank two years before deciding she would go back to school. "I come from a Jewish family," she laughed. "My dad's a doctor. You had to have a graduate degree!"

Accepted at both Harvard's law and business schools, she chose the latter, believing she needed a better understanding of how organizations worked. Between her first and second year she got married. Though the marriage lasted only a year, she graduated near the top of her class as both a Baker and a Ford scholar; with her former husband in Washington, D.C., she fled to the West Coast, where she joined McKinsey & Company in

California, working on health care. McKinsey gave her no more joy than her marriage. "You don't do anything," she explained. "You just tell other people what to do." She left after one year.

Summers was then deputy treasury secretary under Robert Rubin in the Clinton administration. The two had kept in contact and, again, he recruited her as his special assistant. For the next four and a half years, she worked for Summers; when he was elevated to treasury secretary she became his chief of staff. But when the second Clinton term ended in January 2001, she had to move on. Washington had taught her some surprising things. "Over the years," she said, "I got less naïve. I no longer thought, *The private sector is bad. The public sector is good.*" At Treasury, her most "exciting" meetings had been with technology companies. In America, she believed, "economic growth was all technology driven." She decided she wanted "to go and be an operational executive in a tech company, a make-the-trains-run job."

In early 2001, she moved out to San Francisco. Her sister lived there, and it was the technology capital of the world. She took time to clear her head, and in any case, with the dot-com bust still reverberating, it was a difficult time to seek a job. She signed up for cooking classes and relished her free time. She was offered an executive position by eBay, but she had her sights set on Google. "When I came out of the government, I wanted to do something that I believed in," she told me. "I went to Google because Google had a higher mission, which is to make the world's information freely available. But they weren't offering me a job."

Schmidt talked to her in the fall of 2001, and like all top applicants, she met with Brin and Page as well. When Schmidt offered her a position in late 2001, she was excited, but on closer inspection wasn't sure it was a real job. "I was supposed to be a business unit general manager, but there were no business units, and therefore nothing to be managed," she said. Schmidt "called me every week and said, 'We're profitable this week too!'" Friends advised her to "work for a real company," one that earned steady profits. "I met Eric and said there is no job. He looked at me and said, 'You're looking at this the wrong way. None of this matters. Growth matters. Get on a rocket ship and all things take care of themselves.'"

She was employee number 268. Her title was business unit general manager, even though, as she had noted, there was no business unit. There was also no CFO, which is perhaps why Eric Schmidt assigned her a top secret mission, kept even from their venture capitalists, to investigate a potential round of private financing to pump money into a four-year-old company that had yet to have a profitable year. Among the people Sandberg spoke with was Mary Meeker, the author of the seminal Internet report at Morgan Stanley. Their discussions, Meeker said, made her take greater notice of Google. "Before Sheryl arrived," said Meeker, "they were so quiet and private. She was part of a push to bring people in." Months and many meetings later, Sandberg made a PowerPoint presentation to the founders and Schmidt. The consensus of the people Sandberg consulted was that Google should be valued at one billion dollars. The consensus of the founders and Schmidt was that they would not pursue more investment capital because this valuation was, she said, "a total insult."

The project was shelved. "I needed another job. I knew I wanted to work for Omid Kordestani, who runs all business and operations. We were launching AdWords CPC." Kordestani planned to expand the AdWords staff from four to eight. "Omid said to me, 'I need a tractor. You're a Porsche. Why do you want this job?'"

She thought their ideas for selling ads were innovative. If they worked, they would be efficient—by cutting out sales teams—and bold, giving advertisers an incentive to make the ads more relevant. Advertisers would rank higher on the search results page based not just on the price they bid per keyword, but on the number of clicks their ads received. The more clicks, the lower the price, and the higher they would rank.

Advertising, Schmidt said, had not been viewed "as a priority" by the founders—nor, according to Doerr, by Schmidt. And, indeed, Schmidt had become convinced that since Google had succeeded in building the best search engine, the money would follow. But by 2002, at the helm of a four-year-old company that had yet to have a profitable year, Schmidt knew it was time to focus on money. But he also knew Page and Brin had definite ideas about what was "evil." Senior software engineer Matt Cutts recalled that a credit card company (it was Visa) offered five million dollars to put a link to their credit card logo on the bottom of Google's home page. But Page and Brin wouldn't budge, nor would they relax their strictures against advertisers paying for search results. "Google was really trying to do right by their users," said Benjamin A. Schachter, then the senior Internet analyst for UBS. But they weren't building a profitable business.

Moritz was becoming restive, openly wondering if Schmidt was tough enough. A Google insider with direct knowledge said that in 2002, Moritz pressed for Schmidt to be fired. Another insider said the unhappiness with Schmidt was at first shared by others who also worried that he wasn't tough enough, that he was moving too slowly to galvanize a management team, to challenge the founders, and most especially, to find a revenue stream.

Schmidt remained calm, at least outwardly. By late 2001, he knew of the effort at Google that Sandberg was now working on to devise the new version of AdWords, the advertising program associated with search. In AdWords as it worked through 2001, advertisers paid Google the old-fashioned way, based on a cost per thousand (CPM) whether the searcher clicked on their ad or not. What Google was quietly exploring was switching to a cost-per-click model, an idea that built on the Overture model. In addition to Sandberg, Omid Kordestani assigned Salar Kamangar, the author of the original Google business plan, to serve as a bridge between the engineering and the sales team as they improvised.

This began a long and intense period of brainstorming. The team liked the idea of charging by the click, thinking it was a way they could farm out not just search, as they had done with Netscape and Yahoo, but also advertising. "We knew we needed a lot of ads, and to have a lot of ads we also had to syndicate," Kamangar said, performing the search function for sites like Yahoo but also selling ads for them. He knew that Page and Brin would resist allowing advertisers to pay for placement within search results. He also knew advertisers were wary. The CPC model was associated with low-quality ads that were harder to sell and were known as "remnant advertising." Advertisers like to determine where and when their ads appear, and if they allowed a company like Google to put their ads on other Web sites, and allowed the Web sites to choose the times they would appear, the advertiser would lose control. Was there a system to serve both users and advertisers?

For months they came up empty. Members of the team remember Kamangar walking about with two fingers pressed to his lips, muttering, "I'm thinking, I'm thinking." One day, he said, a "lightbulb went off." What if Google combined the cost-per-click model with a measurement of whether users found the ad relevant? Google engineers could come up with an algorithm to measure the quality of the ads, he thought, assuming that more clicks meant users liked the ads. To sell them they could use what economists call a Vickery Auction, an idea suggested by a colleague, Eric Beach. In a Vickery Auction, named after William Vickery, the twentieth-century Canadian economist and Nobel laureate, after Google set a minimum bid price per keyword, the advertiser bids, say, fifteen dollars for a keyword. If the next bid is ten dollars, the winner only pays one cent more than the second highest bidder, saving nearly five dollars; the second-place bidder pays a penny more than the price bid by the third, and so on. The advantages for Google were many. By charging per click, Google could syndicate its ads—sell them on other Web sites as well as on Google search. The more ads it sold on different platforms, the more data Google collected, and thus the more reliant on Google advertisers became. And Google could automate the entire system, minimizing the size of its sales force.

The advantages for advertisers were manifest. They knew they were not being gouged, because they only paid a penny more than the next highest bidder. They benefited by being charged only when the user clicked on the ad. This gave them an incentive to produce a better ad because better ads produced more clicks, which lowered their cost per click. And by charging per click, Google opened online advertising to many small businesses who normally had nowhere else to turn but the Yellow Pages. By allowing Google to syndicate ads, advertisers were achieving the online equivalent of one-stop shopping offered by network television, whereby ads appeared on hundreds of local stations. And because the system was automated, advertisers were spared the expense of a monitoring system. They would simply transmit to Google their keywords, their bid per keyword, their monthly budget, and their billing information. And then using Google Analytics, they could monitor the results online.

Page and Brin made a major amendment to the new AdWords before it was inaugurated in February 2002. At the annual technology, entertainment, design (TED) conference in Monterey, they engaged in conversation with the Israeli entrepreneur Yossi Vardi. Vardi is a bear of a man with a walrus mustache and a friendly, even impish manner. His company started ICQ, the Internet's first instant messaging system, and sold it to AOL for four hundred million dollars. He and the Google founders discussed search ads—how to make them unobtrusive and yet relevant to users. Vardi suggested that they could use two-thirds of the page for search results and wall off the text ads from the search content the way a newspaper walls off ads. They could do this by placing a thin blue line between the search results and a smaller gray box on the right-hand side of the page containing the text ads and links to the advertiser. Users could either click on the link or not. Vardi's idea, Brin recalled, was the genesis for the way ads were displayed. Page and Brin decided the ads should be small, a couple of lines long, imposing a limit of ninety-five characters, and insisting that they be informational.

It was unclear when the new AdWords was introduced that it would be what it became: a Google money machine. "The AdWords is brilliant because it allows you to scale the advertising solution to what you need," said former Microsoft executive Nathan Myhrvold. It democratizes advertising, allowing Google to use it for either small or large advertisers. It was also, Myhrvold believes, pirated from Overture. The rival search engine thought so too, and later that year filed a patent infringement lawsuit against Google.

A year later, a second money gusher—AdSense—would spring from the CPC model. At the time, Paul Bouchet was developing Gmail and working on software to match words sent in an e-mail with keywords selected by advertisers, allowing small text ads to instantly appear. Brin wondered why they couldn't apply this innovation to a new program that would help bloggers and any Web site make money. This idea would be called AdSense. If a reader was looking at an analysis of computers on a Web site like Engadget, an HP or a Dell ad could appear. Similarly, readers of a story about the law in an online newspaper might see a law firm's ad, while people looking at a Web site devoted to pancreatic cancer could see ads for pharmaceuticals. Google would serve as the matchmaker, delivering the advertising and sharing the revenues. As with AdWords, the advertiser would pay only when the ad received a click. And as AdWords democratized advertising, luring small advertisers online, so AdSense would become a way for Web sites to generate income. The effort was led and architected by Susan Wojcicki, vice president, product management, who later received the prestigious Google Founders Award—paying about twelve million dollars—to honor her efforts. AdSense, Danny Sullivan told *USA Today*, "basically turned the Web into a giant Google billboard. It effectively meant that Google could turn everyone's content into a place for Google ads."

Eric Schmidt recalled how Brin lobbied him for money to market the program. "He and an engineer developed a system of showing ads on people's blogs or Web sites. They came to show this to me. It was not an exciting demo. And Tim Armstrong's sales guy is assigned to help them out. Now we've got three people out of control! So Sergey comes in and said, 'I need to buy inventory to make this happen.'"

"How much?" asked Schmidt.

"I need a million dollars," said Brin.

"We don't have a million dollars!" said Schmidt.

"Sure we do," said Brin.

"I didn't give a precise answer"—a couple of hundred thousand dollars, said Schmidt, chuckling. (Susan Wojcicki remembers that he alloted them a marketing budget of two hundred thousand dollars.)

Weeks later, Schmidt asked Brin, "Sergey, how much money did you spend?"

"A million and a half dollars," said Brin.

"Sergey, you said one million!"

"No, you didn't give me a precise figure!" said Brin.

"What does that tell you about them?" Schmidt said of the founders.

"He had the idea. He assembled the activity. He figured out who his opposition was—which was me, in a friendly way. He told me about it because he wanted my support. And he evaded my guidance. And as a result, built a multimillion-dollar business." (By 2004, AdSense would produce about half Google's revenues.) Schmidt paused to chuckle again, then said, "You see why I work with these people!"

The chuckle is appropriate, for Google would not have succeeded without a measure of luck. As Larry Page confessed to a Stanford class, discovering the advertising formula that would work "probably was an accident more than a plan." A reminder that timing, serendipity, luck—not just a smart strategy or brilliant execution—sometimes determines success. With programs like AdSense, Google did not aim to build a huge Web-based political constituency, but it did. As its advertising dollars rained on Web sites, Google was hailed as a benefactor. Not only was Google not evil, it was beneficent. Google would call these content Web sites partners, and give them about two-thirds of the ad dollars, with Google pocketing the rest. Many small businesses would be discovered and thrive. It was largely overlooked at the time that automated AdSense cut out the advertising middleman. Or as Wojcicki told me, "It changed the way content providers think about their business. They know they can generate revenues without having their own sales team." In the online world, Google was potentially dis-intermediating not just the media buying agency but the sales forces of content companies.

AdWords and AdSense would solve the mystery of how Google could monetize its search engine. For the first time, in 2001, Google turned a profit: $7 million on revenues of $86 million. The next year, revenues more than quadrupled to $439 million, and profits jumped to $100 million. Google's search index included three billion Web documents. Not surprising, among the top ten searches on Google in 2001 were these: *World Trade Center, Osama Bin Laden, anthrax*, and *Taliban*.

In 2002, Urs Hölzle, who is now Google's senior vice president of operations, was undecided whether to return to his tenured faculty position at the University of California at Santa Barbara. AdWords made that decision simple. Google had finally found a way to make money. "Now we could fund all these things we couldn't fund before," he said, "2002 was when we said, 'We can afford to spend more on machines!'" This was also the year Google discovered, as Eric Schmidt would tell me several years later, "We are in the advertising business." Ignited, the Google rocket took off.

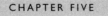

CHAPTER FIVE

Innocence
or Arrogance?

(2002–2003)

Eric Schmidt now fully shared Page and Brin's faith in Google's ascendancy. What set Google apart, he came to believe, is that while people like him always assumed "Google would be an important company, the founders always assumed that Google would be a defining company." The scope of Google's ambition was presaged by something Page said when he and Schmidt spoke before a Stanford class in 2002. "If we solve search, that means you can answer any question," Page said. "Which means you can do basically anything."

Their audacity was displayed in May 2002 when Google made its most ambitious—and riskiest—deal yet. With its new AdWords in place, Google was eager to start syndicating ads, and even though it was doing about 150 million searches a day, it wanted to do more. AOL would be their vehicle. Because AOL later went into a tailspin, it's often forgotten how dominant the company was. Webheads would sneer that using AOL was "the Internet on training wheels." Yet it was AOL's user-friendliness that helped popularize the Web—and which attracted thirty-four million paid subscribers in 2002. For Google, AOL was a ripe target, a giant portal with an enormous audience. But search rival Overture was doing AOL's searches and advertising, and besides, as AOL's then executive vice president, Lynda Clarizio, said, "No one knew who Google was." Overture's contract ended in May 2002, and the founders were determined to snare it.

"I want us to bid to win!" Page declared at an executive staff meeting, according to Susan Wojcicki.

"You're betting the company if you do that," Kordestani warned.

"We should be able to monetize the pages," Page responded. "If not, we deserve to go out of business."

With $10 million in the bank, Google promised AOL 85 cents of each advertising dollar collected, and guaranteed a minimum annual payment of $150 million in revenues. "We could have gone bankrupt," Brin said.

"Overture offered more money," said former AOL president Robert Pittman. But Google offered a better search engine, a more inventive approach to reaching smaller advertisers, and higher minimum guaranteed payments.

Google won the bid, to the surprise of many industry watchers. It was a milestone, "probably the biggest" deal Google has ever done, Brin said. "Every time you did a search on AOL, it said 'Powered by Google,'" recalled Nick Grouf, CEO of Spot Runner, an Internet based advertising agency. "By cutting a deal with Google, what AOL did was surrender the front door to its walled garden" of consumer data. The deal "affected how we thought about doing partnerships and deals," said Tim Armstrong. And the partnership would become a huge moneymaker for both Google and AOL.

The deal enlarged Google's appetite. Schmidt remembers the day in 2002 he walked into Page's office and Page surprised him by showing off a book scanner he had built. It had been inspired by the great library of Alexandria, erected around 300 B.C. to house all the world's scrolls. Page had used the equivalent of his own 20 percent time to construct a machine that cut off the bindings of books and digitized the pages. "What are you going to do with that, Larry?" Schmidt asked.

"We're going to scan all the books in the world," Page said. For search to be truly comprehensive, he explained, it must include every book ever published. He wanted Google to "understand everything in the world and give it back to you." Sort of "a super librarian," he said. "Where are all the books?" Page asked.

"The Library of Congress," Schmidt said.

"Good, we'll do a deal with the Library of Congress!" Page said.

"You're Larry," Schmidt said. "Nobody gives a shit about you."

"Well, how can we get to the Library of Congress?" Page asked.

They arrived at the answer simultaneously.

"We call up Al Gore," Schmidt said. "He's friends with the guy who's in charge of the Library of Congress." At the same time, Page proposed to his alma mater, the University of Michigan, that Google would pay to digitize the seven million books in its library. After Page had the university's consent, he flew to Washington to make a deal with the Library of Congress. Google would soon sign up Stanford, Oxford, and the New York Public Library, among others. They established an internal team under the joint direction of Dan Clancy, who had a Ph.D. in artificial intelligence and had worked at NASA, and Adam Smith, a former investment banker who had served as vice president of new media at Random House. Clancy offered another reason to support the effort: to promote reading among young people who did their reading online. "I sampled college students and asked, 'How many of you went to a library in the last year?'" Only half raised their hand. "There's so much information on the Web that students accept secondary sources." He hoped to combat this. Adam Smith saw their effort "as a book-promoting vehicle," bringing the work of authors to a wider audience. About 90 percent of the more than twenty million books ever published were out of print, and Sandler and Smith had a goal of digitizing ten thousand books each day.

But in their rush to fulfill this mission, Google did not first pause to extensively consult with American publishers and authors who owned the copyrights to many of these books. "If we had done that," Brin said, "we might not have done the project." Because they didn't do that, Google would later have a lawsuit to contend with.

THE FOUNDERS USUALLY FOCUS on different things. Page devotes more time to how consumers interact with Google, hence his chosen title, president of products. Brin spends more time on technology, hence his title, president of technology. The titles can be misleading, because "we overlap a lot," said Brin. It's also inexact because each founder has unpredictable interests or quirks. Brin, for example, thrusts himself into the middle of strategy sessions for many business negotiations, which is welcomed by his fellow executives. He is also a principal proponent, according to vice president of people operations Laszlo Bock, of Google's massage programs and child care centers, while Page is more assertive about which engineers to hire, the food served, and the size of cafeterias. Within Google, this sometimes creates confusion. For example, Bill Campbell, who is in many of the key meetings, said he believes Brin is most focused "on the end user experience" and that Page is more focused on "the product development process to get there." On the other hand, employee number 1, Craig Silverstein, thinks Brin "brings more of an operational focus."

"We're pretty lucky because we have both of us plus Eric," said Brin. "We are able to choose the things to focus on. It's a great luxury." Because "I can't escape being a bit of a tech nerd," Brin said, he spends a lot of time on technology. But so does Page. "These things are subtle. We overlap a lot."

What both bring, said Nick Fox, the group business manager, ads quality, is "an ability to push you down paths you wouldn't have thought about before." When Fox first joined Google and watched Page and Brin at TGIF, "I thought they must be two guys who had a great idea and got lucky." But he quickly concluded they always had "great insights," and an ability to provoke thought. He offers this example: They were in a meeting discussing new ways to advertise with search and how to move beyond the text ads Google relied upon. Brin was holding a plastic bottle of water, and said, "Let's turn this bottle upside down. If I'm a butcher and I'm trying to get customers into my store, maybe a text ad is not an effective way to get customers into my store. But maybe if I was able to film a video of myself showing all the fresh food and great prices and I'm just talking about my store with a lot of passion, maybe this is the way I can get people to come into my store." It was not the typical auto dealer ad announcing a President's Day sale, Fox said. "You don't think about ads of people talking passionately about their store." For various reasons, such ads are still not part of search, but to Fox that is less important than the ability of the founders to "turn the way people think about something upside down."

Alissa Lee encountered this upside-down approach. In the first five years of Google's life, one or both founders insisted on interviewing each applicant. Brin was introduced to a Harvard Law graduate, Alissa Lee, by David Drummond, who was the company's outside counsel in the late nineties and became Google's corporate counsel in 2002. Lee was a contracts lawyer, and in the course of her interview, Drummond remembers, Brin said, "'I really need to see how you will practice law. I need you to draw me a contract. Don't spend a lot of time on it. Draft it and send it to me and to David so we can review your work.'" And then came the Google test: "'I need the contract to be for me to sell my soul to the devil.'" Brin remembered his request and recalled: "I just figured that if I'm interviewing an attorney I should validate their work product."

Lee remembered repeating the question, not sure she had heard it correctly. Brin told her he wanted the contract e-mailed to him in the next thirty minutes. "Amid the surreal oddity of it all," she recalled, "I had forgotten to ask him all sorts of lawyerly questions, like what sort of protections he needed, what conditions he wanted to attach, and what he wanted in return for his soul. But then I realized that I had missed the point. He was looking for someone who could embrace a curveball, even relish it, and thrive in the process of tackling something unexpected. I'm not sure he actually looked at what I sent him, but something in my crazy sale agreement or in my response must have satisfied him."

"She was a clear hire," said Drummond. Today Lee is Google's associate general counsel.

John Doerr encountered a similar upside-down approach when Page asked him what he thought of Google's buying a Boeing 767.

"I think that's a terrible idea," said Doerr.

"Why?"

"For the ethos and egalitarian nature you want to have in the company," Doerr answered, "you're never going to get away from the public perception of two Silicon Valley entrepreneurs owning a personal 767."

"Look at the numbers," Page said, showing Doerr a sheet of paper revealing that for seven million dollars they could purchase the 767, and for another ten million dollars they could install improved engines and a new interior. "A totally upgraded 767," Doerr realized, "cost less than a G-5." And it could fly longer distances and accomodate thirty-five people, transporting engineers and the founders or Schmidt around the world to visit Google sites. "They went ahead and did it." They later purchased an additional plane, a Boeing 757.

WITH INTENSE PRODDING from the founders, the Google engineering shop was innovating at a furious pace. Among the new projects developed at this time were Desktop Search, Froogle (later changed to Google Product Search), Google Maps, Google Print (renamed Google Book Search), Google Docs, to allow users to create and edit documents, presentations, and spreadsheets, and Pyra Labs, to facilitate the creation of blogs. The founders were particularly enthusiastic about the idea for a new e-mail system. Unlike providers such as AOL, Google's e-mail would be free, and would allow its users to easily search their own e-mail archives for content and contact names. And while Yahoo's free e-mail offered its users 4 megabytes of storage, Google's Gmail would provide 1 gigabyte, 250 times as much. To the engineers, it seemed clear that this was enough storage that a user would never have to delete e-mails. In the interest of efficiency, the first version of Gmail did not include a delete button. This had an unforeseen effect: Users feared that Google would peek at e-mails. And Paul Buchheit's e-mail scanning software—the same program that had grown into AdSense—only fanned this fear. For Google, it was a way to make money from e-mail by placing ads when certain keywords were typed. But critics said it was an invasion of privacy, that Big Brother was watching everything. Google's engineers failed to absorb the lesson of Microsoft's Passport program. Introduced in 1999, the program stored personal information and allowed access via a log-in name and password. Its release triggered a storm of protests, complaints that Microsoft would access this personal data for its own business reasons. Perhaps a reason Google failed to absorb the lessons of Passport was because Google believed its intentions were noble and that Microsoft's were probably not.

Terry Winograd, the Stanford professor, was a consultant on Gmail and described a "huge debate" over the program. "We said, 'People want to delete things. There should be a delete.' Larry, among others, said, 'We want them to start thinking differently.'" Page said that because Google was offering so much storage, users could keep everything, and went on to argue: "If you delete stuff, you might later on decide you want it. Plus, you spend time thinking about whether I should delete this or not." The "engineering optimization side," said Winograd, claimed this was an inefficient use of users' time.

The Electronic Privacy Information Center, a public interest research center in Washington that focuses on privacy and civil liberties issues, demanded that Gmail be shut down, declaring that it was "an unprecedented invasion into the sanctity of private communications." Of course, a computer, not a human, was scanning the e-mail, as most e-mail providers do to prevent spam. At first, the founders and Schmidt tried to defend the no-delete button and the advertising feature of Gmail, believing the small tempest would pass. It did not, and Google was forced to add a delete button. For Winograd this was an early sign of troubles to come. He has enormous respect for his former students (and gratitude for the Google stock grants that made him a rich man), but what he saw in the Gmail debate was that Google relied so much on science, on data and mathematical algorithms, that it was insensitive to legitimate privacy fears—and, later, to fears they would dominate the search market. Winograd describes his two former students as impatient: "Larry and Sergey believe that if you try to get everybody on board, it will prevent things from happening. If you just do it, others will come around to realize they were attached to old ways that were not as good." The attitude, he said, "is a form of arrogance: 'We know better.' The idea that somebody at Google could know better than the consumer what's good for the consumer is not forbidden."

Only die-hard Google bashers, however, would deny the idealism that drives many of the decisions Brin and Page have made at Google. In the wake of 9/11, Krishna Bharat, an Indian-born engineer who joined Google in 1999 and today has the title principal scientist, was moved by the awful events of that day to ponder its lessons. One lesson, he believed, is that Americans were largely ignorant of other peoples and creeds, including radical Islam. There was too little international news in print or on television. Bharat said he wanted to "broaden horizons, allowing people to see other perspectives, to see what the Arab street is saying today. It is hard for the *New York Times* to do justice to that." Devoting his 20 percent time to this project, Bharat devised a program that would be known as Google News, initially offering free access to almost five thousand worldwide news links. The placement and selection of stories is made, Google announced, by "computer algorithms, without human intervention." Google News would be ad-free, meaning Google would lose money from this effort. Like digitized books, Google News was advanced as a promotional and sales vehicle. It would, Google said, broaden newspaper readership, and allow newspapers to sell advertising once a user clicked on the newspaper's link. "We send traffic to newspapers," Bharat said. However, newspapers didn't all jump up and down with glee.

One of the major dissenters was the Associated Press. Founded in 1846 to provide news stories to newspapers in exchange for annual fees, the AP had begun to extend this franchise online, selling national and international news to portals like AOL, MSN, and Yahoo. But as Jim Kennedy, the AP's vice president of strategic planning, described it, Google News was sifting news stories, "making copies and taking pieces of this content and posting it as if it were their own news." Google claimed it was fair use, said Kennedy, since it was posting only part of the article and providing a link. Google said it was both creating reader traffic and promotional value for the news sites. The AP, which is a wholesaler of news, claimed Google was commoditizing their content and insisted on a license agreement. Google resisted, and the AP considered bringing a lawsuit.

Did Tom Curley, the CEO of the AP, think Google was naïve? "No, there is nothing naïve about these guys," he said. "They have a very, very aggressive legal view. They have pushed the envelope. . . . They know exactly what they're doing. They have the greatest business ever invented. They are taking everybody else's work and they are figuring out how to do a deal with most other people in which heads, they win, and tails, most everyone else loses." He cited the 80 or so percent Google said it pays its large content partners in the AdSense program. Since Google sells the ads, he said, it charges a commission of about 15 percent off the top, leaving about two-thirds—not 80 percent—for the content creators. "That's not enough."

Eric Schmidt disputes this portrayal. "This is a company that [at the time] had only three or four business development people," he said. Those people alerted Schmidt that the AP felt Google was stealing their content, he said, but "we had a lawyer at the time who advised that this was fair use." Google refused to pay. The AP claimed that for news Google was becoming "an end user," not a search site that sent people elsewhere. The idea, Schmidt said, had "never occurred to us."

Reeling from shrinking revenues, newspapers fretted that Google was depriving them of compensation for their content. They feared Google was expanding from search to the news business. And they were offended that Google thought an algorithm could perform the work of an editor. "Google is driven by engineers who believe that what is most popular is most valuable," said L. Gordon Crovitz, then the publisher of the *Wall Street Journal*. When the space shuttle *Columbia* disintegrated, killing its crew of seven, the Google algorithm allowed the story to rank low and thus disappear from Google News. "Their presentation of news devalues brands. Unlike traditional journalism, it does not communicate to readers the level of authority or authenticity of information." Over time, he said, Google would blur an understanding of which journalism was most reliable, making news more of an undifferentiated commodity. But the wails from newspapers and publishers were fairly muted throughout 2002 and 2003. The anxiety Mel Karmazin felt after his 2003 visit had not yet gripped the old media.

Nor was Google focused on extinguishing external fires: it had its own internal flare-ups to douse. The founders continued to be uncomfortable with Eric Schmidt's efforts to impose streamlined management, fearful it would squelch Google's entrepreneurial spirit. Google was a company rocketing to financial success on the brilliance of its founders and engineers, yet hobbled by them as well. "Larry and Sergey didn't like management," Schmidt said, and they let the new managers know this. They were, he said, "unduly harsh."

In early 2003, Google had four product managers: Salar Kamangar, Marissa Mayer, George Harik, and Susan Wojcicki. To oversee them as senior vice president, product management, Schmidt recruited Jonathan Rosenberg, who had been a senior manager at Apple and other tech companies. Page and Brin were restive with still more managers being added, and Schmidt was caught in the middle. A series of summit meetings was held, with no resolution. Schmidt was not then convinced that relying on four product managers was the best approach. But, he said, "at the time, Larry was having a relationship with Marissa. It was a very complicated set of issues. Eventually, Marissa announced that we should rank all our projects. A great idea. Unfortunately, the top one hundred on the list had three hundred things on it." And then "there was this huge to-do because Larry doesn't agree with the list, and the engineers are not working on what they're claiming to be working on, and the management, which he doesn't like anyway, is getting away—getting too bureaucratic." Page asked everyone to prepare a list of exactly what he or she was working on and insisted on getting the reports directly, said Schmidt, in order "to completely avoid being filtered by all these management types, which includes me!"

This was round two of the founders' unease with Schmidt. Page and Brin would whisper to other Google executives, said one recipient of these whispers, "What does Eric *do*?" This executive believes Page wanted to reclaim his CEO title. Sometime in the summer of 2002, Coach Campbell again intervened. With the fervent support of John Doerr, the coach set out to make the marriage work. Before 2003 was very old, the three men achieved harmony. Asked in 2008 to describe the most important milestones in Google's success, Doerr does not cite the myriad deals with Yahoo, AOL, or revenue gushers like AdWords or AdSense. Instead, he said, "The biggest milestone was for Larry and Sergey and Eric to conclude they were going to work together. It did not happen overnight. They learned to adapt. Bill was very helpful in that, and I was too, in a less key way."

By the end of 2003, the Google rocket was cruising. Its search now controlled 60 percent of the market outside the United States, which produced nearly a third of its revenues. Many of its search competitors—AltaVista, Infoseek, Excite, HotBot—had crashed or would soon crash. Yahoo and Microsoft had jumped into the search business, but Google soared far above them. Already it was common to say "I'll Google it," rather than, "I'll search it."

Google's employee roster nearly tripled in size between 2002 and 2003, reaching 1,628 at the start of 2004. Like a child outgrowing his clothes, the company had become too big for its two-building campus on Bayshore Parkway in Mountain View. Its new campus, christened the Googleplex, was a stone's throw from the old one, faced the same mountains and desertlike expanse, and sprawled over so much territory that Google provided bicycles for employees to travel between buildings. It is a measure of Google's confidence in its own future growth that the company leased 1.5 million square feet of office space in four multistory buildings that once housed Silicon Graphics, and would eventually purchase an additional fifty-six buildings and 2.5 million square feet of building space on sixty nearby acres in Mountain View.

Although its growth was extraordinary, Google remained below the radar of most media companies, unlike Microsoft in the nineties or IBM in the eighties. "Don't be evil" was a heartfelt, galvanizing slogan for Googlers, but it was also an effective way to brand Google as a nonthreatening, almost cuddly, company. Google had bumped into book publishers and the AP, but it was not yet widely perceived as anything more than a narrow search company. As a private company, it was not required to reveal its profits or aims, and so the menace Google might pose to the old media—to broadcast and cable television, to advertising, to movies and print and telephone—was not yet apparent. This was about to change.

CHAPTER SIX

Google Goes Public

(2004)

To grow, Google needed investment capital, but its growth forced a difficult decision. In 2003, Google passed the five-hundred-shareholder mark, and federal regulations stipulate that a year after reaching this threshold companies had either to offer their shares for sale or open their books. Either way, the innards of the Google rocket would be revealed. Page and Brin didn't want to go public, said Schmidt; they were fearful of revealing to competitors proprietary information and the company's true trajectory, but also of having to cope with what they considered the short-term mania of Wall Street. They abhorred the idea of doling out fees to investment banking advisers, of going on road shows to sell their story to investors, of allowing Wall Street to set the initial stock price—in short, of doing things the usual way.

The founders knew an initial public offering of stock was necessary, but they refused to listen to the experts, or to Schmidt and the three other board members: John Doerr, Michael Moritz, and Ram Shriram. They approached the IPO as if it were a science problem, with Page and Brin crafting their own solution. Instead of allowing bankers to arbitrarily set the floor price of the stock or allocate shares at a predetermined price to favored clients, the founders came up with a more egalitarian method. They would run an auction similar to the one Google used to sell advertising. Google would set a floor price, and anyone who made an online bid that matched or exceeded it could acquire a minimum of five shares. Instead of paying the usual 7 percent fee to Wall Street underwriters who were necessary to sell stock, they would cut this fee to about 3 percent. And to protect what they saw as Google's "core values" and maintain a long-term focus, they would implement a dual class stock ownership. The class A shares sold to the public would receive one vote; the class B shares, retained by the founders and by Schmidt and senior managers, would receive ten votes per share, and would comprise 61.4 percent of the voting power.

When the founders proposed this stock structure, Doerr and Moritz objected, and strenuously. Like many on Wall Street, the two board members recoiled at the thought of treating some shareholders as second-class citizens, and of potentially insulating management from accountability to shareholders. "It seemed to me vaguely undemocratic," said Doerr. Shriram was caught in the middle. "I didn't want to take a position until we reached agreement on the board," he said. The VCs had another concern, said a participant in these discussions, about the precedent this might set with their other start-up clients. But the founders had done due diligence, consulting with Barry Diller, who serves on the board of the Washington Post Company, which, like the New York Times Company, has two classes of stock. Diller noted that other companies, including Warren Buffett's Berkshire Hathaway, also have dual voting stock.

The founders were unbending, and Coach Campbell was called upon to help coax Doerr and Moritz to go along. To be even more transparent about their intent, Page and Brin decided to prepare "A Letter from the Founders," to accompany the SEC filing. Written by Page, the letter began, "Google is not a conventional company. We do not intend to become one." To ensure Google's continued creativity and focus on users, rather than investors, they would be unconcerned with "quarterly market expectations," did not "expect to pay any dividends," and would not partake in the usual corporate ritual of offering "earnings guidance" by predicting quarterly performance. "A management team distracted by a series of short-term targets is as pointless as a dieter stepping on a scale every half-hour," the letter declared. They would make big investment bets, even if these only had "a 10% chance of earning a billion dollars over the long term." They would continue to "run Google as a triumvirate," even though this management structure "is unconventional."

They minced no words about the implications of this stock structure: "The main effect of this structure is likely to leave our team, especially Sergey and me, with increasingly significant control over the company's decisions and fate, as Google's shares change hands." They were also telegraphing that the two founders, who together owned 32 percent of the shares, were more equal partners than Schmidt (who owned 6.1 percent), or Doerr, Moritz, and Shriram (with 8.7, 9.9, and 2.2 percent respectively). Years later, Page described his and Brin's motivation: "We were concerned in going public that we would have to change the way we operated, compromise our principles. It ended up being a good way of stating upfront the kinds of things we were thinking about and making sure that everybody who was participating was comfortable. By going public you take on a lot of shareholders, and the shareholders obviously have some amount of rights. But we, who are running the company, also have some degree of rights. We felt like it was better to be explicit . . . and allow us to be able to do the kinds of things we wanted to do." While candid, the letter could have used the skill set of someone with a liberal arts education; say, an editor. Eight times in six pages they repeat a variation of the same messianic vow: to make "the world a better place."

When Google announced it was going public in the spring of 2004, it had to disclose its finances in an SEC filing. As Google's director of global communications and public affairs, David Krane said reporters suddenly realized, "Holy shit, this is a business story we missed here!" Krane and his then boss, Cindy McCaffrey, were bombarded with queries, but because SEC rules require a "quiet period" from companies between the time they file and the time their stock goes on sale, they could not answer. Reporters would call and say, "I need to talk to Sergey. I need to talk to Larry. I need to talk to Eric." The pressure "to get the Google story" was intense. Once, Krane spotted a photographer hiding behind a bush at the Googleplex, hoping to snap a picture of the founders.

On the eve of the auction, there was rampant speculation about the price the stock would fetch. On the day of the offering, August 19, Page did a highly unusual thing: he wore a suit, not his usual black T-shirt and jeans. He and Schmidt had flown overnight to New York to open trading on the NASDAQ floor. They were accompanied by investment bankers and a team of about ten Google executives, including Marissa Mayer. They went back to Morgan Stanley and watched, rapt, as their stock was traded, rising one minute, falling the next. They had suggested in their IPO a floor price of eighty-five dollars, but were hoping to better that. They were now engaged in a spectator sport, one with enormous personal financial consequences. "Will it break one hundred dollars? Will it break one hundred dollars? I kept asking," said Mayer. She and Page and Schmidt and the others were mesmerized by the Morgan Stanley trader who spoke so fast to those on the trading floor that the Googlers found him unintelligible. They watched him finally coax the stock to settle in at one hundred dollars. At last, he rose from his chair and, as if he had put a baby to sleep, calmly told them, "It likes to trade at one hundred dollars."

Page, Schmidt, Mayer, and David Krane hopped into a waiting SUV that took them to Google's New York offices, which were then on West Fortieth Street. As soon as the car doors closed, recalled Mayer, Page pulled out his cell phone and announced, "I'm going to call my mom!" The others pulled theirs out and chorused, "I'm going to call my mom!" When they got to Google's offices, Page and Schmidt and Mayer went back to work, meeting for ninety minutes with a team of engineers.

Where was Brin? He had stayed out of the public eye in Mountain View, working. Page and Schmidt had urged him to come to New York, but he refused, saying, "It would send the wrong message." By treating this as a normal workday, he declared that the IPO was not about getting rich but about building Google.

The stock reached $108.31 the next day, and by January 31, 2005, had jumped above $200. It soared, in large measure, because investors had for the first time peeked at Google's ledger sheet. They saw that Google's revenues had shot up from $86 million in 2001 to $1.5 billion in 2003, and seemed destined to double by the end of 2004. Net profits reached $105.6 million in 2003, and were expected to almost triple the following year. They saw that the young AdSense program now contributed half of all revenues, and that Google raced well ahead of its two primary search competitors, with nearly twice the users of Yahoo and more than three times Microsoft's. Google had little debt, and though Yahoo had terminated their search contract, it had generated only about 3 percent of Google's revenues. They also saw that the Overture patent lawsuit hanging over Google was withdrawn by its corporate parent, Yahoo, which exchanged its warrants for 2.7 million Google shares. And they saw that Google's skilled work force was deeply invested in their company's success, with Google regularly setting aside about 12 percent of its revenues to award nearly 40 million stock options to its employees.

Envy raced through the corridors of traditional media companies. By the standards of media conglomerates (or investment bankers), Google's compensation was extremely modest. Schmidt was the highest salaried employee at $250,000 and received a bonus of $301,556 in 2003, and Page and Brin each earned a salary of $150,000 and a bonus of $206,556. But the value of traditional media executives' stock holdings were usually leaden. By contrast, a total of 19 million share options had been granted to Google employees, more than half of these at an option price of 49 cents per share, and none at a price above $15.95. When the stock price leaped with the IPO, it produced more than nine hundred Google millionaires. Eventually, four employees—Page, Brin, Schmidt, and Omid Kordestani—and the three outside directors would become billionaires. Andy Bechtolsheim, who signed the first check, owned 1.5 percent of Google's stock, and David Cheriton of Stanford, who tirelessly promoted Google, owned 1.4 percent. Stanford University, which received stock and royalties from Google for their investment in Brin and Page, owned nearly 1.7 million shares. If the first thirty Google employees held their stock, said a knowledgeable insider, by 2008 they would each be worth about $500 million; the next seventy employees would each be worth about $100 million. Even Bonnie Brown, the first masseuse hired by Google in 1999, who smartly opted for stock options and a lower hourly rate, retired a millionaire and established her own foundation.

There was more to unsettle traditional media companies. On page 80 of the Google IPO was this strategic declaration: "We began as a technology company and have evolved into a software, technology, Internet, advertising and media company, all rolled into one." And on page 11: "In addition to Internet companies, we face competition from companies that offer traditional media advertising opportunities." Google went on to say that, increasingly, they would be vying with these media companies to induce advertisers to shift their ads online. In an appendix that accompanied the filing, Google produced a chart showing that while magazine and newspaper advertising declined between 2000 and 2007, and television ads only rose 8.8 percent, Internet advertising jumped 101.9 percent, becoming "the fastest growing medium for advertisers."

While Wall Street focused on the money Google was making, Benjamin A. Schachter, then the senior Internet and video game analyst for UBS, focused on the dollars they were investing in computers and servers and data centers, two hundred million dollars in 2003 (and soon to climb to nearly three billion dollars annually). "This said they were doing much more than selling advertising. You don't need that computing power for text searches. You need it for mobile phones and applications, for cloud computing." A "cloud" of servers could store a consumer's information and hold a suite of software products, including spreadsheets, word processing, and calendars.

Google has dozens of data centers all over the world (the exact number is a state secret at Google), and within these data centers are housed what may be the world's most massive computer system, millions of PCs that have no keyboards or screens and are arranged in stacks and have been repurposed as servers to process searches. The servers in these data centers provide an array of software services that users can access from any device. By geographically spreading these data centers all over the world, Google became more efficient. "In a second, light can go around the world seven times," said software engineer Matt Cutts, who joined Google in 2000. "That's a couple of milliseconds between a data center on the East Coast and a data center on the West Coast or in Europe." When we log onto Google, it instantly identifies our approximate geographical location from the Internet Protocol address on the browser that connects us to the Internet. Thus the query is dispatched to the closest data center, which produces a speedier result.

But the data centers are meant for more than search. Eric Schmidt, Schachter noted, has been proselytizing for cloud computing for two decades, since he was a Sun executive touting "network computing." That same year, 2004, John Markoff of the *New York Times* spotted it too. While others saw Microsoft training its guns on search, he saw Google taking aim at Microsoft's software. The scale of the Google computer system, as well as the backgrounds of its management, he wrote, "suggests that while Microsoft may want to be the next Google, the Web search company has its own still-secret plans to become the next Microsoft."

A STRIKING TAKEAWAY from the Google IPO and letter is that Google's two thirty-one-year-old founders were driving the company with a clarity of purpose that would be stunning if they were twice their age. Their core mantra, which was echoed again and again in their IPO letter, was that "we believe that our user focus is the foundation of our success to date. We also believe that this focus is critical for the creation of long-term value. We do not intend to compromise our user focus for short-term economic gain." The IPO declared, as they had from day one, that Google will "not accept money for search result ranking or inclusion"; that no attempt is made to keep users in a walled Google garden but instead to steer them quickly to their destination; that if the ad does not attract user clicks, it will be dropped "to a less prominent position on the page, even if the advertiser offers to pay a high amount." And those ads deemed more relevant because they attract more clicks, move to the top "with no need for advertisers to increase their bids." Since Google only gets paid when ads are clicked, this ranking system "aligns our interests equally with those of our advertisers and our users. The more relevant and useful the ad, the better for our users, for our advertisers, and for us."

How did Page and Brin achieve such clarity?

Page's answer: "Being less experienced, you have benefits and you have costs. We were willing to do things differently because we didn't know better. I think our propensity to do that is higher than most people's. I'm not sure it's clarity. It looks like clarity in retrospect because you see the things that work." Page's modesty is becoming, but falls short of a full explanation.

Brin gave a parallel answer: "A lot of it is common sense, a combination of common sense and questioning rituals. Experience is a benefit, but it can also be a handicap." He also attributes their success to their math backgrounds and a thirst "to be precise." The idea to give employees 20 percent of their time to pursue their own passions he credits to graduate school, where "you're always going off" on your own projects. Stanford was a huge influence: its bikes and buses, its open cafeteria tables and time to work on your own projects. "They wanted to replicate the Stanford culture in the business world," said Ram Shriram.

The precision argument is picked up by senior vice president of Operations Urs Hölzle, who said the logic flows from a focus on the user. Start there, and it is relatively easy to decipher whether users want a Google home page cluttered with ads, or want relevant ads, or want to rapidly move to different sites. "They predicted things that did not make sense to me, but turned out to be true. Larry said, 'The ad results have to be better than the search results.' I thought he was wrong. Yet today studies show that people value the ads as an essential part of their search results."

One of their mentors at Stanford, Terry Winograd, thinks their "clear, coherent point of view" is "an engineering point of view: Don't assume things are done the right way because they were always done that way. Question everything." And after you question, revert to "an engineering optimization attitude: 'Make it more efficient.'" What stands out to another Stanford mentor, Rajeev Motwani, the Stanford professor Brin remained closest to and who died in a tragic accident in 2009, are their one-word questions: "The number of times they made me change my opinion by asking, 'Why?' They asked like a child."

It would be a mistake to ascribe Google's success to the generic category of engineers. Larry Page brilliantly conceived search, and Sergey Brin's math skills were vital to its success. But Google also succeeded because it forged teams of engineers who were not territorial, who formed a network, communicating and sharing ideas, constantly trying them out in beta tests among users, relying on "the wisdom of crowds" to improve them. Building communities of engineers and hackers and users was the ethos they shared. They believed it was virtuous to share, for it embraced the construct framed by Eric Steven Raymond in a paper originally presented at a conference of Linux developers in 1997, "The Cathedral and the Bazaar." Instead of a solitary engineering wizard crafting software as if it were a cathedral and releasing it when perfected, Raymond argued that the Linux model was more like "a great babbling bazaar" that would ignite the creativity of communities of engineers and users. This ethos was one that infected Page and Brin and Google engineers, led them to the clarity of a free search engine designed to serve users.

Eric Schmidt had another theory: Page and Brin actually have more experience than their age suggests. He recounted a recent discussion he had had with Page. He and the founders were upset with a product user interface presentation they attended. Page said the problem was that the engineers were young and had no experience. "The reason you and I agree on this is that I started on this when I was very young, and I've been thinking about it for a long time," Page said. At first, Schmidt was stunned, wondering how Page grouped himself with someone who was two decades older. Then it dawned on him that Page nearly matched him for experience. Like Brin, he said, "He looks like a kid to you, but he's been in the industry as long as I have in a way."

The experience of the founders stems, as well, from four things they shared. First, each was raised in an academic home, where clear thinking was prized. They were trained to be precise. Each also "are quintessential Montessori kids," said Marissa Mayer. "They didn't have a lot of structure. They got to do what they want to do. They were taught to question authority and think for themselves. They fundamentally believe that people on many levels know what's best for themselves. Like the Montessori kid who paints when he wants to paint." Montessori, Page said, taught Brin and him "to question everything." A third vital shared life experience was Stanford. The fourth was that Page and Brin shared each other. "There's kind of a strength in the duo," said Coach Campbell. "So when they come out the door at the other end, they are even more convinced than they were going in."

"We agree eighty to ninety percent of the time," Brin said of his relationship with Page. Page thinks they agree about two-thirds of the time, but said their disagreements are usually over small things. "If we both feel the same way," Page said, "we're probably right. If we don't agree, it's probably a toss-up. If we both agree and nobody else agrees with us, we assume we're right!" He smiled as he said this, an awkward, tight smile, yet one that conveyed both merriment and resolve. "It sounds like a tough thing to say, but that's sort of what you need to do to make progress."

Susan Wojcicki, who rented them her garage, believes they gave each other strength—strength "to be different. They think alike. They had a shared vision. So when things got tough, they were able to support each other in being different." They don't always agree, said Jen Fitzpatrick, who is Google's engineering director and was among the first thirty Google employees, but "having a mental sparring partner is a good way to drive your own thinking."

"Having the two of them being completely in sync" is a huge advantage, said Kordestani. He remembers his experiences as an executive at Netscape, where the three senior executives—founder Jim Clark, CEO James Barksdale, and the browser's inventor, Marc Andreessen—"were not in sync." Pulling in different directions, Netscape lost its focus.

Page and Brin bucked each other up in another way: they burned with an idealism that sometimes bordered on messianic. They launched Google with a fervent belief that advertising tricked people to spend money, that the Internet would foster a democratic ethos that would liberate people. They gave employees their 20 percent time, Page told Schmidt, in order "to force a conversation" with managers, removing some managerial power.

There is a real sense of loyalty to Page and Brin at Google. Their vision has made Googlers obscenely rich. Employees love the freedom that the 20 percent time and generous benefits grant. Like Steve Jobs or Bill Gates, their knowledge can be intimidating, though terror is not commonly part of their motivational arsenal. Their approach can be subtle. Sheryl Sandberg recalled a project she supervised in her role as vice president, global online sales and operations. The story she related could be interpreted as an illustration of a company careless about how much is spent, or as a reason employees like Sandberg saluted the founders. At the time, her project awarded free search ads to nonprofit groups. "Some companies would be worried about the bottom line. Larry and Sergey just wanted to know why the program was not bigger, faster," she said. She increased the size of the effort—too fast, it turned out. "We were giving much more ad inventory to a handful of nonprofits than we should have." She trekked to the founders' office in Building 43 to explain. Page was there alone, and she explained her "really big mistake," said she "should have noticed," and apologized.

Page interrupted her, she recalled. "He said, 'I'm so glad these are the kinds of mistakes you're making because it means you're moving quickly and doing too much. I'm going to be very upset when the mistakes you're making are by going too slowly and missing opportunities.'" She volunteered a ten-point plan to avoid similar mistakes, asking if he wanted to review it.

"No, I totally trust you," he told her.

Of course, clarity is not a trait unique to Google's founders. Steve Jobs has demonstrated prescience with several transformative innovations: the first Macintosh, Pixar, the iPod and iTunes, and now the iPhone. Bill Gates was clear about the value of software, a clarity IBM lacked when it ceded the operating system to Microsoft. By insisting that craigslist.org be a free site for most classified ads, Craig Newmark knew, he said, that by sacrificing revenues "people saw values we believed in and picked up on it." He knew he was building trust.

Page and Brin's clarity was abetted by the CEO they chose as their partner, Eric Schmidt. Aside from the bumps they had the first few years, it is the overwhelming opinion of those who work with them that the three men have a smooth working relationship. Sheryl Sandberg observed that the reason the troika "works is that whoever you go to for an answer, that answer sticks." When you have two parents, a child can usually play one off against the other, she said. But at Google even if one of the three disagrees, he will back the decision. Brin said of Schmidt, "Eric is the leader for the company. Larry and Eric and I all share in the top-level leadership, but mostly Eric takes on the hardest challenges. Larry and I can spend more time on products and technology."

Success in the Valley requires more than good engineers and passion, said Bill Campbell, pointing to the brilliant engineers and divided management that could not save Netscape, or how the passion of founder Jonathan Abrams, who founded Friendster, the pioneer social network site, was no substitute for missing management, and is a reason Friendster was eclipsed by Facebook. "I can't imagine that anyone could have done what Eric has done. He matches what this company needs. You've got founders that have their unique passions, and they have an unusual amount of strategic insight. Applying that to a business model and making sure that the trains are running on time—and at the same time never losing the technology vision—is a feat. Eric's technology skills mean that no one can bullshit him. You can bullshit me. I'm not an engineer."

Being an engineer, alone, is not enough. Oracle has thrived for a long time as a company founded and headed by Larry Ellison, who is not an engineer. Ditto Apple under Steve Jobs. This point is made by Dan Rosensweig, the former COO of Yahoo who is today the CEO of Activision Blizzard's Guitar Hero franchise. What makes a successful CEO, he said, "is a balanced appreciation" of the many factors, including engineering, an entrepreneurial and business culture, plus good management. In defense of his friend Terry Semel, he added, "When Terry ran a movie studio he wasn't a director or an actor. Yet he and Bob Daly ran one of the great studios."

The youth of the founders sometimes leads to sneering that an adult like Schmidt was essential to managing Google. "It borders on insulting to say that Eric provides 'adult supervision.' It is insulting to both," Elliot Schrage said. Yet there are times when Schmidt does supervise, playing a role he likens to "a catcher" who retrieves "loose balls." For example, at the conclusion of a Google Zeitgeist conference, the founders and Schmidt hosted a lunch for fewer than a dozen journalists in a conference room on campus.

In an earlier interview, I had asked Schmidt how he felt about the federal Patriot Act, which grants the president superseding power to tap phones or e-mails to investigate potential terrorism. "I'm not a big fan," Schmidt said. "I'm offering you my personal opinion as a citizen." At the press lunch, the three men sat at the head of a long table, and as a preface to a question I mentioned that two years earlier Google had challenged a Justice Department subpoena that the company share information about search queries involving pornography, and Google took them to court and won. Given that, I asked, what was Google's posture toward the Patriot Act?

"I'm not an expert on the Patriot Act," Brin began, "but it's certainly a long-standing issue prior to the Patriot Act. . . ."

"Can I?" Schmidt interrupted. Not waiting for permission, he proceeded to say: "The best way to answer this question is to say it's the law of the land and we have to follow it."

"Or in some cases we fought it in court," Brin began again, referring to the court victory on whether Google must turn over search requests involving pornography. Again, Schmidt interrupted, steering Brin away from any possible don't-be-evil proclamations. Schmidt said, "We fought it legally, and we followed the law, and we won in court."

There are times when Schmidt appears obsequious to the founders, as when he introduced Page at the annual meeting of Google shareholders as "the best business partner in the world." But then, "every once in awhile," a Google executive said, "he does this unintentional condescending thing, and he does it in public settings."

What Schmidt clearly brought to Google was experience the founders lacked. Experience often brings seasoned judgment. "Eric is the person who said, 'We did this at Sun,'" said Sandberg. "Eric instilled some business discipline. Before Eric started, our engineering team was going to build a finance system." She recalled that he told them "This is not a good use of our resources. We'll buy the software program." Michael Moritz, who as a director was unhappy with Schmidt's toughness during his first year at the helm, now said, "I've become a huge cheerleader and fully paid-up member of his fan club. He's done the most important thing for a chief executive, and that's to recruit and lead a wonderful management team."

Andrew Lack, then the chairman and CEO of Sony Music, who is a friend of Schmidt's, remembers an incident at the 2005 World Economic Forum in Davos. Arthur Sulzberger, Jr., the chairman of the New York Times Company and publisher of its flagship newspaper, spoke at a dinner attended by Schmidt and about fifty media executives and journalists. Schmidt remembers the evening vividly, thinking, "I was the guest." What he did not know, said Lack, was that he "would become a target." Sulzberger, who despite his august position can be surprisingly supercilious, rose and accused Google of "stealing his business," his advertisers, his content. Sulzberger has another side, as a staunch defender of journalistic values—a reason many in the *Times* newsroom believe he nobly stands between them and the financial barbarians—and he then made an eloquent plea for the importance and future of newspapers, before coming back to Schmidt and underscoring his animus toward Google.

The room was tense when Schmidt rose to respond. He defused it with humor, said Lack, referring to himself "as the skunk at my garden party. I can feel in this room, shall we say, a certain indifference towards my contribution to all of our work together, and I feel sorry about that, because I think there are great contributions to be made working together." Schmidt acknowledged that Google and the Internet can negatively affect newspapers and other media businesses, but ended by urging them to talk and search for ways to work together. Sulzberger said he had "no recollection of the specific incident," adding, "You can certainly check with Eric on this." Eric Schmidt confirmed Lack's account.

"I admired Eric for the way he handled himself," Lack said. "There was no armor to him, no bluff, no bravado."

By 2004, relations between Schmidt and the founders were harmonious. The founders are happy with Schmidt, said one longtime Google executive who did not want to be quoted, because "Eric does everything they don't want to do." Bill Campbell sees it from another angle. He lavished praise on Page and Brin for their entrepreneurial brilliance and inquisitiveness. But he added, "Here's the part you don't see: Let's assume they had ten ideas they thought were great. Let's assume they applied six of them. That gauge of what you can apply and what you can't is where Eric comes in big time. These guys decide this is what they want to do, and Eric will say, 'This is worth fighting for. This is a really important thing. Let's go do that. Let's pull that, it will take us a little off track.' What Eric has, and the founders are the first to say, is judgment, judgment, judgment. He knows when to take their initiatives and drive them to a conclusion, or to talk them out of it."

SOMETIMES ENGINEERS CAN BE CLEAR about the wrong thing. By relying so heavily on algorithms and science, the Google founders—and Schmidt— have sometimes been clueless about right side of the brain issues, as they were with their original approach to Gmail, or book search, or their clumsy dealings with traditional media companies. Google collects an enormous amount of data about the people who use it. It asks users to trust them with private information, much as a credit card company asks users to trust it won't share card numbers. The difference is that Google's business model is based on selling advertising. And the data Google collects—the amount of time users spend with an ad or reading something, what they click on, what they search for, what they seem to like or dislike—is invaluable to the advertiser. Although Google does not hand over the data to an advertiser, it does use the data to help advertisers target customers. As Winograd points out, Google is really saying, "'We're smart guys. We have integrity. Trust us.' They see things not from an institutional, political point of view but from this personal and engineering point of view: 'We would never do that sort of thing.' They believe that in their hearts." Winograd believes them too. But the engineer's passion, he said, drives them to also believe that they are "smart enough to make sure that it won't happen by acci- dent." With the air of an empathetic but rigorous professor grading a smart but innocent student, Winograd arches a huge white eyebrow and con- cludes that this entails "a certain amount of technical arrogance—'The system cannot fail, cannot fail.'" But the system can fail, he added, because it is managed by fallible human beings, not machines.

Google, at least abstractly, is aware of this danger. Their IPO filing ac-knowledged that "privacy concerns" could sabotage the trust the company requires from users. In disclosing to investors the various ways in which Google could fail, they write: "Concerns about our collection, use or sharing of personal information or other privacy-related matters, even if unfounded, could damage our reputation and operating results. Recently, several groups have raised privacy concerns in connection with our Gmail free email service. . . . The concerns relate principally to the fact that Gmail uses com-puters to match advertisements to the content of a user's e-mail message."

If users lost trust in Google, believed their private data was being exploited and shared with advertisers (or governments), the company reg-ularly judged one of the world's most trusted brands would commit sui-cide. Do Google's engineers, in their gut, believe they could lose the user trust they have earned? Unclear. What is clear is that there is often a fine line between certitude and hubris.

CHAPTER SEVEN

The New Evil Empire?

(2004-2005)

I n Edgar Allan Poe's story *The Purloined Letter*, an incriminating letter disappears from the private residence of the French queen. The Parisian police prefect takes on the case, but even after an extensive search, he cannot find the letter. And though he manages to narrow the search to a chief suspect, a government minister, he lacks evidence to arrest him. The prefect decides to consult the noted amateur detective C. Auguste Dupin. He explains that each night for three months, he has slipped into the minister's home to assiduously search for the letter, removing cushions, the bottoms and tops of bedposts, the floorboards, the bindings of books—without success. The prefect is agitated; the suspect is a mere poet, he says, and he cannot believe such a "fool" could outwit him. Dupin, however, disagrees; he thinks the prefect and his detectives are the foolish ones, limited by their experiences, their routines, and "their own ideas of ingenuity." They could not comprehend the acumen and cunning of a mind schooled not just as a poet but as a mathematician who follows his own "mathematical reasoning."

Months go by, and the prefect returns, still unable to prove the minister's guilt and ready to sign over the reward. Dupin, after persuading the prefect to sign a check, pulls the letter from his desk drawer. He explains that he cracked the case by climbing inside the supple mind of the suspect and imagining what he would do to conceal the letter. He imagined that the minister tricked the police by not attempting to conceal the letter. Rather, to avoid detection the letter was soiled, slightly torn, and crumpled in a card rack lying in plain sight in the middle of the minister's room. Dupin found the letter where it had always been: under the nose of the prefect and his detectives.

Until 2004, most traditional media executives treated Google the way the prefect treated evidence: they failed to see the digital threat right under their noses. But soon after the IPO, their heightened awareness was captured in an eight-minute Flash-based movie that virally spread across the Internet. Called *Epic 2014,* it was a faux documentary by two young journalists, Matt Thompson and Robin Sloan. With a voice-of-God narrator, it recounted how year by year a new media giant, Googlezon (the merged Google and Amazon), acquires or murders media companies, including the New York Times Company. By 2014, this Orwellian colossus employs its algorithms and computers to snare advertising and customize packages of news for individuals, whose wants are revealed by the cookies Googlezon gathers to track the behavior of its users.

Not surprisingly, this depiction jarred Googlers. When Sheryl Sandberg joined the company in late 2001, she believed she had a public mission, a mission parallel to the one she felt as a ranking member of the Clinton administration. Yet to her shock, not long after the IPO, she first heard Google referred to as the "evil empire." She was attending a Google conference—"I was standing there with our partners and they said, 'How do we sustain ourselves against the power of—' I thought they were going to say Microsoft. Instead they said, 'Google.'"

The hostility, said Eric Schmidt, "did not begin until Google went public and people realized how much money we were making." The reaction had more to do with fear than envy. It took Microsoft fifteen years to exceed one billion dollars in revenues; it took Google just six years. The evidence was now visible that Google was attracting more Internet advertising than anyone else, and these dollars were being siphoned from traditional media. This was perceived as a threat to most traditional media companies, and perhaps none more so than the advertising industry. Google was able to sell advertising with just a few search words, and without charging the same 2 to 5 percent fee extracted by the media buying agencies. The buy was better targeted. And for advertisers it was more efficient, for Google only charged the advertiser when the consumer actually clicked on an ad. "There's that same 'think big' attitude about markets and opportunities," Steven I. Lurie, a former Microsoft executive who had friends at Google, told the *New York Times* at the time of the IPO. "Maybe you can call it arrogance, but there's that same sense that they can do anything and get into any area and dominate."

IT WAS IN THE CONTEXT of this growing backlash that the fight with book publishers, begun a few years earlier, started to come to a head. Like the Googlezon film, the uproar over digitizing books seemed to surprise Googlers. In their assessment, by scanning books and making them part of search, they were performing an ambitious and noble public service— they thought of the effort as their "moon shot"—and they assumed that they could do this without seeking permission of the copyright holders. Google knew that only about a third of the more than twenty million books ever published were no longer protected by copyright. But the mission was to scan *all* books. With books under copyright, Google said it would merely show "snippets," which it claimed was permissible under the fair use clause of copyright law. Google did not precisely define the maximum number of words in a "snippet." Nor does the law, but the rule of thumb is that fair use involves only enough text to briefly explain a book or briefly quote from an article or song.

Google believed it had provided protection to authors and publishers. In its contracts with libraries, Google said that if, within three years of the digital transfer of material, "Google decides not to use that content" (a particular book) because of a copyright dispute, the library would destroy the digital copy. They believed authors and publishers would see Google

Books as a wonderful way to promote authors and their works, and to bring back books no longer in print. Google had earlier launched a Partners Program, signing up publishers who agreed to allow snippets to be shown for certain books, along with a link to an online bookseller. But publishers did not agree to allow all books to become part of search. The gulf between Google and the publishers and authors was vast. Google wanted to push the envelope of copyright, expanding the definition of fair use to allow more extensive quotations from books. It stressed the rights of search users, echoing the views of Web pioneers like Kevin Kelly, the "senior maverick" at *Wired* magazine, who said that in return for government copyright protection, authors and publishers had a "copyduty" to "allow that work to be searched." Google was offering to pay the cost of moving and scanning the books; what publisher—or library or university or author—could refuse that offer?

One clue of Google's fundamental attitude toward books—and fundamental innocence of the publishing process—is a conversation I had with Brin while reporting this book. It was the second of our three interviews and upon entering the small conference room down the hall from the second floor glassed office he shares with Page, Brin playfully ribbed me for writing this book. "People don't buy books," he said. "You might as well put it online." He meant: You might as well publish it for free.

"You might make more money if you put it online," he said. "More people will read it and get excited about it."

There's little evidence that such a free book succeeds, I said. Stephen King tried it, and gave up the effort because he thought it was doomed.

"I guess that's true," he acknowledged a little sheepishly.

Following Google's business model, would he expect authors to generate their income by selling advertising in their books? If there was no advance from a publisher, who would pay to cover the writer's travel expenses? (I made thirteen week-long roundtrips to Google from New York, rented a car, stayed at hotels, and paid for dinner interviews most nights.) With no publisher, who would edit and then copyedit the book, and how would they get paid for their work? Who would pay lawyers to vet it? Who would hire people to market the book so that all those potential online readers could discover it? The usually voluble Brin grew quiet, ready to change the subject.

But our rhetorical go-round hinted at something fundamentally true about Brin and Page and the dynamic company they have forged. Their starting predicate is that the old ways of traditional media are usually inefficient, and scream to be changed. This is a reason Google fundamentally misread the reaction of publishers and authors. While Google did reach various agreements with a variety of libraries, including Harvard, Stanford, the University of Michigan, Oxford University, the Library of Congress, and the New York Public Library, publishers did not like the idea of not getting paid for the use of their books. The Association of American Publishers denounced Google's plan as an invitation to piracy, for the books stored on servers would be vulnerable to hackers. Publishers claimed they could be hit by the same thunderbolt that struck the music industry: free downloads.

Richard Sarnoff, the chairman of the Association of American Publishers and the executive vice president of Random House, said, "Google went to libraries and said we will digitize all your books and just use snippets of copyrighted books. They said it would be good for libraries and for users. This is true. But we have laws in this country which govern what we can do and not do. Like copyright, which prevents people from copying things for their own commercial use. And this is for Google's commercial use, for search." The publishers demanded that Google seek their permission before digitizing any book that was still protected by copyright. "The Internet is a grazing medium," Sarnoff said. "Books tend to be a longer term experience." Grazing can be a great way to promote a book, he said. "But we want to be extremely careful to make sure discovery does not become consumption." To illustrate his fear of piracy, he pulled out his iPhone and said that the small device can hold fifty thousand books, all easily downloadable. This, he noted, is the approximate capacity of a midsize bookstore. In October 2005, the publishers announced that they had filed a lawsuit.

Paul Aiken, the executive director of the Authors Guild, wanted authors to share in any profits from their books, but said his primary concern was piracy. He mentioned "the huge risk" posed by backup copies in Google's possession and the libraries. "Google is giving back to the University of Michigan a digital copy of each book for their own use. What happens to the University of Michigan copy?" What happens, he said, when they share the copy with other Michigan libraries? What happens "if they lose the backup?" Or it's hacked into? Sarnoff was also concerned that Google's definition of "a snippet" was vague. A longer snippet from a novel is likely too brief to rob the book of value, he said. But a snippet of a reference book may be "taking real value" from the author. In a fundamental sense, the differences between Google and its Silicon Valley allies, who want to share information, and publishers and authors, who want to be compensated for it, boil down to a definition of property rights. On the Internet, it is common to make copies of pages and share the information of those who produce content. In traditional media, such "sharing" is often considered theft. The Authors Guild also filed a lawsuit against Google.

To David Drummond, Google's senior vice president of corporate development and chief legal officer, the difference came down to this: "Fair use is as important a right as copyright infringement. It is a balance that is struck between encouraging people to innovate, and a public sphere." He defined a snippet as similar "to a Google search. You see just two or three lines." He rejected the idea of sharing revenues with publishers and authors for the snippets that would appear in a book search, likening a Google search to a book review, which no one claims as a violation of copyright law. As for pirated copies from the libraries, he said, "We've got provisions in the library agreements that they agree not to abuse. We would hope that these are major institutions that take their copyright responsibilities very seriously. These are also research organizations that have not insignificant expertise in data security." The president of Stanford, John L. Hennessy, who is on the Google board, agreed that university libraries have to "guarantee" the security of digital books. But he wants to keep the focus on "finding a way to move forward," to bring the information in books to people. "We need to rethink our copyright framework that is still a rem-

nant of the past. In the digital age, for example, why should the library buy
a physical copy of a book? Why can't the library just buy a digital copy?"
Physical books, he adds, are "too big. They cost too much to store. They're
too hard to deal with, and they're too hard to search."

Columbia University law professor Tim Wu supports Google's efforts
to digitize books, which he also sees as essential for comprehensive search.
But he thought Google was being evasive. "If they had a copyright lawyer
among their founders," he said, "they never would have started the company. The basic business of a search engine is to copy everything. To make
your copy, and then search it. The first thing that happens, arguably, is infringement of copyright law. I say 'arguably' because there's never been a
case on it. From day one, Google went out and copied the whole Internet.
Can you imagine a company starting in the film world and the first thing
they did was make a copy of every film in existence? That company couldn't
have gotten started. The Web is always about copying, but copyright law
is all about making copying illegal." There is an unavoidable disconnect
between the two.

Over the next several years, the Association of American Publishers and
the Authors Guild lawsuits wended their way through the legal system.
While they did, another disconnect surfaced: a contradiction between
Google's push to liberalize the intellectual property rights of others while
protecting its own. Buried in Google's 260-page 2004 IPO prospectus is this
admission: "Our patents, trademarks, trade secrets, copyrights and all of
our other intellectual property rights are important assets for us. There are
events outside of our control that pose a threat to our intellectual property
rights." They cited the politics of other nations, the various legal interpre-
tations. Then they provide a sentence that could have been uttered by a
publisher: "Any significant impairment to our intellectual property rights
could harm our business or our ability to compete."

Looking back, many of Google's nonengineers admit, when asked, that
Google made a mistake by not more closely consulting and coordinating
their efforts with publishers and authors. "I think that's true," said Megan
Smith, Google's vice president of business development, who explained that

"we moved too fast" and "involved the Authors Guild much later" than we should have. "We're a technology company," chimed David Eun, vice president of strategic partnerships. "We thought people would understand that we had good intentions." Asked if Google was guilty of innocence or arrogance, Paul Aiken of the Authors Guild said, "It's probably both."

MEL KARMAZIN THOUGHT it was arrogance. Having left Viacom earlier in 2004 after an unhappy half decade with Sumner Redstone (and before it was split into two companies, Viacom and CBS), he was now the CEO of Sirius satellite radio, which blankets the United States with a cornucopia of radio options. He described an early meeting he had with Tim Armstrong, Google's sales chief. "The first thing he said was, 'We have so many advertisers that we don't have enough content in which to put all of this advertising, so we would like to get into selling radio advertising.'" Armstrong proposed to sell national satellite radio spots the way Google sold search words, in an auction.

"How much money will you guarantee me?" Karmazin asked.

Armstrong made an offer that Karmazin considered way too low. "I believe the system would have been successful," Karmazin now said, "but it would have had the effect of lowering prices." Again, he was struck, as he had been on his 2003 visit to its campus, by Google's boundless ambitions. Again, he believed that its mathematical approach was all wrong. Google didn't understand that you were "selling the sizzle, not selling a cost per point"—each rating point signifying the size of the audience is sold at a set rate. "You're selling a spot in *Desperate Housewives*." To those at Google, Karmazin was slavishly following a formula that digital technology had proved wasteful.

It wasn't just Google that loomed as a threat to traditional media. Yahoo was pushing into content—hiring a former Hollywood executive, Lloyd Braun, to produce and package shows for the Web, in addition to such popular features as Yahoo Finance—and in 2005 had more than four hundred million worldwide users. That year, Yahoo generated profits of $1.1 billion, and was valued by Wall Street at a whopping $50 billion, equal to the combined value of Viacom and CBS or to the Walt Disney Company. Jaws dropped when media executives read in 2005 that Yahoo CEO Terry Semel cashed in $230 million in stock options, and had another $396 million yet to exercise.

Google believed, with merit, that traditional media too often blamed digital companies for events they did not cause—for the disruptive impact of the Internet, for slowed or declining profits, for their shrinking stock price or budget cutbacks, for their rampant insecurities. It was inevitable that the Internet would alter the way consumers received and used content. But Google became a convenient piñata.

The company gave its critics a big target to swing at: in 2005 alone, Google acquired fifteen smaller digital companies and partnered with various others, including a smaller search engine, Barry Diller's Ask.com, to which Google directed advertising as it now did for hundreds of thousands of Web sites. Google had 7,000 employees working out of 62 offices, 30 of them outside the United States, which produced nearly 40 percent of its revenues. By the end of 2005, the company had indexed 8 billion Web pages in 116 languages; its revenues soared to $6.1 billion and its net income to $1.5 billion.

Meanwhile, the tide was running against traditional media. In December of 2005, 77 percent of Americans had Internet access at work and 37 percent of all adults had high-speed access to the Internet. The slight but steady decline in newspaper circulation suddenly steepened in 2004 and 2005. The circulation of daily newspapers would plunge 6.3 percent between 2003 and 2006, with Sunday circulation falling 8 percent. Newspaper advertising revenues, which had grown on average in the high single digits since 1950, beginning in 2001 fell in four of the next seven years, and in 2006 began to fall more steeply. With investors convinced that companies like Google would grow while newspapers would not, the stock price of newspaper companies also plunged—falling 20 percent on average in 2005—leaving them less capital to diversify by acquiring growth businesses. With search and Google News and other news aggregators culling reports from all over the world, readers could easily fetch their news for free online. Newspapers cried that Google and other Web sites that aggregated news lacked what elite news-

papers offered: bureaus in Baghdad and state capitals, investigative reporting, professional editors, and familiar brand names that often stood for
quality. But readers could effortlessly view their stories through Google
News or Google search. By the end of 2005, 40 percent of American broadband users said they got their news online.

Much of the rest of old media was also challenged. Book sales were
steady, but not robust, and the industry was anxious about the decline of
independent bookstores and the new leverage exerted by giants like Barnes
& Noble and Amazon.com. This anxiety was only inflamed by Google's
thrust into digitizing books. The movie and television and music industries were fretting about piracy. U.S. content and software companies lost
an estimated $6.9 billion in revenues to piracy in 2005, and in China about
90 percent of all content and software was pirated. About one billion songs
per month were swapped on illegal file-sharing networks. Although digital
companies claimed piracy was hard to control, media executives rarely
believed this. They believed digital companies were building their own audiences by stealing their content, particularly that of music companies. The
lubricant of trust was missing. "I don't believe they have any incentive to
solve it," said Sony CEO Sir Howard Stringer. With the rise of high-speed
Internet connections, Hollywood knew its movies and TV programs were
becoming more vulnerable to hackers and illegal downloads.

Television broadcasters were antsy about new user-generated online
video companies like YouTube, a site that threatened to steal not just eyeballs from TV but perhaps its content as well. And YouTube was not their
foremost threat. New consumer choices drained audiences from traditional
media. Three years earlier, in 2002, there was a total of 308 cable and video
networks, a number that had tripled from just eight years earlier, and would
double over the next four. The radio industry was also squeezed by newer
technologies that allowed the iPod and Internet and satellite radio to subvert their traditional ad-supported broadcast model. The phone companies
nervously watched their traditional landline business erode, and with the
2005 acquisition by eBay of Skype, a largely free Internet phone/voice service, and Google's voice-chat software also released that year, the erosion
would accelerate. The cable companies were unsettled—as were all existing

media—by how new media, from sharing networks like MySpace.com or Meetup.com to video games, captured the attention of their customers. MySpace was only three years old in 2006 but already had seventy million members.

And, of course, there was the advent of online advertising, which alarmed the traditional advertising industry. Google was able to sell advertising with just a few search words. The buy was more efficient because it was cheaper, better targeted, and Google only charged when the consumer actually clicked on an ad. Google could render traditional ad agencies extraneous middlemen to their clients. Irwin Gotlieb, the global CEO of GroupM, the world's largest media buying and planning agency with a pool of sixty billion in advertising dollars, said that the bigger problem for his business was not Google supplanting his services, but its market power. With the IPO placing a value on Google greater than GroupM's parent, the WPP group—plus the world's four other advertising/marketing giants combined—Google had very deep pockets.

The CEO of one media conglomerate describes the media paranoia Google provoked as intense, adding, "It's where Microsoft was. That paranoia is even greater about Google. The service is free. It's hard to see how anybody knocks them out when it's free. The brilliance of its business is that consumers love them. Consumers never loved Microsoft. They never loved the phone company. They don't love the cable company. Because we have to get money! Advertisers get a better deal than they've ever gotten. Consumers get a better search. And it's all free." What terrifies media companies, he added, is Google's ability and appetite to reach into other businesses, from mobile phones to computer operating systems to video and advertising and even banking. "Name a business that they're not going to disrupt."

In Google's 2004 annual report, published in the spring of 2005, the founders gave old media executives more cause for concern. In the report was a letter to their shareholders announcing what they called their 70-20-10 strategy. "Seventy percent of our effort goes to our core; our web search engine and our advertising network," Brin wrote on behalf of himself and Page. He went on to say that it was desirable for Google to diversify and that is "why we allocate 20 percent for adjacent areas such as Gmail and Google Desktop Search. The remaining 10 percent is saved for anything else, giving us freedom to innovate." The letter cited some new products Google invented or acquired: Google Maps, which allowed users to map directions; Google Earth, which provided satellite images of the earth's nearly sixty million square miles, allowing users to zoom in to search teeming Calcutta streets or war-torn Baghdad; Google Scholar, which allowed researchers to access academic papers and research; Google Video, which allowed users to search television programs; and Gmail. Any media company paying attention saw that Google was not just a search engine.

Even new media was put on notice when, in 2004 and 2005, Google swooped in at the last minute to beat both Microsoft and Yahoo in auctions. The first came in October 2004. Brin and Page were on an overnight flight, heading to a Madrid sales conference on a chartered Boeing 737, when they learned from Omid Kordestani that AOL Europe was close to switching its European contract with Yahoo. (Although AOL was losing subscribers, it still had more than twenty million worldwide in 2005, making it a valuable platform to generate more searches.) "We told the pilots to head to London," where AOL's European headquarters were located, recalled Brin. The founders' families were aboard to accompany them from Madrid to Rome, where they were to receive an award from the prestigious Marconi Society for their scientific contributions. When they awoke, they were astonished to find that they were not in sunny Madrid but instead at Stansted Airport outside gray London.

Brin and Page drove to AOL's European offices. Jonathan Miller, the chairman and CEO of AOL at the time, recalled the jolt he felt Monday morning when the head of AOL Europe phoned. Miller thought they had a deal with Yahoo, but now his European executive described the proposal made by Brin, who takes the lead in business negotiations: "He offered a number that was 40 percent higher than Yahoo's. And he told us we had two weeks to get back to them." There were, added a still stunned Miller, "no lawyers, no nothing."

Google won the prize.

The second victory came a year later, in the fall of 2005. Tim Armstrong was attending meetings in Mountain View when Eric Schmidt entered and whispered, "We're about to lose AOL to Microsoft." The merger between AOL and Time Warner was not working; the touted synergies had not materialized. Into this chaos stepped Microsoft, determined to catch up in search. Back when Google was still headquartered in a garage, Gates and Microsoft had had it within their grasp to build a powerful search engine when it purchased an online advertising company, LinkExchange. Although the creator of LinkExchange, Ali Partovi, then twenty-six, told Microsoft that his partner, college dropout Scott Banister, had come up with a way to include ads in with search using keywords and that a search auction system would be "the next big thing," Microsoft spurned the advice and declined to start a search engine. As first reported by Robert A. Guth in the *Wall Street Journal,* Microsoft believed the pot of gold lay not in tiny search text ads but in portals like their own MSN. But now Microsoft had launched its own search engine, Live Search, and with its deep pockets was seeking to replace Google as AOL's domestic search engine.

Armstrong and others hammered out a counterproposal and showed it to Schmidt, before Armstrong flew back to New York to meet with Time Warner executives. Microsoft executives were on one floor, Google executives were on another, and Time Warner shuttled between them. At one point, Armstrong said, Microsoft left, "thinking they had the deal done. We stayed." Schmidt flew to New York, as did Brin. In the end, Google and AOL reached agreement to become worldwide partners, with Google pledging to make more AOL content available to Google users, guarantee minimum annual advertising revenues to AOL, and invest one billion dollars to acquire a 5 percent stake in AOL.

Silicon Valley companies, accustomed to thinking of Microsoft as a foe, were now becoming uneasy about Google. When Yahoo executives read Google's financial reports, they were punched in the nose with the realization of how much more successful and efficient Google was in selling search advertising. Google's search business was growing twice as fast as Yahoo's, and was attracting more text ads. Yahoo poured engineering resources into a new automated ad-sales system, code-named "Panama," vowing that it would help them catch up. Microsoft and Yahoo conducted talks to see if there was a way to slow the Google juggernaut. And eBay, which had long sold advertising on Google, grew alarmed that Google had started a classified-advertising service that competed with its listings, and had inaugurated Google Checkout, which competed with its PayPal online payment service. So fearful of Google was eBay that the *Wall Street Journal* reported on its front page in 2006 that eBay was holding secret talks with Microsoft and Yahoo about allying against Google. Bill Gates further stoked the fever of fear when he told *Fortune* magazine that Google was "more like us than anyone else we have ever competed with."

GOOGLE'S MANEUVERINGS AND DEALS may have made it unpopular with various media companies, but these did not tarnish Google's image with the public. What happened in China did. In 2002, a Chinese-language version of Google search was launched, and then Google News in 2004. As user traffic mushroomed, the Chinese government found some of the news politically objectionable. China didn't want users to be able to search for news about "free Tibet" or for photos of Tiananmen Square protests. At first, Google refused to engage in any self-censorship. Often, the Chinese government banned Google searches. Senior Google executives believed they had to make a choice between denying Chinese citizens *some* political searches and denying them *all* searches. Google decided to comply with Chinese laws, stripped its news results of offending material and eventually, in 2006, created a separate search Web site, Google.cn, on which it would offer politically sanitized searches in China. If a user searched for a picture of Tiananmen Square on Google in London, *The Guardian* reported, the iconic picture of one man blocking a tank's path appeared; if the same search was conducted on Google.cn, a picture "of happy smiley tourists" appeared.

Having escaped as a child from an oppressive government, Brin was anguished by the decision. Four years later, at Google's annual shareholder meeting, two resolutions were introduced calling on Google to support human rights and oppose all forms of censorship in China; the resolutions implicitly rebuked Google. Page and Schmidt and Google management had the votes and defeated the resolution. Instead of vigorously opposing Google's decision, Brin meekly abstained. When a shareholder rose to ask for an explanation, Brin gave a long tortured reply that vacillated between "I agreed with the spirit of the resolutions," and "I am pretty proud of what we've been able to accomplish in China."

Google rationalized its decision. Executives said they were complying with Chinese law, as they complied with German law to screen Nazi materials or would later comply with the government of Thailand by blocking YouTube videos that "defamed" the king. It said it was serving Chinese users, who still received more information from even a bowdlerized Google search than from any available alternative. It said that the Internet would, over time, help democratize China. And it said it would be transparent and notify users when search requests were blocked.

Google could also justifiably claim that it did not cross the line Yahoo had when, perhaps inadvertently, it shared with the Chinese government the e-mail accounts of prodemocracy journalists, resulting in long jail sentences for two journalists. But there was another reality Google confronted, and it was acknowledged in testimony made to Congress in February 2006 by Elliot Schrage, Google's vice president, global communications and public affairs. Baidu, a Chinese search engine, had seen its market share jump from just below 3 percent in 2003 to 46 percent in 2005, he testified, while Google's plunged to below 30 percent, and was falling. China was steering its citizens away from Google. "There is no question that, as a matter of business, we want to be active in China," Schrage said, adding, "It would be disingenuous to say that we don't care about that because, of course, we do." What Schrage and Google were less transparent about was that Google had invested in Baidu, and presumably had to win the concurrence of the Chinese government in order to do so. The next year Google sold its 3 percent stake.

Perhaps for the first time, Google executives were feeling defensive, troubled that folks thought they had violated their "Don't be evil" pledge. In the wake of China and the Google IPO, Eric Schmidt said he expanded his own job description. "It took me a while to figure out that we had to reach out to traditional media," he said. "It's part of acknowledging they are incumbents." But he, like Google, was just making nice. "I'm happy to be diplomatic," he added. "But I'm about winning!" What wasn't clear was: Winning what? And at whose expense?

Schmidt was not diplomatic with Elinor Mills, a reporter for CNET News, a Web site that contains various online networks, including business news, technology, video games, and television programs. Mills in 2005 was working on a story about how much private information Google collected. As part of her research, she used Google search and Google Maps to run a quick search on Eric Schmidt. She located his Atherton home and address on Google Maps, his approximate net worth, political contributions, and a fair amount of other personal information. Then she published what she found, writing, "That such detailed personal information is so readily available on public Web sites makes most people uncomfortable." It certainly made Schmidt uncomfortable.

"CNET was informed," wrote Randall Stross, "that Google was unhappy with the use of Schmidt's 'private information' in its story, and as punishment, Google as a matter of company policy would not respond to any questions or requests submitted by CNET reporters for one year." Schmidt's and Google's reactions invited derision; Schmidt was accused of a "hissy fit." Google executives tried to reason with Schmidt, to coax him to apologize, to end the ban. Months later, without offering an apology, Stross wrote that Google "quietly restored a normal working relationship with CNET."

Google was becoming more defensive but also began to slowly worry about a potential threat far more powerful than any competitor: government. Google was alienating media companies, and when these companies speak, Washington listens. These companies are a major source of campaign funds and jobs; they provide the stage and microphone for elected officials. By 2005, broadcasters and telephone companies and others were raising questions about Google. Google may have been a multibillion dollar company, but it was unprepared to fight back. It had no political action committee; for a long time its only Washington presence was a one-man office located in suburban Maryland. This office reported to both David Drummond and Elliot Schrage in Mountain View. Drummond was supposed to oversee policy, and Schrage communications, which led to some confusion as the two often go hand in hand.

Although Google was not yet alarmed, it was on notice. At the weekly executive committee meetings, they talked about beefing up their presence in the nation's capital. Brin volunteered to stop off in Washington to say hello to various government officials the next time he was back east visiting his parents in Maryland. But the the trip was hastily planned, as Brin admits: "Because it was the last minute, we didn't schedule everything we wanted to." Among the key people he didn't get to see was Senator Ted Stevens of Alaska, then the chairman of the commerce committee, with jurisdiction over the Internet. (Senator Stevens's knowledge of the Web appeared limited. He once referred to an e-mail by saying that "an Internet was sent by my staff.") The *Washington Post* depicted the poor reception as a snub of Google; it probably didn't help matters that Brin's outfit that day included a dark T-shirt, jeans, and silver mesh sneakers.

Brin did manage to meet with senators John McCain and Barack Obama, and the topic was "network neutrality," an effort by Google and others to ensure that the telephone and cable companies who provide high-speed access to the Internet didn't charge higher fees to Web sites with heavy traffic. Around the time of Brin's visit, an organization called Hands Off the Internet, financed by telecommunications companies, ran full-page newspaper advertisements accusing Google of wanting to create a monopoly and block "new innovation"; one ad featured a grainy photograph of a Google facility housing a sinister-looking "massive server farm." Brin saw it for the warning it was. "I certainly realized we had to think about these things, and that people were going to misrepresent us," he said. "We should be entitled to our representation in government."

Like Microsoft in the late nineties, the Google leadership, "composed of ideological technologists," as Schrage put it in 2007, was slow to appreciate the political and the human dimensions of the technical decisions it made. Schrage's résumé spans a law degree, years of teaching, a senior executive position at The Gap, and work as an international consultant on corporate social responsibility. He acknowledged that Google engineers were new to the ways of Washington. "Some call that naïveté. Some might criticize this; others might applaud it. No question that people here regularly discuss Microsoft's experience and use that as a cautionary tale."

Later, meaning to explain rather than criticize, Schrage told me, "One can make the argument that the genes of technological innovation are frequently in conflict with emotional intelligence. Successful technological innovation is all about disruption. Effective emotional intelligence is all about collaboration, how you get talented people to work together and enjoy it."

Collaboration was central to the thinking of Lawrence Lessig, who was widely hailed as an Internet oracle and was then teaching at Stanford Law School. Lessig had just been treated as such at Facebook, where he'd been invited to speak to its employees and expounded on the virtues of an open Web. Afterward, we had dinner at Il Fornaio in Palo Alto, which is a favorite Valley canteen, and there he asked, and answered, a central question people increasingly posed about Google: Is Google becoming what Microsoft was in 1998?

"The argument is that in an important way, they are the same," he said. "In fact, whether now or soon, Google will have more power than Microsoft did at the time. Google's power will extend to more than one layer of the network." Microsoft's power was its ability to leverage its potent operating system to control the various applications that use the operating system. So Microsoft offered a free browser to knock out the Netscape browser and attacked Java software that might "facilitate competition with the underlying operating system."

Google's power flows from a different source, he said. "They have produced this amazing machine for building data, and that data has its own 'network effect'"—the more people who use it, the more data generated, the more advertisers flock to it. "Everything sits on top of that layer, starting with search. Every time you search, you give Google some value because you pick a certain result. And every time you pick a result, Google learns something from that. So each time you do a search, you're adding value to Google's data base. The data base becomes so rich that the advertising model that sits on top of it can out-compete other advertising models because it has better data. . . . The potential here is actually that the data layer is more dangerous from a policy perspective because it cuts across layers of human life. So privacy and competition and access to commerce, and access to content—everything is driven by this underlying layer. Unlike the operating system, which couldn't necessarily control the content that you got.

"The way they are different is that I don't think there is any evidence that Google has misbehaved in the way Microsoft misbehaved when they tried to leverage the operating system to protect themselves against competition. So far, they've been good guys. But that leads to a question: Why do we expect them to be good guys from now till the end of time?"

Lessig, who benefits from the broad education and reading many Googlers lack, was nevertheless alert to how Google, like Microsoft, might become intoxicated by power and succumb to the same human failures. Of Google, he said, "I fear theirs is an old story about how good people deceive themselves. As Microsoft did in the nineties, you become so convinced that you are good that you become oblivious. I sense that is true at Google today. They've drunk the Kool-Aid."

PART THREE

Google Versus the Bears

CHAPTER EIGHT

Chasing the Fox

(2005-2006)

Rupert Murdoch, the audacious and sometimes outrageous media mogul, made another move in July 2005 that unnerved his peers. He was in the habit of doing so. For four decades Murdoch's News Corporation had been playing bold offense, forcing other media companies to defensively respond. Starting with a single newspaper in Australia, and then England, he build a newspaper empire in both countries, and forced the modernization of newspaper work rules in England. At a time when the audience for the three broadcast networks was aging, he had pioneered the Fox broadcast network, with its youth-oriented programming. He established satellite broadcasting that blanketed much of the globe. He eclipsed the once-dominant CNN in ratings with the Fox cable news network. Journalistically, his impact could be pernicious—spurring tabloid television with his syndicated *A Current Affair,* fomenting shrill, nineteenth-century press partisanship with Fox News, *The Sun* in London, and the *New York Post*. But even as he was disdained in certain quarters, he was always carefully watched. Media companies chase Rupert Murdoch as hounds do a fox.

Murdoch again shocked his peers when he acquired MySpace.com in July 2005 for $580 million. After just two years of existence, the youth-oriented social network and music site had sixteen million monthly visitors; that number would quadruple over the next fourteen months.

Before Murdoch's announcement, it was expected that Sumner Redstone's Viacom would lay claim to MySpace. It was a natural fit with Viacom's MTV, with its own youthful audience of more than eighty million monthly viewers. And it was widely believed that Viacom CEO Tom Freston was close to making the acquisition. But before he could, Murdoch swooped in with a higher offer, which Redstone refused to match. Within months, Redstone had replaced Freston, grousing to associates that had he been more aggressive he could have sealed the MySpace deal. Actually, what happened, according to a Viacom official involved in the negotiations and confirmed by others, was this: "Rupert made a preemptive bid. Sumner told Tom he did not want to get into a bidding war." The parsimonious Redstone had flashed a red light to Freston.

By acquiring MySpace, Murdoch intended to instill in News Corporation a fresh Web-centric sensibility. By contrast, when Viacom tried to instill its MTV television sensibility online with a music site called MTV Overdrive, it stumbled. In early 2007, MySpace cofounder Tom Anderson announced to the German magazine *Der Spiegel*, "I think we have replaced MTV. MySpace is more convenient. You can search for things, while MTV is just delivering things to you. On MySpace, you can pick your own channel and go where you want. That's why TV viewership is dropping among the MySpace generation." MySpace had the traffic and the buzz. MTV had the profits, of course, which MySpace did not have. But Murdoch was nonetheless perceived as once again having set the pace for media companies.

IN THE YEARS SURROUNDING the MySpace deal, Internet visionaries began to dominate discourse in the media, and the prospect of new online challenges attracted some of old media's most creative minds. New media was invading the entertainment business, becoming a magnet for talent, for those wanting to stretch their muscles or pad their wallets. Believing that new media would define the future, more than a few executives fled old media. Viacom lost one such prominent executive, a man named Albie Hecht. After successfully creating music videos earlier in his career, Hecht oversaw the creation of MTV Network's Spike TV, which pitches its programming to young adult males, and then was president of Nickelodean Entertainment. But in 2005 Hecht, then fifty-two, suddenly stepped down, saying he wanted to get back to creating products rather than managing them. It was seen as a blow to Viacom. "I left because one of the lessons right now is that the small, fast-moving company with a specific mission can strike. The Viacoms and the rest of them are having a hard time. They take entrepreneurs and make them executives. They take authentic brands and turn them into their brands. And they put bureaucracy into place and reduce the risk taking and speed to market. That's a killer combination." Big companies, he said, are too impatient because they can't explain to public shareholders how they will quickly get a return on start-up investments. He wanted, again, to be a fox.

Hecht, a full-throated enthusiast partial to T-shirts, khakis, and white sneakers, set out on a "vision quest" similar to the one Barry Diller took when he left as CEO of 20th Century Fox in 1991, purchased a PowerBook laptop to explore the new online world, and embarked on a ten-month odyssey to decide where to stake his future. Diller decided that cable would dominate the media's future. Hecht came to a different conclusion. He had visited studios, directors, writers, producers, digital animation studios, anyone who set out to create programming for the Web. "What kept coming back to me," he said, "was that the most exciting people, the most exciting work I saw, was all on the Web." One night as he watched his seventeen-year-old son, his thinking congealed. "He was up in his room," Hecht said. "He's on the phone. He's watching TV. He's playing a video game. He's IMing. He's reading—thank God he reads! All at the same time! You look at that and you go, 'This is a new world with new media and new audience behavior. You have to capture that audience by capturing the way they are engaged.'" His son was not just receiving information or entertainment. He was interacting. This audience wanted different modes of storytelling.

Hecht's son was typical, according to a 2005 study of media usage among eight- to eighteen-year-olds by the Kaiser Family Foundation. The study reported that young people nationwide spent a daily average of six hours and twenty-one minutes with media; when multitasked activities like reading or listening to music were included, the daily total is eight hours and thirty-three minutes, more than "the equivalent of a full-time job." Nearly four hours per day was expended watching TV, videos, DVDs, or prerecorded shows, and 40 percent of this time youngsters were multitasking, usually by simultaneously going online. Outside of schoolwork, sixty-two minutes were spent on the computer, forty-nine minutes playing video games, and only forty-three minutes reading. School homework consumed an average of fifty minutes per day. A later study by the market-data firm, Forrester Research, found that Americans between the ages of eighteen and twenty-seven spent nearly thirteen hours per week on the Internet, nearly two and one half more hours than they spent watching TV.

When he left Viacom, Hecht established a company, Worldwide Biggies, in a brownstone office not far from Times Square. With venture capital funding of nine million dollars, and a staff of twenty-two, they create interactive Web shows and video games and other multiplatform activities. "I use the word *engagement* as the new metric, as opposed to *viewing,*" he said. "Some people call it leaning forward as opposed to leaning back." In the products they produce, they look for "six levels of engagement." The audience must be able to (1) watch (on any device); (2) learn (by searching for information about it on the Web); (3) play (games); (4) connect (social networks, IM); (5) collect (microtransactions involving money on the Web); and (6) create (user-generated content). "If we have four of the six, we put it into development. If we get six out of six, we think we have a hit." He has since created successful Internet games and a popular mockumentary series on Nickelodeon called *The Naked Brothers Band.*

The new hits will differ from the old ones, he said. Storytelling will have to change. "We're learning that now. Some of it is that a story isn't necessarily a story. Facebook is a story. What's the story? 'I'm going to look at what Albie is doing now. I'm going to go on my Facebook page and it said that Albie is now doing an interview. And just yesterday Albie posted

seven pictures.' That's a story." Hecht, like many a high-concept Hollywood executive, thinks in formulas, but his are broader (in a business
sense). He said games are about "experience," TV about "character," and
movies about "stories." In the stories Worldwide Biggies is working on, he
said, "If we can move someone so they love this character, and they're
moved through a story, and they're playing a game, and they're connecting
with their friends about that game, and they're collecting objects in that,
and at the end of this experience they have created their own video of this
experience, we'll have moved them into a different type of storytelling."

He believes the Web is not just a distribution platform. Rather, because
of its interactive nature, he believes, "The platform itself is content." Hecht
feels like an entrepreneur again. "It's all about the new Wild West for me,"
he said.

JASON HIRSCHHORN WAS ANOTHER Viacom refugee. He grew up in Manhattan wanting to be a music entrepreneur. When he was fifteen, in 1986,
New York City bars were lax about checking the IDs of teenagers, until the
"preppy" murder case. A teenager, Jennifer Levin, left an East Side bar with
Robert Chambers late one night in 1986. Her body was found that morning
in Central Park. Bars cracked down on minors, and kids could not easily
congregate.

Borrowing his father's empty briefcase, Jason approached the owner of
the old Fillmore East, where he had been bar mitzvahed, and made this
offer: on nights the place was closed he would fill the hall with teenagers,
in return for half the gross. No alcohol would be served. The owner agreed
to the experiment. Jason called all his private school friends and asked
them to call their friends; this extemporaneous network became viral.
Seven thousand teenagers showed up. "We grossed seventy thousand dollars the first night," he said.

When Jason was a senior at New York University, he discovered the
wonders of the Internet. "You could ask questions and find things," he
marveled. He started building a music-trading site. From his East Ninety-
sixth Street apartment, and with an assist from his sister, he built a site, the

CD Club Web Server, that offered users advice on how to work the CD clubs and catalogues to get the most for their money. *Consumer Reports* described it as a great resource, prompting Columbia House, a music catalogue, to phone to tell him to take down their trademarks.

"Why don't you just advertise?" he asked, half joking.

Instead, they proposed to pay ten dollars for everyone he signed up. "All of a sudden," Hirschhorn said, "I'm making thirty thousand dollars a month!" With this money he built Musicstation.com, which linked to other music sites. He created a music search engine that scanned the Web and television to find music, place it in categories, and fashion a music index. Not long after, five media companies got into a bidding war to buy his company. A lifelong MTV fan, he chose Viacom in early 2000. He was twenty-eight and "I was the lone digital guy." Over the next six years, he was promoted six times, becoming the youngest senior executive at Viacom, the chief digital officer of the MTV Networks. Soon after Viacom pulled back from its bid to buy MySpace, a bid he had instigated, he resigned. While he won't criticize the failure to acquire MySpace, he was frustrated. "I was an entrepreneur who came into a big company and tried to treat it as a start-up," he said. "Big companies don't innovate. They operate. Frankly, I think MTV should have owned the Internet."

He was thirty-five and opted to take what he said was a 90 percent pay cut and accept equity to become president of the Sling Media Entertainment Group. Sling Media sells a product, the Slingbox, which allows users to watch their home television and DVR on their PC, MAC, or mobile devices. His editors selected what they think of as "the best stuff, putting it on the front page" of a Sling media guide. They plan to make money by selling ads and sharing revenues with their content providers. One day, he hopes, Sling Media will also create its own content. Sling Media aims to become another distribution platform, letting users watch what they want when they want it on various devices, and letting Sling gather data on user preferences which they would share with content partners. Once again, Hirshhorn struck gold. Soon after he joined, Sling Media was sold for $380 million to EchoStar Technologies, the satellite television company. "We've built a virtual cable distributor online," he said. He knew that the

Slingbox, like Apple TV, could prove to be a dud, or that he could feel re-strained operating under a new corporate owner. But Jason Hirschhorn was very rich and had a sandbox to play in.

For a while at least. Chafing under the constraints he felt working within a traditional media company that he said "did not move fast enough into the digital age," in late 2008 Hirshhorn did what he had done at Viacom and left in search of another sandbox. He found it in the spring of 2009, when the company he wanted Viacom to buy—MySpace—had slumped and Murdoch brought in new management, including Jason Hirshhorn as chief digital officer.

MARC ANDREESSEN HAS SPENT much of his life working in the digital sandbox, achieving the fame and financial success others seek. A large man with an immense, shaved, egg-shaped head, his restless leg hammers the floor, and he speaks rapidly in a booming voice. His professed motto is, "Often wrong, never in doubt." A self-made multimillionaire at age thirty-eight, Andreessen has often been right. As a computer science major at the University of Illinois at Urbana-Champaign, he worked at the univer-sity's National Center for Supercomputing Applications. Inspired by Tim Berners-Lee's vision of open standards for the Internet, in 1992 he and a coworker, Eric Bina, created an easy to use browser called Mosaic. The browser worked on a variety of computers, facilitating the hypertext links that allow Web surfing and Google search, helping users to effortlessly hop from site to site. After graduating in 1993, he moved to California, where he met Jim Clark.

The former founder of Silicon Graphics, Clark shared Andreessen's con-viction that the browser could be a transformative technology, and he had the money to advance that dream. Not long after, Andreessen became co-founder and vice president of technology for the company that would be-come Netscape Communications.

With Netscape's IPO in 1995, Andreessen became very prominent in new media circles. He also became very rich, and even richer when Netscape was sold to AOL for $4.2 billion in 1999. After a brief stay as chief technology officer for AOL, Andreessen started Loudcloud, a Web-hosting company that sold software and consulting services. After its own IPO in 2001, Loudcloud was sold to EDS and changed its name to Opsware, with Andreessen remaining for a time as chairman.

He had no interest in being a CEO, though. "I'm a well-trained introvert," he told me. "Being with people drains me of energy." He had a wide range of interests, though, and deep pockets, and he wanted to marry both. He chose to become an angel investor. He put money into Digg, a social news site, and Twitter, among others. He joined the board of eBay. He wrote a blog that displayed his eclectic and wide range of interests—in books, TV shows, movies, politics, press criticism, Wall Street, debt to capital ratios.

The investment about which Andreessen is most passionate is Ning, a social network that enables those who join—artists, musicians, students, educators, a fan club for the Jonas Brothers, a snowboard community, etcetera—to create their own communities of interests. The idea came out of his association with Gina Bianchini, who met Andreessen soon after she received a master's degree from the Stanford Business School and started a company in 2000. When her company was sold in 2004, Bianchini and Andreessen brainstormed her idea of forming a social network among those who seek like-minded communities and his idea of providing a platform on which to build them. They named the site Ning because that was the best name they could agree on that cost no more than $10,000, he said. The site would have two revenue sources: Google's AdSense to reach advertisers wishing to communicate with each community and those niche channels willing to pay a monthly fee to Ning for a range of services, including $19.95 per month for space to sell their own ads with Google or to forgo ads entirely. By the summer of 2008, Bianchini said, there were 465,000 social networks on Ning, with 10 million registered users, 40 million unique users each month, 5 billion monthly page views, and 116 employees working from a building in Palo Alto. As chairman, Andreessen has an office there, but appeared only a couple of days each week, and rarely in the morning. "I wouldn't be sitting here without him," said Bianchini. "He funded Ning and made me CEO. He put up the money, and he took only 50 percent of the equity."

His closest friend, Ben Horowitz, who worked with him at Netscape and in early 2009 became his partner in starting a $300 million venture capital fund, describes Andreessen as a Renaissance man. "You can talk about the economy, fashion, military strategy, whatever, with Marc. I don't know anybody else like that who goes across so many domains."

Andreessen likes to be alone, to stay up most of the night surfing the Web and reading, and rising late and avoiding meetings. He found a kindred spirit in Laura Arrillaga, who teaches at Stanford's Business School and is the daughter of Silicon Valley's wealthiest real estate tycoon and Stanford benefactor, John Arrillaga. "Laura reinforces my hermitlike tendencies," he said. "We love to be home." They are, he said, "dream customers" for old and new media. "We have more DVDs. We have Blue-ray Discs. We do downloads. We're a huge iTunes customer. We've got, between the two of us—she still uses her old house as her office—eight or nine Direct TV dishes. We're about to add Comcast's Video on Demand, because I want to try that. We're about to add a Windows' Media Center PC." They have a Vudu box, Apple TV, two Tivos, several PVRs and DVRs, and numerous high-speed Internet connections. In all, their monthly subscription bill comes to about $2,500, he said.

Although he consumes old media, Andreessen delights in tossing grenades at it. As late as 2005 and 2006, he said, traditional media was "totally putting their head in the sand. They were in complete denial." He cited YouTube, the burgeoning video Web site, as exhibit A: "YouTube ends up being this hub for tens of millions of people to watch video. In two years, it's going to be a direct competitor to TV networks and cable networks. A direct competitor with more users and viewers. . . . All of a sudden, that's a new hub. It's like the old joke: 'Where are they going? I'm their leader and I must find them!'"

He sees the Internet as a medium that will soon have 2.5 billion users worldwide, an audience far larger than any reached by traditional media. And the audience will be composed of those who "want whatever they want when they want it." They will want to skip commercials and watch movies or TV programs on multiple devices and be able to get DVDs of movies the day they are released in theaters. "When has the music industry and the movie industry and the TV industry ever had a market that big to deal with before?" Andreessen said. "And when has distribution ever been this cheap?" The costs that burden traditional media, from paper to printing and manufacturing to trucks to sharing revenues with movie theaters, could be drastically reduced, he said. "An entrepreneur looks at that and says, 'Oh, my God, it's a monster opportunity!' Somebody who is protecting an existing business says, 'Oh, my God, I'm going to go out of business!' Now they're both right. It depends on whether they radically make the changes they need to make."

GOOGLE WAS BOLDLY MAKING CHANGES. It outmaneuvered Murdoch, Viacom, and Yahoo and stunned the media world when in October 2006 it purchased YouTube for $1.65 billion. The deal eclipsed any that Google had done before, and the potential impact of YouTube was vast. Since its start in February 2005, YouTube by the fall of 2006 was attracting thirty-four million monthly viewers, or four out of every ten video Web site visitors. And this number was soaring. What visitors viewed on YouTube was mostly "user-generated content," or short homemade video clips: a pet trick, an artfully told joke, firsthand footage of the devastation from Hurricane Katrina, Janet Jackson's "wardrobe malfunction" at the Super Bowl—that users uploaded and sent to YouTube. Increasingly, though, YouTube was expanding its audience with clips from *Saturday Night Live* and *The Daily Show with Jon Stewart,* with sports highlights and music videos; these, too, were recorded and shared by users, arousing piracy concerns.

The reason YouTube was persuaded to sell, said cofounder Chad Hurley, then twenty-nine, was simple: They feared the site lacked the resources to cope with its explosive growth. "When we started, we thought one million daily uploads would be great." Instead, they were getting a hundred times that many. "We thought we'd burn up our bandwidth. We worried our servers would go down." The marriage to Google, he said, meant more investment capital, more servers and computers, more brainpower, more help finding partners and figuring out how to place advertising on their site. "We needed resources to scale the company. We only had a staff of sixty people dealing with the weight of the world. An option was to raise more money and hire more people and take a long time. But we were visible, unlike the early Google. We had competition. We were challenged by the old media." He and his cofounder, Steve Chen, were enamored of Google's focus on users and its emphasis on the long term. "They wanted to give us the freedom not to have to maximize revenues right away."

YouTube and Google's ambitions were immense. Hurley described the site as "a democratic platform" for user-generated and "independently produced content." He vowed that the "creative people who produced content would have more opportunities in the future without answering to a network." Had network executives heard those words, their paranoia would, no doubt, have been stoked. They would have been even more perturbed to hear Eric Schmidt say that YouTube's real challenge was to figure out how to sell advertising. "If that works," he told me, "it will seem like the birth of the CBS network in 1927."

Because YouTube was making no money, there was a fair amount of sneering from media executives. Like Napster, they said YouTube would be hobbled by copyright lawsuits and would be unable to monetize its enormous traffic. "Right now," Microsoft CEO Steve Ballmer declared, "there's no business model for YouTube that would justify $1.6 billion. And what about the rights holders? At the end of the day, a lot of the content that's up there is owned by somebody else." That "somebody else," the broadcast and cable networks believed, was them. YouTube, they asserted, built its success on their backs; thirteen of the twenty most popular videos on the site, the *Wall Street Journal* reported in early 2007, were professionally made, not user generated. Sumner Redstone, whose Viacom owned *The Daily Show With Jon Stewart*, told Charlie Rose, "There are some issues with YouTube. They use other people's products. The only way they avoid litigation now is they stop doing it if you call them."

To acquire YouTube, Google tapped its enormous market capitalization. The company's stock value at the time the deal was announced was $132 billion, giving it a competitive advantage over the largest media companies on earth, none of which was worth more than one-third this amount. Those still oblivious to the challenge posed by Google were awakened by the YouTube acquisition. "They can buy anything they want, or lose money on anything they choose to," said Irwin Gotlieb. "I can only do things that are rational to do for my business."

Media companies were chasing a new fox. It did not go unnoticed by Gotlieb—or other savvy executives—that Google was expanding its online advertising portfolio to include video. Or that YouTube users would only swell Google's unmatched database. More ominous for traditional media, Google, despite its denials, was now in the content business. Like the television networks, YouTube publishes content produced by others and sells advertising. The more consumers linger on YouTube, the more pages they view, and the more page views, the more YouTube's ad rates rise. In search, Google sped users off its site without any particular interest in their destination; with YouTube, it had a stake. The purchase of YouTube represented something else as well. Their Google Video store, announced by Larry Page nine months earlier at the Consumer Electronics Show, was a flop. "YouTube was an admission by Google that they couldn't just build things," said Danny Sullivan, longtime editor of *Search Engine Land*.

WHAT FOLLOWED was a protracted round of negotiations between the broadcast and cable television companies and Google. The discussions revolved around three issues: money, copyright, and trust.

Money was a stumbling block. Traditional media companies sought a version of the system they had long relied upon: an up-front license fee from distributors to air their content. Google agreed to pay something but argued that with a new distribution platform they should not be locked into old and expensive formulas. YouTube, Google argued, was a terrific promotional platform that would expand traditional media's audience. The networks countered: *Show me the money!* Cable networks also claimed that if they licensed their content to YouTube for a lower price than they charged distributors, cable systems owners would demand the same discount.

After months of negotiations, traditional media walked away. "They didn't value our content at a price point we thought was worthwhile," said

NBC/Universal CEO Jeff Zucker. "They built YouTube on the back of our content, and wouldn't pay us." NBC, like other television and cable networks, refused to allow their programs to appear on YouTube, though the network has not loudly protested as YouTube clips boosted the ratings of, for example, *Saturday Night Live*. Philippe Daumann, the CEO of Viacom and Sumner Redstone's longtime legal adviser, complained that it was frustrating to negotiate with Google. "Every time we thought we came down to a certain point, they changed their mind," he said. "And they changed the people in the negotiations. I learned that Google had an interesting management structure. I talked to their CEO, and then when Eric went down a certain path he had to have a discussion back in Mountain View with his two associates. Often there would be a total change in direction."

Schmidt countered that Viacom made demands Google could not meet, including an insistence on large up-front license fees. Because YouTube had "no revenue at the time," he said Google proposed to share advertising revenues rather than pay an up-front fee. We would "give the majority of revenue to them," said Larry Page, "as long as it's real revenue." Viacom and others declined. Asked how he justified locking into an agreement with, say, AOL, to guarantee payments when AOL chose Google as its search engine, Schmidt said, "We had competition at the time." This suggests that with YouTube, Google was not looking over its shoulder at Microsoft. Google's position was at least partly shaped by a belief that it had leverage in this negotiation.

The more consequential issue, said Daumann, was not money but copyright protection—protection against what he referred to as "theft." YouTube was taking Viacom's content, he continued, "not as an experiment, not consensually, but rather they just take it and say, 'Why don't you watch what happens!'" Google said it was the legal responsibility of old media to tell them what should be yanked from YouTube and said it would immediately comply. Old media disputed this interpretation of the law, insisting that the responsibility, and the expense, of policing belonged to YouTube. Jeff Bewkes, the CEO of Time Warner, echoed Daumann's concern. The problem is that once Time Warner's content appears on YouTube, he said, "it gets redistributed to five other places—MySpace, Gorilla, whatever. Those people are now the new sources of the thing." He added that Google maintained they were not responsible if another site lifted Time Warner's content from YouTube, giving them "deniability in the event of theft."

The third issue, trust, was in some ways the most vexing. Daumann was insulted when Google tried to assure him of the promotional value of YouTube. "I don't need somebody else to say, 'It's good for you!' Let me decide what's good for me. Maybe I'm totally wrong. Maybe I'm totally stupid, and maybe it would be better for me to put all of my shows on YouTube immediately. Maybe I'm just an idiot. But it's my right to be the idiot. I think YouTube is an effective promotional tool. We put trailers all over the Internet. We don't run a walled garden here. We have deals with just about everyone—except YouTube." He held a hardening conviction that Google was a pirate. Google held a hardening conviction that traditional media wanted to halt progress and slip their paws into Google's pocket.

Bewkes, unlike Daumann, was willing to believe that Google "was well intentioned," blaming engineers who are thinking not of his copyright concerns but of solving the "engineering problem of getting it out there." Asked what a company like Time Warner wanted from YouTube, he conceded, "It's difficult to figure out." Like his peers, he wants "what we have wanted for seventy-five years, for our copyrights not to be stolen and used by other commercial enterprises who get paid and we don't, and they choose the time it is exhibited without ever contacting us." But in this new world where every media company gropes for a way out of the tunnel, he said, "There is a question of the best way to do that." Web programmers like Albie Hecht thought old media was stuck in denial. "You either find a way to make your product available to the public in the right way, or they're going to get it anyway," he said. "So you can either create another generation of video as opposed to audio pirates, or you can do the smart thing and give it to them," and figure out a way to monetize it.

The chasm between new and old was as wide as the gap between Mel Karmazin's view of how to sell advertising and Google's view. They each spoke of piracy, but old media thinks it is preventable and new media says it wants to try but is dubious that absolute prevention is possible. They each spoke of content, but by content they meant different things. For traditional media companies, it is usually defined as full-length, professionally produced TV programs or movies. For YouTube, it is shorter-form clips, mostly user generated. In many ways, the debate is pointless since both user-generated and slickly produced content commands attention. "Content is where people spend their time," said Herbert Allen III, the forty-one-year-old investment banker who is president of Allen & Company. "Content is not just what's on Comedy Central. Content is Facebook too. Content is how the consumer chooses to spend time."

What is really at stake, Allen suggested, is control of the thriving distribution platform that is the Internet, a platform "of endless choice and immediate fulfillment. Media companies are used to the exact opposite. They have thrived on the pricing power that comes from complete control of distribution. Since the consumer has already voted in favor of the Internet, media companies will have to find a new economic proposition for their content. Media companies have to embrace the fact that the consumer is now firmly in control."

IRATE AND ANXIOUS as they may have been, as 2006 drew to a close, the TV companies were scrambling to find Internet platforms. Some, like the local broadcast stations that formed the backbone of the networks, were largely bereft of an Internet strategy. Other media companies made a genuine effort not to resign themselves to their fate. Among the most active suitors of the new media was Robert Iger, who became CEO of the Walt Disney Company in 2005. He purchased Pixar, the groundbreaking digital animation studio, from Steve Jobs in early 2006. Iger's predecessor at Disney, Michael Eisner, was mistrustful of Jobs, and Iger was warned to keep him at arm's length. Instead, he invited Jobs, now his largest shareholder, to serve on the Disney board. "I figured that if things go well for Disney, they'd go well for him," Iger said. "If things didn't go well for Disney, I'd have more than Steve Jobs to worry about. And to have someone like that in the boardroom when we're discussing technology was great. I love working with him." Iger felt he was building into the company's DNA a digital, user-first perspective. He remembered asking Jobs how often he visited Apple's design lab or technology center, thinking he'd say once a week. Jobs told him he visited three or four times a day. Iger said that now "I try to spend one hour a day surfing the Internet. I just surf and look."

But at least one inspiration came from old media. "The first thing I did after becoming CEO was read Elisabeth Kübler-Ross," said Iger, referring to the five stages of grief described in her book *On Death and Dying*. "First came the denial phase. Then the anger phase. Then the bargaining phase. Then depression. Then acceptance. That's what the music industry did. They listened to a cacophony of voices and let those voices drown out the most critical audience, which was its customers." Determined not to repeat the mistake of the music companies, he became the first network and studio owner to license his shows and movies on Apple's iTunes. ABC station managers and movie theaters protested. He was not swayed, insisting that ABC and Disney were in the content business, not the network or movie theater business, and reminding critics that the average age of those who streamed shows on computers or handheld devices was only twenty-nine. To be relevant to young people, he said Disney had to break old habits. In the first year on iTunes, he said, Disney streamed a hundred million shows and movies. Although iTunes represented just 1 percent of Disney's revenues, it generated $44 million in revenues in 2006, a figure analysts projected would mushroom to over $320 million in 2008.

Murdoch and others made moves. Seeking to bring fresh storytelling to the Web, Murdoch signed seasoned Hollywood producers Marshall Herskovitz and Edward Zwick to create a slickly produced series called *Quarterlife,* for MySpace. NBC Universal's corporate parent, General Electric, announced that it was placing $250 million in an equity fund to invest in digital companies with robust growth prospects, including Albie Hecht's Worldwide Biggies. Comcast, which has more subscribers than any cable company, would launch Fancast.com, an ad-supported cable Web site that hoped to attract full-length content from all suppliers. Viacom and CBS joined others in investing $45 million in Joost.com, a YouTube rival that chose not to display user-generated content but instead to offer full-length programs from MTV, Comedy Central, and CBS, sharing ad revenues in exchange. The TV giants discussed forming their own Internet platform to compete with YouTube. Although many participated in the discussions, only two initially joined: News Corporation, which as the new owner of MySpace saw YouTube as a direct competitor, and NBC Universal. The new platform was named Hulu, and it would look very much like television on the Internet, with full-length programs from the two networks interrupted by commercials in the old-fashioned way.

Sumner Redstone declined to join Hulu; Viacom's content, he believed, appealed to younger viewers than Fox's or NBC's, and in any case, he and Daumann wanted control over where their content appeared. CBS, which was split off from Viacom but which did not lose Redstone as its controlling shareholder, came close to a licensing agreement with YouTube, but pulled back. Redstone didn't want CBS to make such a deal; nor did its network peers. Like Redstone, CEO Les Moonves said CBS would not agree to display its programs exclusively on Hulu. "The issue of the moment is whether Google is going to dominate advertising," observed private equity investor Steven Rattner, then managing principal of the Quadrangle Group, which invests in media companies. "The airlines always kept McDonnell Douglas in business because they did not want to depend on just Boeing. Everybody wants at least two suppliers."

Still, CBS established a more cooperative relationship with YouTube and Google. This reflected, at least in part, the different nature of the two businesses. As a cable program and movie supplier, Viacom got the bulk of its revenues not from advertising but from the license fees cable distributors like Comcast and Time Warner paid them. Unless YouTube offered a reasonable license fee, Viacom risked blowing up its cable business model. CBS, a broadcaster reliant on advertising as its sole source of revenue, saw YouTube as a worthwhile experiment to tap into new revenues that might replenish the revenue CBS lost as its audience shrank.

CBS also had a more assertive digital strategy. Les Moonves decided that he would not treat the Internet as a single distribution channel that his network could control; instead he would spread CBS content on over two hundred Web sites. He had to overcome resistance from the traditionalists in CBS. Jeff Fager remembers the contentious 2005 meeting he attended. Fager is the executive producer of *60 Minutes*, the longest running program in evening television history, and he wanted to expand his audience. He had worked out a proposed agreement with Yahoo that would give the Internet site a total of sixteen clips, up to two minutes long, from the CBS show each week. Yahoo would sell advertising against these clips. Fager pitched the deal to a roomful of CBS executives. He assured them CBS News would retain control of the editing process, that he would have a staff of seven to edit these pieces, that Yahoo had agreed to pay half this staff cost and to split the advertising revenues. "I argued that we needed to reach a larger and a younger audience and to find new revenue sources," he recalled. The average age of his Sunday evening audience was approaching sixty. "The resistance was: 'Why do we want to give one of our best brands to the competition?'" They would be diluting the exclusivity of a venerable CBS program found nowhere else. CBS executives wrongly thought of the Internet as just another distribution platform, and anyone airing *60 Minutes* should pay big bucks. They did not see the Internet as a transformative medium, a medium with thousands of Web sites that could serve as CBS platforms, an interactive platform, a promotional platform that would lure younger viewers to CBS. "The sentiment in the room was not to do it," said Fager.

But Les Moonves intervened. "Look at all the new people we can introduce to *60 Minutes*," Moonves remembers saying. "And since we don't syndicate *60 Minutes*, we are not cannibalizing it. There is no downside for us." That was the decision, and soon 150 million Yahoo visitors would view *60 Minutes* clips each year on Yahoo, far more than the 10 million streamed on CBS.com. (Of course, one day *60 Minutes* video streams might produce big bucks, but not yet; the experiment was cancelled in 2008, after producing only one million dollars, to be split annually with Yahoo!)

Moonves also announced another partnership, with YouTube, in the fall of 2006. CBS would allow the video service to air short-form clips, usually none longer than three minutes, from its entertainment, news, and sports divisions, with CBS and YouTube sharing any advertising revenues. CBS would also become the first network to agree to test a new YouTube technology that would identify its pirated content on YouTube. "We're pleased to be the first network to strike a major content deal with what is clearly one of the fastest growing new media platforms out there," Moonves declared in the joint press release. Redstone blessed the deal, said a CBS executive, because showing clips of CBS long-form shows was a promotional platform to enhance their value, while showing clips of short riffs from such Viacom programs as *The Daily Show With Jon Stewart* would rob them of value. In the not too distant future, CBS would follow Murdoch's lead with a major digital acquisition, CNET.

CBS's switch to playing offense coincided with the appointment in 2006 of Quincy Smith as president of CBS Interactive. "I think Quincy is one of the most advanced thinkers in this space," said David Eun, who was a Time Warner executive before becoming Google's vice president for strategic partnerships; he now works out of Google's New York office as their principal negotiator with traditional media companies. Smith's task, in part, he continued, "is to go back and educate his very smart colleagues that this will not kill their business," because YouTube is not "a destination" that competes with CBS, but rather another platform. The challenge to media companies is to get "their content to where the audience is." Eun credits Moonves: "What he's decided is that he has to change. He needed someone and he empowered him." Of the geekspeak that gushes from Smith's mouth, Moonves said, "I understand half of what he's saying, on a good day! But the important thing is, he understands everything."

SMITH IS PROUD to be called a geek, though this was not what was expected of him when he entered the world. He was born in December 1970 on Manhattan's Upper East Side. His father, Jonathan Leslie Smith, became the youngest partner at Lehman Brothers; his mother, Elinor Doolittle Johnston, was a Bennington College graduate and the editor of *Art + Auction Magazine*. A computer was Quincy's childhood pet.

He enjoyed a privileged childhood—Collegiate, Phillips Exeter, Yale philosophy major—that suggested a life on Wall Street, or the CIA. His ponytail did not. He cut it, though, for his first job as an analyst for Morgan Stanley's Capital Markets group, in 1994. But computers and technology were what really inspired him. He moved the next year to the technology group in Menlo Park, under Frank Quattrone. He worked on the 1995 Netscape IPO, going on the road with cofounders Marc Andreessen and Jim Clark, and with CEO James Barksdale. In October 1995, he joined Netscape as their chief deal maker and Wall Street liaison. He helplessly watched as Microsoft bundled the free Internet Explorer browser in with its dominant operating system, weakening Netscape.

Andreessen's company was profitable, but Netscape was sold to AOL for $4.2 billion in 1999, where the browser lives as the open-source Firefox. Smith left and joined the Barksdale Group to invest in Internet start-ups.

It took just part of his time, and Omid Kordestani, whom he had worked with at Netscape, tried to lure Smith to Google in 1999. He had several interviews, including one with Page and Brin, but was rejected. "I didn't graduate with a Ph.D.! I didn't even go to business school," he said. "The coach"—Bill Campbell—"wanted me to join a couple" of the companies he was advising, but Smith stayed with the Barksdale Group until early 2003, when he joined Allen & Company. "The day I joined," remembers Smith, "the coach stopped talking to me. He said, 'I have no respect for investment bankers.'"

For the next three and a half years Smith labored on a number of big deals, including the Google IPO. He was introduced by Andreessen to his future wife, Kat Hantas, who coowned a small Hollywood production company with the woman who was then dating Andreessen. In the summer of 2006, Les Moonves called and Smith began to do advisory work for CBS. Moonves said he wanted to hire a new digital executive to move more audaciously into the digital space. Smith funneled people in to see Moonves. After each interview, he said, "I felt the harpoon." Moonves wasn't satisfied with the candidates. He entreated Smith to take the job. The clinching argument came, Smith said, when Moonves told him: "You know, I used to be an actor. One night I was going to a premiere and my agent called and said, 'Good luck. We're all in this together.'"

"No we're not!" Moonves told the agent.

"That's the line that got me," said Smith. This was an opportunity to be an actor, not an adviser. "The day I joined CBS," Smith said, "I got an e-mail from Bill Campbell: 'Welcome back to work. Now don't fuck up the quarter!'"

In a sedate company partial to charcoal suits or blazers, Smith called people dude, wore his wavy black hair long and his sideburns down to the bottom of his earlobes, favored loud purple shirts and chinos and shiny Adidas JAM's that were popular in the hip-hop world. He wanted to move fast, yet knew he had to help bring traditional CBS along gradually, Sumner Redstone included. When CBS budget executives questioned him about how much his proposed digital schemes would cost, he tried to instruct them that they should refer to these not as costs but as "investments." He recognized the differences between his old friends in the Valley and his new friends at CBS. He said, "Every win in my external world is a loss inside." He wanted to quarterback a digital offense, yet knew he also had to play defense for the network. "When you're Google or Facebook you're all offense," he said. But he understood that traditional companies have legacies to protect. "In our world you have sixteen reasons not to move too fast." He credits Moonves for pushing change. "They are letting me do a lot. Are there certain things I'd like to do more? Yes." He won't identify these, but he was acutely aware that he had to persuade, not just act.

When he acted he would do so based on a bedrock belief that "the Web is not simply a more efficient video distribution system. The bigger opportunity for the Web is as a new media." He didn't believe CBS would ever make "a material amount of our broadcasting dollars from rebroadcasting full episodes" of its programs online. He believed the Web would require CBS to devise fresh forms of programming, to create new and shorter ways of telling stories. He could proudly point to the fact that in its first month as a channel on YouTube, CBS clips got twenty-nine million views, making it the single most watched content on the site. It offered, he thought, great promotional value.

He described his job by recalling a conversation he had with a friend before accepting Moonves's offer. He repeated the friend's analysis as if it were his own: "'Your problem is that traditional media is sitting in a castle.

If you ask them to run outside in the middle of the rain of arrows and go down a river and cross a bog to go up a hill to get to what we don't know is over there, we can't assure them it is out of arrow range. No promises. Facing that option, traditional media is going to stay in the castle. And what's going to happen to the castle? Those arrows are going to turn into catapults. You have to do something to escape.'" Smith adds his own coda, a kind of halftime talk to stir his new team: "You can be good in television and radio. But you're a media guy. Don't you want to be good online? It's a new medium. And aren't you better than those geeks in Mountain View? Right now they're kicking your ass!"

As QUINCY SMITH AND CBS were reaching out to Google, Google fitfully tried to assuage traditional media's concerns. Eric Schmidt blamed Google's lack of outreach on its newness. "When you're a small company," he told *Time*, "you sort of have to do everything yourself, and as you get more established, you begin to realize you'll never get everything done by yourself." Google reached an agreement with News Corporation's MySpace that was similar to the one they had made with AOL. In return for being chosen as MySpace's search engine, Google guaranteed the social network nine hundred million dollars in revenues over the next several years. YouTube made a series of smaller deals to pull in content from old media, gathering what company officials said at the time was a total of one thousand content partners, including the National Basketball Association, CBS, Sony, The Sundance Channel, and a channel to air the full library of *Charlie Rose*.

Before 2006 came to an end, Google tried to send a signal to traditional media that its intentions were honorable. It reached an accord with the Associated Press and three other wire services—the Canadian Press Association, AFP (Agence France-Presse), and the UK Press Association—thus eliminating the possibility of lawsuits dating back to 2004. The agreement allowed Google News to host and carry complete or partial stories as well as pictures from these wire services, and for Google search to link to these wire service stories; in return Google agreed to pay an undisclosed license fee. This was an acknowledgment that a wire service like the AP, whose articles are syndicated to countless newspapers, posed particular problems for Google search. Every time a user did a search, a waterfall of the same AP story appeared from different newspapers, clogging the search results. Google called this "duplicate detection," and announced that the agreement with the wire services "means we'll be able to display a better variety of sources with less duplication. Instead of 20 'different' articles (which actually use the same content), we'll show the definitive original copy and give credit to the original journalist." Google justified paying a license fee to the AP and other wire services—but not to newspapers—by claiming that since these four news agencies "don't have a consumer website where they publish their content, they have not been able to benefit from the traffic that Google News drives to other publishers."

Solving one problem created another, though. More than a few newspapers tried to make the same deal and were rebuffed, said a senior executive at Dow Jones, parent company of the *Wall Street Journal*'s Digital Network. "If they're really about the user, they should want to say, 'Some sources are better than others.' We've had many conversations with Google. The bottom line from their perspective is that they are not interested. They are about algorithms and links and 'the wisdom of crowds.' But is that really best for the user?" And since the *Journal* charges for its online edition and is behind a firewall, Google cannot offer full links to *Journal* stories as they do with other newspapers.

Amid declining sales, the anxiety of newspapers was inflamed. It was not difficult to incite newspaper owners. The average daily circulation of the largest 770 U.S. newspapers fell 2.8 percent in the first six months of 2006, and 2.5 percent the prior six months. Although online traffic for the top 100 newspapers rose 8 percent in the first half of 2006, and online ad dollars grew even faster, the gains did not compensate for the losses. The rule of thumb is that an online ad brings in at most about one-tenth the revenue as the same ad in the newspaper. There are two reasons for this: readers spend much less time reading a paper online than they do a newspaper, and because ad space is not scarce on the Web, advertisers pay lower rates. A regular newspaper reader of the *New York Times* spends thirty-five minutes each day with the print version, according to Nielsen, while those who read the *Times* online spend only thirty-seven minutes a month reading it. These figures can be misleading, because they average in the occasional visitors who may spend a minute or less online with those who are online devotees. Nevertheless, there is a wide disparity between online and print newspaper readers. Those who can read the paper online for free help explain the drop in newspaper circulation. And those who spend less time with newspapers have less time to scan the ads, which helps explain the drop in advertising. Advertising in major newspapers, which grew barely 1 percent in 2005, would actually drop 1.7 percent in 2006 and 8 percent in 2007. Coupled with the other dismal facts—the falling value of newspaper stocks and their rising debt load—only added to their agitation.

Inevitably, resentment toward the AP spread among newspapers. The AP is a nonprofit cooperative owned by its fifteen hundred or so newspapers. It employs a staff of about four thousand, and because the AP smartly diversified, a third of its revenues come from selling video and online news to its members. While most of its newspaper constituents struggle, the AP's revenues grow annually at about 5 percent. The licensing agreement with Google promised to boost these revenues. Unable to share this growth, U.S. newspapers began to petition the AP to lower the fees it charged them. As part of their cost cutting, the *Chicago Tribune*-owned newspapers, along with about 7 percent of the AP's U.S. newspapers, announced plans to cancel their relationship, a step that, contractually, takes two years.

In the spring of 2007, Rupert Murdoch summoned all his News Corporation newspaper editors and publishers from around the world to a retreat at his ranch in Carmel, California. There they spent a couple of days wrestling with one terrifying question: What is the future of newspapers? Their conclusions, according to Jeremy Philips, the News Corporation executive vice president who prepared the agenda, were bafflingly mixed. The short-term outlook for newspapers promised more declines in advertising, circulation, and classified ad revenues; the long-term prognosis—if the papers could hold on—promised lower costs for printing, paper, and distribution online. "The headline is a paradox," said Philips. "The macrotrends underlining these businesses have never been stronger. The consumption of news is greater than ever before. And the cost of delivering news is lower than ever before." He noted that the online version of *The Times* of London and the *New York Times* have ten times the readers as their print editions had. On the other hand, he continued, "The microeconomic trends are problematic. The advertising available has declined because there are more places to advertise. Newspapers have lost control of classified advertising. In addition, the migration to online leads to a revenue gap because the print reader is more valuable today. And young people are reading fewer newspapers. This is a long-term trend." In a world where online links to content obscure the brand names that produce it, the economic vise tightens faster for small and midsize newspapers as their costs rise and their revenues decline.

THE CONTROVERSIES DID NOT HINDER Google's growth. At the end of 2006, it had 10,674 full-time employees, about half of them engineers. It had reached $10 billion in revenues, a year ahead of Wall Street analysts' expectations, and $3.5 billion in profits, meaning that for every dollar collected, a hefty thirty cents was profit. (Amazon, which was sucessfully branching out from selling books to selling other goods, made a profit of about two cents on every dollar; Wal-Mart made almost four cents.) Google pleased many of its partners—from AOL to MySpace to thousands of Web sites—then paying them a total of $3 billion from its AdSense program. In their annual letter to shareholders, the founders spoke of improvements in search and pitched their new products. However, the core of their thirteen-page letter consisted of endorsements from those who benefited from Google, including Quincy Smith of CBS, who was quoted as saying: "You-Tube users are clearly being entertained by the CBS programming they're watching as evidenced by the sheer number of video views. Professional content seeds YouTube and allows an open dialogue between established media players and a new set of viewers."

There was much in the annual letter to sharpen traditional media's concern about Google's intent. User-generated content was "central" to the site's success, the letter said, and these users would "become the broadcasters of tomorrow." Page and Brin spoke of their new efforts to sell radio and newspaper advertising, declaring, "Our goal is to create a single and complete advertising system." This system, they added, was one in which Google was "helping advertisers of all sizes buy and place offline ads more effectively."

A rain of arrows would soon be aimed at Google. Quincy Smith thought this was a mistake. "I've never seen a company so loved on Wall Street and by advertisers, yet so despised by media companies," he said. "Media companies don't understand that the platform is the business. Google is a platform. They help you monetize your content." For many media companies, however, this was a risk they were unwilling or unable to take.

CHAPTER NINE

War on Multiple Fronts

(2007)

Once you get to a certain size, you have to figure out new ways of growing," said Ivan Seidenberg, CEO of Verizon. "And then you start leaking on everyone else's industry. And when you do that, you sort of wake up the bears, and the bears come out of the woods and start beating the shit out of you." Seidenberg was speaking of Google, with whom he started jostling in 2007 to prevent Google from entering his mobile phone business. The Verizon bear was now awake to the perceived Google menace, as was Viacom.

Of the two, Sumner Redstone was the more openly belligerent. In late 2006 and early 2007, he demanded that YouTube immediately remove one hundred thousand clips of Viacom's copyrighted content. Viacom CEO Philippe Daumann became convinced that Google was "very lackadaisical" about the content that appeared on YouTube. He cited Al Gore's movie, *An Inconvenient Truth*, which Paramount released and which appeared on YouTube in its entirety. "We got frustrated. We told them to take our content down." How come, he asked, YouTube could successfully block spam and pornography and hate speech from appearing, yet said it couldn't block copyrighted Viacom content from being displayed? Redstone, who had long championed the idea that content was king, was furious. He and Daumann resented having to pay what they claimed to be one hundred thousand dollars a month to monitor what appeared on YouTube.

Google countered that only the copyright holder knows what content is under copyright, said Eric Schmidt, citing the Digital Millennium Copyright Act, which makes monitoring a shared responsibility. "The law basically said that the copyright owner monitors, and then we expeditiously remove, and we've done that," he told *Wired* magazine. "And it's well documented, because Viacom told everybody that they gave us one hundred thousand video takedowns, which we did very, very quickly. And what was interesting was that our traffic to YouTube has grown very strongly since then. So one of the arguments that they made was that somehow YouTube was built on stolen content, which is clearly false." He said Google was testing various technologies but had yet to solve the piracy puzzle. Viacom did not believe a technology company could fail to find a remedy—unless it lacked the will.

In March, Viacom filed a lawsuit in federal court charging Google and YouTube with "massive intentional copyright infringement" and asking for $1 billion in damages. Viacom said YouTube effectively stole almost 160,000 clips of its programming and allowed these to be shown more than 1.5 billion times. YouTube's Chad Hurley doesn't deny there were copyright infringements, but he insisted they were not deliberate. His argument was twofold: First, YouTube is just "a clip site. We don't want full programs." And second, Web videos are so new that "everybody's still trying to figure it out." Viacom, he believed, sought clear answers when there were none. Hurley, like top executives at Google, believed the litigious Redstone was using the lawsuit as leverage to negotiate a better deal. Schmidt grows uncharacteristically agitated when Viacom's suit is mentioned. At a 2008 conference at which Philippe Daumann spoke and castigated Google for stealing copyrighted materials, Schmidt sought me out and growled, "Everything Philippe said was a lie. And you can quote me!"

There were those who recognized Viacom's concerns yet thought Redstone was wrong. Esther Dyson, an early and prominent investor in digital media, said, "As a business, I think they are behaving foolishly—like the music companies. They are fighting their customers. What they should do is use YouTube as a platform and share in all the revenues." Those who agree that YouTube is a platform, not a content competitor—including some who work for Redstone but dare not be quoted—think the lawsuit is a declaration of war when what is needed is an agreement that encourages more trial and error.

Many media bears sympathized with Viacom even if they didn't join the lawsuit. "If we're putting up programming for free, why should cable or DirecTV pay us for content?" asked Mel Karmazin. And if consumers can get the content online or on iTunes, he said, unless the digital company pays a substantial licensing fee "you're trading analog dollars for digital dimes." Moreover, once a copy is made, it is easily duplicated and shared.

Anxiety about piracy was not peculiar to television. On the eve of Viacom's lawsuit, all the major Hollywood film studios jointly protested that Google was selling keywords such as *bootleg movie download* or *pirated* for two Web sites it knew to be illegally downloading their movies. Google assured the studios it would prevent a recurrence. But although those keywords can be blocked, there will be others. Even the company that a decade earlier aroused the same fears Google now did, Microsoft, publicly accused Google of a "cavalier" approach to copyright, charging that Google was making "money solely on the backs of other people's content."

Undeterred, Google vowed to take the case all the way to the Supreme Court. Because Google was already warring in the courts with publishers and the Authors Guild, this battle with Viacom opened a second front in the war with old media. And soon there would be other skirmishes, including those with new media companies like Facebook, the fastest growing social network. With more than forty million active users in the summer of 2007, Facebook "doubles in size every six months," said founder Mark Zuckerberg. Then twenty-two, Zuckerberg is a Harvard dropout who in the early days of his company's life slept on a mattress on the floor of a Palo Alto apartment he rented near his office, allowing him to move effortlessly between work and sleep. His baby face is framed with curly hair, and because he is thin, with a relatively long torso, one is surprised that he stands only five feet eight inches tall.

He arrived for dinner at an outdoor Thai restaurant in Palo Alto sockless, wearing Adidas sandals and a green T-shirt, and ordered lemonade that he sipped through a straw. He was on guard to avoid saying anything boastful about Facebook, or intemperate about rivals. He said he did not feel competent to discuss almost anything but Facebook. He lacked Brin's unguarded zest or Page's quiet confidence. But his long pauses when asked about Google, and the way he shifted uncomfortably in his chair, suggest the tension between the two companies. He was somewhat less circumspect about MySpace, his main competitor among social networking sites: "What they're doing is very much different from us. On a fundamental level, what they're doing is not mapping out real connections. They're helping people meet new people. Rather than using the social graph and the connections people have in order to facilitate decentralized communication, they're using it as a platform to pump and push media out to people. They call themselves a next-generation media company. We don't even think we're a media company. We're a technology company."

Facebook is not a content company, he said, just as a telephone company is not. In fact, in some ways Facebook is like a telephone conversation, with all your friends on the same call. But on this call, your friends can share photographs, text, political summons to action, video, and music, or can click to make purchases. "There is a big misconception around what social networks are," Zuckerberg said. "People think there are communities, or media sites, where people are going to meet new people or make new connections or consume a lot of media. But what they really are is a completely different paradigm for people sharing information. The traditional media models are all centralized. What we're enabling here is decentralized individual communication. When that happens with a certain level of efficiency, it starts to become easier for people to communicate and get a lot more of their information through this network than through a lot of the centralized approaches they used before."

This is precisely why Google, starting in 2007, began to worry about Facebook. If Facebook's community of users got more of their information through this network, their Internet search engine and navigator might become Facebook, not Google. As media companies agonized that Google and YouTube were capturing more eyeball time, Google began to have the same concerns about Facebook. What if Facebook became the equivalent of AOL's former walled garden, the home page, the place its users went not to roam but to comfortably nest? Google depends on more and more people surfing the Web. Relations were further strained when Microsoft outbid Google in October of 2007, laying claim to 1.6 percent ownership of Facebook and establishing Microsoft as Facebook's advertising sales agent.

There was another reason Google fretted about Facebook. The social networking site operated on a different business model than Google's. Like Flickr (Yahoo's photo-sharing site), Twitter, or Linux, they are part of what Lawrence Lessig, in his book *Remix: Making Art and Commerce Thrive in the Hybrid Economy,* refers to as hybrids—companies that take the shared efforts of many and build communities that help create commercial value. They are not strictly part of a "commercial economy," as Google, Amazon, and Netflix are, according to Lessig, nor are they strictly part of the not-for-profit "sharing economy," as Wikipedia and the open-source Linux operating system are. The hybrids, wrote Lessig, are those that combine making money with sharing—as Red Hat did by offering Linux for free but selling consultant services to corporations; as Craigslist does by offering 99 percent of its listings for free; as YouTube does by allowing users to freely share videos; and as community-building sites like Facebook do. Google was free, but it was not building a community.

While Google warily watched Facebook, a real skirmish broke out between Google and the bear that is the advertising industry. Ad executives had been uneasy for some time that Google would displace media-buying agencies. But there were additional concerns. How many more ad dollars would Google siphon from traditional media companies? Would Google disintermediate the sales forces of these companies? Might Google bypass advertising agencies and develop a direct relationship with advertisers? If Google's automated auction system brought the cost efficiencies Larry Page touted, would it not inevitably lower old media's advertising rates as well as the fees ad agencies charged clients? Perhaps the overriding concern was the one identified by Herbert Allen III, who said of Google: "They want to be the digital advertising network for all forms of advertising. They want to be the advertising operating system, sitting in the middle of all advertising." Google was indeed "fucking with the magic."

Concern turned to fright in April 2007 when Google paid $3.1 billion to purchase DoubleClick, outbidding Microsoft and Yahoo. "There's no way Google would have acquired DoubleClick if not for their fear of Microsoft," said a DoubleClick executive close to the negotiations. The executive said that because Microsoft and Google were bidding against each other, DoubleClick was able to inflate its sales price by about $1 billion.

In the world of online advertising and marketing, DoubleClick was as dominant in its arena—placing display advertising—as Google was in placing text ads. DoubleClick provides the digital platform that allows sites like MySpace to sell online ads and advertisers and ad agencies to buy them, with DoubleClick culling from its database the information that targets the ads. The acquisition gave Google "an opportunity to be the infrastructure backbone for all ad-serving on the Internet," said a worried Wenda Harris Millard, then Yahoo's chief sales officer. In addition to potentially controlling the plumbing, DoubleClick offered rich new data-mining possibilities. By combining DoubleClick's data with its own, Google would house an unrivaled trove of data. As Randall Rothenberg, the CEO of the Interactive Advertising Bureau, said the day the deal was announced, "You can dive deep into that data and say, who were those people, where do they live, what were they doing when they looked at those ads?"

DoubleClick's promotional materials boast that they "track more than 100 metrics," including which ads users download, how long they view them, where they scroll, what links they click on, if they view an ad and later visit the site, what products interest them, what ads "resonate the most," what they buy and choose not to buy, and how much they spend. According to then CEO David Rosenblatt, the company delivered as many as twenty billion online ads each day. For the "sell side" (the content providers, who in the online world are called publishers), DoubleClick provides tools that help them evaluate the inventory they have to sell and where to target it, delivers the ads, and reports the results. For "the buy side" (advertisers), it provides the same service.

Google's purchase of DoubleClick triggered a flurry of digital advertising acquisitions. Within months, Yahoo, AOL, Microsoft, and the WPP advertising/marketing colossus each swallowed online marketing agencies that compete with DoubleClick, with Microsoft spending six billion dollars, twice what Google had paid, to buy aQuantive. Why the rush to acquire digital ad agencies? And why was DoubleClick sold?

Since DoubleClick and Google share the same one-square-block building on West Fifteenth Street in Manhattan, CEO Rosenblatt joked that the free food was an enticement. But the main reason was that he saw the sell side changing. DoubleClick had promised to transform the business of selling remnant ads, the roughly 30 percent of an ad seller's inventory that is hardest to sell: the least read part of the magazine, the least watched TV shows, the least listened to radio programs. Selling these remnant ads was becoming more expensive for DoubleClick, and Rosenblatt feared that a Google or a Yahoo would come along and offer to sell these for free in exchange for an opportunity to sell more of a client's premium advertising, luring away his customers. DoubleClick needed to widen its scope. "We were selling transmissions. We were not in a position to sell cars," he said. In Google, Rosenblatt saw not just "the single best monetization engine on the Web," and a company with a base of over one million advertisers, but more vitally, a fellow and necessary "middleman" who did not compete with clients by entering the content business.

DoubleClick offered Google a way to pool the two databases and their networks of advertisers. But DoubleClick also brought something Google lacked: a dominant online position in display advertising (banner and video ads), which meshed nicely with YouTube's video offerings and Google's narrower text-based expertise. Tim Armstrong, Google's president, advertising and commerce, North America, envisioned three advantages for Google: better measurement of all online advertising, from text ads on search results to display ads on YouTube; better targeting of ads, which pleases both consumers and advertisers; and finally, higher fees for these better targeted, better measured, ads. Google's game plan, said Richard Holden, its product management director, is simple: "We'd like to create one-stop shopping for advertisers."

With reason, the advertising bears translated "one-stop shopping" to only-stop shopping, provoking dread about market domination. Rosenblatt, a bald, cheerful man of forty-one with a bright smile that provides cover for the technologist within, rises and goes to the whiteboard in his office to draw what he envisions as the future of advertising. Between "buyer" and "seller" he elongates an "ad exchange," a clearinghouse for all online inventory to be sold. There could be many of these, but Rosenblatt, who would become Google's president, display advertising, makes clear he hopes the Google/DoubleClick exchange will be dominant. This new approach can be much more efficient, he thinks, likening it to how online trading siphoned business from brokerage houses. Imagine, he said, that "instead of just selling remnant advertising to the exchange, the seller said, 'We'll expose all of our inventory onto this ad exchange. Maybe we'll carve out a small percent—maybe ten percent—of the really premium stuff and our sales force will sell that directly. But this other stuff'"—he acknowledged that the distinction between remnant and premium ads can be arbitrary—"'I don't know where the line goes. I don't want to figure out where it goes. Instead, I want the ad network to bid.'"

Why shouldn't a media buying agency, such as Irwin Gotlieb's GroupM, conclude that DoubleClick/Google might gobble his piece of the advertising pie by offering to charge, say, 2 percent rather than his 4 or 5 percent? And by promising better data about what ads worked? Irwin Gotlieb did see DoubleClick and its ad exchange as a potential disrupter. He was uncomfortable with the wealth of data that Google would now possess, and could one day refuse to share with advertisers. He was uncomfortable with Google's dominant market share. He was wary of its deals with EchoStar satellite television and Clear Channel radio and some newspapers, allowing Google to serve as the media-buying middleman for their online ads. He was rightly concerned that Google could be trying to usurp his role.

If that was Google's intention, Gotlieb did not believe they would succeed. He welcomed Google reaching into the long tail to match advertisers with smaller Web sites. But he did not think Google/DoubleClick could make inroads with brand advertisers, in part because these clients want to be serviced, to have relationships with media agencies they can consult. And he also expressed skepticism that Google would loom as large in the future as it now does. "If you and I were talking about this in 1998, we would have been talking about AOL," he said. "Two years later we would have been talking about Ask Jeeves."

IN THE ADVERTISING WORLD, if you say "Irwin," insiders instantly know whom you mean, just as people in Hollywood know who Warren and Barbra are without hearing their surnames. In four decades in the advertising business, Irwin Gotlieb has seen fads come and go, though he hasn't changed his hairstyle (his bouffant, graying mane sits flat atop his head, like the deck of an aircraft carrier) or his attire (dark suits and ties). He is confident that with the largest worldwide market share of media buying—estimated to be 19 percent—GroupM is secure. He disputes the notion that there is a sharp definitional difference between new and old media. "As all media moves to digital delivery," he said, "the distinction between media types is going to become less relevant, or perhaps irrelevant. Hypothetically, if I'm reading my newspaper on an electronic display and I see a photograph of a touchdown in the Super Bowl and I click on it and get to see a sixty-second video of that touchdown play, am I now reading a newspaper or watching television? Or does the distinction cease to be relevant?" And whether the consumer is leaning forward over a PC, or leaning back to watch TV, or a combination of the two with a mobile device, he believes each medium will be "addressable," which means his agency will know a lot about that consumer, and each medium will allow the user to click a button for additional information or to make purchases.

Irwin Gotlieb approaches life with the air of a knowing skeptic, one who is conversant in nine languages, including Japanese, Russian, Polish, and Hebrew, and has lived all over the world. He believes Google, like most businesses he has observed in his sixty-one years, is a great company that does one thing brilliantly, but "will probably be leapfrogged by something that two Ph.D.'s in China are working on."

Irwin Gotlieb knows China, and much of the rest of the world. He was born in Shanghai in 1949 to Jacob Gotlieb and Genya Diatlovitzky, who were second cousins and Belarusian émigrés; when he was a year old, the family left for the newly forming Israel. His father, Irwin said, bribed an official to allow them to exit with valuables, including small antiques and precious metals. Because Jews could not pass through the Suez Canal, the refugee boat took six months to arrive. A year later his father flew alone to Japan—Irwin does not know why—and several weeks later the family flew to join him. In Japan, his father suddenly had a new career as an exporter of pearls and an importer of diamonds. Irwin knew his father wasn't a trained jeweler, and he knew Asian currencies "were not worth the paper they were printed on," but he did not know how his father came to that business, or who funded it.

Irwin lived in Japan until he was fifteen and was a precocious student. His parents encouraged him to attend college in the United States and he was accepted by New York University, arriving alone at fifteen with a stipend of cash from his parents. He rented an apartment, learned to speak English, and served as his father's U.S. representative, working with Japanese and Chinese diamond dealers. In keeping with the many secrets held by the Gotlieb family, he never told his parents that he dropped out of college ten days after entering. "They were teaching me stuff I already knew," he said.

He met Elizabeth Billick, a paralegal, in 1968, when he was nineteen. They eloped the following year, fearful that his father, who at the time was not speaking to Irwin, might try to block their marriage. Irwin displayed the stealth of his father. "My mom and dad went to their graves," he said, "not knowing that I didn't go to school and that I eloped."

He had a friend in advertising and it sounded like "a fun business," so Irwin, at age twenty, sent a résumé to various agencies. Over the next five years he worked for two of them, amassing a quiverful of skills: cash and barter syndication, spot buying, research, planning, network TV negotiations. He was recruited by Benton & Bowles in 1977 to run their national broadcast group; over the next twenty-two years he helped build their overseas business and also supervised the production of prime-time shows and made-for-TV movies. Throughout, he dabbled in computer software, creating the first application to measure the audience that ads attracted, and building software to manage ad inventory. "I wrote my first full-blown software system in 1973," he said. In 1979, he built "the first Monster system—eventually two million lines of code," he said, which became the standard yield management software that determined prices, modeled the national marketplace, and allocated ads. His last job at Benton & Bowles was CEO of MediaVest, their media buying and planning agency. In 1999, Sir Martin Sorrell, the CEO of the WPP Group, who was knighted in 2000, recruited him to become global chairman and CEO of Mindshare, a MediaVest competitor. Sorrell acquired other media-buying and planning agencies, and in 2003 Gotlieb was elevated to run them all under the rubric of GroupM. Today, 73 percent of his company's revenues come from outside North America.

Gotlieb's background well served GroupM's global expansion. "The fact that I didn't grow up in the United States was incredibly helpful as the business began to morph globally," he said. His techie background better prepared him to understand and compete against the Googles and Double-Clicks. His friend Michael Kassan, who had a successful advertising career and founded and is the CEO of Media Link LLC, which serves as a consultant to Microsoft and AT&T, among others, remembers the time he and his wife visited the Gotliebs' Westchester home and watched a movie in his screening room. "In Hollywood, a screening room is a show-off room," he said. "At Irwin's, he takes you behind the wall and shows you the wiring and how he does it himself."

Gotlieb tries to stay a step ahead. When digital recorders allowed viewers to dodge TV ads, he pushed to place his clients' products in programs, establishing a production arm of the agency to do it. He grew his digital staff, which now numbers more than two thousand employees. He invested in various companies with technologies that gather consumer data. Invidi, one of those investments, is a software system that resides in a cable box and monitors viewer behavior. It collects data on what we watch, what we like, and how much time we spend watching ads, and can correlate reams of television-watching data with other data collected from motor vehicle records, credit cards, purchase cards, and other credit-rating services and databases. The technology allows the advertiser to show different ads to different potential customers watching the same program.

Gotlieb doesn't think Google, outside of its search advertising, can rival GroupM because most advertising was "not in the sweet spot of their capabilities." Like Mel Karmazin, he believes that engineers cannot replicate what his sales force can do. They can't do product placement, an increasingly popular form of advertising requiring subtle judgment to avoid offending viewers. They miss the "art" part of selling ads, the judgment required to build a brand, the relationships that seller and client forge and that spark ideas. "As complex as the Google processes are, as robust as they are," Gotlieb said, "there is an inherent oversimplification because it is purely quantitative."

ASSUMING THAT GOTLIEB is truly undaunted by Google as a competitor, his would have been a lonely voice in the advertising community. Sorrell, the CEO of the WPP Group, worried that DoubleClick would allow Google to "take our client data." He began to refer to Google as a "frenemy," not quite a friend or enemy but a rival power to guard against. With mounting anxiety, executives noted that Google TV Ads was selling advertising for EchoStar's fourteen million set-top boxes and for Astound Cable, a small cable company. Google's sales pitch was that it could find new local advertisers and help advertisers better locate their targeted audiences. The way it works, according to Keval Desai, the product manager and director for the project, is that Google finds the advertisers through ad agencies or by dealing directly with companies that advertise and brings them to one of one hundred satellite channels. Once the ad airs, Google has software in the set-top box that collects data and analyzes the results. Among the things they learned, he said, turning to a series of slides to make his point, is that when grouped together the shows that have "less than a half of one percent audience share can have a share equal to ESPN." Unlike the Nielsen ratings, which make an estimate of the audience's size by extrapolating from a relatively small sample, Google takes a digital measurement of actual homes. Desai said they learned that advertisers were spending half their dollars on the twelve largest cable networks when they could be reaching audiences of comparable size by grouping smaller networks together. Because the ESPN and other large cable network spots are much more expensive, Google is saving advertisers money, removing the "inefficiencies," as Google had told Mel Karmazin they would. Or as Desai now said, "This slide fucks with the magic!" Through a digital box "we can measure second by second" what ads and programs viewers are watching or turning off, and share this information with advertisers within a day.

As Google's director of media platforms, Eileen Naughton, said, "It is absolutely our intention to be in every cable box." To accomplish this, she knew, would require the cooperation of the cable companies that own the box. And that cooperation depended on trust. Naughton said, "Google aims to improve the advertising quality in traditional media." If traditional media trusts her word, then Google is servicing them, not supplanting them. If they mistrust Google, they will never allow its software to invade the cable box. A decade ago, when Bill Gates tried to persuade the cable companies to trust Microsoft to be the operating system for digital cable boxes, he didn't get past first base.

Television executives had reason to be paranoid about the seventy billion dollars spent each year on TV advertising, as did advertising agencies. Not only was Google telling its customers they could do a better job of targeting ads and telling them which spots worked, but it was also extolling its array of other products. Among them were Google Print Ads, which by early 2008 was selling ads for seven hundred newspapers and allowing them to use an "ad creation tool" to craft inexpensive advertisements; Google Audio Ads, which was hoping to build on the deal it had made with Clear Channel Communications, the largest radio station owner in the United States, to sell 5 percent of ad inventory; and Google TV Ads, which on the

Google Web site is described as "a searchable directory of specialists" to create television commercials. Was Sorrell right? Was Google intent on taking over the media buying function? "Yes, he's right," said Terry Semel, the former Yahoo CEO. "Google and Yahoo are always working on platforms to sell ads. All [of the new Google programs] at the end of the day will have the capability to sell ads in any medium."

So why would a company like Procter & Gamble need a middleman media buyer like Irwin Gotlieb's GroupM? Smita Hashim, the group product manager for Google Print Ads, said "that's a good question," and conceded that, "the roles will start shifting." But Hashim, like Desai and others at the company, quickly assert that Google requires the "expertise" of ad agencies. With passion, Desai insisted that Google is engaged in a "win-win" game. If these programs succeed, the advertising revenues of traditional media as well as Google's will rise. This is a familiar Google refrain, one that relies on what might be called Google "magic": everyone wins. If old media gets with the program, makes a push to be more Internet-centric and share with Google, there will be no losers, no zero-sum games in this brave new digital world.

But these claims did not allay the anxiety of Sorrell, who feared Google would vie to obviate his creative teams as well as his sales and media-planning teams. The wellspring of this concern was not the Google TV Ads program, which does not generate the kind of slickly produced commercials his agencies create. He was troubled by Google's hiring of Andy Berndt, who was copresident of one of Sorrell's ad agencies, Ogilvy & Mather. Berndt was recruited in 2007 to run a new Google unit, the Creative Lab. Google denied that this was an attempt to enter the advertising business, and Berndt said his job is to focus on the Google brand, "to remind people why they love Google," and to create ads only for his new employer. His staff consisted of just twenty people, he said, and would expand to only thirty-five. He said "the short version" of why he joined Google is simple: "When the spaceship lands in your backyard and the door opens, you just get in the spaceship."

To most consumers, Google remained an iconic brand, a force for good, a company that made search easy and fast and free; a company that retained its bold, entrepreneurial spirit and was both a beneficent employer and a benefactor to shareholders.

To most media industries, Google was becoming a dreaded disrupter. The engineering efficiencies touted by Google were also perceived as threats to the sales forces of the television and radio and print industies. Weeks after the DoubleClick purchase, Beth Comstock, then the president, integrated media, for NBC Universal, and now the chief marketing officer for its parent, General Electric, said, "If Google could introduce us to tens of thousands or even a thousand advertisers we currently can't have, that would be a great thing. But when they start moving up the pyramid and they think you can put a self-serve model to what we know of as a very highly customized, high touch, more intuitive kind of business—it's a content cocreation in some cases—you can't do that with self-service and algorithms." In her dealings with Google, she said, "There is this undertone of: Is that all they're looking for? Why are they into television advertising?" Are they intent on replacing NBC's sales force? She would have gladly outsourced the selling of remnant advertising to Google; what she wanted to retain control of was the selling of premium advertising. Like Karmazin, she wanted her salesperson in on the process, persuading clients to spend more.

Days after the DoubleClick transaction, Microsoft and AT&T publicly called on federal regulators to block the deal, saying it would reduce competition and give Google access to too much private data. Sorrell called on regulators to review the acquisition, declaring, "It raises issues as to whether we are happy to let Google have our clients' data and our own data, which Google could use for its own purposes." A senior executive at Time Warner, who did not want to be identified because its AOL division is a Google partner, told me at the time, "You always have to worry when someone gets so much more powerful than all the competition out there. This is why I come down to this: I hope the government starts understanding this power sooner rather than later."

Tim Wu, a professor of law at Columbia University and a former Supreme Court clerk, looks at the issue from a different angle. He said he's not "worried about Google becoming large." One can make the argument, for example, that size brings standardization, he said. "I'm less concerned how they're behaving in their own market than what a company does to other markets." Will Google use its power to unfairly dominate other markets, as Microsoft used its operating system dominance to cripple the Netscape browser? "If Google remains true to its mission of being an 'honest broker,' I'm pleased. If they have an agenda, that's when I become fearful." He wasn't sure Google had an agenda, but was plainly worried: "If they're willing to block sites to placate China, are they willing to block sites to placate powerful advertisers?"

Here the issue of privacy becomes entwined with the issue of power. Together, Google and DoubleClick amass a mountain of consumer data. The more "personalized" this data, as Eric Schmidt said, the better the search answers. "When I decide to go to the movies," said Schmidt, "I'd like to rely on the recommendations of friends. How do we capture that? The more we know who you are, the more we can tailor the search results."

Of course, when a company retains as much data as Google does and also proclaims, "We are in the advertising business," as Eric Schmidt does, this arouses more privacy concerns. And since Google believes advertising is information users want if it is "relevant," it follows that sharing data serves users, which exacerbates these fears. Or as Sergey Brin told Wall Street analysts during Google's third-quarter conference call in October 2007, "I am really excited to tell you today what we have done over the past quarter in ads and apps. As you all know, for advertising our real philosophy is to create a win-win between advertisers and customers by presenting users with really relevant information which is interesting to them, but is likely to cause a transaction to commence." With technology making inroads toward improving how users' real desires are gauged and finding patterns of behavior, the data-mining discipline Sergey Brin studied at Stanford enters a new age. The pressures on Google—and all sellers of advertising—to share more data will intensify.

Privacy fears escalate when Google executives express peculiar ideas about privacy—ideas that suggest they don't grasp the reasons people are fearful. Each fall, Google hosts a two-day Zeitgeist Conference on its Mountain View campus, inviting a cross section of people from various fields. Much of the conference is moderated by journalist James Fallows, and a cavalcade of prominent scientists, musicians, artists, public officials, and others make presentations or appear on panels. The last event of Google's Zeitgeist is when Brin and Page come on stage—in jeans, of course—to answer Fallows's and the audience's questions. At the 2007 conference, Randall Rothenberg of the Interactive Advertising Bureau rose to ask Brin to access the importance of privacy.

Brin declared that "the number one" privacy issue was "stuff that is untrue about people on the Web." Because information "travels so fast" online, and because "anyone can publish anything," these untruths gain currency. The number two privacy issue, he said, was the "hijacking of credit cards." He dismissed concern about the information collected on cookies "as more of the Big Brother type"—in other words, fantasies. "Do they [users] trust what you're doing? That's not so much a privacy issue." By this logic, if we trust Google, there is little reason to fear they will misuse our data. Afterward, at a small press lunch with the founders and Schmidt, Page signaled his agreement with Brin. "Sergey is just saying there are practical privacy issues that are different than the ones debated." As was true when the founders pushed to add a delete button and allow Google's Gmail scanning technology to more aggressively deliver ads when users typed certain keywords and to forgo a delete button—a mistake Brin told me showed "we just weren't good" at anticipating fears, but "I think we've now learned"—once again, Brin and Page displayed an inability to imagine why anyone would question their motives and a deafness to fears that can't easily be quantified.

CHAPTER TEN

Waking the Government Bear

While a full chorus of incensed media—advertising agencies, publishers, newspapers, television and telephone companies, and tech companies like Microsoft—complained about the growing power of Google, the Bush administration, steadfast in its belief that a free market provides its own regulation, was silent. Stepping into this breach was Brooklyn-born public interest advocate Jeffrey Chester, executive director of the Center for Digital Democracy in Washington, D.C. Chester founded this two-person organization with an annual budget of two hundred thousand dollars in 2001. He has mounted a ferocious campaign to induce the world's governments to handcuff Google. Its first petition was filed before the FTC in the fall of 2006, prodding them to investigate how online marketing encroaches on privacy. In the spring of 2007, Chester, then sixty-two, began to press for an antitrust investigation of the rapid consolidation of the online advertising sector, and urged the FTC to reject Google's proposed merger with DoubleClick. He petitioned the European Commission to do the same.

A voracious reader of trade publications, Chester became obsessed by what he saw as the pernicious power of the Internet to compile data on consumers. Chester is difficult to ignore. His Brooklyn-accented voice is loud and piercing. He hounds people. He speaks passionately and rapidly, leaping in midsentence from privacy to monopoly to a conversation he had that morning with an FTC staffer. He wears horn-rims and short-sleeved shirts with the neck open and the pockets bristling with pens. His tiny office on Connecticut Avenue is adorned with movie posters that assail McCarthyism and corporate power. He has little regard for the advertising industry, but knows that if he railed against commercialism and consumerism it would open him up to attack as a left-wing former social worker, which, of course, he is. So he sticks to the privacy issue. "The basic model for interactive advertising," he said, "combines this very powerful data-collection business designed to know your interests in a daily, updated way that is then utilized to create very powerful multimedia to get you to behave in some fashion, whether it's buying a product or liking a brand."

Marc Rotenberg, the executive director of the Electronic Privacy Information Center, rents a single office to Chester's organization and works just down the hall. He is in nearly all ways Chester's opposite. He wears charcoal business suits and has degrees in law and computer science; no pens can be found in his shirt pockets. But he and Chester work closely together to advance privacy protection measures. Rotenberg believes the central question should not be, Is Google invading people's privacy? Rather, it should be, Why does Google need to collect all of this information?

GOOGLE'S SERVERS NOW CONTAIN a tremendous amount of data about its users, and this database grows exponentially as search and a variety of Google services multiply. With the latest techniques to discern what really motivates consumers—often categorized as "behavioral targeting"—companies and advertisers will know even more. Some forms of such targeting are widely seen as helpful, such as when Amazon extrapolates from the browsing and purchase histories of a customer to recommend books. Other forms might be alarming to the lay consumer. New technology will allow cameras built into television set-top boxes to be armed with algorithmic models that read our facial expressions and tell advertisers what we do and don't like; Nielsen is investing in brain reading—called NeuroFocus—which is meant to take the guessing out of why consumers react to what they see on a screen or read or listen to.

New smart phones collect enormous amounts of data. Mobile telephone companies gather and store digital data on calls made and received and how long each lasted. In addition, the chips in the phone's GPS track a user's location, the length of stay, and other mobile users she is in touch with. Tapping this sort of data is known as reality mining, and is a cousin to Brin's data mining. Although telephone companies don't share the names of customers, they have begun to sell this data to companies seeking to market products. Phorm, an American company with offices around the world, proposed to go one step further, approaching telephone and broadband Internet service providers with software that tracks each consumer's online activities, so that a nameless portrait of each consumer can be created. In return for supplying the data, the telephone and cable companies can open a new revenue spigot. By late 2007, Phorm had done three deals in England that could potentially yield data on two-thirds of Britain's broadband households.

Publicity about Phorm aroused the ire of Tim Berners-Lee, a senior researcher at MIT and the inventor of the World Wide Web. Because Berners-Lee refused to patent his invention, to cash in financially, or to become a talk-show celebrity, his opinion carries heft. In a rare interview with the BBC, Berners-Lee expressed outrage: "I want to know if I look up a whole lot of books about some form of cancer that that's not going to get to my insurance company and I'm going to find my insurance premium is going to go up by 5 percent because they've figured I'm looking at those books."

The data did not belong to Phorm or the telephone or cable company, he said. "It's mine—you can't have it. If you want to use it for something, then you have to negotiate with me. I have to agree." This seemed to be the view of many European Union officials, for they were gathering evidence to determine whether to impose restrictions on this practice; however, there have been positive comments from the UK authorities.

Because the financial rewards will be so huge if corporations can capture and use this data, pressure to do so will increase. Describing the effort to track the identity of an online user, Irwin Gotlieb invokes an imaginary user searching for an SUV: "If you're searching for an SUV and you price out a couple of them and you go to a site that requires you to register, I now have your name. If you want pricing, dealer costs, you've got to give me your name, your e-mail address. Now as soon as you do that, we've got more on you. There are lots of ways we can track you. If I've identified you with your address, I can go to DMV records and see what cars you own. I can then go to Experian and see what your credit history is. And if I find out you're in the last month of a thirty-six-month lease on a Land Rover . . ." He doesn't finish the sentence but smiles, as if he's trapped his prey. "I can't do that today. In a few years I can."

There's no question that new technologies spur ways to improve services, and also to quietly redefine privacy. A home becomes less of a castle. Google's Street View has cameras on city streets that reveal street activity and traffic—and also license plate numbers and the faces of a passersby. If you know the address of a celebrity (or an old girlfriend), it allows close-ups. Similar closed-circuit television cameras on streets and in stores help police solve crimes, but might also catch an old paramour or celebrity smooching. Cell phones help parents track the location of their children, but can track much more. Part of YouTube's appeal is that it shares private moments. Facebook is a glass house, a complaint sometimes voiced by parents of teenagers who share their sexual exploits. Marketing companies create ads that annoyingly pop up when people are online, offering a premium—free telephone calls—in exchange for permission to monitor your activities.

Google's Web site acknowledges that it collects information about its users, but not names or other personally identifying information. It does, however, collect the names, credit card information, telephone number, and purchasing and credit history of those who sign up for such features as Google Checkout, a service that enables customers to make online purchases. In its five-page Checkout privacy policy, Google said that it may also "obtain information about you from third parties to verify the information you provide." Google said it "will not sell or rent your personal information to companies or individuals outside Google"—unless individuals give their "opt in consent." But even if consumers choose not to opt in, Google still retains a wealth of personal information, which it is free to use to better target search or YouTube advertising. This data, mingled with its search data and the data gathered by DoubleClick, induces privacy anxiety. Companies like eBay and Amazon.com, among others, also retain credit card and other personal information, but there is a difference: Google uses this data to assist advertisers, and eBay and Amazon do not have advertisers to assist.

This is where the specter of Big Brother enters the discussion. "In *1984,* Winston Smith knew where the telescreen was," observed Lawrence Lessig. "In the Internet, you have no idea who is being watched by whom. In a world where everything is surveilled, how to protect privacy?"

Big Brother comes in different guises. Under the federal Patriot Act rushed to passage after 9/11, the executive branch can, without a warrant or users' knowledge, gain access to what Americans e-mail, search, read, say on the telephone, watch on YouTube, network with on Facebook, or purchase online. There are tens of millions of surveillance cameras on our streets and in buildings. Candidates for public office can be harmed by damaging leaks to reporters of the most private information, as nearly happened to Supreme Court nominee Clarence Thomas when his in-store video rentals were leaked, suggesting he was partial to pornographic films. Advertisers can pay Google and other companies to access better targeting data. Telephone or cable companies can offer free services in exchange for a record of a consumer's every click, encoding the knowledge of every song they listen to, product they buy, ad they like. In recent years, AOL (among other companies) was publicly embarrassed when it extracted and shared the names of some users from the Internet protocol address found on every browser on every computer.

Google may be viewed with suspicion by many media industries, but it enjoys a well-deserved reputation for earning the trust of users. In its 2007 annual ranking of the world's most powerful brands, the *Financial Times* and the consulting firm Millward Brown awarded Google a number one rating. Still it is hard to imagine an issue that could imperil the trust Google has achieved as quickly as could privacy. One Google executive whispers, "Privacy is an atomic bomb. Our success is based on trust." The Interactive Advertising Bureau's Randall Rothenberg employs a different image: "Privacy is one of those third rails with unknown amounts of electricity in it. People think about advertising and worry. That's part of America's don't tread on me attitude." Yet Rothenberg is unsure about the amount of electricity in the privacy issue because he is acutely aware that Americans hold contradictory attitudes toward privacy; they tend to distrust governments, businesses, or advertisers that can spy on them, yet "if they really cared enough about privacy they'd never have credit cards. They'd never subscribe to cable TV." They wouldn't parade their most private thoughts on Facebook. So how does a company like Google locate and not step on the third rail?

To find that third rail requires a degree of sensitivity not always found in engineers. Yet Google has at times been sensitive. When, in 2006, the Justice Department subpoenaed a number of Internet companies to turn over all child pornography search queries, Google, opposing the request as a "fishing expedition," took the U.S. government to court and won. (The judge ruled that Google had to turn over fifty thousand suspicious URLs, but none of its user's names.) "Unfortunately," said Schmidt, "our competitors"—including Time Warner, Yahoo, and Microsoft—"did not hold the same position, and complied." He is outspokenly critical of the Patriot Act, which he believes violates privacy and grants the president too much power. Schmidt implicitly agrees that privacy is a do-not-step-on third rail: "If we violate the privacy of our users, then we'll be hosed."

Trust is essential to Google, as it is to much of modern commerce. If we didn't trust waiters or Amazon, we couldn't use credit cards. If banks didn't trust that we'd pay back loans, they would not grant mortgages. Sergey Brin notes that users don't like intrusive ads or junk mail, and Google deserves credit for siding with users against these, even sacrificing revenues to do so. From a user's perspective, Google is not wrong when it says the more information it has about our search histories, the better the search results will be because it can anticipate a user's intent. And it is also undeniably true that many users search the ads to comparison shop. "We think of the ad as content," said Google's vice president of engineering, Jeff Huber. The portrayal of Google as Big Brother frustrates people who work there. "It's a fear of the possibility rather than the reality," said Huber.

FEAR OF "THE POSSIBILITY" was enough to motivate privacy advocates. In May 2007, the Bush administration decided that the Federal Trade Commission (FTC), not the Justice Department, would look at whether the merger might violate antitrust laws, and the commission quietly began a preliminary investigation. Chester pushed for the FTC to broaden its probe to include privacy, and the agency scheduled a town hall meeting in November to explore those issues. "*I* got the hearing," Chester boasted. "There's nobody watching the store."

Chester is not the stereotypical lobbyist, the ingratiator, the affable fund-raiser, the guy you'd join for a drink or a steak dinner at the Palm. Chester annoys people, concedes a senior FTC staffer, "but he is responsible for the hearing." Chester helped persuade Democratic senators on the Judiciary Committee to conduct a one-day hearing in September 2007 focused on the merger and online advertising. Knowing that European governments have more stringent privacy protections, he urged the EU to hold up the merger until Google better explained its privacy policies. Chester stayed in touch with government regulators elsewhere. He filed additional complaints with the FTC. He had no expectation that the FTC would reject the merger. His best hope was that the FTC would compel Google to admit that its warehouse of data required more stringent privacy safeguards. Chester and Rotenberg were more hopeful that the European Union would reject the merger; and privately, Google officials conceded that an EU rejection would scuttle the deal.

By the end of 2007, it was apparent that privacy issues were gaining traction, spurred by a crescendo of news stories about real or potential invasions of privacy. Many were chilled when President Bush declared that under the Patriot Act he did not need judicial or congressional approval to wiretap the phones of anyone the executive branch suspected of consorting

with, or knowing, alleged terrorists. It was revealed that telephone companies, at the request of the Bush administration but without court approval,
turned over oceans of data concerning the phone calls and e-mails of
individuals.

There is often an inherent conflict between privacy and Google's belief
that data is virtuous. Eric Schmidt, as we've seen, said that the more Google
knows about a user, the better the search results. His and the founders'
ideal? For Google to know enough to be able to anticipate the user's true
intent in a search query, eventually getting to the point where Google
could improve the user's experience by supplying a single answer to a question. Better targeted ads, Google believes, serve the consumer as well as the
advertiser. In an October conference call with analysts to discuss Google's
third quarter and its new products, Schmidt said, "We're working on expanding our breadth of ads, offering all sorts of new types of ads—gadget
ads, video ads, others coming. And each of these initiatives gives advertisers
new and interesting ways to build relationships with their customers. So by
building these deeper ad solutions, we really can deliver more value." More
"types of ads" equals more data, which equals more assistance to advertisers, which can be a service to consumers, but also an invitation to nibble
at privacy constraints. Schmidt insists Google would never risk violating
user privacy because Google's success pivots on user trust. Rotenberg counters, "If people knew what Google was doing, they'd lose trust."

In a voice as steady as a dial tone, Schmidt said Google users can click
to "opt out" of allowing Google to track its cookies by clicking on the
Privacy choice on the Google home page and following the instructions, a
feature most users are probably not aware of or have a difficult time finding. Rotenberg, Chester, and others say that instead, Google should allow
users to opt in, meaning that they would have to actively volunteer their
cookies. That would be a mistake, Schmidt said, because the quality of a
Google search would be inferior if it stored none of the cookie data; that's
what helps Google better answer a search question. Without information
about the user, Google would not be able to narrow search results based
on prior searches. Without a cookie, an American living in Paris would
receive search results in French, not English. Schmidt disputes the notion

that advertisers have become as important to Google as the user, reciting the company's official first two principles: One is "the quality of the search as seen by the end user. The second one is the quality of the ads as seen by the end users, not by the advertisers."

When asked why consumers should trust that Google would not abuse the private data it collects, Sergey Brin in 2007 told me that the fears people have are tied to a distaste for advertising and to a fear of Big Brother, which is sometimes "irrational." He wondered: "How many people yesterday do you think had embarrassing information about them exposed as the result of some cookie? Zero. It never happens. Yet I'm sure thousands of people had their mail stolen yesterday. . . . I do think it boils down to irrational fears that all of a sudden we'd do evil things."

Irrational or not, Google was assailed from many sides and compelled to play an unaccustomed role: defense. Nick Grouf, CEO of Spot Runner, an advertising/marketing agency that counted among its investors Martin Sorrell's WPP Group, believed Google was engaged in too many battles. He said that traditional media woke up to the Google threat not when the company did its IPO or was sued by book publishers, but when it bought YouTube. "When you pay $1.6 billion for a site that is on the cover of every newspaper and magazine, and is the centerpiece of the zeitgeist as the future of media"—suddenly Google was widely perceived as a media company. By 2006 and into 2007, Grouf said, Google was battling with television and newspapers and book publishers and Microsoft and eBay and advertising agencies. "It's hard to compete on all fronts. And people start to whisper: 'These guys have gargantuan ambitions.'"

In November, the FTC held a two-day town hall meeting on privacy, a series of tame panel discussions that became more a seminar than an inquisition, disappointing Jeff Chester. The commission decided that the often-baffling issue of privacy would be excluded from the decision of whether to approve Google's acquisition of DoubleClick. The focus, instead, was on whether the marriage was anticompetitive. It was difficult to argue that the merger harmed competition when, within months, companies such as Microsoft and Yahoo and AOL and the WPP all acquired digital advertising companies of their own. The FTC prefers "to wait for a violation before we act," an agency official said on the eve of the approval of the merger. The EU did compel Google to make concessions and to tighten its privacy policies, but it, too, would approve the merger.

By mid 2007, Google was worried about the many restive bears it had provoked. It began to reach out to Washington. To allay privacy concerns, the company announced that it would reduce from two years to eighteen months the information it keeps in its database about the Web search histories of its users. Claiming that privacy laws were out of date, Google put out a press release proposing uniform international privacy rules and perhaps laws that recognized how the Internet and technology posed new privacy challenges. Instead of one "uber cookie" that permanently tracks a user, Google said it was experimenting with "crumbled cookies" that would disappear over time.

The public battles probably made Google's executives somewhat wiser. Google was only guilty, they believed, of naïveté, not arrogance. "The product brand was very strong," said Alan Davidson, Google's senior director of government relations and public policy, who is a computer scientist as well as a lawyer and who oversees Google's Washington office. "The political brand was very weak. Because we were not here to define it, it was being defined by our enemies." He paused a moment, and added, "*Enemy* is a strong word. It was being defined by our competitors." Gigi Sohn, the president and cofounder of Public Knowledge, a nonprofit organization that lobbies for both an open Internet and more balanced copyright laws, said that like many Silicon Valley companies, Google chose to have a smaller presence in the nation's capital. But Google was more extreme, she said. "They were almost alone among Silicon Valley companies in failing to recognize that you have to play in the sandbox. If you want progressive spectrum policies, the free market does not ensure that."

Google's one-man operation in Washington expanded in 2007 to include twenty-two staffers. Among them were Jane Horvath, a former senior privacy attorney in the Bush administration's Justice Department; Johanna Shelton, former senior counsel to Democrat John Dingell, then chairman of the House Energy and Commerce Committee; Robert Boorstin, a former speechwriter for President Bill Clinton; and Pablo Chavez, former chief counsel to Republican senator John McCain. To advance its Washington agenda, Google had established its own PAC (NETPAC), and soon hired three outside firms to lobby on its behalf: the mostly Democratic Podesta Group; King & Spalding, where Google relied on former Republican senators Connie Mack and Dan Coats; and Brownstein Hyatt Farber Schreck, which had recently hired Makan Delrahim, a former deputy assistant attorney general who'd been in charge of the Antitrust Division in the administration of George W. Bush. "We've been under the radar, if you will, with government and certain industries," observed David Drummond, the Google senior vice president who oversees all of the company's legal affairs and policy interaction with governments. "As we've grown, we're engaging a lot more."

The most immediate concerns of Google's Washington office were the privacy issues raised by the acquisition of DoubleClick. By the end of 2007, Google was battling the image that it was the Microsoft of 2000. "No question that people here regularly discuss Microsoft's experience and use that as a cautionary tale," said Elliot Schrage, the vice president of global communications and public affairs. On the subject of Microsoft, Brin said, "Microsoft is a bit of an unusual company. They don't seem to like any of us being successful in the technology space."

So Google sought to demonstrate that it was reaching out to media companies as well as to Washington. To preserve copyrights, YouTube announced that it was testing new antipiracy software to block unauthorized content from being uploaded and viewed. In an ecumenical spirit, the word *partnership* was constantly invoked by Google executives. Repeatedly, they celebrated its "more than 100,000 partners," the more than three billion dollars it then distributed annually to Web sites and mostly small business partners in its AdSense program. As 2007 progressed, said General Electric's Beth Comstock, relations with Google thawed and by summer, G.E.'s NBC negotiated for Google to sell some of the network's remnant ads. "In the end, I was less concerned that Google was out to replace our entire sales force," she said.

Google, however, was still clear-eyed about the inevitable gap between its engineers and traditional media. Google's engineering prowess would, inevitably, make the consumption of media and the selling of advertising more efficient, Larry Page told me one afternoon as we sat in the small, bare-walled conference room steps from his office. So was it inevitable, I asked, that "Google would sometimes bump into traditional media?"

Without hesitation, he corrected me. "I would say, always," he said in his deep baritone, emitting a subdued chuckle. His was not a boast; rather, it was a candid recognition of reality. He believes Google's engineers can eradicate most inefficiencies if given the time and resources.

Page had reasons to feel confident. Google had a great year in 2007. Measured by growth, it was Google's best year, with revenues soaring 60 percent to $16.6 billion, with international revenues contributing nearly half the total, and with profits climbing to $4.2 billion. Google ended the year with 16,805 full-time employees, offices in twenty countries, and the search engine available in 117 languages. And the year had been a personally happy one for Page and Brin. Page married Lucy Southworth, a former model who earned her Ph.D. in bioinformatics in January 2009 from Stanford; they married seven months after Brin wed Anne Wojcicki.

But Sheryl Sandberg was worried. She had held a ranking job in the Clinton administration before, joining Google in 2001, where she supervised all online sales for AdWords and AdSense, and was regularly hailed by *Fortune* magazine as one of the fifty most powerful female executives in America. Sandberg came to believe Google's vice was the flip side of its virtue. "We're an engineering company in that products come first," she said. "A lot of the reason we're winning is because our engineering is better." Reminded that she once was quoted as saying Google made a mistake in not speaking to publishers and answering their questions before announcing plans to digitize all books, she added, "Sometimes we make mistakes here because we move too quickly."

Eric Schmidt would, inadvertently, prove her point. In August 2007, he piloted his Gulfstream G550 to Aspen, Colorado, to give the keynote speech at a dinner held by the free-market oriented Progress and Freedom Foundation. In the speech, he described four "basic principles," as he referred to them, that he believes are vital for media and tech companies to embrace: freedom of speech, universal broadband access, net neutrality, and transparency. Missing from his prepared remarks were thoughts about privacy and copyright—and how far Google might push the permissible boundaries. (When, for instance, does anticipating a user's wants become an intrusion? When does fair use become copyright infringement?)

A few weeks later, seated in his tiny conference room on the Mountain View campus, I discussed that speech with Schmidt. Why, I asked, didn't he mention privacy in his Aspen talk?

There was a long pause before he said, "No particular reason. It's sort of a given. If we violate the privacy of our users, they'll leave us."

And why no mention of copyright?

"Maybe it was the altitude! I was just chatting away." Besides, he said, copyright "was not an absolute right" and had to be balanced by fair use.

Isn't it true that Google wants to push the envelope on privacy and copyright?

"That's probably correct," Schmidt conceded. "If there's a legal case, we're going to favor the legal one that favors users."

"Google, if it were a person, has all the flaws and all of the virtues of a classic Silicon Valley geek," said Columbia's Tim Wu, who between jobs teaching law worked for a spell in the Valley. "In some ways, they are very principled." He cited Google's 20 percent time, saying that few "money-crazed companies would allow" such a thing. "But they have this total deaf ear to certain types of issues. One of them is privacy." Why? Because, he said, "They just love that data because they can do neat things with it."

CHAPTER ELEVEN

Google Enters Adolescence

(2007–2008)

For all its democratic ethos, its belief in "the wisdom of crowds," at Google the engineer is king, held above the crowd. The vaunted 20 percent time that is parceled out selectively by management to nonengineers is given universally to the half of Google employees who are technically trained. Salaries for engineers are relatively modest—a beginning engineer starts at around $100,000 (versus about $50,000 for nonengineers), and rises to about $300,000, including a bonus—but stock rewards are extravagant. Google rewarded its employees with $868.6 million in stock in 2007, a one-year increase of more than 90 percent.

The importance the company attaches to engineers is spotlighted by the time Google's founders and CEO Schmidt devote to meetings with them. Their Tuesday, Wednesday, and Friday afternoons are crammed with Google Product Strategy (GPS) reviews. Teams made up mostly of engineers meet in a long, dimly lit, low-ceilinged conference room named Marrakesh, on the second floor of Building 43, next to the office that Page and Brin share. Industrial gray carpet covers the floor and melts into the gray walls. A massive, pale oak custom-made rectangular table stretches almost the full length of the room; at one end are billowy red-velvet couches, and at the other, large, flat LCD screens. Whiteboards line the walls. There are two projectors, so time is not wasted unloading and reloading projectors during multiple presentations, and all cables and wires are color coded to minimize time locating the right connections for laptops and other electronic devices.

Meetings last from fifteen minutes to two hours, and are scheduled one after another, like airport takeoffs and landings. "If you want to talk to Larry or Sergey, you can at one of these meetings," said Vice President Megan Smith. "If you work at another company, can you get to the CEO within seven days? Probably not." Often at these meetings, said Tim Armstrong, "Larry is going to take one side of the argument and Sergey is going to take the exact opposite side, and what you're going to see is that everyone is going to argue in the middle and at some point it is going to be clear what the answer is." This is a process that allows Page and Brin to learn, he said, "who comes to the meeting prepared" and who has the passion and guts to challenge them.

A meeting on October 9, 2007, did not quite follow this pattern. Brin and Page were to meet with an engineering team to review their proposal for an upgrade of AdWords 1.0. Since its introduction in early 2002, some parts of AdWords had been substantially upgraded while others had not. Small businesses complained that the system was too complicated. Larger customers, such as eBay or Amazon, complained that they wanted new features, including an ability to organize their accounts by products and to break out expenditures by country. To make these functions work, Google needed to enlarge its computers that retained data and enhance the speed of the advertising auctions. To demonstrate their commitment to a new architecture, the founders decided to skip 2.0 and christened this effort AdWords 3.0. The purpose of this session was to receive, and review, the new product teams' recommendations.

Everyone around the conference table sat on gray-mesh ergonomic swivel chairs. Page was wearing his usual jeans, and a gray T-shirt under a black sports jacket; he sat in the middle of the table, a coffee cup in hand. Brin arrived a few minutes late in jeans and a black crewneck sweater, and plopped in the seat beside Page. More nattily attired in a blue V-necked sweater over a light blue dress shirt and gray slacks, Schmidt sat at the head of the table with a translucent container of salad and a Diet Coke. Schmidt opened the meeting by calling on the team leader, vice president of engineering Sridhar Ramaswamy, to describe the teams' recommendations.

The upgraded system they proposed, said Ramaswamy, would be less complicated for advertisers, would produce search results faster, and would be "scalable" in that it would allow for the retention of more data. But, he cautioned, it was not quite the gut renovation that had been requested; it would be too expensive and require diverting too many engineers to both speed up AdWords, as Page had urged them to, and to make the sweeping computer changes needed to accommodate Page's database growth projections.

To a nonengineer, the hour-long discussion was often incomprehensible— "three-tier architecture," "middle-tier API," "UI tier," "end-to-end solutions," "no latency," "Java script bindings for third parties," "10 percent CTR," "SQL base." But no translator was required to observe that Page and Brin were unhappy. At first, the founders were stonily silent, sliding lower in their chairs, and occasionally leaning over to whisper to each other. Intermittently, Page looked away from the engineers; Brin, appearing alternately distracted and irritated, would rise and stretch his legs on the empty chair beside his. Schmidt began with technical questions to the product team, but then he switched roles and tried to draw out Page and Brin, saying, "Larry, say what's really bugging you."

The room was quiet for perhaps ten seconds before Page responded. When he did, he scolded the engineers, saying they were not ambitious enough. Brin concurred, adding that the proposal was "muddled" and un-Google-like in its caution. "I named this 3.0 for a reason," Page interjected. "We wanted something big. Instead, you proposed something small. Why are you so resistant?"

The engineering team leader held his ground. Ramaswamy said that his entire team concurred that the founders' proposed changes would be too costly in money, time, and engineering manpower. Page countered that a significantly improved AdWords would make it easier for advertisers and result in greater revenues. "You are polishing up the program. I wanted to have a redesign."

Schmidt stepped in to summarize their differences. He noted that Brin and Page were focused on the outcome, while the product team focused first on the process, and concluded that the engineering improvements would prove too "disruptive" to achieve the goal.

Brin said that neither he nor Page wanted to add patches to the system, something Microsoft has been criticized for when they stuff more code into their already bloated operating system. "I'm just worried that we designed the wrong thing," Brin said. "And you're telling me you're not designing the optimum system. I think that's a mistake. . . . I'm trying to give you permission to be bolder."

Schmidt achieved a cease-fire by asking the product team to make its slide presentation. It demonstrated how the new product would actually work for advertisers, allowing them to manage their accounts. The discussion now went round and round with Schmidt finally stepping in to summarize the technical changes that would be made, the engineering challenges, the different approaches proposed by the team and by the founders. As he spoke, I kept wondering: When Terry Semel was CEO of Yahoo, or John Sculley CEO of Apple, could either of those nonengineers understand what their engineers were saying? Could they challenge them? (I would ask this question of Semel, who said the Yahoo founders, Jerry Yang and David Filo, both engineers, often accompanied him to similar meetings. Besides, he said, "I'd make people describe things in English!") Semel brought good judgment and people skills to Yahoo when he arrived in 2000, but the question begs to be asked: Did Yahoo slip technologically because the CEO could not wrap his brain around the technology? Was that why Apple slipped technologically after Steve Jobs had been fired? (While Jobs does not possess an engineering degree, he seems not to need a translator.)

Schmidt, sensing that a resolution was not possible at this Google meeting, told the product team to report back with a detailed design "which is responsive to Larry and Sergey's criticism," one that laid out "what it takes to build a good product," and what it would cost in time and money. He took care to balance this rebuke with praise: "But this is very well done. I love it when people show me the flaws in our products."

Neither founder was happy after the meeting. "I hope they try to do something a little more ambitious," Brin said two days later. He compared the project to renovating a house. "Once you get into it, you know it's going to take some time and effort, so you may as well do as good a job as you can. We prefer not to do too many small things when we know where we'd like to get to." Page was disappointed in what he described as the engineering team's "self-imposed, bureaucratic response." He sounded harsh, and a few seconds later he softened his words: "It's hard when you're so focused to see the big picture. It's sort of easy for us. We just say, 'If you're going to make changes at that rate, we're going to go out of business. It's just not OK. It's all of our revenue. We're obviously doing some things wrong. We need some sort of reasonable plan to fix these things in our lifetime. Our lifetime means years, not multiple years.'" Ultimately, Ramaswamy and his team came back with an AdWords 3.0 proposal that went more than halfway toward the one proposed by the founders; Google has been rolling out the new system in stages.

THE MEETING DEMONSTRATED that the ethos that had launched the Google rocket—to shoot for the moon, not the tops of trees—was intact, no matter how much the company had grown. Page and Brin's passion for technology was apparent, as was the way they push engineers to act boldly. At meetings they feed off each other, punishing engineers and product managers who think they have devised a "new" solution when, the founders say, they have merely devised a "cute" solution, not a fundamental one. Or as Schmidt said, "They think about what should be, and they assume it is possible."

Page describes his and Brin's role as supplying the "big picture," and by way of illustrating what he sees as a management rather than a technological innovation, he cites the work of Gordon Moore at Intel and his Moore's law. "People think it's this wild statement about how the universe is, but it's actually a management innovation. Moore's law was a statement saying, 'We're going to double the performance [of integrated circuits or computer chips] every eighteen months, and let's get organized to do it.' They spent billions of dollars doing that. If you didn't have Moore's law, you wouldn't have that advancement. It's actually causal in another way." The management pressure to double performance helps assure it.

IN SPITE OF GOOGLE'S RAPID GROWTH, or because of it, by 2007 the company had become a target for lawsuits and sneers. Leading the chorus was Microsoft CEO Steve Ballmer. In 2007, he had labeled Google "a one-trick pony," and had derided the company at nearly every public opportunity since, telling reporters, "they have one product that makes all their money, and it hasn't changed in five years. . . . Search makes ninety-eight percent of all their money." Irwin Gotlieb, who is not in Ballmer's adversarial camp, nevertheless shared the view that Google's attempt to broaden its reach had been a failure. "Google is extremely good with search," he said. "They are good with AdSense. They are not as good with display advertising. I believe they've lost a fortune on selling radio ads, they've lost a fortune on selling print ads, and they are now losing a fortune on selling television ads." Tad Smith, the CEO of Reed Business Information, which produces eighty publications and Web sites, asked, "Where is the new pony? Apple came up with a new pony, the iPod and iPhone. Microsoft came up with Office. Google is throwing a lot of things against the wall, and so far only one has stuck to the wall. And Google's search growth will slow."

Eric Schmidt had a ready rejoinder to Ballmer: "I like the trick!" And justifiably so: the trick yielded more than sixteen billion dollars in revenues and four billion dollars in profit in 2007. Schmidt went on, "The Google model is one-trick to the extent that you believe targeted advertising is one-trick." Google now had about 150 products available, and he believed the other efforts—YouTube; DoubleClick; mobile phone products; cloud computing; selling TV, radio, and newspaper ads—could sell targeted advertising. Yet with almost all of its revenues pumping from only one of 150 wells, the question—can Google find another gusher?—was "a legitimate question," as top Google executives like Elliot Schrage conceded at the time.

At the start of 2008 there was evidence that the gusher was tapering off. Search advertising was slowing. In January and February, comScore, a research firm that tracks online activity, reported that Google searchers were clicking on fewer text ads. Wall Street analysts predicted Google's revenue rise would stall, and the stock price dropped; from its pinnacle of $742 on November 6, 2007, it had plunged 40 percent by March 2008. The press, lusting for a new narrative, fixed on this one: the Google rocket was crashing. "Goodbye, Google," read the headline in *Forbes.com.* Reporters buzzed, incessantly, about dire days ahead. Google was spinning them, they believed, when people like Tim Armstrong explained that the company was trying to make the ads "more relevant" and had deliberately reduced the number of ads appearing with search results to reduce clutter and produce better information. Google said clicks without purchases meant the ads were not useful to the user, so they were eliminated. Reporters were deeply skeptical when chief economist Hal Varian in early 2008 cautioned, "The clicks are not what is relevant. The revenue is."

But events would demonstrate that the press and Wall Street analysts are often handicapped by two imperatives: don't be late with bad news, and don't be the lone blackbird left on the pole. In April 2008, when the company released its first-quarter results, the narrative changed. Google's revenues had surged 42 percent compared to the first quarter of 2007; its profits had jumped 30 percent, and as Varian had suggested, its ad clicks had risen 20 percent. "Google Inc's Go-Go Era Apparently Isn't Over," said a report in the *Wall Street Journal.* The *Times* headline was: "Google Defies the Economy and Reports a Profit Surge." As the report showed, Google hogged three quarters of all U.S. search advertising dollars, compared to only 5 percent for Steve Ballmer's Microsoft.

Yet Ballmer had a point. Google had not figured out how to make money on its surfeit of products. YouTube accounted for one of every three videos viewed online, three billion of the nine billion viewed in January 2008. The impact of this new medium would forever change the way politics are conducted. Seven of the sixteen candidates who ran for president in 2008 announced their candidacies on YouTube, and more people saw a taped version of the July 2007 Democratic presidential debate there than live on CNN. YouTube succeeded in democratizing information. It became a viral hub where a candidate's flubs or fibs were exposed by a video. When Mitt Romney became a born-again crusader against abortion, videos were posted of the former governor of Massachusetts championing a woman's right to an abortion. Overseas, when Venezuelan strongman Hugo Chavez shut down *El Observador*, an opposition newspaper, it began broadcasting on YouTube.

However, YouTube made no money. Its bandwidth and computer costs were steep, and it paid for some of its content. Three senior Google executives with knowledge of these figures said at the time that YouTube would lose money in 2008, and these losses would grow in 2009, with revenues initially projected at about $250 million and losses totaling about $500 million. There were those, like Gotlieb, who believed "they'll never make money on YouTube." He thought online display ads would annoy viewers, and that most advertisers sought predictably ad-friendly settings for their ads, something a site dominated by user-generated content could not ensure. Like many Valley start-up founders, Chad Hurley and Steve Chen believed, as Google's did when they launched, that if they first built traffic, money would follow. By February 2008, Schmidt said he had summoned teams from YouTube and Google to "start working on monetizing it."

"You didn't tell us to work on it," a surprised Hurley said, recalled Schmidt.

"Well, times have changed," said Schmidt.

Schmidt was not unhappy with YouTube or its founders. He believed YouTube was becoming nearly as ubiquitous a Web activity as e-mail. But Schmidt wanted a business plan; he announced that his "highest priority" in 2008 was to figure out a way for YouTube "to make money." He knew that online video ads had to be different from television ads. Ads that appeared before a video started would be annoying. Internet users wanted to see the video as soon as they clicked on it. Thirty-second ads anywhere in an online setting were too long. The ads couldn't feel like an interruption, certainly not a long interruption. Schmidt's joint teams came up with several novel advertising schemes. Schmidt said he didn't know if they'd work, but "if any of them hit, it is a billion-dollar business. Of course, it's now zero." To minimize insecurity at YouTube's headquarters in San Bruno, he dispatched Coach Campbell to visit regularly and to calm the troops and help coax a monetization plan.

There was another potential cash cow to pursue. In 2007, Google began to aggressively move to claim a slice of the mobile phone business, which then counted three billion users worldwide—three times the PC market—a number Schmidt expected to grow by another billion in four years. The success of Apple's revolutionary iPhone, with its easy access to the Internet, was an eye-opener: the iPhone delivered fifty times more search queries, Google found, than the typical so-called smartphone. A mobile device was no longer just a telephone or a PDA, and portable access to the Internet advanced Google's interests; the more people went online, the more Google benefited.

But Google was frustrated that many of its programs functioned poorly on mobile phones. They were frustrated that telephone companies, not consumers, decided which applications would appear on their mobile phones. "As compared to the Internet model, where we've been able to make software that basically is able to run everything and works for people pretty well, it's been very difficult to do that on phones," Page said. Google's mobile quarterback was Andy Rubin. A former Microsoft employee, Rubin had left to cofound a mobile software company called Android, which Google had acquired in 2005. As the senior director of mobile platforms for Google, Rubin set out to make Android an open-source operating system—open to improvements from any software designer because the source code was visible, not proprietary, and peers could collaborate to offer and improve different software applications. This was a direct assault on the telephone companies, which policed what software applications could be displayed for consumers.

Rubin likened the current mobile market to what happened in the early eighties to PCs. Original hardware makers, such as Wang or DEC, were supplanted by IBM, which in turn was supplanted by the manufacturers of clones. As the hardware became commoditized, the price of the PC dropped. At the same time, the cost of the software rose, because a single company, Microsoft, controlled it. "Unless there is a vendor-independent software solution," said Rubin, expressing the ethos not just of Google but of the Valley culture at large, "the consumer isn't going to be well served. What I mean by 'vendor-independent' is you can't have a single source. Microsoft was a single source. What Android is doing is trying to avoid what happened in the PC business, which was to create a monopoly." That is why, he said, Android is an open-source system that "no single entity can own." He is openly disdainful of phone companies like Verizon and AT&T, though he doesn't name them, and obviously feels the same way about Apple's closed iPhone system. "The thing I carry around in my pocket every day," he said, gripping his yet to be released Android phone manufactured by T-Mobile, "is as powerful as the PC was five years ago. So how can I take advantage of that and make it do what I want it to? I'm the one who paid for it! Just because I have a service plan with some whacky wireless carrier doesn't mean they get to dictate what I do with my product that I paid for. Another thing: It shouldn't cost four hundred dollars. That's absurd. If you add up all the components, somebody is making a lot of money."

For Google, Android represented a perfect storm—its idealistic desire to promote an open, more democratic system meshed with its business interests. The more people who had access to the Internet, the more Google searches or Google Maps would be used, and the more data collected. And those using the Android operating system for mobile phones might also use it for their laptops, allowing Google to charge for this software or share in the mobile ad revenues.

There was another issue to be addressed with mobile phones: spectrum space. All radio frequencies—whether for cell phone calls, broadcast television or radio signals, or other wireless devices—travel over spectrum space that is assigned and regulated by the Federal Communications Commission. Google lobbied to ensure that the new wireless space would be open and not controlled by just a few telephone giants. Ivan Seidenberg, the CEO of Verizon, disputed Google's contention that his was a closed system: "Since we think we have the most reliable network, we'll publish standards and let people connect to any device they want to." The FCC sided with Google, and in July 2007 ruled that the telephone companies could not control what applications were used on this new spectrum. Soon after the FCC announcement, Google raised the stakes by threatening to bid in the January 2008 spectrum auction, establishing itself as a telephone company.

Google had no intention of providing telephone service or producing hardware for a Google phone. They would not say this publicly, however, because by fanning speculation—and the speculation was incendiary—they kept people guessing and increased their leverage over the wireless telephone companies. They also brought themselves closer to achieving three objectives: to make Google programs, including such new features as voice search, work on wireless devices; to reduce the cost of mobile phone service and Internet connections by allowing advertisers to subsidize them; and to extend to mobile devices the company's dominance in online advertising. Google believes that ads on mobile devices could fetch premium prices. With GPS positioning married to Google's immense database, an advertiser could know who purchased cashmere sweaters or golf clubs and if a consumer was outside a store that had a special sale on, an alert could appear on the mobile screen informing her. Because this would be what advertisers and Google excitedly describe as "a service" or "information" rather than a traditional ad, the hope was that consumers wouldn't be annoyed by these intrusions. In November 2007, Google announced that it was working with thirty-three corporate partners, including T-Mobile, Samsung, Intel, and eBay, to launch Android as a free operating system.

In the auction, few companies could match the financial bids made by the giant telephone companies. Google could, though, and to enter the mobile phone business and ensure that Android would work seamlessly, they needed to. But Google didn't want to become a telephone company. So it made a let's-hope-we-lose floor bid of $4.6 billion for a block of wireless spectrum, conditioned on the FCC's agreement to guarantee that the winner of the auction open its hardware and services to third parties.

Of course, Google's mobile phone ambitions would collide with powerful telephone companies and with Nokia, the world's number one mobile phone manufacturer. They were allied in fear that their business model was under assault. They worried that their dominance would be diminished. Who would receive the advertising revenues? Who would claim ownership of the valuable data generated? Would their own hardware be cloned, like PCs? "Now that they want to dominate the planet on phone calls," Seidenberg said of Google, "they've provoked the bear."

Neither Seidenberg nor representatives from AT&T or Nokia joined in Google's November announcement of the first truly open mobile operating system. A traditional Google corporate ally, Steve Jobs, also did not join because Apple's iPhone provides a mobile operating system, one less open than Google's. This was a little clumsy, because half of Apple's eight directors serve as Google directors or advisers, among them Eric Schmidt, Bill Campbell, and Al Gore. At Apple board meetings, Schmidt told me he now recused himself from mobile phone discussions.

In the auction, that commenced in January, all bidders were instructed not to reveal their bids. When it was over, Verizon and AT&T had won, paying a total of $16.2 billion for two wide swatches of spectrum. In an April "all hands" meeting with Google employees, either attending or on a video hookup, Schmidt confessed, "We had the very good fortune of entering the spectrum auction for $4.6 billion, and not winning. We sweated it out!" Both Verizon and AT&T would pledge to open their networks. AT&T announced that it would sell phones with Google's Android system, and Verizon announced that it was open to consider any Android prototype. (By the summer of 2009, Verizon had yet to submit an Android application; nor had any phone company, save T-Mobile.) One former federal official was cynical about what he called Google's "fake bid." He believed Google had a sweetheart deal with Verizon, that the telephone company knew all along Google would not make escalating bids and that all Google really wanted was assurance that Verizon would open its system to Android. He was dubious that Verizon's system would be open for anyone but Google, who deny a sweetheart deal.

BY THE SPRING OF 2008, Google was buoyant. Rejecting the one-trick pony charge, Schmidt said that with mobile phones, plus search, plus its array of software products, and YouTube, he explained why it was conceivable that Google could become the first media company to generate one hundred billion dollars in revenues. He described to me "a planning process where we said, is it mathematically possible for Google to become a hundred-billion-dollar corporation? And not over any particular period of time, just, is it possible, are the markets big enough?" He estimated the annual worldwide advertising market as "somewhere between seven hundred billion and a trillion dollars. Is it possible for Google to become ten percent of that? And the answer is yes, over a long enough period of time."

How?

"First place, you're not going to get there with small little advertising deals. You need these big initiatives . . . the number one big one right in front of us is television. Big market, well monetized, easily automatable. Second one is . . . mobile." The third was "enterprise," by which he meant web-based services—"cloud computing"—offering various software applications and IT services for corporate customers, organizations, and individual consumers.

Brave words, but throughout 2008 Schmidt's company made no money from its mobile or YouTube or cloud-computing efforts. Google did not let up. It was still talking to cable companies, Schmidt said, about partnering to target advertising for cable's digital set-top boxes, and for Android to become the operating system for cable mobile phones—should cable decide to enter the thriving wireless market. Google joined with cable companies, Intel, and wireless providers, such as Sprint Nextel Corporation, to invest a total of $3.2 billion in WiMAX, a technology promising faster wireless connections to the Internet than those offered by Verizon and AT&T.

Jeffrey L. Bewkes, the CEO of Time Warner, acknowledged his company's discussions with Google and laid out the reasons they had not yet been resolved and might not be. On the one hand, he said, unabashedly, if the cable companies could get together they would have "a Google-type ability to do targeted digital advertising." Google, he said, "has the search data and the cookies through its searches. But the cable companies not only have that, they have everything that you do on your cable broadband connection, they've got everything you've signed on and saw. And they have everything you watched on television. And they've got their customer's name and credit card information." On the other hand, he sighed, the cable companies have a difficult time acting in concert, and the data is useful only if they aggregate it. That's where Google has the advantage. It is willing to organize cable companies' data, combine it with its own, and extend it to all mobile devices. Which begs another question, he said: Who owns the data, the cable company or Google? And if the cable companies let Google in the door and grant them access to its data, "you can never build an alternative because Google's will always be that much more efficient."

Cloud computing was another new Google initiative. Like other corporate giants with massive data centers and servers—IBM, Amazon, Oracle—Google was intent on launching its "cloud" of servers. The cloud would allow a user to access data stored in the Google server from anywhere; it would reduce corporate costs because companies could outsource their data centers; and it would subvert more expensive boxed software sold by Microsoft and spur the development of inexpensive netbooks whose applications are stored in the cloud. Because all these software applications can function on a browser, escaping the dominance of Microsoft's operating system, in the future, said Christophe Bisciglia, the twenty-eight-year-old chief of cloud computing, "The browser becomes the operating system. Applications have outpaced browsers, which is why we did it"—introduced a Google browser in 2008.

While cloud computing offered consumers portability, it potentially offered them less control. Just as a consumer loses access to the Internet every time a broadband connection is down—for instance, when YouTube was silenced for several hours on February 24, 2008, when the government of Pakistan tried to block a YouTube video critical of Islam and wound up shutting down the worldwide video service, or when Gmail's one hundred million users were disrupted for just over three hours exactly one year later, on February 24, 2009, or when Google search and Gmail went dark for an hour on May 14, 2009. "We're sometimes going to have problems," Bisciglia admitted, "just as we do when our hard drive crashes."

And what is the business plan?

"The more people on the Internet, the more clicks our ads get," Bisciglia said.

While these aggressive Google efforts resemble those of other corporations' always angling to continually grow profits, they were also reminders of the "Don't be evil" idealism that animated the company. In its annual letter to shareholders released on the last day of 2007, Google announced it was entering the energy sector, investing tens of millions of dollars in new technologies with the goal of making renewable energy cheaper than coal-fired plants. "If we are successful," the founders declared, "we will not only help the world, but also make substantial profits." Their profits would rise because the energy costs to operate Google's data centers would fall. They acknowledged that solar power is "more expensive," yet vow to use it to power a third of the Googleplex and to subsidize it for seven years. Consistent with their fervor to spare the environment, Page and Brin made personal investments in Tesla Motors, a Valley company intent on producing an electric sports car.

They established a philanthropic arm, Google.org, and recruited an esteemed epidemiologist and world health expert, Dr. Larry Brilliant, to run it. They pledged to divert to this foundation one percent of Google's profits, with three goals: to ascertain the quality of water and health care and other services country by country; to gather enough information to try to predict and prevent catastrophes, whether these be forces of nature or disease; and to make energy-renewable investments. Page and Brin sound more like social workers than hardheaded businessmen when they extol Google Earth as a vehicle to spot imminent disasters and offer to make "a gift" of this technology to disaster relief organizations. Google put up thirty million dollars to fund the X Prize Foundation's Google Lunar X Prize, which would be awarded to the private team that designs the best robotic rover to traverse the moon's surface and send high definition video images back to earth.

Google also launched Google Health, an effort much like the one announced by Microsoft and by AOL cofounder Steve Case's Revolution Health Group LLC. Each aimed to give citizens a safe place to store health records online and share them with doctors, and search for the best medical advice online. Google recruited Dr. Roni Zeiger, a primary care physician who returned to Stanford for an advanced degree in medical informatics, hoping to devise ways to democratize medical information. He joined Google in January 2006, after a typically rigorous interview. "They asked for my high school grades!" Zeiger laughed. He was dead serious about his mission. "Google gets more health questions than anyone on the planet," he said. Zeiger realized that "Google's skills could help people organize their own health information." He vowed, "We'll never sell anyone's health records." And in a March 2008 speech, Eric Schmidt promised to keep the site free of all advertising.

There is a shared, and perhaps blinding, belief on the Google campus that Google was altruistic, an attitude reflected in "Don't be evil." On a stage he shared with Page at the Global Philanthropy Forum after Google embraced the slogan, Brin declared that "'don't be evil' serves as a reminder to our employees," but it "was a mistake. It should really say, 'Be Good.'"

One can interpret Brin's remarks as a reflection of his idealism, or his naïveté—or both. To simply say a corporation should be good ignores the range of choices a company is compelled to make in conducting its business. How "good" was Google when it complied with German laws not to disseminate Nazi literature? Google's searches were following German law, which is good. It was censoring search results, which is bad. When in 2008 Google closed its Phoenix office and laid off a handful of employees because the company did not believe the office was essential, it was being good to shareholders. But those employees most certainly did not see Google's action as good.

BUT THE SPEED OF GOOGLE'S ascent and its expansive commercial ambitions came to overshadow its noble ambitions. Google grew up very fast. In their first annual letter to shareholders, in 2004, Page and Brin wrote of Google: "If it were a person, it would have started elementary school late last summer, and today it would have just finished the first grade." Three years later, *Search Engine Land*'s Danny Sullivan thought Google had prematurely entered its awkward teenage years. "The story of Google today is perhaps the adolescent period they are going through. How do they deal with the challenges of the growth they are going through? You are going to go through this wave of people leaving Google. They don't need to work there anymore. And it's not going to be fun, which will change the culture."

"Google's become a big company," said Paul Buchheit, who left Google in 2006 to start Friendfeed.com. "It's a very different environment." As with most big companies, he said "priorities become based more on what looks good internally. You become distant from the users. When you get bigger, some engineer comes up with this crazy project, but he's four or five layers from Larry. These layers in between are going to serve up all sorts of weird barriers." There's little incentive, he said, for individuals to innovate because the bureaucracy becomes cautious, overwhelmed with a terror "not to look dumb." Asked for a more concrete example, the engineer who distilled Google into a powerfully simple slogan retreats to this sweeping analogy: "It's an entire system. Think about the Soviet Union. They had lots of brilliant people. But there was an economic system there that encouraged certain kinds of behavior. They failed to innovate because the system was wrong." Buchheit's critique is echoed by Scott Heiferman, CEO and cofounder of the social network site Meetup.com, who has hired some former Googlers who left the company because it got too big. "Google did not invent YouTube. They tried and failed with Google Video. Google did not invent Facebook. They tried and failed with Orkut." Aside from search, Heiferman said, "Google has actually failed at most things."

Ask Google executives to describe their biggest future concern, and more often than not they say size. Growing too big and losing focus is Omid Kordestani's foremost worry. At Netscape, he said, the company drifted away from founder Jim Clark's vision of it as a company whose browser enabled Internet communication. "Suddenly we became more of an enterprise company than a Web company, even though we started the browser." When Netscape rushed too quickly to issue an IPO in 1995, he said, pressure was on to generate more revenues, to perform on a very public stage for the press, to "focus on quarter to quarter" performance.

"For the last year my biggest worry was scaling the business," Schmidt said in May 2007. "The problem is we're growing so quickly. When you bring in people so quickly there's always the possibility you'll lose the formula. How do you manage engineering teams that are not on one campus? How do you manage across time zones? How do you keep the culture?"

IN ADDITION TO the natural concerns with rapid growth, critics both inside and outside Google believe the company has real management weaknesses. Paul Buchheit believes Google has succumbed to the disease of bigness that he says afflicts "every big company" and has become bureaucratic. There are many bottlenecks at Google. A former Google executive criticizes "micromanagement at the top," and said a prime example is that the founders and Schmidt, or their designees, "have to sign off on each hire. That's OK when you are hiring five new employees." In 2007 and early 2008, Google was hiring 150 people per week. Because most decisions about new employees, deals, or policy "have to go to the top," the process is slowed. Echoing a common thought, an executive who is a Google corporate ally and works closely with them said, "In many ways, it's a very disorganized company. It looks to me like they are caught in this interesting conflict between a company that is overmanaged and undermanaged. They have a control mechanism at the top that has inordinate control. And at the same time, there is too much freedom." He lists two complaints: "You can't get answers out of Google when you want to schedule something," so there are long waits. And "they are structured to allow way too many people to participate," which results in endless meetings.

The founders get diverted by issues that should not require their attention. Eric Schmidt described a Monday management committee meeting in March 2008 during which they discussed how, under California labor laws, a review was necessary to determine whether their many massage therapists should become full-time employees. The significant plus was that they would receive full benefits. The significant minus was that tipping would be prohibited. The issue had first been raised at the TGIF meeting the previous Friday. The founders, massage regulars, were agitated. Schmidt, who said he has "never had a massage at Google, and never will," was impatient, and blurted, "You guys are in charge of this."

"'We're on it!'" they said.

That afternoon, Page and Brin scheduled another meeting to resolve the issue. "This is where the team really works well," Schmidt explained. "I knew what I wanted, which was to get the hell out of the meeting! Larry and Sergey knew they had to get involved in an employee issue." The founders resolved the issue by making them "variable part-time employees" and allowing tipping to be continued as long as it was reported. This incident can be viewed as an example of teamwork; it can also be seen as an example of micromanagement.

The founders' zeal for efficiencies extends to the unusual way they manage their time. They used to share three assistants. No longer. They share an office on the second floor of Building 43 without secretaries or assistants to guard the entrance, keep them on schedule, or answer phones (which don't ring anyway). A staircase whose banister is festooned with a large green kite leads from their regular office on the main level to a glassed loft where they work on desktop computers with oversized screens, circled by unpacked cartons on the floor, a large massage chair, and gym equipment so that Brin can stretch his cranky back. A helmeted spacesuit with the name Sergey Brin on a breast pouch is splayed on a hanging stand facing the offices below. (Brin has applied and left a $5 million deposit for one of the six seats on Space Adventures' *Soyuz* spacecraft's 2012 orbital trip.) Another staircase allows them to slip out of the building and to the parking lot where they daily leave their commuting vehicles, including two Priuses, two $109,000 Tesla Roadster electric sports cars from the company they've each invested in, and a couple of bicycles.

Asked why they have no assistants, Page gave a revealing answer. They do have an assistant "from time to time," he said, but "the amount of time it takes me to actually schedule is not very high because of Google Calendar. Occasionally, I have to go back and forth with somebody, but usually they'll meet when I want to meet anyway. It's not like I have to negotiate very much." He laughed, gently. "I'm not sure it would work for everybody, but for me it's worked pretty well. Also, it's actually allowed me to have more time. People are willing to ask an assistant: 'Will Larry come and talk at this thing?' But if they actually have to e-mail me about it, they think twice. It's not that anybody in the company can't e-mail me. It's that they realize they shouldn't be using my time that way. So the number of requests I've gotten has gone down, which is kind of nice."

What isn't so nice for Google executives is that they often don't know where the founders are, or if they will attend meetings. Page and Brin resist being tied to someone else's schedule. With no assistant to contact, the way executives learn if one or both founders will attend a meeting is if they see that Page or Brin has placed the meeting on his online Google Calendar, which senior Google executives share. Sometimes, Schmidt said, the founders show up unscheduled for the wrong meetings. Sometimes they disappear— Larry suddenly to tour a cafeteria to make sure it seats no more than one hundred and fifty, which he insists is the maximum size to inspire a team culture; Sergey or Larry to disappear from the office (if the wind has picked up) to pursue their kite-surfing hobby, which relies on a small surfboard and wind to propel the kite and skim across the water.

Schmidt defends management chaos, or at least a degree of it, as a style that fits the founders, and he offered an illustration. For months he tried to get the founders to craft a corporate strategy memo for the future, believing their "brilliance" produces unique insights. He couldn't pin them down. Finally, on a business trip to Seville, he opened his e-mail and up popped a draft from Brin. "Perfect," he thought, and shared it with Page, who was on the trip. Page made his edits, then Schmidt did some edits and circulated the draft to Google's management with a "What's missing?" note. "Why couldn't I get them to write this in a normal way?" Schmidt asked. "That's not the way their minds work. Their ideas are much better than mine. I can't write the memo, and in that you see why they are the founders."

Whatever their brilliance, each member of the troika running Google has the same liability, said an industry insider who knows them well. "None is an inspirational leader, a great salesman, or a great speaker." Their brilliance and success move people, but not their words or the symbols they evoke. They are not Steve Jobs, not gifted salesmen or evangelical leaders.

Page and Brin differ from Jobs in another significant way. Al Gore, who has had a ringside seat at the management of both Apple and Google, said that he deeply admires the founders of each company, but "a genius like Steve comes along only once in several generations." Jobs has demonstrated his genius over a longer period of time than Page and Brin, he believes, and also has benefited from something the Google founders lack: "Steve has the great if painful experience of failing, and coming back." The wisdom that comes from failure has not yet punched Page and Brin.

It was time in the spring of 2008 for executives to make tough choices among the 150 products Google produced. Why 150 products? "That can be stated as criticism, but it can also be stated as strategy," Schmidt responded. "The goal of the company is customer satisfaction. You should think of Google as one product": customer satisfaction. This response summons memories of Yahoo's famous Peanut Butter Manifesto. Composed in November 2006 as an internal memo by Yahoo senior vice president Brad Garlinghouse, it was leaked and caused a stir in the Valley. Garlinghouse wrote:

> We lack a focused, cohesive vision for our company. We want to do everything and be everything—to everyone. . . . I've heard our strategy described as spreading peanut butter across the myriad opportunities that continue to evolve in the online world. The result: a thin layer of investment spread across everything we do and thus we focus on nothing in particular.

Search gives Google more of a focus than a self-proclaimed "media company" like Yahoo might have. Yet a departed Google executive, who like many who voice criticism of Google's management chooses to do so anonymously, said, "Google could do fewer products and make less investments. They are doing too many products and peanut buttering everything."

Why?

"They've never had to make hard choices," answered the former executive.

"The company is so successful that it can do anything. They think they can make energy. Why? They have passion. That's what makes Google great. The question is when things get hard, can they make tough decisions?"

The CEO of an old media company described a visit he and his COO made to Google a few years ago. They were doing what Mel Karmazin had done: take a tour of Google and have a meal with the founders and Schmidt. As an executive led them around, they paused to look at the gallery of photographs of the projects Google had launched. The Google executive explained the 20 percent time each engineer was given. The COO asked, "Has there ever been a project started where someone said, 'OK, it's not what we thought it was. We should get rid of it.'?"

"I don't think so," answered their tour guide.

When I pressed a longtime Google executive to recall the products the company had canceled, he came up with just two: Google Answers and Google Catalog Search. "This is a company that doesn't set priorities," said another former Google executive. Part of the reason, this person said, traces to the founders. "It's the Talmud of the founders. The word of God. And everyone interprets the word of God at Google."

It's very hard not to defer to founders who have been right so often. But here's where Schmidt is criticized for not imposing his will. One reason, said a former Google executive, is because "He hates confrontation." A second reason, said another former manager, is because "Eric runs the company—unless there's someting Larry really cares about. Anything Larry cares about, he runs. Like products." Brin is said to assert himself on fewer things, but on advertising and privacy policies, business deals, or "Google's approach to China, Sergey rules." The prominent CEO of one company that does business with Google said he found Schmidt "odd, as if he's holding something back. In the guise of someone who is straight—a sincere, decent, thoughtful, kind man—he is something different than all of those qualities. In his business dealings people will tell you that if he said, 'OK, I agree to this,' you will find that he actually hasn't done so. If you confront him, he said he couldn't. Or he forgot. Or he gives you gobbledegook."

Why? "He is not the decider," the CEO answered. "Yet in certain areas he pretends that he is. Eric is smoothly duplicitous."

Silicon Valley venture capitalist Roger McNamee of Elevation Partners calls "Google the most impressive company I've ever seen." Yet in mid-2008 he also said, "I am very disappointed in Eric Schmidt. He got off to a great start because he was wise enough to leave a crazy culture alone. The Google culture has become a monster."

Even Coach Campbell, who has no direct managerial responsibilities, is not immune from criticism. "He's more a crutch than a coach," said a former Google executive, who believes Campbell compliments too much and challenges too little. A senior Google executive observes that until late 2008, Google never had an internal budget that apportioned capital, made choices about what resources to allocate; instead, it projected expenditures and revenues month by month. He blames the CEO for this, but also asked of the experienced coach, "Where was Bill?" He said Campbell spends too much time dispensing hugs. "I find him all hat and no cattle."

MARC ANDREESSEN was of two minds about Google. On the one hand, he believed, "Google is in a great position," particularly with YouTube, which he thought will find a way to monetize. On the other hand, he cautioned against Google's "trying to do everything. You saw their energy initiative! History suggests that people have circles of competence and when you go outside the circle, they fail."

Columbia's Tim Wu concurs. "Google is a precocious company. Great grades. Perfect IPO. A typical high school standout," he observed. "The basic problem is whether they remain true to their founding philosophy. I don't just mean 'Don't be evil.'" Will they stay focused on search, on "their founding philosophy, which is really an engineers' aesthetic of getting you to what you want as fast as you can and then getting out of the way?" Or will Google become "a source of content, a platform, a destination that seeks to keep people in a walled Google garden? I predict that Google will wind up at war with itself."

Brin rejects this analysis, but when asked what his biggest worry was, he answered simply, "I worry about complexity. I admire Steve Jobs. He has been able to keep his products simple."

Advertising pressures may add to Google's complexity, for there is a built-in tension between the interests of users and of advertisers. Recall the aversion the founders once had to banner ads because, they said, "they don't give the user the best experience." And now Google heralds its purchase of DoubleClick as a means to get into the banner advertising business it once shunned. Because Google now admits to being in the advertising business, which produces almost all its revenues, they will have to answer this question: Is Google's customer the advertiser or the user?

"I don't think I'm worried about that changing at Google," Brin said. He would not make the same argument for others. "I see other Web sites making trade-offs that I wouldn't," including allowing "pop-ups and pop-unders," or online publications that allow "eight columns of ads on the side and one teensy article."

But with such a wealth of data at Google's disposal, their advertising customers will want more. And if Google's growth sputters, pressure to satisfy advertisers will intensify. Richard Sarnoff, now the president of Digital Media Investments at Bertelsmann AG, whose great-uncle was David Sarnoff, the founder of NBC radio and television, likens these potential advertising pressures on Google to those faced by his great-uncle. "He had a vision of what radio and television could be in terms of being informational, educational, cultural, relevant. He said, 'OK, we've got radio. Let's put Tchaikovsky on!' . . . The reason the broadcast media didn't end up being this public trust type of programming but became primarily—let's call it lower-culture entertainment programming—is that radio and television was just so good at delivering audiences to advertisers. Business being what it is, whatever you're good at, you concentrate on, you maximize, and that ends up delivering value to your shareholders. Google, like NBC in those early days, finds itself being a phenomenally effective way of delivering consumers to advertisers. The question is: To what extent is that going to change the very lofty principles that the company was originally founded on and that made them effective in the first place? Google is at that kind of crossroads." Advertising pressures on Google will build. "What I have seen is that their very success has allowed them to resist such pressure—so far."

All of these concerns, not to mention the luxury of being rich, contributed to the exodus of Google employees. George Reyes, the company's long-serving CFO, with nearly three hundred million dollars in company stock, decided to retire at age fifty-three. Seeking to get on the ground floor of a hot new digital company, a number of other Googlers left, including executive chef Josef Desimone. Many who left did so out of frustration. The most prominent of them was Sheryl Sandberg.

Frustrated by what friends say was sometimes chaotic management at Google, and wanting broader responsibilities to address these, Sandberg left in March 2008 to accept the title of chief operating officer at Facebook. Venture capitalist Roger McNamee, an investor in Facebook and a close friend of Sandberg's, introduced her to founder Mark Zuckerberg. "Sheryl created AdWords," he said. "The idea had many parents, but the execution was hers." Her title, vice president, global online sales and operations, did not reflect her importance, he said. And he believed she was junior to some "tired executives." In the effort to keep her, Google offered her the CFO job, which she declined. "She wanted to be a COO," said Schmidt. "Sheryl is a terrific executive. But we don't want a COO."

By the time Sandberg stepped down, her Google team had grown to four thousand employees, with AdWords and AdSense then yielding 98 percent of the company's revenues. "Sheryl is a person who balances the left brain and the right brain. All of us could learn from her," said her close friend Elliot Schrage, who lost an ally in his ongoing efforts to persuade the engineers to think more broadly. Schrage soon followed Sandberg, accepting a position at Facebook similar at first to the one he'd held at Google. (Months later, he was also put in charge of overseeing Facebook's relations with outside developers.)

Sandberg's departure was jarring. Her move drew attention to Facebook, the new rocket, and highlighted the strained adolescence of Google. It brought some sadness as well, for Sandberg was popular, and not just among Googlers. When media executives like Donald Graham, CEO of the Washington Post Company, or Arthur Sulzberger, Jr., of the New York Times Company visited Google, they often separately went to her home in Atherton for cocktails or dinner with Sandberg and her husband, David Goldberg. Before she left Google, Graham tried to hire her for a senior position at his company. She was the friendly face at Google that some traditional media company executives trusted enough to let their hair down and ask: How can Google help my troubled business?

Google executives were stumped as to why Sandberg would take the job at Facebook. She wasn't given the same broad responsibilities as most COOs: vital parts of Facebook—product management and development, engineering, and finance—would continue to report to founder Mark Zuckerberg. And they didn't understand why she would leave for a company that, according to one Facebook insider, had generated only $150 million in revenues in 2007 and was bleeding money.

Google was already anxious about Facebook, and Sandberg's defection elevated their discomfort. True, Facebook wasn't making money, but neither had Google in its first three years. Facebook had 123 million unique visitors in May 2008, according to comScore, a 162 percent increase over the previous May. For the first time, Facebook had passed its rival, MySpace. Also making Google anxious was Facebook's alliance with Microsoft, which owns 1.5 percent of the social network site and sells its advertising. Microsoft was coming after Google, aggressively allying with traditional media companies—agreeing, for instance, to sell online advertising for Viacom, to license and display its television and movie products on its MSN and Xbox 360 platforms, and expending half a billion dollars to advertise on Viacom platforms.

Google and Facebook were not yet joined in battle, observed Marc Andreessen, who joined the Facebook board in the summer of 2008, but they were engaged "in a little shadow boxing." Mindful of his experience at Netscape, he said he believed that Google and Microsoft had already fallen into the trap of becoming obsessed with what each was doing. Of Facebook and Google, he said, "It would be a mistake for either company to rush to compete too quickly. The danger there is that you orient your strategy to what others are doing. Then the press wants to write a conflict story: Google versus Facebook."

ALTHOUGH ITS FINANCIAL PERFORMANCE was sterling, the first quarter of 2008 was the winter of Google's discontent. The company was becoming more defensive. It was under attack for its privacy and China policies, for its growing dominance in search, for its perceived threat to copyright owners, for its disruption of such traditional businesses as advertising, for its efforts to muscle into the mobile telephone business. The government was peering over its shoulder. Like other giant corporations, Google's power, and sometimes its behavior, threatens to sabotage its trusted brand. A Microsoft executive, clearly enjoying the rain of criticism falling on Google, candidly observed, "People dislike Google for the same reason they disliked us: arrogance." A major difference between the two is that while Microsoft's dominant operating system was difficult to avoid, people can escape Google with a single click of a mouse.

Microsoft's engineering culture, like Google's, had missed the warning signals that its actions had aroused the government bear. And Microsoft, like Google, truly believed it was advancing the public good. Microsoft's Internet Explorer was, after all, given away for free. A single dominant operating system meant that PCs could more easily communicate with one another, as Microsoft liked to say. Both companies were capable of being blinded by righteousness—the flip side of hubris. Unlike Microsoft, Google was managed more chaotically.

The smart question asked of Google was the one Adam Lashinsky of *Fortune* posed in early 2007: "Is Google's culture great because its stock is doing well, or is its stock doing well because its culture is great?"

WHAT WASN'T AT QUESTION was Google's success. Measuring it by growth, profits, and market valuation, it's difficult to claim that Google's management has not worked. And a reason it has worked, so far at least, is that it is, in the words of Google director Ram Shriram, "controlled chaos—meaning that there is some method to the madness. If you have too much structure, you have less innovation." Instead of describing Google management as chaotic, Brin said, "I'd prefer 'less structured.'" He cited Google's youth as a partial explanation: "We're only in this business ten years."

Former vice president Al Gore recounted a private conversation he had with Brin and Page several years ago in the boardroom near their office. Gore worried aloud whether Google was maintaining its focus on potential new search threats and continuing to prosecute its technological lead in search. "They had to go to another meeting," Gore recalled, "and said, 'If you can stay, Al, we'd like to bring in the engineers and scientists in charge of this part of the business.' Ten of them came into the boardroom. Larry and Sergey left. I spent another three hours. And then when it was over, I gave Larry and Sergey an oral report."

Four weeks later, Gore said, laughing, "I went up to their office and found that all ten of these people had been moved in. All ten of them!" He described how Page and Brin had to cram twelve computer monitors into the glassed two-story office, and "move around some of their toys—a remote control helicopter, flying messenger boards, whatever the latest new supercool toy is." These ten people stayed—"until they satisfied themselves that they had an ongoing system for maintaining hypervigilance in the organization on the continuing innovation necessary to make sure they were always at the cutting edge of the highest quality search experience available on the Internet. . . . I defy you to think of any other executives in the world who would have a team like that into their personal office for weeks on end."

Gore may have been a prod, but the execution of innovation at Google is due to the focused passion Brin and Page bring to Google. Barry Diller, who had that unsettling session with Page and Brin in the early days of Google, when Page would not look up from his PDA to talk to him, now thinks what might be construed as rudeness was really focus. "They had their own method of communicating and processing," Diller said. "They give much less quarter than other people do to common business courtesies. They've stayed true to this. It's a spectacular strength. It means you never get defocused by the crowd." At Google the focus is on the engineer is king culture Brin and Page had the precocity to impose.

True to its open-sourced, wisdom-of-the-crowd ideals, Google has created a networked management. It is bottom-up as well as top-down management, and it unleashes ideas and effort. "There is a pattern in companies," Page explained, "even in technological companies, that the people who do the work—the engineers, the programmers, the foot soldiers, if you will—typically get rolled over by the management. Typically, the management isn't very technical. I think that's a very bad thing. If you're a programmer or an engineer or computer scientist and you have someone tell you what to do who is really not very good at what you do, they tell you the wrong things. And you sort of end up building the wrong things; you end up kind of demoralized. You want to have a culture where the people who are doing the work, the scientists and the engineers, are empowered. And that they are managed by people who deeply understand what they are doing. That's not typically the case."

CHAPTER TWELVE

Is "Old" Media Drowning?

(2008)

On a sunny July afternoon in Sun Valley, three friends who had competed and cooperated for a quarter century—Robert Iger, the CEO of Disney; Les Moonves, the CEO of CBS; and Peter Chernin, the COO of News Corporation—gathered for sodas. They sat beside a tranquil pond, but their world was not serene. By the summer of 2008, the economy had started its swoon. The shrinking of the audience for their broadcast networks and TV stations had accelerated. Their stock prices were getting mauled. "At least we've had a good run," Chernin said, half joking.

"Yeah," Iger replied with a laugh, "but I feel like we've gotten to the orgy and all the women have left!"

"We sound like three old men sitting in Miami Beach with blankets over our legs!" Moonves cracked.

The network and station business was once much easier. "The era when I worked at ABC was fantastic," recalled Michael Eisner, who was a program executive at the network before leaving to become CEO of Disney in the early eighties. "There were three networks, and all I had to worry about was 'Did we have a good show?' Even if we had a bad show, we did OK."

What does it feel like to be a media executive navigating these swiftly churning waters? Before he became CEO of Sony, Sir Howard Stringer spent much of his life in traditional media, starting as a researcher for CBS News and becoming an award-winning news producer, president of CBS News, and president of CBS Broadcasting. Today, seated in the Sony dining room in New York, he said, "If you read every piece in every newspaper and magazine about new technology, you would walk into the East River! There are so many options out there, simultaneously, that it's a dizzying experience. For every time you see an opportunity, you also see a threat. Every time you see a threat, you see an opportunity. Or if you see a threat, you're afraid you're missing an opportunity. That's the one-two punch of the technological marathon we're all in. You worry about missing a trend. You worry about not spotting a trend. You worry about a trend passing you by. You worry about a trend taking you into a cul-de-sac. It means that any CEO or senior executives of a company have to induce themselves to have a calm they don't feel, in order to be rational in the face of this onslaught."

Sony, like others, had reason to fret about missed trends. Before Stringer was CEO, the company that in 1979 had introduced the Sony Walkman was being challenged in 2001 by a stylish upstart, Apple's iPod. By 2003 Apple's iTunes offered singles that could be downloaded simply and for just ninety-nine cents, hampering the sale of albums by record companies like Sony. Although the Walkman was still the dominant portable music player in 2003, the iPod was gaining. I asked then CEO Nobuyuki Idei, are you worried about the iPod?

No, he replied, dismissing the question like a man brushing lint off his jacket. *Sony and Dell know manufacturing. Apple does not. Within a couple of years, Apple will be out of the music business.*

Probably no other traditional media business has been so disrupted by the digital wave as has music. And none was slower to respond to the challenge. Music companies like Sony gave an incentive to digital pirates by insisting that their customers buy entire albums rather than allowing them to purchase individual songs. The music companies failed to understand that technology awarded power to consumers to mix and choose their own music, failed to strike an accommodation with Napster and other music download sites, failed to create a digital jukebox like iTunes, failed to enter the lucrative concert business for their artists, failed to start a TV platform like MTV. Edgar M. Bronfman, Jr., the CEO of the Warner Music Group, said, "It's fair to say we didn't get it"—meaning the digital revolution. "But I'm not sure what we could have done." He added, "The record business is in trouble. The music business is not." He believes the music companies were murdered by technological forces beyond their control. In fact, they committed suicide by neglect.

A glance at the record company business suggests the depth of its travails. Into the nineties, best selling albums sold at least 15 million copies, said Jeffrey Cole of the Annenberg School's Center for the Digital Future at the University of Southern California. In 2007, the top-selling album registered only 3.7 million sales. People are listening to more music, but paying much less. Some performers, such as Madonna, bypass traditional music companies altogether. Following the predigital model of the Grateful Dead, who built their audience by encouraging fans to tape their performances, acts like Coldplay made single songs available for free over the Internet. (When released, Coldplay's album *Death and All His Friends* shot to number one.) In 2007, worldwide digital music sales rose to 15 percent of all music sold, up from less than 1 percent in 2003. Yet this rise could not compensate for the decline of more expensive compact disc sales, which fell 10 percent that year. Music companies were in the business of selling albums, and since their sales peak in 2000 of nearly 800 million, album sales in 2007 plunged to just over 500 million. This helps explain why music company revenues have dropped significantly from $14.2 billion in 2000 and will dive to $9 billion by 2012, according to Forrester Research.

In one sense, newspapers share this dilemma. Most newspapers enjoy healthier profit margins than music companies, but these are shrinking. Investors punish their stocks because, compared with a Google or Apple, newspapers have dismal growth prospects. The speed with which the world of newspapering has changed was captured in interviews conducted by the *Los Angeles Times Magazine* with six former editors of the *Los Angeles*

Times newspaper. William F. Thomas, the editor from 1971 to 1989, suggested that the so-called good old days were akin to what was commonplace at Google: "I never experienced any real restraints on anything we wanted to do for budget reasons. . . . The only limit I recall was when they started enforcing a no-first-class rule." By the time John S. Carroll took the helm in 2000, the newspaper's corporate owners were seen as predators, people who understood math but not journalism, and Carroll, like his two successors, chose to quit in 2005 rather than obey directives from Chicago. With the benefit of hindsight, this fine editor blamed not just his former bosses, but himself as well. Carroll told the magazine that, like most editors, he was preoccupied with the fireman's part of his job, answering news alarms, covering and editing daily stories. "If I had it to do over again, I might have taken some time off and tried to figure out where the Web was going and tried to do something about it." This mistake—not to treat the arrival of the Internet with urgency, not to pour resources into a vibrant online newspaper—was one that most of his peers made as well.

In 2007, newspaper advertising, which accounts for about 80 percent of most U.S. newspaper revenue, fell 9.4 percent, according to the Newspaper Association of America. Adjusted for inflation, ad revenues were 20 percent lower than in their peak year, 2000. Circulation had dropped about 2 percent each year after 2003, and some papers, including the *Los Angeles Times* and the *Boston Globe,* lost about a third of their circulation in those years. The falloff in both advertising and newspaper sales would accelerate as more readers went online to sites like Google, Yahoo News, the *Huffington Post*, or *Gawker.*

The flight of advertisers from magazines was usually not nearly as severe, in part because advertisers believed they got more value from glossy, picture-filled pages. But even before the 2008 recession leveled magazines, many had slipped. Business magazines, said Time Inc. editor in chief John Huey, were battered by a severe drop in auto and tech advertising. Condé Nast would feel compelled to close *Portfolio* magazine in early 2009 and just months later *BusinessWeek* was put up for sale. And the weekly news magazines, whose pages age rapidly in a time of instant news, were so bereft of advertising as to appear anorexic. *U.S. News & World Report* at first announced that it would switch from a weekly to a biweekly publication schedule, then within months retreated further, saying it would only publish monthly.

It is true that if we add Web site visitors, newspapers and magazines had a net increase in readers. Twenty million unique visitors came each month in early 2008 to the largest newspaper Web site, the *New York Times*. The rub is that because the online audience pays less attention to ads and spends less time with an online newspaper, advertisers only pay 5 to 10 percent of what they do for the same ad in a newspaper. According to Jim Kennedy, vice president and director of strategic planning for the Associated Press, newspaper revenues in 2007 totaled sixty billion dollars, with online revenues accounting for only four billion of this total. Theoretically, a newspaper that abandoned print to publish online could save 60 to 80 percent of its overall costs, having done away with the expense of paper, printing, and distribution. To date, however, with the exception of the *Wall Street Journal* and the *Financial Times*, few if any daily newspapers have succeeded by charging for online subscriptions. With online newspapers generating minute advertising and zero circulation revenues—and with younger readers migrating online and exhibiting less loyalty to a particular news brand—newspapers that attempted to publish only online would undoubtably subtract more revenue than they would add.

Hemmed in, the print press in 2008 engaged in a blizzard of cost cutting. *Newsweek* shed two hundred jobs, Time Inc. six hundred; the San Jose *Mercury News* cleaved two hundred newsroom employees. The headcount at the world's best newspaper, the *New York Times,* dropped almost 4 percent in a single year, and the McClatchy chain, which historically prided itself on its no-layoff policy, began laying off employees in September and by the spring of 2009 had reduced its workforce by 25 percent. After years of patching and pasting to get by, newspapers seemed to be in free fall. The Tribune Company cut five hundred weekly news pages in its papers and laid off employees, then filed for bankruptcy. The *Philadelphia Inquirer* and the *Philadelphia Daily News* would soon follow, as would others. The New York Times Company, with a bulge of debt payments due in the spring of 2009, sought a second mortgage on its headquarters building and accepted a $250 million loan at an inflated interest rate of 14 percent from

Mexican billionaire Carlos Slim. The *Christian Science Monitor* shut down its daily print edition and went online, as would the *Seattle Post-Intelligencer*. Gannett, the nation's largest newspaper publisher with eighty-five dailies, watched its stock price drop 87 percent in a twelve-month period.

Not everyone in the news businesses was on a starvation diet. Three wire services—the AP, Reuters, and Bloomberg—defied the industry trend. There were several reasons for this. The bleak economic climate for newspapers, ironically, benefited the wire services. As newspapers contracted, they outsourced more of their news gathering to the wire services. ("The cold our customers caught," said Thomson Reuters CEO, Thomas Glocer, "has been good for Reuters—unless the patient dies! That would be bad for Reuters.") And unlike most newspapers, the wire services moved early to tap new sources of revenue. The AP, according to its CEO, Tom Curley, "gets about 20 percent of our revenues from digital sources." The AP's 2008 revenues totaled $750 million, which means digital sources—Google News and Yahoo and advertising from newspaper and broadcast links and other customers—generated about $150 million. And broadcasting revenues were even larger. More than half the AP's worldwide revenues now came not from the fees newspapers paid but from its broadcast and online operations.

Bloomberg and Reuters, for their part, were sitting on data-generating gold mines. Bloomberg, like Reuters long before it merged with Thomson, started as a collector and provider of financial data; essentially, it was in the service business, not the news business. The value of this business is demonstrated by contrasting two business transactions. In 2007, when Rupert Murdoch acquired Dow Jones, parent of the *Wall Street Journal* (and former owner of Telerate, a data business it failed to invest in and eventually sold), he paid five billion dollars. In 2008, when Merrill Lynch sold its 20 percent ownership in Bloomberg, the company was valued at a whopping twenty-two billion dollars. Both Bloomberg and Thomson Reuters tapped a rich revenue source from the terminals they rented to companies, and with readers hungry for business information from around the world, they expanded into news. According to Thomas Glocer, by 2008, Reuters had 2,600 reporters, and six hundred broadcast outlets as customers for its video news service; its profit margins topped 20 percent. Unlike newspapers, the three wire services were publishers who did not have the expense of paper, printing presses, or distribution.

On stage at the Dow Jones/*Journal*'s annual All Things Digital Conference in San Diego in May 2008, Murdoch noted that newspapers had lost 10 to 30 percent of their revenues and almost all were engaged in a frenzy of cost cutting. He said he saw this as an opportunity, and would pour more resources into the *Journal*, aiming to siphon general and business readers from the *Times* and the *Financial Times*. The jury was out as to whether by going after general readers of the *Times* he would over the long run chase business readers from the *Journal*, but to date his strategy has been a modest success. Comparing the *Journal*'s circulation in the six months ending March 2009 versus the same period ending in March 2008, the Audit Bureau of Circulations reported that the *Journal* was the only one of the top twenty-five newspapers to gain (just under 1 percent) circulation.

Murdoch was well aware of the newspaper industry's plight. Some newspapers, he said, "will disappear." As more news is aggregated online, it weakens the value of a newspaper brand. "What really is going on underneath this news aggregation," said Tad Smith, CEO of Reed Business Information, "is that for journalism the return on investment for going out and hiring other journalists is negative. What that means is that Google has created an environment where the way to make money in the media world is with OPC: other people's content." Smith experienced firsthand the plight of print publications when his parent company put his division up for sale in 2008 and was unable to find a buyer to pay what it considered a fair price. They took Smith's division off the market.

Eric Schmidt bridled at the suggestion that Google was somehow the fall guy for an Internet that had inevitably changed the rules of the game. "There is a systematic change going on in how people spend their time," he said. "I think it's important that Google understand that we are one of the companies that is making that happen. It's very important that we be polite about it, and not be arrogant or obnoxious, because there is real damage being done. But also, our rationale is that it's the end users who are choosing this. This is not a concerted effort by us to do anything other than adapt to the way end users behave. If looked at that way, we have a shared problem. We need newspapers' content. And it's critically important that they continue." When users do a Google search or come to Google News and click on a newspaper story, he said, they are taken to that paper's Web site, which increases its traffic and its ability to sell more online ads. Schmidt and newspaper proprietors have no illusions that Google can magically restore the economic vitality of newspapers. Google rubbed salt in the wound, however, when after seven years of being ad free, Google News in 2009 for the first time started accepting small text ads, triggering renewed newspaper complaints that Google was enriching itself on their content.

Book publishing "is in so much better shape than the music industry or certainly the newspaper or magazine industry," said Authors Guild executive director Paul Aiken. He thinks the physical format of a book—and therefore the publishing business model—is not as easily altered. Nor is book publishing dependent on fickle advertisers, as are newspapers and magazines. But when asked if he was an optimist about the future of books, Aiken paused before candidly responding, "Sometimes."

The reasons to be wary are many. Book sales were relatively flat in 2007, reaching $3.13 billion in the United States, a rise of less than 1 percent from the previous year. And according to a 2007 study by the National Endowment for the Arts (NEA), when adjusted for inflation, money spent to purchase books "has fallen dramatically." Publishers rarely say aloud what this study suggested: books are losing younger readers. "Nearly half of all Americans ages 18 to 24 read no books for pleasure," the study found, and the percentage of those 18 to 44 who read books was sliding. It is true that the following year, 2008, the NEA reported a modest increase in reading. But if one asked publishers, or educators, whether they had high hopes for the expansion of book reading, few would say yes. Publishers also fretted about whether Google Books would bring them the same piracy woes that bedevil music and movies; about the disappearance of independent bookstores and the squeeze on their profits from big distributors like Amazon and Barnes & Noble; about publishing houses' increasing dependence on blockbusters, making it harder for them to justify publishing so-called midlist books that often make editors proud but lose money; about the folks who sign their checks but who often treat publishing as just another business and not an endeavor that can replenish the culture. That one day books would be printed on demand or that online book sellers could reach into the long tail and resuscitate books that were no longer in print was a distant shore to most book publishers in late 2008, when they imposed layoffs akin to those at newspapers. One publisher, Houghton Mifflin Harcourt, followed its round of layoffs by announcing that it would temporarily suspend the acquisition of new books.

Broadcast radio, with the notable exceptions of sports and talk radio, was also losing altitude in 2008; revenues began a steady decline in 2006, which has since accelerated. Les Moonves announced in July 2008 that he was selling fifty of his Infinity Broadcasting's smaller-market stations. With his CBS stock hammered by investors who saw no growth prospects in the saturated radio market, he said he would sell his entire station group for the proper price, which he cannot get. Similar maladies afflicted satellite radio. Even with nearly twenty million customers and a merger between the two satellite services, Karmazin's Sirius XM Radio, burdened by huge programming and satellite and debt costs—and by the emergence of new digital competitors that allowed consumers to program playlists for themselves—teetered near insolvency. All of radio is besieged by too many ads and too many choices—from Internet radio to podcasts to iPods to MP3 players—that siphon off listeners because they empower them to become their own disc jockeys.

Traditional advertising companies were growing, but only because they were no longer focused exclusively on creating advertising and selling it. They had merged and morphed into four worldwide marketing conglomerates—the WPP Group, the Omnicom Group, the Interpublic Group, and Publicis—with public relations and marketing and direct mail and polling and research and lobbying and political consulting divisions. Ad spending in the United States grew an average of about 5 percent from 1963 to 2007, peaking at $162.1 billion in 2008, according to Gotlieb's GroupM. This was about 36 percent of the estimated $445 billion spent globally on advertising. Yet ad spending was less than half of what was spent on what is euphemistically now called "marketing." A media campaign no longer consisted of buying ads on the three networks and a few other places; now a campaign might combine ads on TV and in magazines, a viral effort online, search ads, in-store sales promotions, telemarketing, polling, public relations—all of which was more expensive. The increased expense, and spending, spurred media buying agencies to merge into superagencies, such as Irwin Gotlieb's Group M. These media buyers now had enormous clout, which they exercised over traditional media companies that relied on advertising.

While advertising in most traditional media was declining or growing incrementally, online advertising was soaring. The advantage enjoyed by digital media is transparency. The client (advertiser) knows more about the audience, more about who actually responds to the advertisement. Marketing thus becomes less opaque, robbing ad agencies and sellers of their ability to sell what Mel Karmazin called "the sizzle." This is a primary reason online advertising jumped 30 percent each year, topping twenty-three billion dollars in 2008. This transparency and the additional supply of media outlets, as well as a suspicion that advertising and media agencies had not sufficiently adjusted their fees downward, shifted leverage to the true buyer, the client.

Seeking to surf the Internet wave, companies like WPP bid aggressively to acquire digital advertising and marketing companies. They and others invested in digital advertising exchanges like Spot Runner, which creates an online dashboard of local media platforms on which small businesses advertise, and offers a roster of prefab commercials that can be cheaply customized. Want to buy a thirty-second TV spot in Santa Barbara? Nick Grouf, the CEO of Spot Runner, said he can reach into "the long tail" of local media and purchase it for a mere twelve dollars. This makes television advertising accessible to small business—pizza parlors, pet stores, hair salons—that would previously have found it unimaginable. "We told local businesses this and their jaws dropped," said Grouf. "We're democratizing the business, opening it up to small business." By selling ad space once seen as undesirable, the digital technologies that allow advertising exchanges, such as Google's AdWords and AdSense, shake the advertising business to its core.

Technology was the frenemy of all traditional media businesses. According to an Annenberg Center study, the average American family classified as poor spent $180 per month on media services—mobile, broadband, digital TV, satellite TV, iTunes, and the like—that did not exist a generation ago, and the average American household spends $260 per month. (Irwin Gotlieb's GroupM data pegged the number at $270.) By providing consumers with all these choices, new technology inevitably disrupted traditional habits. The audience that had once belonged to broadcast television moved to cable, to video on demand, to DVDs, to YouTube and Facebook and Guitar Hero. TiVo and DVRs allowed viewers to become their own programmers. This was great for viewers but not so great for the television business. It meant that viewers were often skipping the ads broadcasters relied on for revenue, and programs being watched were not being counted in the Nielsen ratings, weakening ad rates. And networks are soon to be slammed by another disruption: surveys show that those between ages fourteen to twenty-five (called millennials) are watching less television and spending more time on the Internet and with video games. Television executives like to argue that this is really good news for the broadcast networks. Yes, they will say, the live viewing audience for ABC, Fox, CBS, and NBC plunged 10 percent in the year 2008. But, they boast, their ad revenues continued to inch up, because in an age of niche media and fragmented viewership, no other medium delivers a mass audience. If they took a truth serum, though, they would admit that one day their advertisers will also fragment. They would also admit that their investment in local broadcast stations, which once yielded profit margins of 40 to 60 percent, were now a drag on their growth.

The U.S. movie business was growing overseas, but was under attack everywhere else—from Internet piracy to DVD and video sales and rentals that were declining in the face of competition from movie downloads. Equally worrisome, personal video recorders empowered viewers to ignore ads promoting new movies. "We're not like a car or prescription medicine company where you can build a brand over a long term," said Michael Lynton, Chairman and CEO of Sony Pictures Entertainment. "You have to build a brand in five weeks. If they skip over your ads, you're in trouble." Flat screen TVs, DVDs, and movie downloads drained customers from movie theaters. Video games were stealing the attention of teenagers. And that burgeoning business—now taking in twenty-one billion dollars a year worldwide and expected to double by 2012—was expanding from action games for teens to mass-market Wii games for adults to play with their kids, or with one another. Telephone companies watched their lucrative landline phone business rapidly lose customers to Skype Internet calls and mobile and new cable phone services. Yahoo and Microsoft were tossed in the digital storm. With better search and advertising technology, Google's search widened its lead. With the promise of cloud computing and free software applications, Google menaced Microsoft's packaged software business. Everywhere they turned, new technologies were disrupting businesses faster than they could respond.

MORE THAN A QUARTER CENTURY AGO, as the age of cable TV materialized, the three television networks were slow to recognize the seismic shift that cable heralded, missing their chance to own rather than compete with cable networks. They were not alone in disdaining the new. When Robert Pittman cofounded MTV in 1981, Coca-Cola and McDonald's refused to buy advertising, saying they would not advertise on a television network that did not reach at least 55 percent of the nation. Pittman did persuade Pepsi to place some ads, and for the next several years Pepsi had a de facto exclusive advertising platform that greatly boosted its market share. It took Coca-Cola and McDonald's four or five years, Pittman recalled, to change their minds. Likewise, most traditional media companies in the Google era concentrated more on defending their turf rather than extending it. Belatedly, most have begun to dip their toes, and in some cases entire feet, into new media efforts, hoping that technology could also be their friend.

In the summer of 2008, CBS became the first full-scale traditional media company to open a Silicon Valley office in Menlo Park. Quincy Smith, who had been promoted to CEO of CBS Interactive, supervised the office and averaged two days a week there. Under his prodding, CBS made a number of digital acquisitions. The biggest was the $1.8 billion CBS spent to acquire CNET, whose online networks generated revenues of $400 million. It was a pricey acquisition—three times what Murdoch spent for MySpace in 2005—but CEO Moonves said he hoped the digital acquisition would add "at least two percentage points" to CBS profits and growth rates. CBS had also become one of YouTube's biggest suppliers, uploading eight hundred one- and two-minute clips per day from CBS programs. It was also among the first traditional media companies to strike a deal with YouTube to treat pirated video, as Brian Stelter reported in the *New York Times*, "as an advertising opportunity." Instead of ordering YouTube to remove the content illegally uploaded by citizens, CBS and a few others granted YouTube permission to sell ads off these and to split the revenues. Smith said CBS had about two hundred partners, and was selling digital copies of its shows on Yahoo, iTunes, and Amazon. Smith's digital group now had 3,300 employees in its various ventures, and Moonves predicted that the group would generate revenues of $600 million for CBS in 2008, with $90 million to $100 million of that as profit.

Almost daily in 2008, old media announced new media efforts. Seeking to extend its programming to other platforms, NBC said in January 2008 that it would customize shorter content that it called promo-tainment and sell ads on nine other platforms, including screens in gyms, subways, and the backseats of taxicabs, on gas pumps, and at supermarket checkout counters. In its competition with YouTube, NBC and News Corporation's Hulu video site had, by October 2008, signed up Sony and Paramount and other studios. Hulu offered a choice of about a thousand network shows, and reached an estimated 2.6 percent of the online video market—far below YouTube—but in a promising ad-friendly environment that would soon make it the second ranked video site. CBS, which declined to join Hulu, later established its own site, TV.com, to serve as an online platform for its present and past programs and for those of other content creators. Disney sold ABC programs and movies to iTunes, defending Apple's then policy of a single price for programs, movies, or music on the grounds that it was simple and clear and better served consumers. In April 2009, Disney's ABC gave a boost to Hulu by joining NBC and Fox as an equity partner. By mid 2009, Hulu—like YouTube—was still not profitable.

Local stations scrambled to create Web sites for their news and weather and to lower their ad rates in order to sell inventory to small businesses. A consortium of the six largest cable operators started Canoe Ventures, an effort to forge a single national digital cable platform to sell and target ads and collect the kind of user data Google gathers. HBO experimented by offering some of its programs for free online. Viacom joined with MGM and Lions Gate to create Epix, a premium cable channel with a Web site to stream their library of movies. All the movie studios sought to improve picture quality by offering films shot in high definition and by replacing costly reels of film they sent movie theaters with digital copies. Trying to demonstrate that it was not "a dumb pipe company," Verizon rolled out its cable video service, called FIOS, and announced plans to spend twenty billion dollars by 2010 to ensure its success; by the summer of 2008, FIOS was available in one million homes. AT&T promised to offer video services for mobile phones. Spurred by the success of Apple's iPhone, mobile phone companies moved to transform their devices into PDAs that were really powerful minicomputers. People who had grown up in the television business, such as Disney's former CEO, Michael Eisner, or MTV's Albie Hecht, and Jason Hirschhorn and Herb Scannell, switched careers to become Internet programmers.

And yet all of these efforts failed to answer two lingering questions: would these efforts make money? And would storytelling change on the Web? Eisner said he believed it would not, that though there are many more platforms to display stories, stories need space to be told. He didn't believe attention spans had shrunk, that multitasking diverted attention, or that interactivity would reshape storytelling. "If the story is really good, they'll stay with it," Eisner said. "I don't think a lot of the rules for storytelling are unique for the Internet." I think Jason Hirschhorn was closer to the truth when he said that the way storytelling will change is that the audience—as Google's YouTube demonstrates daily—will "do a lot of snacking." Everything will speed up, probably including the decline of old media.

CHAPTER THIRTEEN

Compete or Collaborate?

To achieve a balance of power against Napoleonic France, Prince Metternich of Austria helped organize the weaker European monarchies—Austria, Prussia, Russia—into an alliance. And in the Congress of Vienna, which followed the defeat of Napoléon, he maneuvered to maintain peace in Europe by forging an agreement among these nations to prevent the rise of another superpower. They would achieve a delicate balance of power among European nation-states, with no nation dominant. As in nineteenth-century Europe, today's traditional media companies must decide how to deal with the new superpower, Google. Do they aggressively compete or do they collaborate? Can they achieve a balance of power? The strategy media companies choose will pivot, as it did in Metternich's day, on whether they assume they are strong or weak. If executives of old media believe their business model is strong—that content is king—their strategy will likely veer from those who believe they are gravely threatened. If executives feel particularly vulnerable, convinced that they require substantial financial and security guarantees before risking their copyrighted material, they are likely to focus on these fears rather than on their best hopes for the Internet. And if they distrust Google's intentions, cooperative agreements will be elusive.

Although Google appears less vulnerable than Napoléon turned out to be, many traditional media companies chose to stick out their chests. Viacom filed a lawsuit, as the book publishing industry had. Fox and NBC refused to join Redstone's lawsuit but teamed up to create Hulu as a rival to YouTube out of fear that YouTube would cannibalize their audience and cheapen the value of their content. "The economics around these digital properties are not yet fully formed—that's five years away," NBC Universal CEO Jeff Zucker told a Harvard audience in early 2008. "We can't trade today's analog dollars for digital pennies."

Zucker's dollars-for-pennies claim is "not the right way to look at it," said David Rosenblatt, Google's then president, global display advertising, and the former CEO of DoubleClick. "That implies that the preservation of your existing business is more important than understanding what the new economy will be. My great-grandfather was in the ostrich-feather business. He went out of business in the early part of the twentieth century because ostrich feathers, which women wore attached to their hats and had worked well in carriages, no longer fit into automobiles. He could have said, 'I need to find smaller feathers to preserve my business.'" Despite these entreaties, Zucker, like many of those in traditional media, viewed Google as a frenemy.

Microsoft, like Viacom, treated Google as an outright enemy. This was never more evident than during the winter of 2008, when it made a Murdoch-like bid of $44.6 billion to acquire Yahoo, a valuation of $31 per share, or 62 percent more than Yahoo's stock price at the time. The battle that ensued left Microsoft and Yahoo bloodied and embarrassed, each wounded by self-inflicted blows.

There were reasons for Microsoft to pursue Yahoo. On paper, it was a way to increase Microsoft's then meager 9 percent share of the search market and to boost the $3.2 billion in online advertising Microsoft totaled in 2008, a figure dwarfed by Google's more than $20 billion; it was a way for Microsoft to piggyback on Yahoo's lead over Google in display advertising; it was a way for Microsoft to combine its MSN portal and e-mail with

Yahoo and achieve a dominant market share; it was a way to shore up Microsoft's defenses against Google's cloud computing offensive.

Yahoo clumsily resisted. After initially rejecting the offer, Yahoo CEO Jerry Yang and his board feigned interest; then again said they were not interested; then swallowed a poison pill so costly—saying at first that it would award each of its fourteen thousand employees a two-year window in which, if Microsoft won, they could quit and pocket generous severance benefits—that Yahoo was later compelled to abandon it. Yang and his board then said they'd accept thirty-seven dollars per share; then lowered this to thirty-three dollars; then said they'd consider selling just their search engine and not the rest of Yahoo. Microsoft's moves were equally maladroit. Steve Ballmer called off discussions, then put them on, then off again; he sought partners to make another run at Yahoo; then threatened to mount a proxy fight to remove the Yahoo board; then said he was no longer interested in Yahoo. By the end of 2008, the general he had placed in charge of Microsoft's battle plans, a man named Kevin Johnson, had left the company.

This comedy continued at the Dow Jones/*Wall Street Journal*'s annual D Conference in San Diego. Ballmer and Yang met privately that day, May 27. In the opening session that evening, Ballmer, answering pointed questions from *Journal* columnists Walt Mossberg and Kara Swisher, insisted, "We are not rebidding for the company." But he opened the door a crack, saying, "We reserve the right to do so." The next day on stage, Jerry Yang answered their questions and said the opposite, declaring that Microsoft had slammed the door shut and "was not interested anymore in buying the company." In November, Ballmer told his annual shareholders' gathering that Microsoft had "moved on" and was "done with all acquisitions discussions" with Yahoo. In December, he said he was interested in acquiring Yahoo's search business "sooner than later."

Yahoo shareholders were bludgeoned by these gyrations. In January 2009, Yahoo's stock was trading at around $12.00 per share, well below its $19.18 price on the day Microsoft made its initial bid a year earlier. Each company appeared indecisive. As the venture capitalist Roger McNamee observed, "The two biggest forces competing against Google have banged heads and knocked themselves unconscious."

Microsoft was unaccustomed to losing. The ever-competitive Ballmer, a Microsoft adviser admitted, was filled with "jealousy" and rage that Google was doing what Netscape had done a decade before, not merely challenging but "mooning the giant." Jealousy and rage are not the sturdiest foundations for rational decision making.

Microsoft seemed to affect Google's testosterone level as well. Sergey Brin told the Associated Press that Microsoft's takeover bid was "unnerving." It would grant Microsoft near-monopoly power, not just over operating systems and browsers but would also "tie up the top Web sites, and could be used to manipulate stuff in various ways." Eric Schmidt insisted that he believes in sitting down and talking to everyone. But did this include Microsoft? Reflecting a professional lifetime of being on the other side of the Redmond giant, Schmidt said, "If Microsoft wanted to do a business deal with us, we'd do it. You betcha. But we'd bring a tape recorder!"

Jitters aside, Google would find a way to gain advantage from the Yahoo-Microsoft melee, but not without getting bloodied itself. The company's Executive Committee and Board of Directors held meetings to devise a blocking strategy. They discussed petitioning the Justice Department to obstruct the merger, using the same antitrust arguments Microsoft had employed to try to stop Google from acquiring DoubleClick. They wrestled with whether to make their own bid for Yahoo, but decided it would be difficult to integrate two large companies with different cultures and assumed, in any case, that the government would disallow on antitrust grounds a merger of the two dominant search engines. They reached out to Jerry Yang and in the spring jointly devised a roadblock strategy; they announced that Google would become the selling agent for a large portion of Yahoo's search ads. "It gives them a tool to avoid being swallowed by Microsoft," Eric Schmidt said at the time. Asked in September 2008 what was the most important Google event of the previous six months, Schmidt said, "the Yahoo business deal. . . . It was a setback for Microsoft."

Google's effort to have the Justice Department block Microsoft's bid for Yahoo brought to mind Ralph Waldo Emerson's delicious observation that "a foolish consistency is the hobgoblin of little minds." Like other corporations, Google and Microsoft extol the virtues of government's leaving them unfettered, free to innovate—except when they call on government to intervene in order for them to gain a competitive advantage. But antitrust concerns were a real issue for others. The Association of National Advertisers, which represents major companies such as Procter & Gamble, petitioned Justice to block a Google/Yahoo alliance. The World Association of Newspapers, which represents eighteen thousand newspapers, urged both the Justice Department and the European Union to block the deal. This opposition unnerved Page and Brin. According to a member of Google's senior management team, the idea that Justice was more concerned about Google's becoming a monopoly than Microsoft provoked an uncomfortable discussion at a September 2008 executive committee meeting. The founders, this executive said, were "very upset" to be compared with Gates's "evil empire." They ranted about how Google was making the Web more accessible, not trying to kill competition. That the government could think they were trying to squelch search competition, or might possess too much leverage over advertisers, baffled them. They could not comprehend the anti-Google sentiment that was building.

This executive committee meeting coincided with the annual Google Zeitgeist press luncheon, and there I asked Brin and Page, "How do you feel when people accuse you of potentially doing evil?"

Not surprisingly, they didn't really answer my question. "If you look at our products, search being our most popular one," Brin said, "we don't lock anyone into search."

"The value to the world," said Page, "of having access to everything for free everywhere, all the time, really fast, without degraded service anywhere, has really been a tremendous thing."

A decade earlier, Bill Gates had felt similarly hurt that the government would call his motives into question by filing charges that Microsoft, which provided 95 percent of PC operating systems in America, was a monopoly. This blind spot to public fears, to emotion, prevented Gates from properly reading people, from anticipating the challenges that would materialize in Washington. Now Page and Brin seemed to have the same blind spot.

This emotional opaqueness was on display on the second day of the 2008 Zeitgeist. Al Gore was to conclude the conference by interviewing Page and Brin. The three men chatted on stage for a few minutes when Page interrupted to say that Brin wanted ten minutes to share something. Brin stepped to a microphone and riveted the audience for about ten minutes with a precise, impersonal account of his mother's recent diagnosis of Parkinson's disease. He explained that his wife, Anne Wojcicki, had co-founded 23andMe to study genetics, including the genetics of Parkinson's. He said the evidence of a genetic link to Parkinson's was at first slight, but studies had recently unearthed one gene, LRRK2, in particular a mutation known as G2019S, that in some ethnic groups creates a familial link through which the disease travels.

Brin said he had dug deeper, reading genetics journals, searching for pieces of DNA shared with relatives. Ultimately, he learned that he shared with his mother the G2019S mutation. He spoke as if he were talking about someone else. The implications of this finding are imprecisely understood, he said. What was clear was that he had "a markedly higher chance of developing Parkinson's in my lifetime than the average person." Sounding like a scientist, he pegged the odds "between 20 percent to 80 percent, depending on the study and how you measure it." This knowledge left him feeling "fortunate," he said; the mutation had been discovered early in his life and he could reduce the odds through exercise, certain foods, and by employing his substantial wealth to support further research. With the audience seated in stunned silence, he concluded, "That's all I wanted to say," and sat down.

Compared with Steve Jobs, who had declined to discuss his own health and issued opaque statements even as he grew visibly ill, Brin was admirably forthcoming. Yet it never seemed to occur to him to turn his attention to introducing to the audience his very pregnant, beaming wife, soon-to-be mother of a child who might very well carry that same gene. Certainly it did not seem to occur to him to display emotion, to allay the concerns his comments would arouse among Google employees or shareholders. What was billed as "a personal statement" was really a science lesson. The way Brin dealt with his DNA mirrored the way Google dealt with Washington, politics, or traditional media: just give us the facts, don't blur them by discussing your fears or feelings.

The Justice Department did finally intervene against Google, informing the company that if it did not terminate its ad sales partnership with Yahoo, it would be sued for antitrust violations, just as Microsoft had been the previous decade. Three hours before Justice was to file antitrust charges, Google dropped the deal.

Microsoft did not capture its prize, at least not through 2008. However, by the end of that year Microsoft seemed eager to return to the bargaining table, if only to purchase Yahoo's search business. Gates's company continued to lose search market share, and emerged from this battle with Yahoo looking feckless and defensive, not the posture one assumes before a foe with Napoleonic power.

In the confusion, other media companies maneuvered to achieve their own best balance of power. In tactics worthy of Metternich, Time Warner pursued simultaneous discussions with Yahoo, Microsoft, and Google about either selling off AOL or forming a partnership. The News Corporation schemed to combine with Microsoft to bid for Yahoo and, at other times, with Yahoo to block Microsoft.

Among the more interesting aspects of this drama was witnessing Microsoft cheered on as an underdog. "Microsoft," said Philippe Daumann, the CEO of Viacom, "is the one company that can most effectively challenge Google's emerging dominance." A victorious bid by Microsoft would provide advertisers with more leverage, Irwin Gotlieb said. "We're always better off with more than one strong party." He added, "The real concern is that once Google has an eighty percent market share, they can change the auction rules."

At Microsoft's annual two-day forum for advertisers on its Redmond campus in mid-May of 2008, the company's new head of advertising, Brian McAndrews, was the first to speak. He described the online advertising opportunities Microsoft was offering, and sketched for attendees Microsoft's pitch to advertisers: "We seek ongoing input from you." He did not cite Google by name, but his meaning was clear: *We seek to work with you as partners, and the other guy does not.* On the final day of the forum, Irwin Gotlieb was eating scrambled eggs at a breakfast buffet, greeting people as they came by to shake his hand or lay a palm on his shoulder. Microsoft's sales pitch, he told those who came to ask his thoughts, is not new. "They've been saying it for a while. Microsoft has never been perceived by people like us as someone who is looking to destabilize an existing business model because they feel like it." They were not vying to enter the advertising business the way others were. He, too, did not invoke Google's name, nor did he have to.

Microsoft intended to close the forum by presenting a new plan to overtake Google, a plan it privately touted as "a game changer." Company executives took care to brief people like Gotlieb beforehand, seeking not just his input but his enthusiasm for a program they hoped would attract more advertisers, more purchases, and more searches. For the unveiling of this plan, Bill Gates, who would step down the next month from his day-to-day duties at Microsoft to concentrate on the work of his foundation, appeared on stage to announce what he called "a milestone." He was tieless and jacketless, his sandy hair uncombed, and he stood at the foot of the amphitheater and described the program they called Cashback. The idea was that Microsoft would offer a cash rebate to consumers who did their searches on Microsoft and clicked to purchase products from more than seven hundred merchants, including Barnes & Noble. In essence, Microsoft was offering a reward for consumers who used its search engine rather than Google's. Yusuf Mehdi, senior vice president of strategic partnerships at Microsoft, helped shape Cashback and described it as "maybe a genius idea," a program that would transform Microsoft into "the Robin Hood of the search business." The initiative offered Google "two bad choices," he said: duplicate Cashback and lose income, or don't and lose market share.

Mehdi and Microsoft were spectacularly wrong. The program did not excite many of the ad agency people in attendance, partly because the Microsoft program already had a name in the advertising community: it was a rebate program. Perhaps it failed to excite because Microsoft didn't come up with a catchy name and a finely tuned sales pitch—"geeks acting

like marketers," muttered one attendee. In the press too, Cashback failed
to generate the headlines or excitement Microsoft anticipated. Still, the
jury was out. "If consumers perceive that the search process on Google and
Microsoft are the same," predicted Sir Martin Sorrell, "what Microsoft is
offering will be important."

By November 2008, the verdict was in. Cashback had not boosted Microsoft's search share. Google's search market share in the United States
had risen from 57.7 percent a year before to 64.1 percent. In September,
when I asked Eric Schmidt about Cashback, he could not resist: "All
attempts by Microsoft to give people back money they paid them is great!"
By January 2009, the two executives who headed Microsoft's advertising
efforts, Brian McAndrews and Kevin Johnson, would depart.

Meanwhile, Sorrell, whose WPP steers an annual total of between five
hundred million and eight hundred million dollars of his clients' advertising dollars to Google, grew more agitated. What enraged him, he said on
a panel at the Cannes International Advertising confab in June, was that
Google was now reaching out and talking to his ad agency clients directly,
something he claimed Google had vowed not to do. In WPP's annual report, Sorrell noted that although WPP and the next three largest marketing
companies combined had 50 percent more revenues than Google, their
combined market value was 75 percent less. He expressed hope that Google
was now working "to develop the constructive side of our relationship."

Had he attended Google's 2008 national sales conference, held June 11
and 12 at San Franciso's Hilton Hotel, he would have been more alarmed.
In the main ballroom, Eric Schmidt and Tim Armstrong were onstage.
Below them sat a Google sales force of fifteen hundred people, one-third
of whom had been hired in the past year. Why did Google need such an
army of salespeople? "Because our customers must talk to someone at
Google," Schmidt said.

Many of these new Googlers were account executives, like the people
who work for Sorrell or Gotlieb. And their mission, Schmidt emphasized
in his remarks, was to share with advertisers the targeting techniques that
made search advertising a rousing success. Online, he said, Google was
pouring engineering resources into making itself the leader in display ad-

vertising on YouTube. In traditional television, he said, they started by "reaching into the long tail" and he expected that "over a five- to ten-year period . . . we'll become a very significant player in traditional television because of our targeting. The same thing when you look at radio or print." Consumers of traditional media, he continued, "are scared. They're scared of what they're reading in the paper. They're scared about what's happening in their company. You show up and you offer a new message, a message of hope, a message of change and opportunity."

Page and Brin showed up unannounced, and Schmidt spontaneously invited them to join him onstage. The troika sat in oversized armchairs and had a lighthearted colloquy before turning to the audience for questions. The first two were from a sales manager named Seth Barron, and both concerned missing pieces in Google's effort: "How do we make it easier for agencies to work with us?" he asked first. It was a question that would have pleased Sorrell. The second question would not: "What resources do we need to be able to effectively compete for deals and eventually do bigger and better deals with companies like the Procter & Gambles and Mars of this world?"

"Today," said Schmidt, "we lack the tools. We've identified this as a big hole in our strategy, and we're either going to build them or buy them."

"The piece that is missing is production," said Barron. "The creative execution, the operational execution—those are the factors where we stumble today, and where our competition has world class solutions." Later, Schmidt said that the "competition" Barron referred to was Yahoo and Microsoft and display advertising. But these are not the companies that produce "world-class solutions" to the puzzles of advertising. The true answer is probably that Google's real "competition" is WPP and GroupM and their peers—the biggest players in the business of advertising.

THERE ARE THOSE WHO ASSUME Google has a master plan for world conquest, as Napoléon did. By early 2008, it was not unusual to encounter a traditional media executive who at the end of an interview whispered, "Have you read Stephen Arnold's study on what Google is really up to?"

Stephen E. Arnold heads a consulting firm, Arnold Information Technology, and starting in 2002 he and a team of researchers spent five years digging into Google's various patents, algorithms, and SEC filings. Then, for a hefty but undisclosed fee, he sold his voluminous report to various media companies. The title of the report, "Google Version 2.0: The Calculating Predator," telegraphs Arnold's stark conclusion:

> Analyzing "the Google" in a deliberate and focused way, we find that while Google may have started out to "do no evil," it has, to some, morphed from a friendly search engine into something more ominous. Googzilla, fueled by technical prowess, is now on the move.

Where is it moving? The gruff Arnold, who responded to a phone call but refused to speak on the record to anyone who was not paying him, in his book often drops the scientific method in favor of a more fevered tone. Conjuring a monster, he repeatedly refers to the company as "Googzilla," and writes that "Google stalks a market . . . then strikes quickly and in a cold-blooded way." Behind Google's free food and volleyball games he sniffs a public relations scheme to "misdirect attention. Like a good magician, Google is able to get its audience of competitors and financial analysts to look one way." Meanwhile, "Googzilla is voracious, and it will consume companies presently unaware they are the equivalent of a free-range chicken burrito. . . ."

Arnold and his researchers have uncovered enough information from their study of Google's patents and algorithms to terrify media companies. As Wal-Mart reshaped retailing, Google, he believes, aims to become a digital Wal-Mart, an online shopping powerhouse that allows consumers to shop for the best price, an essential middleman that offers efficiency and data to advertisers, and shovels revenues to Web sites and services to merchants, including back-office computers that find the quickest and cheapest way to reroute their delivery trucks.

The world would have been better served if its leaders had been more paranoid in the 1930s; media companies would be better served if they were less paranoid and defensive today. If Google is destroying or weakening old business models, it is because the Internet inevitably destroys old ways of doing things, spurs "creative destruction." This does not mean that Google is not ambitious to grow, and will not grow at the expense of others.

But the rewards, and the pain, are unavoidable. When Google Earth started displaying paintings from the Prado in Madrid, allowing users to zoom in and see the art as an up-close digital photo, it was giving many people access to art they would never see, granting them the time to study paintings that security guards in the bustling museum would never allow them. This was a wonderful opportunity to extend the public's appreciation of great art. But perhaps we'll learn that it wasn't so wonderful for the museum's box office. Just as the invention of the telephone crushed the telegraph, so motion pictures crippled vaudeville, television eclipsed radio, cable weakened broadcasting, and iTunes shattered CD music album sales. In some cases, new technologies brought new opportunities. The movie studios, after huffing about television, belatedly discovered a lucrative new platform to sell their movies. Exposure on YouTube has broadened the audience for *Saturday Night Live*. If advertisers can sell their ads more cheaply and better target them through Google, should they fret that they are harming Irwin Gotlieb's business? What we don't know is whether the new digital distribution systems will generate sufficient revenue to adequately pay content providers.

David L. Calhoun spent his career at General Electric, where he rose to vice chairman. He left to become chairman and CEO of The Nielsen Company in 2006. When Calhoun joined, Nielsen had long dominated the audience measurement field but was facing a challenge from digital technology, including Google's. He believes media company executives spend too much time wailing about disintermediation. He prefers the word "*reintermediate,*" because it suggests a company more focused on offense than defense. The companies that "lean in," he said, are those that embrace change; those who "lean out," resist it. Companies that concentrate on defense "are frozen," he said. "If Google's looking at you, you look like an iceberg. And Google is looking at everybody."

He does not impute sinister motives to Google, though he treats it like a frenemy: "I genuinely think they just want to empower the consumer. Anything that gets in the way, that blocks a perfectly efficient market, is fair game. If there is a moment they can do something to make the consumer more efficient, they will. And you should know that. But they don't lie, they don't cheat, they don't give head fakes." Calhoun seeks to collaborate with Google as well as compete, and in 2007 he entered into a partnership to work with Google TV Ads to provide the demographic data that digital set-top boxes do not now yield.

Of course Google is a frenemy to most media companies. Like all companies, Google wants to grow, and growth usually comes from taking a slice of someone else's business. Because engineers excel at finding efficiencies in the digital world, Google can often offer a more cost-effective solution than companies less focused on engineering. And with 20 percent of their time to concoct new solutions, Google's engineers are constantly dreaming up ideas—like the young engineer who entered Marissa Mayer's office in the fall of 2008.

Mayer has one of the most important jobs at Google: to ensure that all Google products are simple and easy for users. She also has an almost photographic memory, the absolute trust of the founders, and joined Google when it was just a year old, so her memory becomes a virtual library of what has worked and what has not, what the founders would and would not want. Mayer sets aside regular open office hours to encourage Google engineers to stop in and describe the 20 percent projects they are working on; it is where they receive her encouragement, or discouragement. On that fall day, a young engineer sat beside her desk and described the device he was working on to search television digital video recorders. He wanted to know two things. Should he develop this as open-source software that others outside Google could tinker with and improve. (Yes.) Second, he needed clarification about something Larry Page had said when he broached the idea at an engineering meeting. Page, who like Brin doesn't often watch television, expressed impatience with the idea of still another device in the home. Page told the engineer he was thinking too narrowly. The only useful device, he said, would be hardware or software that would allow Google to sell new forms of advertising on any device in the home, from DVRs to TVs to computers. The engineer came to Mayer's office to better understand the thinking of the founders. The project was code-named Mosaic, and would let Google partner and share ad revenues with cable or telephone companies.

In Google's way of looking at the world, she explained, any product that simplifies a task for consumers better delivers "the world's information" to them. Which is another way of saying: Google engineers should imagine that search can be anything that makes a current system more efficient. Searching for a better way to display ads or a better advertising rate—or a better alternate energy source to reduce costs—are forms of search.

The answer is consonant with the Google culture. Understand this Google bias and you'll better understand why it is a wave-generating company that other media companies ride, crash into, or are submerged by.

"I think they're naïve, not evil," said CBS's Quincy Smith. He said his friend Marc Andreessen thinks he's naïve to be so trusting. But Smith doesn't subscribe to a conspiracy theory because "I don't think anybody can be that smart." Not that he'd allow Google to take over CBS's ad sales function—"That would be letting the fox in the henhouse," he said. However, having marinated in Silicon Valley for most of his professional life, Smith approaches Google as a potential partner, not adversary. He wants CBS to play offense. Pacing the floor of his new Menlo Park office, he said that media companies fail to understand that Google is a platform. "CBS has sixty-five thousand advertisers, and only fifteen thousand are core advertisers. Google has millions of advertisers." By placing two- or three-minute clips on YouTube, CBS can sell advertising off those clips. Smith doesn't believe Google is a content competitor. He does believe that the more CBS places its content on Internet platforms, "the less chance there is for piracy"; a two-minute *CSI* clip on YouTube watched by two million people is a fantastic way to enlarge *CSI*'s audience. He is encouraged that CBS CEO Les Moonves wants CBS to play offense. Smith, however, was mindful that he was now a member of the broadcast fraternity—and presumably, though he didn't say it, that his controlling shareholder was Sumner Redstone. "My objective is to be a little bit ahead of the pack, not a lot," he said.

Eric Schmidt, who admitted in September 2007 that relations with traditional media companies were frosty, was more encouraged in September
2008. "The CBS deal is one" example of détente, he said. "We've done a
series of deals. They are slowly happening." Of course, he added, "it would
be much better if I could point to a billion-dollar new revenue stream." To
try to calm advertising agency fears, Google established a forty-person
team to visit agencies and assure them that Google was not a competitor,
just another company that had products their clients would want to use
and that could share valuable customer data with them.

To ease the fears of content providers, Google turned to David Eun, vice
president of strategic partnerships. A soft-spoken man who displays few
rough edges and who once served as a senior executive at Time Warner and
NBC, Eun today supervises a staff of about two hundred employees out of
New York. He and his partnership team made some deals for YouTube.
HBO and Showtime agreed to run a handful of their full programs on
YouTube, accompanied by ads; MGM licensed some of its movies, and
music companies supplied videos. With a new antipiracy technology they
called the Video Identification System (VID), YouTube has now archived
the reference file numbers for companies' content and set its computers to
scan all uploaded material to determine whether numbers match. If they
do, content companies are offered three choices: they can have YouTube
take the clip down; let it run and monitor audience reaction; or sell ads
against it, as CBS agreed to do in late 2008. David Eun pushed for the third
option because he believes content companies, in addition to selling ads off
this content, can collect valuable data. "The audience is telling you what
they like," he said. YouTube can monitor what content is uploaded and
shared with friends, how much time users watch it, or what they click on.
"These are like the presidents of your fan clubs. Would you arrest the president of your fan club?

"The headline here," said Eun, "is that there has been a dramatic shift"
in traditional media's attitude toward YouTube. He singled out Quincy
Smith as "one of the few people who seems to truly understand so-called
new media versus traditional media."

Eun made a larger point about how very different this new medium really is, how control has shifted to users. In the digital world, advertising is not locked into a time and space. Ads are interactive, allowing users to click to remove them from the screen or to fill the screen, to treat them as information and go deeper to learn more and make a purchase, or to forward the ad to a friend. "Traditional media was about bringing the audience to where you decided the content was going to be," said Eun. Media companies would announce when a movie would open, a DVD would go on sale, a record would be released, a show would be scheduled on television, a book published. "It was about control. This is no criticism. That was the business. They created a huge, multibillion-dollar business. In this medium, the new media, it is not about bringing the audience to where the content is. It's about taking the content to where the audiences are. And the audiences are all over the Web." Not just YouTube but thousands of sites become potential platforms.

Because this is a very different model than traditional media is accustomed to, and because they have legitimate concerns about giving content away cheaply, "No one wants to be the first to jump into the pool, or be the last," said a Google executive. The old media companies "are all clumped together. And if one breaks out—as Bob Iger did when he put Disney content on iTunes—then all follow. It is an industry that follows."

Google did achieve a dramatic breakthrough when, in October 2008, it reached an accord with the U.S. publishing industry. The industry agreed to drop its lawsuit, subject to approval from the court; and Google agreed to pay $125 million to settle earlier copyright infringement claims, to reimburse publishers' and authors' legal fees, and to establish a system that will permit publishers and authors to register their books and receive a payment when these are used online. Individuals or institutions will be able to read up to 20 percent of out-of-print but copyrighted books, and either purchase digital copies or search them using Google, and publishers and authors will receive 63 percent of any sales or ad revenues, with Google taking the rest. Libraries will be able to display these digital copies for free; colleges and universities will, for a subscription fee, allow students to retrieve books online. Book titles still in print would be available to be purchased or searched, but only if approved by author and publisher. At the time of the agreement, Google Book Search had already scanned seven million of the estimated twenty million books that have ever been published. By winter, Brin said, Google was "able to search the full text of almost ten million books."

There are two potentially momentous shifts here: First, Google had conceded it must pay for some content. And second, Google was not relying on a promise of advertising revenues to reach an agreement; rather, it agreed to an up-front compensation formula of a sort it had refused to make with other traditional media companies, with the exception of the Associated Press and some wire services. "It's a new model for us," admitted Google's chief legal officer, David Drummond.

This new model was lavishly praised by authors and publishers, but it raised new questions. Was Google going to enter the online book-selling business, competing against an early investor, Amazon's Jeff Bezos? With Microsoft dropping its book search project and no other deep-pocketed competitor jumping in, did the agreement concentrate too much informational power in the hands of a single company? Did Google have the right, as it claimed, to sell digital copies of books whose copyright had expired? If it is true—as the Internet Archive, a competitive book digitizer, claims—that the settlement grants Google immunity from copyright infringement, will the courts permit this? What of so-called orphaned books, those whose copyright owners can't be identified—does Google, as it claims, get to own the digital rights? Will there be any regulation of the prices Google may charge libraries and colleges for access to digitized books? What will be the outcome of new lawsuits challenging this and other aspects of the settlement? And what impact would the publishing accord have on the Viacom lawsuit and Google's dealings with other media companies seeking compensation for their content?

Viacom was quick to link the book copyright settlement with its own lawsuit. In a public statement released the same day, Viacom said: "It is unfortunate that the publishers had to spend years, and millions of dollars, for Google to honor that [copyright] principle. We hope that Google avoids the wasted effort and comes more quickly to respect movies and television programming." Drummond insisted that his company has never favored free content and has not altered its posture: "There is a difference in wanting to push for access, and wanting to push for free access. There are some folks on the Web who think you should get access to copyrighted material for free. We don't." Fair use to Google, he said, was to create a card catalogue to open new sources of information—"allowing books to be discovered, not consumed." The book settlement had no impact on the Viacom lawsuit, he added. "The litigation is in full swing."

Why not offer Viacom compensation for their content, as Google has now done with publishers and did earlier with revenue guarantees to AOL and MySpace? Drummond does not oppose an up-front payment but wouldn't agree to the amount Viacom sought. "A lot has to do with how much they want. They want a lot more, in my perception, than the monetization potential of the content." Having guaranteed MySpace a total of $900 million in ad revenues over several years, and having fallen short of that guarantee, he said of guarantees, "We don't do them as much as we did before." By the end of 2008, however, Google acknowledged it had a total of $1.03 billion of "noncancelable" guaranteed minimum revenue share commitments through 2012. It was widely expected that Google would cancel, or curb, many of those agreements when the contract period expires.

Google at first said it was not in competition with Amazon to sell hardcover copies, because most of the books they want to sell online are out of print. "We are unlocking access to millions and millions of books," Drummond said. But of course, they could be in competition with Amazon—or any distributor—to sell electronic books. (In May 2009, Google announced it would compete to sell e-books.)

Might the book settlement apply to newspapers and open a vein of revenue for them? Drummond didn't think so: "For news, it's a little different. News has to be current. It doesn't have the same shelf life as a book. We are thinking deeply about how to help. Now we send newspapers traffic." He knows newspapers want more, but he said Google has found "no silver bullet yet."

—————

NOR, BY THE END OF 2008, had traditional media companies found the silver bullet. With some exceptions—the thriving worldwide game business being one—most media businesses seemed to be falling off a cliff. Their fall preceded the worldwide recession that struck like a category five hurricane in the last half of the year. The dismal headlines were not pretty.

By the end of 2008, daily newspaper ad revenues dropped 17.7 percent, about double the 9 percent decline of the previous year; average daily newspaper circulation among 395 dailies dropped 7.1 percent.

Magazine advertising pages plunged 11.7 percent in 2008, fell 26 percent in the first quarter of 2009, and were projected to fall 10.9 percent for the year.

The number of viewers tuning to prime-time network shows dropped almost 10 percent, and according to Nielsen, this figure includes viewers who later watch the shows on DVRs. Broadcast network television advertising fell 3.5 percent.

Broadcast radio advertising fell 9.4 percent.

Aside from Internet advertising, whose growth rate dipped in 2008 but still rose 10.6 percent, according to Nielsen the only medium to experience ad revenue growth in 2008 was cable television, rising 7.8 percent.

Record album sales dropped 14 percent.

The number of people going to movie theaters dipped, but thanks to an increase in ticket prices, box office revenues rose by 2 percent. DVD sales, which had been a revenue gusher, dipped to their lowest level in five years.

Book sales of about three billion books fell 2.8 percent, according to the Association of American Publishers (1.5 percent, according to the annual report from Book Industry Trends). And although electronic book sales climbed 7 percent to $113 million, this was a tiny percentage of the just over $11 billion generated by adult books.

Advertising spending in the United States was flat in 2008 at about $162 billion, and was projected by GroupM to fall by 8 percent in 2009. Worldwide advertising spending of about $450 billion grew just 1 percent in 2008 and was projected to fall by almost 7 percent in 2009, according to ZenithOptimedia, the media-buying arm of Publicis, the world's fourth largest advertising/marketing company. Although estimates of ad spending differ, the other major firms predicted similar drop-offs. Total marketing spending—direct mail, event marketing, public relations, etcetera—dropped 1.7 percent in 2008.

In a December 2008 report, Morgan Stanley's Mary Meeker produced a chart that should alarm traditional media. Titled "Media Time Spent vs. Ad Spend Out of Whack," the chart reveals that advertising expenditures don't conform to where consumers spend their time. Newspapers, for example, consume 8 percent of our time, yet receive 20 percent of advertising dollars. By comparison, the Internet garners 29 percent of our time, yet attracts just 8 percent of advertising dollars. At some point, those ad dollars will shift away from traditional media, probably dramatically. Whether or not one factors in the most severe recession to strike the United States since the thirties, change was slamming into traditional media with new ferocity. Unlike the fog in Carl Sandburg's famous poem, it did not creep in "on little cat feet."

CHAPTER FOURTEEN

Happy Birthday

(2008-2009)

I n September 2008, Google was ten years old, which in Internet years virtually qualifies it for senior citizenship. Yet the company did not slow down and move on "little cat feet." Announcements of fresh initiatives kept rolling out.

In the second half of the year, it was announced that the Google Content Network would employ its AdSense program to identify video-hosting Web sites and sell syndicated programs to them. The first show was a new animation series, *Cartoon Cavalcade of Comedy,* created by Seth MacFarlane, whose credits include *Family Guy,* a hit comedy show on Fox. There was Google Ad Planner, which provides advertisers with digital data free of charge to identify the Web sites their desired audience visits. There was the exchange of employees between Google and Procter & Gamble, with P&G saying it hoped to better understand how its present and future customers use the Internet and Google not saying that it hoped to snare a bigger slice of P&G's $8.7 billion ad budget.

There was Google Maps for transit, an online navigation tool to allow riders to figure out subway routes in New York City and other metropolitan areas, and an announcement that Google News would pay to digitize newspaper archives, place ads next to the search results, and share any revenues with the publications. There was a new partnership with General Electric to improve the efficiency of the electric grid; new investments were made in renewable energy that would be cheaper, and cleaner, than coal.

Larry Page, usually parsimonious with his public appearances, mounted a campaign of speeches to persuade the FCC to set aside an unused block of the radio spectrum (known as white space) for wireless devices, including Wi-Fi and other high-speed wireless connections to the Internet. Broadcasters and Broadway theater owners protested that the use of that spectrum by these devices might interfere with broadcast signals and wireless microphones in theaters. The FCC voted 5 to 0 to open the spectrum. Google launched Knol, a searchable user-edited encyclopedia, to compete with Wikipedia; Google strayed still deeper into content by signing up Michael Davies, creator of *Who Wants to Be a Millionaire,* to produce an entertainment-news show called *Poptub,* to be distributed on YouTube and the Google Content Network.

David Calhoun of Nielsen said Google could no longer claim to be a digital Switzerland. "YouTube crossed the line by a mile. YouTube's audience competes with other content." If Google hopes to sell display advertising, as it does on YouTube, Terry Semel believes it will have to own content. User-generated content on YouTube "does not feel safe" to advertisers, he reasoned, and to lure ads Google will need to own attractive content in order to attract advertisers.

Eric Schmidt, when asked if Google had gone into the content business, split hairs, saying that YouTube and the Google Content Network were merely "hosts" of the content, "not authors." This is akin to saying that ABC merely "hosts" the programs it chooses to pay for and air. Schmidt's distinction ignores another salient fact: the more traffic his sites generate, the more data Google gets, and the more dollars it receives for its ads.

And what about Knol?

"Knol is an example of something right on the edge," he conceded. (Not that Knol, which debuted in July 2008, posed a serious threat to Wikipedia. By the following January, it had just a hundred thousand entries and had relatively few page views.)

With all these new initiatives, the opportunity Schmidt was most excited about in late 2008 was cloud computing. It was an idea that had animated him since his days at Sun, when he promoted what was called "the network is the computer." Now, he said, the shift from the PC to the Web was "the defining technological shift of our generation." The excess capacity of Google's data centers, and the variety of applications the company had developed—Gmail; Google Earth; Google Maps; Google Scholar; Google Finance; Google Product Search; Google Calendar; Google Desktop to search all text on a personal computer; Google Docs to do all word process-ing, spreadsheets, and presentations—offered Google enormous growth opportunities. "Eventually, this will be a very large source of revenue for our company," he said, citing a professor in Africa who had told him his schools had no textbooks but as a substitute they used Google search. He was aware that South Korea, which has the world's highest broadband penetration, was already eliminating textbooks and downloading books to laptops.

A Google-invented browser, dubbed Chrome, would provide access to all the applications. Because Google is not in the packaged software busi-ness, all of its applications live in the browser. With billions of people around the world on the Internet, increasingly a browser will become their operating system, the host for all applications. "Everything we do is running on the Web platform," Page told reporters on the day Chrome was announced. "It's very important to us that that works well." When Brin, who arrived at the press conference wearing bright red Crocs, was asked whether Chrome was aimed at Microsoft, he said: "We don't spend our time thinking about Microsoft." In truth, Google couldn't abide being dependent on Microsoft's Internet Explorer, which then had a 72 percent browser market share. Schmidt described Chrome as "the most important product" Google launched in 2008. "The reason is that the browser, like our proposed Yahoo deal, has a defensive as well as an offensive component." Defensively, he said Internet Explorer's dominant position "allows Microsoft to make arbitrary extensions to the browser and close off the Internet"; Chrome would help Google defend against such a move. The offense comes from speed and flexibility. Schmidt maintains that Chrome is faster and, as an open-source browser, will encourage developers to compete to produce innovative applications. Chrome also grants Google "a platform on which to build better apps" and "to collect more data." The data is important, for browsers produce the cookies that track what users do online. Despite its importance to Schmidt, by mid-2009, the Chrome browser was still not available to Mac or Linux users.

Google introduced another major product—Android—in 2008. First announced in late 2007, Android was Google's free, open-source operating system for smart phones. It promised new profits, and new conflicts. With three times as many mobile devices in the world as PCs, Google had ample incentive to jump into this market. They did not fail to notice when Steve Jobs stood up at Macworld in January 2008 and said that four million iPhones had been sold in the United States in the first six months, giving Apple a market share of 19 percent. Since the first 3G phones were sold in July 2008, over the next five months a total of nearly ten thousand applications—among them games and travel and book and finance and social network sites—had appeared for the phone, three quarters of them available to users only for a fee. Every day, Americans send *1.6 billion* text messages on their mobile phones, and 10 percent of Verizon's customers have replaced their wired telephone with a mobile phone, a number that CEO Ivan Seidenberg predicted would soon double. Because his customers use so many more services on a mobile device, including text messages and Internet access, the average monthly Verizon wireless bill is fifty-two dollars, about fifteen dollars more than the average landline bill. In the United States, AT&T and Verizon were each ringing up revenues of more than a hundred billion dollars in 2008.

If the Android phone (as with Microsoft's Cashback, geeks are not always deft with names) sells well, Google will have some leverage over the telephone companies that sell the hardware and control distribution. And it would ensure that Google's applications, including text and voice search, would be featured. The Android also opens up new frontiers for search; as Brin noted in the spring of 2009, "almost a third of all Google searches in Japan are coming from mobile devices." Smart phones will yield more data for Google. And they will allow Google to explore ads or services on these devices to generate revenues.

Schmidt, however, was dubious about how Google would monetize Android: "I would love to argue that mobile is the next business for us. I'm not sure it is." Among the reasons for his caution were that neither of the dominant phone companies was eager to jump into bed with Google. AT&T already had a deal with Apple, and Verizon was standoffish. "We're watching it," said Verizon's Ivan Seidenberg, who added, "We said we'd be willing to consider something like that"—an open-source Android— but he said he was worried more about maintaining the quality of the Verizon system. "We want an open network where we can ensure quality," he said.

"Google's vision of Android is Microsoft's vision of owning the operat- ing system in every PC," Seidenberg said. "Guys like me want to make sure that there is a distribution of platforms and devices. Is it in Google's interest to disintermediate us? Yeah." He let his voice trail off, not wanting to en- gage in verbal warfare. But he said his job is to "make sure we are never out-positioned," never a "captive." Neither Seidenberg's power nor Schmidt's skepticism deterred Google from plunging ahead. (In late 2008, T-Mobile ordered two million units in the hope that its Google-powered smart phone could rival iPhone.)

If mobile's growth prospects are clear, the data questions are not. Do companies have the right to own, or share, data about their users? Who would own the data, the phone company or Google? Is there a privacy line they cannot cross? Many digital companies and advertisers agree with IAC/ InterActiveCorp CEO Barry Diller that privacy is overrated. "Privacy is a much noisier issue than it is for people," he said. Of course, when it suited Diller's interests to position his Ask.com search engine as superior to Google's, his company took out full-page advertisements declaring that its AskEraser would purge cookies of data and Google would not. But surveys suggest that the public disagrees with Diller. A March 2008 poll of one thousand Americans by TRUSTe, an organization that monitors privacy practices on the Web, found that 90 percent thought online privacy was a "really" or "somewhat" important issue, and only 28 percent said they were comfortable with behavioral targeting techniques. Even if the survey was flawed—surely the organization that conducted it had a rooting interest in the outcome—in this instance, Google seemed more attuned to the public's feelings; in March 2009 the company announced that it would allow users to preview and edit the data it had gathered on them and would, as Yahoo has done, allow them to opt out. Because users are automatically opted in, and opting out requires that the user go through an esoteric process of clicks, Google's announcement did not represent a major policy switch. Google demonstrated this when it was among the first major companies to announce that it would employ behavioral targeting, showing ads to users based on their prior activities online. The fact that Google would couple such a new transparency policy with its new behavioral targeting efforts is another reminder that privacy questions will continue to hover like a Predator drone, capable of firing a missile that can destroy the trust companies require to serve as trustees for personal data.

Alternatively, if the public is truly less concerned with privacy questions and more interested in trading data for, say, a subsidized service, or is more interested in the trivial, as the late scholar Neil Postman believed, then privacy will be the least of our issues. A former student of Marshall McLuhan's, Postman taught at NYU for more than four decades and authored a variety of important books, the best-known of which was *Amusing Ourselves to Death*. In that book he argued that the real threat was not the one described in *1984* but one contained in an earlier book, Aldous Huxley's *Brave New World*.

> Contrary to common belief even among the educated, Huxley and Orwell did not prophesy the same thing. Orwell warns that we will be overcome by an externally imposed oppression. But in Huxley's vision, no Big Brother is required to deprive people of their autonomy, maturity

and history. As he saw it, people will come to love their oppression, to adore the technologies that undo their capacities to think. . . . Orwell feared those who would deprive us of information. Huxley feared those who would give us so much that we would be reduced to passivity and egoism.

This much is certain: neither concerns over privacy nor the issues raised by Postman have slowed the ascendance of smart phones. The attraction is undeniable. They are portable and perform varied functions, including playing movies, music, and games. They enable employees to work from more than one location. They can function just as a desktop or laptop does. They can serve as a key to unlock a car or as an ID at an airport or bank, or become a universal remote for a TV. Third World countries that cannot afford a fiber infrastructure can build a low-cost wireless infrastructure that connects classrooms to libraries, individuals or health care facilities to medical expertise.

The question, of course, is how to monetize not just the hardware but also the services and applications. That's where advertising comes in. Smart phones provide advertisers with precision targeting, reaching individuals they know are ready to purchase a car and are close to an auto dealer. Irwin Gotlieb, whose demeanor is normally subdued and steady, could barely contain his excitement as he sat in his office in the Garment District and described the Brave New World he envisioned. "It's a totally different kind of advertising," he said. "You're in Tokyo. It's noon. The population density is scary. You have forty-five minutes for lunch, and you go rushing out of your building and already there's limited restaurant space. So you flip your phone open and up come six restaurants that have seating availability in the next ten minutes. You click on the restaurant you want to go to, telling them you need three seats, and the table is held for you. Is that advertising? Not the way you and I think of a thirty-second spot. But you better believe that restaurant is paying for it. Or it's going to be built into the bill."

He took a sip from his second cup of tea. "Let's take another example," he continued. "I'm standing on Fifth Avenue and I point my phone at a building and on my screen up comes the directory for that building, all the businesses in the building. Some of them are retailers. If I click on a retailer, I may get promotional offers. That's an ad? There are revenue opportunities there. It's a service." He paused again, this time to talk about the power of the tiny handheld device: "The average phone today has more computing capacity, and more storage capacity, than the average set-top box does. They are powerful computers."

The consumer has the power to make choices, but Irwin Gotlieb envisions that he will help steer the consumer to those choices and cash in on them. And if Gotlieb were to deliver the services, Google and Verizon would be excited by the prospect of serving as his facilitator. And maybe one day taking over the delivery of those services themselves.

THERE WAS, HOWEVER, a more pressing concern for the media: the colossal economic recession that struck in the second half of 2008. With advertising and other revenues plummeting, traditional media businesses accelerated their cost cutting. With less revenue and sinking market values, debt obligations became ticking bombs. For the Tribune Company and other newspapers, that bomb exploded. Faced with end-of-year debt obligations, Sumner Redstone was compelled to frantically sell Viacom and CBS shares and to propose the sale of National Amusements, his movie theater chain. He has since vowed not to cede control of his media empire, and renegotiated one of his debt obligations, but by the summer of 2009 it was still not certain he would eventually succeed. The recession pinned down most traditional media companies, hampering their ability to write the next chapter. Their core businesses were declining. It was tough for them to sell assets. They lacked resources to acquire new media ventures, and debt obligations loomed.

The gloom extended to Silicon Valley; at the November 2008 Web 2.0 Summit in San Francisco, there was clearly a dark cloud overhead. Welcoming the thousand attendees, the popular Tim O'Reilly, whose O'Reilly

Media cosponsors this annual event, appealed to the evangelical heart that beats in the Valley. Borrowing a campaign slogan from Barack Obama, he began his presentation by chanting, "Yes we can! Yes we can!" He paused, then continued, "It's true in the campaign! And it's true in Silicon Valley!" But even this enthusiasm couldn't appreciably lighten the mood. O'Reilly conceded that "these are tough times." A number of other speakers agreed, including John Doerr. In his radio announcer's voice, Doerr bellowed that venture capital funding would fall from thirty-seven billion dollars in 2007 to ten billion or even as little as five billion in 2009. "Google is not going to buy these Internet start-ups now," he said, and no one else would either. He advised the executives in the hall to make cuts, to make sure they have eighteen months of cash on hand (and the rest in Treasury bills), to renegotiate contracts, and to be honest with employees but "keep up their hope."

There were some at this conference, like Mary Meeker, whose optimism about the Web was unwavering. Although Meeker gave an unremittingly bleak analysis of the American economy at large, she offered a euphoric analysis of the tech world's "opportunities," expressing her faith that YouTube would be able to make the abundant ad sales that had so far eluded them.

To Doerr and others in the Valley, Meeker's optimism seemed at odds with the facts on the ground. Layoffs spread even here, fueling talk of another dot-com bust. Intel and Cisco would report that their sales were heading south. Nokia predicted that global mobile phone sales would fall 10 precent in 2009, reversing a long trend. With PC sales slumping, Microsoft would cut five thousand jobs, 5 percent of its work force. Twitter, which attracts users but not yet profits, pared employees and installed a new CEO. Sequoia Capital, the venture capital firm that backed Google and Yahoo, convened a fall meeting of the Valley companies it was supporting and began its presentation with a slide that read, "RIP good times." Unless the start-ups had a pool of venture capital and other monies, as Facebook, Linkedin, and Twitter did, investors had become less enamored of the Google mantra: The rise of Google had contributed to another article of faith in the Valley: Information wants to be free, and advertising would pay for it. The recession would, slowly, teach that the new media had fallen into an old trap of relying on a single source of revenue, advertising.

Where once optimism had ruled, rancor and incivility began to rear their ugly heads. Michael Arrington, the editor of TechCrunch.com, an influential arbiter of technology, began to feel firsthand the desperation of tech employees or investors who felt their companies had been victimized by bad press. He wrote a blog in January 2009 about an encounter he had had in Munich. As he was leaving a conference, a stranger "walked up to me and quite deliberately spat in my face." He did not know why. All he knew was that the environment had become rancid: "I can't say my job is much fun anymore. Start-ups that don't get the coverage they want, and competing journalists and bloggers tend to accuse us of the most ridiculous things. . . . On any given day, when I care to look, dozens of highly negative comments are made about me, TechCrunch, or one of our employees in our comments, on Twitter, or on blogs or other sites. Some of these are appropriately critical comments on things we can be doing better. But the majority of comments are among the more horrible things I can imagine a human being to say."

Worse, he told of how "an off-balance individual threatened to kill me and my family." Because the individual had a felony record and carried a gun, Arrington hired a personal security team at a daily cost of two thousand dollars. He hid out at his parents' house. "I write about technology start-ups and news," Arrington wrote. "In any sane world that shouldn't make me someone who has to deal with death threats and being spat on. It shouldn't require me to absorb more verbal abuse than a human being can realistically deal with." To "get a better perspective on what I'm spending my life doing," Arrington said he would take a month off.

GOOGLE WAS NOT IMMUNE to the downturn. Signs of the downturn were apparent on Google search. During the fall, *travel* was no longer among the most popular search words or phrases, but *home safes* was; by early 2009, searches for *bankruptcy* had jumped 52 percent. The "most significant thing that happened at Google" in the past six months, Bill Campbell said in November 2008, "was the realization that there was a flattening of the business." This realization, he said, was driven by Schmidt, who began reviewing "expenses relative to revenue every Monday." Another senior executive at Google credited not Schmidt but the new senior vice president and chief financial officer, Patrick Pichette, "for forcing, for the first time, the company to focus on priorities" and to "allocate capital based on whether there are returns." The founders' push to expand into a multitude of businesses was, for the first time, subjected to a budget analysis and scaled back, this executive said. "While Google's success is hard to dispute, I don't think they are a particularly well-managed company," Mary Meeker said. "Part of the problem was that Larry and Sergey didn't need to care about the numbers because growth was so steady and the company's competitive position was so strong they didn't feel they had to. The downturn in the economy gave the new CFO help in imposing some cost discipline."

Pichette had come over from Canada's foremost telephone company, Bell Canada, where he was credited with slashing two billion dollars from its operating costs. A thin man of modest height, he comes to work lugging a backpack and wearing jeans, a button-down shirt with sleeves rolled up, and a ready smile. Told that he has come to Google at a bad time, he quickly disagrees. "You can argue that I came at a good time," he said. "When everything runs well and works perfectly, at least according to financial results, you don't take the time to ask tougher questions because you don't have to. When you're growing so fast that you're running out of desks, if you talked to people about waste and inefficiencies they wouldn't have listened to you. It would have been the wrong question to ask at that time."

In a March 2009 Morgan Stanley conference interview with Mary Meeker, Eric Schmidt said, "Patrick is particularly good at business reviews, so we've been going through systematically business after business. In our hypergrowth period, we did not have the necessary systems in place. . . . " Pichette was well rewarded; he received a bonus for 2008 of $1.2 million, though he had only worked six months; it was the highest bonus granted by Google. (Schmidt and the founders, as is their custom, take no bonus.) For the first time, Google was contracting. It slowed its hiring, adding only 99 employees in the fourth quarter of 2008, fewer than it added in a week at the start of the year, bringing its employment total at the end of 2008 to 20,222. It laid off some of its 10,000 outside contract workers, sliced 300 jobs at DoubleClick, reduced by one-quarter its 400 job recruiters, and scaled back some of its engineering teams. Taking a closer look at management, Google decided that management was not Dr. Larry Brilliant's forte, and gave him a new title as chief philanthropic evangelist, replacing him with Megan Smith, who would retain her position as vice president for new business development. It delayed the opening of its Oklahoma data center by eighteen months, and closed its office outside Phoenix, which had two dozen full-time employees. After Pichette discovered that in some cafeterias—most buildings have one—a third of the food was thrown out at the end of each day, cafeteria hours were reduced and menus pared. Google also curbed some free services and, according to a longtime executive, engaged in a "hot debate" over whether to continue to offer water in plastic bottles or switch to less expensive filtered tap water. (By 2009, Google was serving filtered water out of plastic cups, which were soon to be replaced by reusable and renewable cups.)

Google also eliminated a few sites, including Lively, its virtual world, and began to welcome ads on such formerly ad-free sites as Google Finance and Google News. Although Tim Armstrong boasted in September that Google Print Ads had "70 percent of newspapers in the U.S. as clients," the program had been encountering resistance from newspapers reluctant to cede control of big clients or sales staffs; as a result, it wound up selling mostly remnant ads, and often for below-market rates. Just months after Armstrong's announcement, the program was terminated. In its day-care program, Google jacked up both the level of services and the cost—from $1,425 per month to $2,500, reported Joe Nocera of the *New York Times*. This elite offering—and its elitist price—seemed at variance with Google's egalitarian ideals, and many employees were irate.

These cuts probably displeased two Google audiences, one external, the other internal. For talented young engineers, who look to join companies that are rockets, Google's actions might suggest a company that had reached cruising speed and might be descending. And as Google coped for the first time with saying no, there was frustration among Google employees accustomed to hearing yes. The founders had sold Google's mission as making the world a better place, not just making money. While the Google rocket soared, hard choices could be avoided; now they would have to be made.

Soon after Google shuttered its office outside Phoenix, the closing was raised at the September 19, 2008, TGIF session. The complaint came in a text message from an employee in London, which Brin read aloud to the assembled Googlers. It said, "What of people in Phoenix who can't relocate? If we don't take care of them, shame on us as a company!" Brin allowed Alan Eustace, senior vice president, engineering and research, to answer. Google, he said, would strive to find openings for those wishing to relocate; for the others, Phoenix was "a robust area for jobs." Brin and Page said nothing, but associates said they were increasingly distressed by Google employees' sense of entitlement. This was a company, not a socialist paradise, and the Phoenix question—like the grumbling when Google pared cafeteria hours and no longer allowed employees to cart home dinners for the entire family—troubled them.

With a cash hoard of $14 billion, Google was better positioned than most companies to withstand the economic shocks, but this did not stop its stock from plunging from nearly $700 per share at the start of 2008 to $307 at the end. The value of Brin's and Page's stock holdings reduced their net worth to about $12 billion each, which they said did not faze them. Although the downturn hit most media companies hard, online advertising continued to rise. Google now claimed 40 percent of all online ads. Revenues and profits climbed more slowly, though, and the company warned in its year-end 2008 filing to the FCC, "We believe our revenue growth rate will generally decline" as the search market matures.

Despite the downturn and its own difficulties, in many ways Google remained a company apart. It did not slash its investment spending on research and development or its data centers, investing a total of $2.8 billion on these in 2008. Its fourth-quarter profit margin grew to a fat 37.6 percent. While much of the Valley was contracting, Google decided to set aside $100 million to start a venture capital fund, Google Ventures, to invest in start-ups. Yes, it pared free snack choices from about one hundred to fifty, but that was still fifty more choices than most companies offer.

YouTube was not contracting. "Display advertising and YouTube will be big in the next twelve months," Schmidt predicted. He was encouraged that a combination of cost cutting and new advertising formats would slash YouTube's 2009 losses from a projected $500 million to $100 to $200 million, according to a knowledgeable Google executive. He believed the unusual traffic YouTube generates will become a magnet for advertising. In March 2009, according to Nielsen Media Research, two-thirds of all Web videos were watched on YouTube, and that month ninety million viewers came to the site, streaming a total of 5.5 billion videos.

Schmidt also believed that Google's Android investment would produce many more Google searches and provide opportunities to play a dominant role in all portable devices. He remained bullish that cloud computing would take off, particularly with the advent of four-hundred-dollar (and dropping) netbook laptops that could be powered by Android and store their data in a Google server rather than Windows. Between YouTube, Android, and cloud computing and its Chrome browser, Schmidt remained hopeful that Google was still on its way to becoming the first hundred-billion-dollar media company.

For its employees, Google did something else that defied the bleak economic times. The company had awarded a total of $1.1 billion in stock-based compensation in 2008; by the end of the year, those stock options had declined below the current Google stock price. So Google announced that any employee whose stock options were "underwater"—priced above the value of Google's stock price as of March 6, 2009—was eligible to exchange this stock for new options pegged to the March 6 price. Although the founders and Schmidt declined to partake, this generous bailout cost the company $400 million. Google reported that 93 percent of employees exchanged their old options for new ones priced at $308.57. It was a magnanimous gesture, and also a way for Google to keep valued members of its team from fleeing to a start-up. Many on Wall Street saw Google's repricing—Google was not the only company to do this—through another prism, as if Google were unfairly granting employees a benefit denied other shareholders.

Asked in April 2009 what he considered Google's biggest accomplishment of the past six months, Eric Schmidt said: "Our safe landing. We want to be the least affected by the recession." There was evidence that Google succeeded. Although it experienced its first quarter-to-quarter revenue decline since going public in 2004, its net income rose 8 percent in the first quarter of 2009; new cost controls sliced expenses by more than two hundred million dollars, and its profit margin swelled to 39.2 percent. Its 2009 revenues were projected to drop by 31 percent over the prior year, but its net income was still projected to grow by 4 percent.

What gave Schmidt more angst was the management upheaval that loomed ahead. With a number of relatively young senior executives blocking the upward path of the next tier, what happened with Sheryl Sandberg was happening with others. In February, Tim Armstrong, thirty-eight, announced that he was leaving to become CEO of AOL. A popular figure at Google, with salesmanship and people skills that are uncommon at engineering companies, Armstrong's departure was widely mourned. Soon after, Singh Cassidy, who also reported to Omid Kordestani and supervised business in Latin America and the Asia-Pacific region, also left. In April, Kordestani, the company's longtime sales chief, stepped aside to become a senior adviser to Schmidt and the founders. He was succeeded by the president of international operations, Nikesh Arora.

Google was not accustomed to such management turnovers. But Schmidt knew he was sitting atop a bigger management powder keg. With the development of Android, and the ambition to expand to provide the operating system for not just mobile phones but also the new generation of lightweight, low-cost netbook laptops, Google was on a collision course with Apple. This risked turmoil at the most senior levels of Google. "Because it is open source, Android is a horizontal system," explained a senior

Google official. "It is not devoted to any one hardware supplier. Apple is a vertical system that serves one supplier"—Apple. Already, as we've seen, Schmidt awkwardly left the Apple boardroom during iPhone discussions. By the summer of 2009, Schmidt and Jobs agreed the situation was untenable because, as Jobs said in a statement released to the press, "he will have to recuse himself from even larger portions of our meetings due to potential conflicts of interest." Schmidt resigned. Arthur Levinson, who is on both boards, will probably have to choose between them, as will Al Gore. Most disruptive of all, Coach Campbell, the colead director at Apple and almost a brother to Steve Jobs, has told friends he would regretfully choose to sever his ties to Google. Tensions between Apple and Google were simmering. By the end of 2009, it was likely they would come to a boil.

PART FOUR

Googled

CHAPTER FIFTEEN

Googled

Media companies can be divided into two broad categories: the few who create waves, and the many who ride them—or drown. The elite companies that generate waves are rare, the wave riders common. A company can be successful—Cisco, Dell, Oracle—yet not fundamentally alter the behavior of consumers or other companies. Dell's approach to efficiently making computers was an innovation, not a disrupter; it did not alter the way consumers behave. Steve Jobs and Apple are wave makers; companies like Dell—or Quincy Smith's CBS and Irwin Gotlieb's GroupM—attempt to ride the wave; newspapers crash into them. The Apple wave started with the Apple II, which launched the PC era in 1977; followed in 1984 by the Macintosh, with its innovative graphical user interface; followed by Pixar studios, which transformed movie animation; followed by the iPod and iTunes and the iPhone. It's probably safe to say that Intel and HP created waves. Ditto Amazon. There are those who say Microsoft doesn't qualify because it rode the waves others invented, but it is inarguable that it has thrived for three decades and changed computing. It is much too soon to know whether companies like Facebook, YouTube, Twitter, or Wikipedia will have a lasting impact.

It is not too early, however, to call Google a wave maker. The planet has been Googled, with the company becoming, as Larry Page has said, "part of people's lives, like brushing their teeth." Google has eliminated barriers to finding information and knowledge. "The Internet," Hal Varian said, "makes information available. Google makes information accessible." The Google wave has crashed into entire industries: advertising, newspapers, book publishing, television, telephones, movies, software or hardware makers. Its power is measured by the companies that fear it and the public that adores it. Google has fostered the growth of the Web by nurturing Web sites with its AdSense and AdWords programs, which have delivered advertising dollars and enabled small businesses to reach new customers. Google's way of building its business—make it free and attract users before figuring out a way to make money—became the template for Web start-ups from Facebook to YouTube to Twitter to Ning. Google is responsible for creating an entire new industry of search marketers and search optimizers who gather by the thousands several times a year under the umbrella of Search Engine Strategies (SES); these companies set out to outwit Google's algorithms so they can advise companies how to jump to the top of search or advertising results. Google has created a new model for an innovative business culture. Its search results provide a graph of our times, revealing which subjects preoccupy us; by studying search data on Google Trends, economists believe they can spot trends and better predict consumer behavior. By making information available, Google has facilitated political participation, as YouTube demonstrated throughout the 2008 presidential campaign. It has made institutions, from governments to corporations, more transparent. And with its open-source Android phone and cloud computing and YouTube and DoubleClick, it threatens to extend its considerable reach.

"Fifteen to twenty years ago, entrepreneurs would have said, 'I want to be the next Bill Gates and Microsoft,'" Michael Moritz said. "Today people's great ambition is to be the next Google. They went from zero to twenty billion dollars in revenues in four hundred weeks! Google has become the front door to the world for many people, the place they go for information. They are probably the most visible service concocted by mankind. Was Henry Ford more recognized in 1925? I doubt it. Because of the Internet, Google has leapt geographical boundaries." Perhaps the only company visible to more of the planet's occupants, he guesses, is Coca-Cola.

During the 2007 Zeitgeist Conference, a prominent media executive in attendance whispered a question to me. He was clear, he said, about the immense value Google was producing for itself. What he said he didn't understand was this: What value was Google producing for society, other than shifting money from the pockets of traditional media to Google's? During a long interview with Sergey Brin that day, I relayed the question. Brin had an easy answer if he wanted it; on the front page of that day's San Jose *Mercury News* was a story about the jobs his company had created and the auxiliary businesses that benefited from what the headline called "The Google Effect." But Brin chose to make a broader point: "It's very simple. People with the right information make better decisions for themselves. People presented with the right commercial opportunities will buy things suited to them."

By way of illustration, Brin described a trip he and his wife had made to Africa. With sophisticated digital cameras in hand, the two of them often jump on the private, customized Boeing 767-200 or 757 that Brin and Page purchased and that transports them to different continents. "One day in Zambia the driver was telling me how he was trying to get all the parts to a computer," Brin said. The driver couldn't locate some parts he needed, and those he could find were five times as expensive as they were in the United States. "He was trying to get a DVD-Rom drive. I said, 'In the U.S. they cost about thirty dollars.' He said, 'What?' He was about to spend two hundred dollars on a DVD-Rom. Imagine if there was information there? He would have been able to get that DVD-Rom drive for forty bucks. He'd be more efficient at his job, and it would help communities as a whole. I certainly believe that information creates value, rather than displaces it."

Google search is of enormous benefit to other companies as well. Refer-ring to the Internet as "a magic box where whatever you want to do, it's all there," Marc Andreessen credited Google with making the box "more magical. Google makes the world a much better place because it makes everything findable. Many companies spend a lot of time and effort to make their stuff more findable on Google. It's a huge source of traffic and income. Facebook used to be closed off from Google—you had to be logged into Facebook to see people's profiles. But then Facebook started publishing public profiles so that when you search on Google for someone, their Facebook profile pops up in the search results. That generates additional incoming traffic and therefore money for Facebook." Web site owners report that Google search often sends them 80 to 90 percent of their vistors. With Google as the Internet's prime navigator, there still remains the question Nicholas G. Carr asked in a 2008 blog post: "Is the company an exemplar or a freak?"

Itay Talgam did not mean to address this question when he appeared at Google's 2008 Zeitgeist Conference, but he inadvertently offered an answer. Talgam, a renowned Israeli orchestra conductor, stood on a small semicircular stage wearing a wrinkled cotton polo shirt with a sweater draped over his shoulders, his sparse hair shooting in several directions. For a half hour, his presentation of how conducting could be a metaphor for transformational management hushed the audience. Music is "noise," he began, and what the conductor does is "make a large group of people work in harmony."

Scanning a century's worth of conductors, he chose to discuss five. Each was outstanding, he said, but only two were transformational. The lights went down and on a large screen appeared a video clip of the autocratic Riccardo Muti, whose stern face and robotic baton movements brought forth from his orchestra no "joy," and suppressed the development of individual artists. Muti's "expression never changes," Talgam said. "He tells everyone what to do. He is a micromanager." The second conductor was Richard Strauss, who seemed to be in another place as he mechanically moved his arms, granting his orchestra more freedom but imposing no authority and offering no inspiration. The third was Herbert von Karajan, who never looked at his orchestra and also failed to inspire. The fourth was Carlos Kleiber, whose face was filled with rapture as he conducted and who, Talgam said, "creates a process" and "a feeling of freedom" while also conveying "authority." Notice, he said, the way Kleiber shot a disapproving glance at a soloist.

Talgam saved his favorite conductor for last. With the fifth clip, we were treated to a video of Leonard Bernstein welcoming an orchestra of high school students from around the world who had been granted one week under his direction to perform Stravinsky's *The Rite of Spring*. The first day of practice, the makeshift orchestra was discordant. But Bernstein did not wield a baton as a symbol of his "authority," Talgam noted. Instead, he stopped the music and spoke of the feelings Stravinsky sought to evoke, of the smell of spring grass, of waking animals. "He empowers people," Talgam said, "by telling them that their world is larger than they think." Cut to a week later, and the high school orchestra sat attentively before Bernstein, who looked on with obvious satisfaction as an assembly of young strangers achieved musical harmony. Without a baton, arms folded, Bernstein conducted only with facial expressions—a curled lip and lowered head for the basses, a raised eyebrow for the higher strings, a nod to the horns, an extravagant smile for the finale. Talgam did not need to tell the audience what they had seen. It was a sublime management seminar demonstrating how unusual leaders liberate those who follow. Bernstein was the boss, but he was not an autocrat. He managed to coax the best out of his orchestra, to make them part of a community.

It was no accident that Google invited Talgam. This sense of being connected to something larger is central to its culture. Employees share offices and work in teams. Google strives to make employees feel that they are part of a network. When Patrick Pichette became CFO, he relied on a wisdom-of-crowds approach to cost cutting. He set up a Web page and invited employees to make suggestions to eliminate waste, which he said unearthed many of the best ideas. Google uses a variant of this network approach when it test-markets whether its users like blue or yellow, one beta product or another. Of course, this faith in quantification is what drove some designers to leave the company and to blog about their frustrations.

These forms of communication are characteristic of what Anne-Marie Slaughter, the former dean of the Woodrow Wilson School of Public and

International Affairs at Princeton, has described as "the networked world," a world that Google has been instrumental in advancing. Diplomacy requires "mobilizing international networks of public and private actors"; CEOs are acutely aware of "the shift from the vertical world of hierarchy to the horizontal world of networks"; the media increasingly is composed of "online blogs and other forms of participatory media" that "create a vast, networked conversation." Society itself is networked, with "the world of MySpace" creating "a global world of 'OurSpace,' linking hundreds of millions of individuals across continents." This world is one where a more open America, and a more open company, has distinct advantages.

Google has devised a management system that liberates its employees. The "Googly" way, said Laszlo Bock, Google's vice president of people operations, is simply to treat employees better. "Google is a platform to say, 'You can trust your folks.' We want to be an example to other companies. The key is the 20 percent time, not the free food. There is a feeling here of intellectual freedom." Even though there was some grumbling from Googlers in 2008—about costly child care, the closing of the Phoenix office—most recognized their work life was charmed. How many companies gifted its employees with new stock options to replace those that had become worthless? Asked what impact Google's employment policies have had on other companies, Page said, modestly, "It's hard for me to know. I've never worked anywhere else. But I feel that we have had an impact. We certainly got a lot of attention for the things we do for employees, and that's positive." It also means, he added, "Our competitors have to be competitive on some of these things."

Marissa Mayer claimed that half of Google's products materialize from the 20 percent time. This has fueled innovation at Google, and has helped wreak havoc on old media companies. The engineers who come to Mayer's office seeking encouragement and company support for their projects often start with the same assumption Page and Brin do: that the tried-and-true ways of doing things are outmoded.

Google Voice, a suite of mobile phone services, provides a good illustration of how the company's engineers think. They began with their favorite question, Why? If we use the Internet for phone calls, they wondered, why can't all telephones have a single number? Why do we need multiple answering machines? Why do we need to switch phone numbers when we move? Why do we need to wait to listen to phone messages? Why can't we convert them to text messages instead? Why can't we record phone conversations if the other party consents? Why can't our phones block telemarketing calls or make sure certain people are screened out? Because it's over the Internet, why can't most calls be free?

For its beta test, in 2007, Google introduced for a relatively small group a service that would work as Google Voice does. It was called GrandCentral, the name of a start-up Google acquired a few years earlier. With their regular phones, in the initial GrandCentral pilot project, users called into a voice mail service, then pushed a button to get a dial tone. They were now on the Internet. It was free and convenient. Users liked it but Google treated it like a "maybe" product, making no commitment to expanding the service. The snickers from those who thought the Google test must have failed, as David Pogue noted in the *New York Times*, became sneers.

In March 2009, Google Voice was announced, and the sneers turned to gasps. Everyone in the telephone business—from telephone companies to new entrants like cable companies to eBay's Internet phone service, Skype, which imposes small charges on calls made on regular phones—had reason to be concerned. Google would at first give away the phone service for free, with a nominal charge for long distance calls, and hoped one day to sell the service to corporations at a low price. What was an advance for consumers was a potential setback for these companies. They were being Googled.

Once again, Google's engineers proved their brilliance. They had devised the simplest, most cost-efficient way to accomplish a task. What impact Google Voice might have on the thousands of jobs in the telephone industry or on local communities was not a question the engineers asked. Nor did they ask about privacy. Because Google would be gathering data on the calling habits of its customers, there were obvious privacy questions. Nor did they ask what the ramifications were for a society if Google Voice succeeded and became as dominant in telephony as Google is in search, online advertising, YouTube, or digitized books. These questions were beyond the pay grade of the engineers.

Many Valley companies, and others, have modeled themselves after what Chris Anderson calls "the biggest company in history built on giving things away." In his book *Free,* Anderson cites the many companies that offer free services, from Twitter to Facebook to MySpace to Yahoo's photo-sharing service, Flickr, to e-mail services to Wikipedia to craigslist to news aggregators like Digg to the free shipping and returns offered by the online shoe retailer Zappos. By offering free services, Google has reinforced the notion that traditional media now wants to combat—that digital information and content should be free. "This is the Google Generation," writes Anderson, "and they've grown up online simply assuming that everything digital is free."

Many Valley companies have now copied Google's 20 percent time, including the one Bill Campbell chairs, Intuit. Facebook offers subsidized housing for employees who live within a mile of the office, free meals, parking, gym memberships, laundry services, and a host of other benefits that mirror Google's. "Google has raised the bar for everybody in the Valley," said Campbell. "Everyone has to respond to the pressure that said, 'If the engineer is good, we better hire him before Google does.'"

Of course, Google has borrowed as well as led. Stanford president and Google director John Hennessy, who once chaired his university's computer science department, believes some Google ideas—such as the 20 percent time—can be traced to Stanford "and the academic world," where Stanford graduate students like Jerry Yang and David Filo on their own time in the computer lab concocted the idea for Yahoo. Page and Brin have acknowledged that they took cues from the generous way Genentech treated its medical scientists, including a 401 (k) plan that matched up to 5 percent of their salaries; this was one of the reasons they recruited its CEO, Art Levinson, to join Google's board. Google has a pet dog policy—allowing dogs to accompany owners to campus, providing an outdoor space, offering veterinary services—that Larry Page said was copied from Netscape.

Nor is Google unique. Netflix drives its employees hard but among other generous benefits, it lavishes unlimited vacation time on them. The e-commerce site Zappos encourages employees to point out any other employee who does outstanding work; that person then gets a fifty-dollar bonus from the company. Zappos also employs a full-time "life coach" who lets employees vent and serves as a corporate shrink.

Google has done something else that sets the best companies apart: it earned its customers' trust. Google regularly ranks among the world's most respected corporate brands. All companies endlessly talk about achieving brand status, but few attain it. They fail because they often confuse brand with name recognition; they don't recognize that brand is a synonym for trust, which is not something that can be purchased with a rich marketing budget. Most consumers trust the information in the *New York Times*, the Think Differentness of Apple, the taste of Coca Cola, the safety of a Volvo, the bargain prices at Wal-Mart or Southwest Airlines. If we think of the Internet as a copying machine that produces free information, as one of the founders of *Wired* magazine, Kevin Kelly, wrote on his blog, then "how does one make money selling free copies?" Kelly's answer: "When copies are free, you need to sell things which cannot be copied." The first of these, he said, was "trust," which is not duplicable. "Trust must be earned, over time."

That trust is founded, in part, on a feeling that a company both serves noble ends and yields wealth for its shareholders. Recall the "Letter from the Founders" that was part of Google's 2004 IPO, in which Page and Brin declared, "Google is not a conventional company. We do not intend to become one." They said they would focus on users, not investors, and that they'd be concerned not with "quarterly market expectations" or paying dividends but rather with protecting Google's "core values." In a Q&A published as part of Google's prospectus, Brin said the company's aim was "greater than simply growing itself as large as it can be. I believe large, successful corporations . . . have an obligation to apply some of those resources to at least try to solve or ameloriate a number of the world's problems and ultimately to make the world a better place." They would try to serve, as Eric Schmidt said, as "a moral force." The combination of free services, coupled with principled stances like its refusal to allow advertisers to rent space on its home page, or its insistence on a customer service that communicates to users that Google wants to get them to their destination quickly and without trapping them, have helped convince consumers that these goals were genuine. When the tsunami struck Southeast Asia in December 2004, Google made a billboard on its home page to alert searchers to the various international relief efforts they might assist. In 2008, Google Flu Trends began tapping the company's database to predict flu incidents well ahead of the health warnings issued by the Centers for Disease Control. "Who would have thought," said Steven Rattner, then managing partner of the venture capital firm Quadrangle, "that a bunch of computer geeks would turn out to be the best marketers of the twenty-first century?" Little wonder, then, that Google in 2009, as in prior years, was again ranked by *Fortune* as one of the "World's 50 Most Admired Companies."

Bill Gates, like Page and Brin, has always believed a corporation should be concerned with looking over the treetops. Before Page and Brin were out of college, he refused to deliver dividends to Microsoft's shareholders, believing this money should be reinvested. But unlike the Google founders, Gates thought a company like his had one obligation: to increase its wealth. He also once said that he would not begin to make large personal charitable gifts until he had stepped down as CEO and could concentrate on making intelligent choices. He changed his mind in part because his marriage to Melinda French Gates broadened his thinking and gave him a partner, because his parents' generous charitable endeavors had an impact, and because age had mellowed him. Starting in 2000, long before Google established its own effort, the Gates Foundation has been extraordinarily generous and smart about leveraging its resources to affect real change. More recently, Gates has enlarged his view of a corporation's role. In a speech to the 2007 graduating class at Harvard, and again in a January 2008 address to business and government leaders attending the World Economic Forum in Davos, Gates called for a "creative capitalism" that relies on market forces to address the needs of poor countries. In an interview with Robert Guth of the *Wall Street Journal*, Gates spoke of the shortcomings of capitalism. He said he was troubled that innovations in education or health care tend to skip over poor people, and he proposed that successful companies spin off businesses that have "a twin mission" of making money and "improving lives."

Over the years, it has not been unusual to hear Silicon Valley companies sound like social service agencies. In 1995, the newly founded Yahoo declared, "We believe the Internet can positively transform lives, societies and economies." Craig Newmark, the founder of craigslist, extols "nerd values," by which he means that he is intent on keeping his listings free for most of his users and refuses to enrich himself by selling his company or taking a large salary. Social idealism has been a core value in the culture of the Internet, from the insistence of Tim Berners-Lee, who believed that the Web should be open and that he would not patent it or enrich himself; to the open-source movement; to Wikipedia, which follows a democratic faith in "the wisdom of crowds" and has adopted a nonprofit model.

Before one dismisses these approaches as the gauzy thinking of left-wing populists, consider how often traditional companies now promote their own "corporate social responsibility"—in part to ecumenically emulate Andrew Carnegie, in part to bathe in the favorable publicity, in part to profit from some of these endeavors, and in part as a reaction against almost daily ethical business lapses. Companies like the Gap and Hallmark donate a portion of their profits to fight AIDS; Starbucks gave comprehensive health care to its employees, including part-timers. General Electric devised what it called an ecomagination strategy to address climate change and reap profits from it. WPP started issuing a Corporate Responsibility Report in 2002, and has promised to reduce its carbon footprint by 20 percent. One of America's most powerful marketers, Jim Stengel, in late 2008 left his job as global marketing chief for Procter & Gamble to fund a private consulting venture to advise companies how to build trust in brands. His task, he said, is to create "emotional equity," by which he means that consumers will believe the company cares not just about their dollars but about them. This is what P&G did with Pampers, consulting parents and designing diapers that felt more like cloth and kept babies warmer. And the Harvard Business School, in 2009, introduced a voluntary oath, which 20 percent of the graduating class signed, pledging to "serve the greater good" and avoid advancing "narrow ambitions."

True, do-goodism is often a marketing ploy. True, the idealism one encounters at Google can be tempered by its business realism, as when Google placated the government of China, or denied that it wanted to snare a chunk of the income of media buyers like Irwin Gotlieb. It is also true that waves can inflict real damage. Google creates jobs, and it also destroys them. This poses life-and-death questions for traditional companies.

I asked Tom Glocer, CEO of Thomson Reuters, "Does Google help or hurt Reuters?" For a moment it seemed that Glocer was not going to answer. "My pause," he said finally, "is the pause of a time frame. To date, they've been neutral to positive." In the short run, Google has served as a spur, compelling traditional companies to "raise the level of our game," just as Wall Street brokers had to improve their services and information to compete against online services like E-Trade or information sources like Yahoo Finance or CNBC. In the long run, he continued, "What everyone's waiting to see is whether 'Do no evil' is true to the credo, their real inner core, or is it just a convenient sort of 'Don't worry, Don't worry'—until they've built up such an amazing personal database about all of our habits and they then go to the *New York Times* and say, 'By the way, if you want the search engine to include your content, you're going to have to start paying us.' . . . They've created with software a narrow strait through which most people need to pass to do an activity that is at the root of much of what we do on the Web. . . . The fear is that an increasing number of businesses depend on Google to get their eyeballs. At a certain point, Google can flip their business from being a utility" to a gatekeeper that charges for access.

This power imposes constant pressure on other companies. "You can't wait for the wave to get there. You've got to start paddling," said Peter Thiel, who was cofounder and CEO of PayPal, and is now president of Clarium Capital Management, a global hedge fund and Silicon Valley venture capital firm. "If you were running a railroad company in the 1940s and people started to fly airplanes, what would you do?" I asked Thiel what *he* would do if placed in charge of a traditional media company. He said there were two choices. Either you push consolidation and cost cutting much further than media companies have done. Or you "do something radically transformative." On paper, the radical solution is more appealing. One question is how to adopt a radical solution, such as for newspaper companies publishing only a free Web edition, without destroying what you're trying to save. One impediment is that in the digital age the transformation often depends on engineers, and media and engineering, as we've seen, are from different planets. "This is not a problem specific to media," Thiel said. "When we started PayPal in 1998–99, we asked, 'Why can't the banks do this?' They did try to copy us, but you needed engineers and the large financial institutions were not able to build it. The caliber of our engineers was significantly higher. Nothing against these companies, but if you're a talented engineer, why would you go to work at CitiGroup? Why would you go to work at a place where your contribution is not seen as central to the success of the organization? If you're a politician, you want to be in D.C. If you're a finance person, you want to be in New York. If you're an aspiring actor, you want to be in Los Angeles. If you're an engineer, you want to be in Silicon Valley."

Most traditional media companies, including those that have a reasonably good relationship with Google, are worried that they will be Googled. But there is a larger context for their insecurity. They are anxious about technological innovations that can quickly disrupt their businesses; about maneuvering in a world where corporate partners are also competitors; about how rapidly their businesses can change; about not being embarrassed by the omnipresent bloggosphere. Not long after he relinquished his CEO job at Disney, Michael Eisner flew JetBlue from Burbank to New York. "When I landed, I opened my BlackBerry and there was my picture on JetBlue. On JetBlue! In a blog saying, 'Has something happened to Michael Eisner that he can't afford a private airline or a big-time airline?'" He laughed about the incident, but used it to illustrate how cell phone cameras and bloggers transform private actions into public acts. The stage has widened.

The Internet and its Google surrogate impose pressure on companies to simultaneously play both offense and defense. Jeff Zucker, CEO of NBC Universal, explained that to be a CEO in the digital age "feels incredibly exciting, and incredibly scary." He is aware of how quickly businesses can collapse, as did Wang and Gateway and Compaq computer, and of the ups and downs of companies like Motorola or Sun or Yahoo. He is wary of too quickly embracing a fad, as CBS seems to have done when it invested in Joost, a free Web site offering licensed full-length TV programming. After winning coveted innovation awards—and the commensurate buzz—when it was introduced in 2007, today Joost stumbles and in mid-2009 exited the consumer video market. Zucker is aware of the danger of throwing overboard the wrong business, as the company that once owned the NBC network, RCA, did when it decided at the start of the seventies to abandon consumer electronics. Convinced that no new breakthroughs were possible in consumer electronic products, RCA stood still while Apple and Microsoft and Sony surged. "What we all worry about," said Zucker, "is destroying value as we innovate. And not letting that paralyze you is really the pressure that I personally feel. The scariness is not that I'm going to miss an opportunity, but that the business model will be destroyed as we're innovating." The "Innovator's Dilemma."

Every media company is speculating on where the digital wave is heading and how to ride it. This much is clear about Google: the company has a big appetite. After I watched the 1,500-strong Google sales force gather at the Hilton in downtown San Francisco, I met Eric Schmidt in a hotel conference room. Pressed to describe Google's growth strategy, he was jawdroppingly candid. "All large media companies are both distribution and content companies," he said, and "we really are competing with the distribution" side of these companies. Google wants to be the agent that sells the ads on all distribution platforms, whether it is print, television, radio, or the Internet. To advertisers, he said, "We say, use us." In addition, he said, "As our technology gets better, we will be able to replace some of their [large companies'] internal captive sales forces. They are not doing that much work; they are not automated. So the eventual goal is, again, to replace some of these sales functions by automation."

So Google will disintermediate the functions of these traditional media companies? Schmidt disputed the word, but not the effect: "Disintermediation is not the correct word to use. It's better sales technology."

He thought mobile phones would probably be "a smaller target for us" because to get on those platforms Google would have to pay large fees and cede control to telephone companies. Perhaps the biggest future opportunity for Google, he said, was YouTube. "If that works," he said of YouTube's effort to sell advertising and, he admitted, to become a content company, "then that's the creation of the equivalent of the CBS network in the 1950s. It's the creation of both content and a monetization mechanism."

Sergey Brin told me that it is Google's willingness "to experiment," to "take risks" and "innovate"—to do the bold things Schmidt described— that will continue to set Google apart. However, companies with large appetites can get fat. Marc Andreessen believes Google aims "to do everything," but is dubious that they can succeed. Andreessen also believes that in the digital age, technology alters the competitive battlefield, just as it did in World War II. Germany in 1940, as New York University professor Clay Shirky points out in his provocative book *Here Comes Everybody*, was not the invincible power "etched in communal memory." Germany teetered near bankruptcy; its army was smaller and its tanks were inferior to France's. So why did the German blitzkrieg succeed? Because its tanks were equipped with a technology the French tanks lacked: radios. These radios allowed Panzer commanders to share intelligence and make quick decisions, leaving French commanders standing still and guessing while German tanks moved in concert. Even if the French had radios, Shirky writes, the Germans held another advantage: "The French regarded tanks as a mobile platform for accompanying foot soldiers. The Germans, on the other hand, understood that the tank allowed for a new kind of fighting, a rapid style of attack. . . ." The technology advantaged Germany, but so did a superior strategy that allowed Germany to prevail.

CHAPTER SIXTEEN

Where Is the Wave Taking Old Media?

One morning in 2007, Joe Schoendorf was breakfasting at Il Fornaio, the Palo Alto restaurant that serves as a Valley canteen. A burly, avuncular man with a prominent mustache, Schoendorf is a principal at the venture capital firm of Accel Partners, a primary backer of Facebook. In his more than forty years in Silicon Valley, Schoendorf has seen companies come and go, but he's still humbled by the eye-blink speed of change. "If we were having breakfast in 1989, there was no Internet," he said. "IBM was number one in the computer business. DEC and Ken Olsen were on the cover of *BusinessWeek* and the cover line was, 'Can They Overtake IBM?' If I said to you that DEC would go out of business, you'd think I was crazy." Today, young associates tell him, "Old media is dead. Television and radio will become dinosaurs. Google is impregnable." Schoendorf's experience teaches him to be more cautious. He has witnessed the quick rise and fall of Lycos, Netscape, Excite. He has seen AOL go from Internet darling to a company few would buy. He respects Google's prowess, but is wary of sweeping prognostications.

Robert Iger, the CEO of Disney, is equally humbled. When he was at ABC, he said, "I put *America's Home Videos* on the schedule. It was user-generated content. How come I didn't envision YouTube?" In fairness to Iger, one could also ask: How come the *New York Times* or CBS didn't invent CNN? How come *Sports Illustrated* didn't start ESPN? How come AOL, which launched Instant Messenger, didn't develop Facebook? How come IBM ceded software to Microsoft? No one knows with any certainty where the wave is headed. "Sometimes you have to guess," said Bill Campbell, who recalled his experience at Intuit. "What you do—as happened at Intuit in 1998—is you say, 'Let's get five things and see what works.' If two work, you have a home run. If three work, you double the stock."

Was Barry Diller right when he said, "The world is moving towards direct selling—no middleman, no store"? Or is this the wishful thinking of an executive whose online enterprise would benefit if his prediction proved true? Or could one say that Google is itself a middleman because it brings together users and information, Web sites and advertisers? Was Irwin Gotlieb correct that consumers "will happily go along" with trading private information to advertisers in exchange for some free services or reduced charges? Will advertising succeed on social networks and YouTube? Will consumers opt to spend less on software by ceding storage (and control) of their data to Google's cloud? Will younger generations raised in digital homes read books, and at what length? Is the Internet safe or is it vulnerable to hackers and viruses? Will the deep recession that commenced in 2008 prompt the Obama administration to become more of a digital cop, imposing new regulations, investing in broadband, strengthening or diluting antitrust oversight? And will this choke innovation, or enhance it?

Yossi Vardi, the Israeli entrepreneur whose company invented instant messaging, once spent three years trying to graph the future. The result was a presentation consisting of four hundred slides. He discarded the slides and substituted what he called Vardi's Law: "If you need four hundred slides to explain it, it really means you don't have a clue." In fact, the questions are more apparent than the answers, and a central question that will profoundly shape the future of old and new media is this: Will users who have grown up with the Web pay for content they now get free?

———

In this back-to-the-future moment, online companies ape broadcasters by proclaiming that their services are "free" because advertisers pay for them. This is the answer touted by *Wired* editor Chris Anderson in his latest book, *Free: The Future of a Radical Price*. He argues that making information free allows digital content creators to use the Internet as a promotional platform to create alternate money streams, including concerts, selling goods and lectures and premium services. In the digital world, he writes, "Free becomes not just an option but an inevitability. Bits want to be free." In his spirited book *What Would Google Do?* Jeff Jarvis argues that online news aggregaters like Google are the equivalent of newsstands that help papers boost online circulation and serve as promotional platforms for the newspapers. By increasing their online traffic, Jarvis posits, aggregaters allow papers to charge a steeper price for their online ads. "I believe papers should beg to be aggregated so more readers will discover their content," he writes. He concludes, "Free is impossible to compete against. The most efficient marketplace is a free marketplace."

There is no question that links increase the number of newspaper readers. Marissa Mayer said that Google search and Google News generate "more than one billion clicks per month" for newspaper sites. But for "free" to work as Jarvis says it will, news aggregaters like Google or Yahoo would have to be gushing money into newspaper coffers. They are not. While Larry Page, Sergey Brin, and Eric Schmidt insist they want to help newspapers, and AdSense does bequeath ad revenues to newspapers, the three men admit AdSense's receipts are relatively modest, too meager to restore newspapers to health. Jarvis is correct that free "is impossible to compete against," but I fear that the consequence will be the opposite of the one he intended. For newspapers, if revenues continue to fall short of costs, free may be a death certificate.

Second, advertising is a wobbly crutch. In economic downturns, ad expenditures are usually among the first to be pared. Indeed, in harmony with the worldwide recession, total U.S. ad spending dropped in 2008, and in 2009 Jack Myers, a respected marketing consultant, projects that total advertising will plunge 12.1 percent. Newspaper ad revenues, according to ZenithOptimedia, will fall from $44 billion in 2008 to $37.4 billion in 2009, or 8 percent; Jack Myers predicted the falloff would be almost three times greater (22 percent). And just as the Internet has disrupted traditional ad sales, it may well disrupt the effectiveness of advertising itself. Consumers now have the tools to easily comparison shop online, to compare prices and performance reviews. The emotional power of a commercial is weakened by the informational power of the Web. Even *Wired* editor Chris Anderson, who once more forcefully advocated that free was the perfect model, has changed his position. Blaming the deep recession, Anderson appended a "Coda" chapter at the end of his book in which he amends what he wrote earlier. He writes that he now believes "Free is not enough. It also has to be matched with Paid."

Third, to rely solely on advertising is to risk becoming dependent on a revenue source whose interests may diverge from those of good journalism. The wall between advertising and news was erected to ensure that news was not at the service of commercial interests. This wall is easier to maintain when newspapers can buttress their ad revenues with subscriptions and newsstand sales. In a February 2009 *Time* cover story titled "How to Save Your Newspaper," former *Time* editor Walter Isaacson quoted Henry Luce, cofounder of the magazine, as saying that to rely solely on advertising was "economically self-defeating." Luce, Isaacson wrote, "believed that good journalism required that a publication's primary duty be to its readers, not to its advertisers." The warning was given life several weeks later when the management of Time Inc. goaded five of its magazines—*Time, Fortune, People, Sports Illustrated,* and *Entertainment Weekly*—to prepare major stories on a new 3-D animated movie from DreamWorks, *Monsters vs. Aliens.* The publications would each receive advertising from three of DreamWorks' corporate partners on the movie, McDonald's, HP, and Intel. Many other media companies have felt compelled to make similar Faustian bargains, potentially trading credibility for dollars. In April 2009, page one of the *Los Angeles Times* featured an ad for a new NBC show that was laid out to look at first glance like just another news story.

It is no surprise that advertisers will always want the most conducive setting for their ads; they want to sell products and have perfectly good business reasons to be concerned with the environment in which their ads appear. The problem is that this impulse leads them to push for more "friendly" news: a senior network news executive said, "I've seen increasing incursions by advertisers into morning show content. Can the evening news be far behind?" Of course, network news has in recent years made itself more of an inviting target for advertisers by allowing the morning shows and evening newscasts to become "softer" and more superficial. Likewise, it is as certain as a sunrise that advertisers will want tamer social networks and more predictable YouTube videos to accompany their products. To better target their ads, they also want to extract as much information about their potential customers as they can. But news outlets or Web sites that share users' private information or allow themselves to be seen as bought and paid for will lose the trust of their customers. An additional revenue source will give them more leverage to resist.

When media companies depend solely on advertising revenues, there is also a real risk to quality. As more people read newspapers online, or watch their favorite TV shows online, or illegally but effortlessly download movies or music, the revenues of traditional content companies will fall. While it is true that too few newspapers do a good job of covering state capitals or city hall, or sustaining investigative reporting or investing resources in international news, those elite papers that do—the *New York Times, Wall Street Journal,* and *Washington Post*—are hobbled; that kind of reporting is expensive. Similarly, a television network's ability to invest in expensive but exemplary programs like *Friday Night Lights, 30 Rock,* or even the more popular fare—*Desperate Housewives, CSI: Miami*—will be endangered.

A total reliance on advertising can menace many new media sites as well. Facebook and YouTube and Twitter have an enormous base of users, but they lose money. Sites like Facebook and MySpace struggle to devise ad-friendly formats, but have so far stumbled. Robert Pittman, the former president of AOL, thinks he knows why: "Wrestling had bigger audiences than some prime-time shows, yet wrestling never monetized well. Why? Because most advertisers didn't want to be associated with it. Environment did matter. We had huge audiences on AOL chat rooms. We couldn't sell it worth a damn. People were communicating. They didn't want to be interrupted by ads. You start running an ad on Facebook and users will say, 'I don't like GAP. Don't put GAP on my page!' It will attract some advertising dollars. But I don't think social networks monetize to the size of the audience they have. The advertiser doesn't want to be in an environment where they feel they are a big negative." Social networks might be able to sell more ads if they share more of their users' private information with advertisers, but when Facebook tried that approach in 2007 with an ad program called Beacon, irate users forced it to install a system that relied on the users' willingness to participate. Eventually, if these sites cannot devise an ad formula that works, they will once again demonstrate—as AOL chat rooms or Friendster.com did—that advertisers may not always follow the audience.

One begins to hear anxious whispers in Silicon Valley that "free" might not be free. "I think people are getting more willing to pay," said Marc Andreessen, who cited iTunes and Amazon's Kindle as successful online pay services. "More and more of what people do, they do online. I think most people like the things they like and are willing to pay for it." Maybe. Certainly there are products that users are willing to pay for on the Web, most notably the music on iTunes. Google generates 3 percent of its revenues by charging corporations for premium services—tailored searches, special software apps, extra Gmail storage—and expects those numbers to rise. Web companies such as Ning and Linkedin charge corporations for extra tools or premium services—including a fee to have an ad-free environment. Those wanting online access to the full *Wall Street Journal,* or to the *New York Times* archives and crossroad puzzle, pay for it. To read the *Times* on a Kindle one must subscribe. In 2008, each of the 40,000 member groups of Meetup.com paid the social network site fifteen dollars per month to host them online. One-quarter of CBS's digital revenues comes from fees or subscriptions. The online dating service Match.com has nearly 1.5 million paid subscribers. By mid-2008, China was generating $2.5 billion in online video game revenues.

Mary Meeker predicts, "Ultimately, while advertising will remain the primary revenue driver for Internet content companies, I think we'll find more and more examples of people paying for content, the way people do to download games on mobile devices. With mobile downloads, where the payment mechanism is integrated, I think you will be able to charge just a little bit a lot of times." A research report from the market research firm Piper Jaffray projected that consumers would pay $2.8 billion to download applications to their mobile phones in 2009, a number projected to rise to $13 billion by 2012. One alternative is a monthly or annual subscription model. Another is micropayments. The impediment to either a subscription or a micropayment system is that with notable exceptions—mobile phones, Amazon, PayPal, Google Checkout, broadband providers—most Web sites do not have the names and credit card information of their users; new users would have to make a considered decision about whether the service was worth paying for before handing over their billing information. "At Ning," Andreessen said of the social network site he funded, "we want to get credit card numbers. We're edging towards it." With over one million Ning niche networks—female writers have one, fans of Enrique Iglesias have one—the credit cards would stack up.

The cable and telephone companies, already in possession of the credit card or banking information of their customers, are well positioned to benefit from a micropayment or metered payment system. Using their broadband wires, they could offer a range of new pay services. Referring to smart phones as "the stealth device of this planet," Ivan Seidenberg of Verizon painted a blue sky: "Your phone will replace your credit card, your keys. It will become your personal remote control to life."

Nevertheless, a chasm yawns between the needs of business and the culture that has grown up around the Internet. Users may love YouTube or Facebook or Google News, but will they pay for them? Schmidt said he is dubious that "social network traffic will ever be as lucrative as business, professional, and educational traffic. When you go to a bar you may buy a drink, but you're fundamentally there for social interaction." Advertising, he believes, will become an annoying distraction.

Stanford president John Hennessy surprised me when he said, "We made one really big mistake in the Internet, which is hard to reverse now. We should have made a micropayment system work. Make it very simple, very straightforward. Let's say I go to Google's home page or Yahoo's and I see a story I want to read in the *New York Times,* and that story is going to cost me a penny. I click on it. I pay the penny electronically. I have a system up that says, 'Any story that costs less than a quarter, give it to me instantly. If it costs more than a quarter, ask me first.' I get a monthly bill. It pays automatically against my credit card. We could have done this easily. The technology is all there to do it. The question is, how do we get back to something like that? We need some people to go out and say, 'We need some approaches other than advertising.'"

In September 2008, I related Hennessy's thinking about micropayments to Eric Schmidt. "A lot of people believe that," he said. "I've been pretty skeptical." Free is the right model, he believed then. "The benefit of free is that you get 100 percent of the market. And in a world where there's no physical limits, it's easy to have so much free. Traditional thinking doesn't work." There are businesses that can succeed by charging, he said, "but it's a one percent opportunity. The lesson that Google sort of learned a long time ago is that free is the right answer. . . ."

It is not, I fear, the right answer for many media businesses. Nor was it the answer Schmidt came to seven months later, when we again discussed charging for content on the Internet. "My current view of the world," he told me in April 2009, "is you end up with advertising and micropayments and big payments based on" the nature of the audience. Each member of the old guard—newspapers, magazines, TV and cable, phone companies—has its own online challenges. None can afford to blithely give away their services, yet neither can they afford to ignore that this is what the public might want.

For newspapers, the trends are clear: circulation and advertising revenues are falling, newspaper readers are aging, debt service and production costs are rising, and stock prices are stuck in the basement. Neither giving away online newspapers nor partnering with Google or Yahoo to sell ads has made an appreciable difference. The bleak headlines did not subside in 2009 as more newspapers shuttered, including the *Rocky Mountain News* and the print version of the *Seattle Post-Intelligencer,* and with the threatened closing of many others, the *San Francisco Chronicle* among them. Declining revenues—newspaper ad dollars fell by nearly one-third between 2005 and 2008—a reflection of new competition. Bloggers increasingly offer a wealth of local information and links that lumbering newsrooms don't know how to match. The changing competitive landscape is being felt at the Journalism School, Columbia University. While the foremost employers of 2008's graduating class continued to be newspapers and magazines, according to Ernest R. Sotomayor, assistant dean, career services, there has been a profound shift. Many students clamor to take online media courses, he responds via e-mail, and to learn "to shoot/edit video, create audio content, Flash graphics and packages, etc." And "virtually all those" who went to work for newspapers or magazines are working on their online versions. Increasingly, said Nicholas Lemann, the school's dean, "many of our students go into 'print' or 'broadcast' jobs that are actually mainly Web jobs." Web sites have become for them, he said, the new Ellis Island, their point of entry to journalism.

Looking back on the investment mistakes made by newspapers, it is not hard to understand the too-sweeping contempt that people like Jeff Jarvis or Marc Andreessen harbor for them. Take the New York Times Company, which, though rightly proud of its flagship newspaper, has made its economic predicament worse with a series of what-were-they-thinking? business decisions. In 1993, at a time when it should have been clear that newspaper growth would slow, the Times spent $1.1 billion to acquire the *Boston Globe*. Instead of investing in new media, the Times purchased small television stations, which they have since sold, and spent more than $100 million to acquire a 50 percent stake in the Discovery Civilization digital channel, with an audience so small Nielsen could not measure it, and which was eventually sold back to Discovery in 2006. Instead of making other digital investments or reducing its debt, the company spent $2 billion to buy back its own stock, whose value has plunged; and it spent more than $600 million on a new headquarters building, which has since been leased out to help meet debt payments. The Times did make some smart moves: it made one big digital purchase, About.com, an online source of information and advice, which has been a modest success;

and it invested to expand its national circulation and advertising base, which helped cushion the paper from a local advertising and circulation falloff.

For the past decade, most other newspaper publishers have proclaimed that one answer to their woes was to offer readers more local news coverage, yet too few invested in local newspapers. Even fewer newspapers vied to make their Web sites innovative.

The Internet democratizes knowledge, allowing us to fetch information from most newspapers, magazines, or books anywhere in the world. It provides choices. It is convenient; Google aggregates information so that it's easy to access. It spreads newspaper stories all over the Web, multiplying the readership. It opens lines of communication to bloggers and readers with valuable information and provocative opinions. And it generates some advertising revenue. But it robs actual newspapers of readers, reduces newspaper advertising and circulation revenue, and makes information in the *New York Times* equal to information from anywhere. Digital news has another side effect: it allows newspaper owners to quantify which stories appeal to their readers. As Larry Page lamented, "The kinds of stories that generate page views"—a Britney Spears meltdown or a Jessica Simpon weight gain—"are not the kinds of stories reporters want to write," or that he personally wants to read, "and that kind of makes it worse."

We are racing through a revolution comparable to the one ushered in by Herr Gutenberg's printing press in the fifteenth Century. The outcome is as unclear today as it was then. "During the wrenching transition to print, experiments were only revealed in retrospect to be turning points," NYU professor Clay Shirky wrote on his blog. He continued:

> The old stuff gets broken faster than the new stuff is put in its place. The importance of any given experiment isn't apparent at the moment.... When someone demands to know how we are going to replace newspapers, they are really demanding to be told that we are not living through a revolution. . . . They are demanding to be told that the ancient social bargains aren't in peril, that core institutions will be spared, that new methods of spreading information will improve previous practice rather than upend-

ing it. They are demanding to be lied to. . . . We're collectively living
through 1500, when it's easier to see what's broken than what will replace
it. . . . Society doesn't need newspapers. What we need is journalism.

Shirky is correct, I believe, that it's vital to preserve journalism, but
wrong about the unimportance of newspapers. By newspapers I don't necessarily mean the printed papers we are accustomed to. I mean a product
that offers readers a variety of news, including news they didn't expect they
would want or need. Maybe it's a book review, or a recipe, or a description
of pension padding by public workers, or the bonuses paid to investment
bankers whose institution has received a federal bailout. Maybe it's a report
on the appointment of a finance minister in a country that's going to be
vital next year. A good online or print newspaper should be like a supermarket, with a variety of choices. No one is forcing readers to pull items
down from shelves. But they ought to have available to them all the information they need to be well-rounded, informed citizens of a democracy.
Even a not very good newspaper—and most are not very good—broadens
the horizons of its readers.

By newspapers, I also mean something often neglected by those who
have a better understanding of technology than of journalism. While good
journalism can be practiced by individuals—think Upton Sinclair or I. F.
Stone—it is often a collaborative effort, the result of teamwork rather than
solitary labor. Story ideas are kicked around in a newsroom. A journalist
reports a story and phones the editor, who makes suggestions and prods
the reporter to probe various angles and seek different interviews. When
the story is completed it is transmitted to the editor, who usually asks: "Are
you sure about this fact? Who's your source for this anonymous quote?
Have you got a second source on that? There was a report in X newspaper
that drew the opposite conclusion. You buried your lede—the heart of your
story is in paragraph ten. Did you talk to Y? This story needs more context." On a big story, other editors will weigh in. This is not meant to dis-
parage bloggers or other independent voices or experts. It is meant to say
that the offhand dismissal of journalistic organizations—which is a cousin

of the belief that a computer can assemble news without editors—will diminish the thoughtful journalism a democracy requires.

I asked Marc Andreessen, as I did others, to make believe he was the publisher of a newspaper. "What would you do?" The answer he shot back at me was a common one: "Sell it!" The problem with this strategy, as the *Rocky Mountain News* and other papers have discovered, is that there are no buyers. And those wealthy buyers who might be tempted to splurge for a newspaper trophy, the way their peers buy sports teams, risk looking like fools, not saviors, like Sam Zell at the now bankrupt Tribune Company.

Pressed further, Andreessen said he'd rush to put the newspaper online and move away from the print edition, as a handful of papers have already done. There are at least two vulnerabilities to this approach, as Andreessen recognized. First, because online newspaper ads today generate no more than 10 percent of what a print ad does, the paper really would be, as Mel Karmazin said, trading dollars for digital dimes. Second, public corporations are dependent on investors, and not many folks will invest in a declining asset. So the market value of newspapers will continue to fall, depriving them of the capital to invest in reporting and, in too many cases, the money to meet debt obligations. It may be true, as Rupert Murdoch's News Corporation's newspaper retreat concluded, that in another ten years online news will generate enough income to save the paper. The quandary is how to get through the next ten years. As Murdoch conceded, more than a few papers "will disappear," either consolidating with others or collapsing. Some of these newspapers are mediocre outposts of former monopolies and will not be mourned. But many are valuable civic institutions that cannot easily be replicated.

Any number of ideas have been advanced to rescue newspapers and journalism. Newspapers are belatedly striving to make online editions more interactive and to better conform to a Web sensibility. Michael Hirschorn wrote a provocative media column for *The Atlantic Monthly* and took a stab at defining a Web sensibility. He wrote that newspapers should take some of their star reporters—he mentions Kelefa Sanneh, the pop music critic for the *Times,* and Dana Priest, the national security reporter for the

Washington Post—and encourage them to create "an interactive online universe," inviting others to share their information, views, or news tips. "Gaming this out in the most baldly capitalistic fashion," he wrote, "the papers then stand a chance of transforming one Sanneh review (one impression) into the organic back-and-forth of social media (1,000 impressions)."

Newspapers are also experimenting with reducing costs by outsourcing functions to online ventures—investigative reporting to former *Wall Street Journal* managing editor Paul Steiger's foundation-funded ProPublica; or international reporting to *GlobalPost*, a privately financed organization whose news operation is supervised by former *Boston Globe* foreign correspondent Charles Sennott, and which pays seventy correspondents in fifty-three countries one thousand dollars for four dispatches a month and gives them part ownership of the enterprise. Bloomberg has proposed that newspapers could outsource their business coverage to them; dozens of newspapers have ceded much of their national political and government coverage to the hundred reporters who work for *Politico*. Another form of outsourcing is for papers to share articles and photographs; this approach is being tried by a consortium of the New York *Daily News, Buffalo News, Times Union* of Albany, and New Jersey's *Star-Ledger* and *The Record*. It has also been proposed that newspapers could be saved by acts of philanthropic generosity similar to the Poynter Institute's ownership of the *St. Petersburg Times;* or by injecting new revenues into newspapers (Yahoo has had some success in selling ads for a group of about eight hundred newspapers); or by various governmental actions, from relaxing regulations to tax breaks to advertising subsidies (as France did starting in early 2009) to—a really bad idea—direct subsidies.

While any of these Band-Aids might help slow the bleeding, two things are essential if print or online newspapers are to have a shot at survival. First, newspapers have to stop acting like victims, bemoaning their fate and clinging to the past. To blame Google is to prescribe a cure for the wrong illness. Second, they have to go on the offense by trying new things, including trying to charge for their content.

I was smacked in the face with this realization when my friend Kenneth Lerer, who started the *Huffington Post* with Arianna Huffington, mentioned in the summer of 2008 that he had hired a single twentysomething employee to launch its local Chicago online edition. The Web site, like Google, was free and offered links to stories in the *Chicago Tribune, Chicago Daily Herald,* and other local papers and Web sites. Aside from inviting citizens to blog, this local online "newspaper" was little more than a collection of links to work done by others. Lerer said there was promotional value for content providers like the *Tribune.* True. He said the more page views their content got the more advertising they'd sell. True. He said that "citizen journalists" often provide valuable information. True. But at a time when most newspapers proclaim local news as their potential salvation, these papers were suicidally supplying the *Huffington Post* with their own murder weapon. By 2009, the *Huffington Post* was discussing similar local editions in as many as fifty cities.

What to do? Eric Schmidt once told me that he thought "Apple's iTunes is a great example of compromise" between old and new media and, of course, users pay for their music there. "Google," Schmidt continued, "has not found the iTunes" model—yet. And unlike music and other forms of entertainment, few will keep replaying a newspaper story on their iPod. Andrew B. Lippman, the associate director and senior research scientist at the Media Lab at MIT, wonders whether the example of ASCAP, the organization that has channeled copyright payments to musicians since 1914, might be a way "for newspaper companies to share revenues." Newspapers and Google have to keep looking.

Even if they locate the right model, the technical challenge is daunting. "Can you put it behind a wall and charge for access? Yes," said Andreessen, who despite his criticism of traditional media still subscribes to the print edition of the *New York Times* and owns some eight thousand books and six thousand CDs. "Can someone still take that content, copy it and mail it to friends? Sure. Can somebody post it on a Web site in Russia and provide it for free? Sure. Can you get the Russian government to crack down on that? You can try. Can somebody put up every copy of the *New York Times* ever published on BitTorrent and make it available in a single pirated download? Sure. You can't stop it. It's bits. If anybody can see it, then there is going to be a way for everybody to see it."

Today, more than one billion people go online and view these bits. They are accustomed to reading news for free. To suddenly try to get them to pay for it would be an imposing task. To prevent leakage, presumably newspapers would need to act in concert. To do so would require discussions, and such collusion might invite antitrust lawsuits. On the other hand, when the survival of newspapers has been at stake in the past, government has allowed joint operating agreements (JOAs) so that two papers can pool printing facilities or other resources to save money. As there's little question that newspapers are endangered, our foremost papers—the *Times, Journal,* and *Washington Post*—might get together and agree to erect a firewall around their content. Responding to a March 2009 request from House Speaker Nancy Pelosi, Attorney General Eric Holder said he would consider relaxing antitrust regulations to allow newspapers to share costs and merge. In 2009, three longtime media executives—Steven Brill, the founder of Court TV and *The American Lawyer;* L. Gordon Crovitz, the former publisher of the *Wall Street Journal;* and business investor Leo Hindery, Jr.—announced that they had formed a company, Journalism Online LLC, in hopes of creating a single automated payment system so that print publications would be paid when their content was viewed.

The rub, of course, is that even if most newspapers agreed to erect a firewall, some would choose not to, probably including wire services like the AP that are now paid by Google for their news. Maybe the *Christian Science Monitor,* which now relies mostly on an online edition, or the *Seattle Post-Intelligencer,* which relies solely on its online edition, will achieve success with these and be unwilling to give them up. There would be leakage, as users shared stories. Or as Jack Shafer of *Slate* observed, an online publication like the *Huffington Post* or *Gawker* could subscribe to newspapers and rewrite their stories, as "Henry R. Luce and Britton Hadden started doing in 1923 as they rewrote newspapers on a weekly basis for *Time* magazine." On the upside, perhaps online citizens would be better able to distinguish between good reporting and bad. If the online newspaper offers content not readily available elsewhere, along with interactive and video and other features, perhaps customers will pay for it.

In March of 2008, I asked Larry Page how he would save newspapers, and he grew uncharacteristically passionate. "I don't know how to do it, or I would," he said. "Or at least try to help." He said he was spending time thinking about it. This was no abstract puzzle; he knew the question was linked to Google. "I do think that our mission at Google ends up being pretty close to this. We try to produce the best information we can. The success of a Google search is based on the quality of the information—is there a good article about this?" He went on to say, "I've been trying to learn more about journalism and trying to understand the issues better. I do think that there is a problem that if you're primarily doing it for profit, it's hard to do a really good job. The kinds of things that generate profits and page views are not necessarily the things that generate value for the world. If you look at really good newspapers, they have dual classes of stock. That's part of our inspiration for doing that."

Could he imagine Google in the newspaper or journalism business? "We look for high-leveraged things," he said. "We're trying to figure out, how does this one employee affect ten million people? I think most content creation companies involve more work. So we naturally steer away from that."

The next day I asked Eric Schmidt, why not pay a paper like the *Times* for its content? "We've been able with the *New York Times* to convince them that they make so much money from the traffic that we send them that they want their content available to Google," he said. "They have the choice of not doing it." In fact, the *Times* does generate some income from Google, but digital income from digital operations accounted for just 12 percent of the company's $2.9 billion revenues in 2008, more than a third of this from About.com. About half of the About Group's revenues, according to Arthur Sulzberger, Jr., comes from Google's AdSense, as does "a significant portion" of its online revenues. Might Google try to buy the *New York Times*? "The official answer is that we have discussed buying the *New York Times* over the years—and there are many such interesting companies," Schmidt answered, candidly. "In every case, we ultimately decided we don't want to cross that line"—to become a content provider and risk favoring Google's own content. "The reason I say we don't rule anything out is that our strategy is always evolving. We might come up with a different answer in a year or two."

A year later, in April of 2009, I asked Schmidt if he had come up with a different answer. "It's the same answer," he said, before adding that Google was working on a product that is targeted at individuals, that knows the stories that interest people and what they've already read and targets text and video to people based on those interests. "In order to do that model we would have to partner with news sources." He mentioned newspapers like the *Times* and *Washington Post* as potential collaborators. Indeed, after leaving Schmidt's office I bumped into the *Times* chairman and publisher, Arthur Sulzberger, Jr., and his senior vice president of digital operations, Martin Nisenholtz, grabbing lunch in the cafeteria of Building 43. They were startled to encounter a journalist, no doubt fearful word would spread that they were meeting that afternoon with Schmidt and the founders to discuss a partnership. How they would monetize such a partnership—share ad revenues, create a micropayment system, pay the papers a license fee for their content? Schmidt said he did not yet know the answer. He did know, however, that the new product would not be "a solution to the problems newspapers have today." But, he added, "the fact that we don't see a solution today doesn't mean that it doesn't exist. This is about invention. One criticism I would make of many industries is that they've lost the ability to reinvent themselves."

In an e-mail exchange afterward, Sulzberger did not portray Google as a villain: "Our industry faces many challenges but I would not lay them at the feet of Google." A major Silicon Valley figure only blames Google for playing a public relations game by appearing sympathetic to newspapers: "Let's suppose you're Google and you fully realize newspapers are screwed . . . and there's not a damn thing you can do about it. Are you better off saying 'tough noogies' or 'we carefully considered all kinds of ways that we could possibly help?'"

NEWSPAPERS—like the more seriously challenged music companies—have seen their decline abetted by the recession but not caused by it. By contrast, the sharp drop-off in magazine advertising that began in 2008 is probably linked to this downturn. Like newspapers, magazines require a robust online strategy. And like newspapers, even in a bustling economy some will perish. But magazines are just as portable as newspapers, and their content usually doesn't have to be read the day they're published. In weekly and monthly magazines, stories often benefit from the luxury of time denied to most daily journalism. There is more context and opinion. There are vivid pictures and color. The paper is glossy, and clean. The ads are more inviting. As a business, magazines probably have better prospects than newspapers.

Few investors would rush to acquire magazines. Even fewer would buy a book publishing company. Their dominant source of revenue is book sales, and these have been fairly flat. The profit margins are slim, and as with newspapers or magazines, the cost of production and distribution is immense. There are long-term questions about what multitasking and the "quick snacks" available online are doing to attention spans. Is it an accident that the fastest growing book category consists of shorter romance and young adult novels? Technology now permits books to be distributed electronically, and upstart publishers have begun to produce paperless books. In turn, writers have to adjust to new pay formulas that involve less money upfront and more profit participation if their books sell. More books will be self-published. And an entirely new class of books—user-generated serial novels written online—now appear on cell phones in Japan, and will elsewhere. For readers, a digital book, like a digital newspaper or magazine, offers a multimedia dimension: video, music, games, interactivity between author and audience.

Early in 2009, Amazon CEO Jeff Bezos said that of the books that were available both in print and electronically at Amazon, 10 percent of these were downloaded and sold on its portable Kindle device. By May, Amazon said the number of electronic books it sold had soared to 35 percent. This figure had nearly quadrupled in a year. Although electronic books comprised but 1 percent to 2 percent of all books sold, it is clear that paper will continue to be replaced by bits. As with newspapers, this will reduce costs. What gives publishers pause is that Amazon, like Apple with iTunes, gets to set the price for these electronic books, and they worry, as advertisers do with Google, that if there are no potent electronic competitors, Amazon will be able to dictate price and publishing terms. This is a reason that publishers welcomed Google's 2009 announcement that it would compete with Amazon to sell e-books.

Bezos has been smart about spotting trends, and he said he is optimistic about the future of books. At the *Wall Street Journal*'s D Conference, he told the audience, "Physical books won't go away, just as horses won't go away. But in the future the majority of books will be read electronically." The reason, he later told me, is convenience: "We humans do more of what is easy for us. The more friction-free something is, the more of it we do." Bezos was sitting on a Sun Valley patio with dark sunglasses shielding his eyes, and was more expansive. He said devices like the Kindle have the advantage of portability, have big, easy-to-read screens, provide online access to other information, and store many books. Most people, he believes, read more than one book at a time, and thus reading is more "frictionless" on devices like the Kindle or the Sony Reader. "The Kindle is an example of a device that is going to make long-form reading more convenient and less friction filled. As a result, you're going to get more long-form reading. If you want more reading, make reading easier. That's what we're trying to do. If you have a book with you, you'll read more."

Broadcast television, like newspapers, suffers from too many choices. In the final two decades of the twentieth century, the new consumer options were cable and then satellite TV. In this century, the Internet offers vastly more diversions, while TiVo and DVRs allow ad skipping and snatch the scheduling power away from network programmers. Although Americans still spend more time watching television than on the Internet, the proliferation of choices weakens the business model of many of these choices. This is especially true for broadcasters who, unlike cable, do not receive subscription revenue and rely solely on advertising. How, broadcast executives privately mumble, can they afford to pay three million dollars or more for each episode of a one-hour drama when ratings are falling? How continue to afford expensive nightly news broadcasts on ABC, NBC, and CBS when their nightly audience has plunged from thirty-two million in 2000 to twenty-three million in 2009? Local television stations, once known as cash cows because they generated profit margins of around 50 percent, have seen those margins collapse as viewers flock elsewhere and networks demand compensation for programming. Jack Myers projects that local broadcast station advertising revenues will drop 20 percent in 2009.

The belief embraced by too many television (and movie) executives that they are in the *content* business—and most digital companies are not—is not just smug but stupid. Content is anything that holds a consumer's attention. If four million people in China subscribe to online games and play an average of six hours daily, as Activision CEO Bobby Kotick says they do, that audience is lost to television and most any other media. If Facebook or YouTube or Twitter is captivating audiences, the number of eyeballs watching CBS will drop. Internet video is growing twice as fast as television viewing, Nielsen reported in early 2009, and eighteen- to twenty-four-year-olds now spend the same amount of time—five hours a day—watching Internet video as American adults spend watching TV.

"To survive," said Quincy Smith of CBS, "media companies have to get out of a broadcast mentality. All of us—broadcasters, cable networks, Hollywood studios—have to display our content on multiple platforms, be it YouTube, TV.com, Hulu, MySpace, or iTunes. We need to use these platforms to promote our content and drive audiences, particularly younger audiences, to our primary platform." Network television can no longer think of itself as a lean-back medium. The Internet, Smith emphasized, was more than just a distribution platform: "On the Web, you build communities. And traditional media has to change its DNA to think about that community. Our most trafficked CBS sites are the ones that create community. The Internet is not just a platform. It's about interactive storytelling."

By the summer of 2009, however, Quincy Smith decided that it was time to move on. He denied he was frustrated trying to turn the CBS ship around, steaming toward the digital world. He expressed admiration for CBS CEO Les Moonves. He desired to move on because he had accomplished what he set out to do. He had engineered the acquisition of CNET. He now presided over CBS Digital's three thousand employees. CBS Digital was generating one hundred million dollars in annual profits and growing 10 percent each year. The challenge now was "blocking and tackling," he said—management. This was not his forte. If he won Moonves's concurrence, he said he wanted to return to what he did best—deal making—and planned to hang his investment banking shingle in Silicon Valley and serve as a digital adviser to old and new media companies. If Smith left, said Moonves, he would want to retain him as a consultant.

The challenge for Smith's potential successor, as for all old media, is to create unique content.

No cable or satellite or telephone system will pay a hefty price for a network series that appears for free on YouTube—or is available in a pirated version. Because Viacom took the extreme (and arguably foolish) position of suing them, Google and YouTube have made considerable progress in coming up with a better (if probably still porous) defense against piracy. And as Google acknowledged in the negotiations—and in its settlements with the AP and the book publishing industry—it has accepted the principle of paying for content. Whether piracy safeguards or deals with YouTube can spare traditional television from further slippage is doubtful. Ultimately, the fate of traditional media is to jump off a bridge without knowing whether there is a net below.

The Hollywood studios have their own concerns about piracy. The biggest box office movie of 2008, *The Dark Knight,* was illegally downloaded around the world more than seven million times, according to the *New York Times.* The Motion Picture Association of America claims that illegal downloads and streaming of movies in 2008 accounted for 40 percent of the industry's revenue loss due to piracy. The audience for illegal downloads of *Heroes,* a studio-produced NBC series, was equal to one-quarter of the ten million viewers who watch it each week on NBC. In their efforts to stamp out piracy, the studios often offend their customers. Sergey Brin described going on a boat in Europe on his honeymoon and watching a DVD he and his wife had purchased. "We didn't finish. So we took it with us, and of course it wouldn't work in other DVD players." The more he talked, the more exercised he got. He recalled the time he purchased *The Transformers,* hoping to watch this science fiction movie in high definition on his new Blu-ray player. But his copy wasn't compatible with Blu-ray. "For a variety of reasons and some kind of piracy paranoia, they make it really hard on you. . . . I kind of feel the studios get in their own way."

Squaring the piracy concerns of studio executives with customers' urge for convenience has thus far eluded a solution. The movie business may be glamorous, but the profit margins are tight. For decades, selling movies to television proved to be richly rewarding, as did VCR and then DVD sales and rentals. Now the revenues from all of these are declining. Downloading movies over the Internet could be the next profitable platform—if piracy can be solved, and if the Hollywood studios were not immobilized by fear of offending big retailers, such as Wal-Mart, which sells their DVDs, and instead partnered to sell their own movies directly.

The cable business is more robust. Unlike broadcasters, cable programming channels like ESPN or MTV that produce content are not dependent on mass audiences because they enjoy two revenue streams, advertising and license fees from cable systems. Cable system owners like Comcast or Time Warner that own the cable wire and distribute content over cable systems also derive revenue streams from both ads and monthly service charges. Digital cable also has this advantage over broadcasting: it is able to offer interactive features like video on demand. Cable networks and online advertising are the only two of the seven media groupings projected to gain ad revenues in 2009, according to media consultant Jack Myers. However, like broadcasters, cable systems are dogged by the proliferation of platforms—YouTube, MySpace, CNET, Verizon's FIOS, local stations, two satellite television providers—that weaken their power as gatekeepers.

By 2009, with cable networks and broadcasters distributing programs for free to various online platforms, giant cable system owners like Comcast and Time Warner were concerned that their programming was being devalued. So they initiated efforts to offer online access to all of their programs, but only to their cable subscribers. The hope was that if cable subscribers could summon any program they wanted when they wanted it, they'd have less reason to fret about YouTube or Hulu, and might lure new cable subscribers. Currently, cable system owners pay much of the thirty billion dollars in license fees collected annually by the cable networks that produce programs. The club cable system owners wielded to prevent the ESPNs from putting their programs online was a warning that they would not continue to pay these steep license fees for programs cable channels were giving away cheaply or for free.

But the cable programmers may hold their own club in the form of new technologies that could replace cable set-top boxes with wirelessly received signals that will allow users to integrate all devices—from streaming video to computers to TV sets to portable devices. In early 2009, Eric Schmidt saw a demonstration of one such sleek wireless box made by the Sezmi Corporation and came away thinking that this new technology posed an imminent danger to both cable and satellite TV systems. If the wireless system worked, the cable or statellite wire could become a superfluous middleman. Sezmi was planning to beta test its system that year and claims that it had already negotiated deals with cable and broadcast networks. TV manufacturers like Sony and Samsung are developing sets with Internet connections, allowing them to bypass the cable gatekeeper.

The cable system owners already lacked leverage over broadcast networks because they do not pay to air the programs of CBS, NBC, ABC, and Fox, all of which were pushing their own online strategies. If people could watch 24 on Hulu, its value to cable would be diminished. By placing their programs on a variety of online outlets—Hulu, TV.com, YouTube, Boxee—broadcasters also ran the risk of sabotaging their business. But if they didn't, they ran the risk of passively watching their business erode. Again, the *Innovator's Dilemma*.

A major challenge confronting the cable and telephone and other distribution companies is to demonstrate that they are not just a pipe that others use to transport their valuable content for a bargain price. Verizon's Seidenberg wants to position the phone company as a disrupter. "We can go directly to Procter and Gamble and they can reach you without having to go through Google. So the world will now move in a direction where distribution will have a more important role." Verizon was experimenting in late 2008 by distributing Prince's music "directly to customers without going through a middleman": the music companies. "We can talk directly to directors and creators of content."

Seidenberg, who began his career as a telephone lineman, was seated in a corner booth at the Regency Hotel, which is a New York power breakfast spot, and he grew blustery as he talked of what Verizon could do to middlemen. "We're going to change ten percent of every relationship. In some

cases, fifty percent. So will there be a need for media buyers? Maybe one!"
He laughed. Because Verizon will own a wealth of data, he envisioned
working directly with advertisers to better target customers. The telephone
companies have a technology known as deep packet inspection (DPI)
that both protects their pipes from security threats and exposes the web
browsing activities of consumers to the kind of controversial behavioral
advertising practiced by Phorm in England.

"It could be the broadcast networks" that Verizon siphons ad dollars
from, Seidenberg said. "It could be the cable networks. It could be a lot of
people." Seidenberg's words, however, bump against reality. Having existed
for so long as quasimonopolies, the phone companies and cable companies
may not be agile and daring enough to move with the speed required. It
sounds hubristic for Seidenberg to assume, for instance, that a company
like Verizon, with minimal experience working with Hollywood directors
or advertisers, could overnight develop the skills to work with actors and
directors, or with Procter & Gamble. And Seidenberg blithely minimizes
the volatile issue of privacy.

Irwin Gotlieb also dismisses anxiety about privacy. He is more focused
on the ability of digital technology to generate more data, which will mean
that "the value of data will escalate dramatically." The critical questions
to Gotlieb will be: "Who collects the data? Who owns the data? Who gets
to exploit the data? Who's the gatekeeper? Who's the toll collector? These
are key strategic issues that need to be resolved"—between the ad agencies
and Google and the cable and telephone companies, among others. But the
data will be crucial because it will allow advertisers to move from guessing
about "multiple correlations"—income, demographics, television programs watched—to "intent," which he described this way: "Today, if I
decide I need to sell a high-end watch, who's the prospect? I can identify
people with discretionary income. I can identify males or females fifty or
older. But down the road, I will know you're a watch collector because I
will have that data on you. How? I will know your purchase behavior. A
lot of retailers have loyalty programs, and they will share this information.
If consumers have searched on Google or eBay to look at watches, all these
searches are data trails. So instead of assuming that because you're wealthy

you might buy a watch, I can narrow my target to the small percentage of watch collectors." And mobile phones offer still more data. Whether the mining of this data will provoke a public outcry is an issue Gotlieb does not stress.

To make the sale, he believes awareness, or brand advertising, will remain vital. He has a stake in saying this, but he seems to believe it: "I am not a proponent of the belief that most advertising is wasted. If I don't create a predilection in you for a Mercedes when you're a fifteen-year-old male, you're not going to buy a Mercedes when you're forty and can afford to. Take disposable diapers. Should you just market to pregnant women? I would argue that maybe the grandmother has significant influence. And maybe you could make little diapers for Barbies, so the eight-year-old girl becomes aware of your brand. Both of these require you to substantially expand your target." And expand the money clients spend on advertising. It also assumes that the public will accept such hard sells.

Gotlieb believes only the agencies possess the skills and experience to engage in such long-term brand building. He refers to his work not as media buying but as "media investment management." Whatever name he chooses, it's endangered, which Gotlieb reluctantly admits. "I'm terribly concerned about getting disintermediated." It's why he thinks his business has to change from middleman to a principal. "I've grown up in a business where the media agency was a pure service business. I was taught from day one to put my clients' interests ahead of my own. It may have been appropriate for the time and place. But it is no longer appropriate today, because we're competing with people who are both vendor and client, as well as agent. Microsoft is a vendor, but owns a digital ad agency. Google is a vendor, but deals directly with clients. As a consequence, unless you're terribly naïve, we have to morph our business from pure service to a mix of service and nonservice." He ticked off several options, including producing and owning content, whether it be television programs or movies; investing in technologies, as his parent company has, to try to capture more data and receive not just fees and commissions but "participate in the profits."

What if a client asks whose interests come first, Gotlieb's or the clients? "That's a really good question," he responded. "But how many people ask

Google that question? If we remain purely a service business, we won't be in business."

Advertising will look very different in coming years. New digital middlemen have already surfaced. Like Google's AdSense, these advertising networks act as brokers, putting Web sites and advertisers together. Computerized ad networks can quickly cobble together Web sites or TV stations that, together, reach an audience the size of an ESPN but at a fraction of the cost. This is a threat not just to traditional media, but to middlemen like Gotlieb. Still another refinement among agencies like Gotlieb's is that, increasingly, the media buyers are beginning to offer to create ads as well. Because the giant media-buying firms operate under the same corporate umbrella as the creative agencies, this could produce civil war within firms.

Gotlieb knows that if he doesn't refine his business model, Google or someone else may grab his clients. Most media (and not a few other industries) are in a race to avoid becoming superfluous middlemen. No matter how much popcorn they sell, movie theaters might face this fate when Hollywood begins to release movie DVDs simultaneously with the theatrical release. It is the danger faced by local TV stations as broadcast networks air their programs online and threaten to sell them directly to cable, and by media buyers like Gotlieb as clients work directly with Google or perhaps Verizon. The Internet and digital technology allows people to download movies rather than buy a DVD, to bypass stores and travel agents and perhaps eliminate financial or real estate brokers, publishers, bookstores, agents, music CDs, newspapers, cable or telephone wires, paid classifieds, packaged software and games, car salesmen, the post office. The Web allows sellers and buyers to connect directly, as they have done on eBay. Inevitably, new technologies will cripple many old media businesses.

One day when I was questioning Eric Schmidt about the travails of old media, he calmly asked, "Do you feel bad that the pager business is in trouble? No, because you use your cell phone as a substitute. When you have a good substitute, it's very, very hard to fight against that." Unless old media companies want to fight their customers, try to deny their desire for new choices and new conveniences, they have no alternative but to figure out how to ride the wave.

CHAPTER SEVENTEEN

Where Is the Wave Taking Google?

G oogle is surfing a huge wave that seems not to have crested. Eileen Naughton is the director of media platforms for Google and works out of its block-long New York office on West Fifteenth Street. Before joining Google, Naughton spent more than fifteen years at Time Warner, where she held a number of senior positions, including president of *Time* magazine and vice president of investor relations during the merger of AOL and Time Warner, when everyone feared layoffs, turf battles, a stock price drop, and senior management at the joined companies vied to mirror the Ottoman Empire, where the wives of sultans poisoned stepsons. When asked to describe the difference between working at Google and at an old media company, Naughton offered a one-word reply: "Optimism."

Google may not have an overarching strategy, but it does aim to be a disrupter. Google has always been guided by a vision enunciated as early as 2002, as we've also seen, when Larry Page told a Stanford class, "If you can solve search, that means you can answer any question. Which means you can do basically anything."

When Google defines its informational mission so broadly, and enters businesses where engineering can eradicate inefficiencies, it is left with a shooting gallery of swollen targets. An "innovative" company like Google, said Brin, enters fields where "we scale," meaning where they have the infrastructure to enter fairly cheaply and without huge diversions of resources. With millions of computers and servers processing searches and collecting and digesting data, this architecture makes it possible for Google to "scale" into cloud computing, to store and search and sell digital books, to host the fifteen hours of video uploaded each minute on YouTube—the equivalent, Brin said, of uploading eighty-six thousand full length movies every week. "Everything Google does extends its reach," Bala Iyer and Thomas H. Davenport wrote in the *Harvard Business Review*. "It is informational kudzu." And although Google likes to say they don't compete with media companies and prefers to call them "partners," Iyer and Davenport write that by working with advertisers and newspapers, magazines, television, radio, mobile telephones and Web sites, it "is quite possible that what Google learns across various media as it solves problems for the ecosystem partners may position it to become the competitor that it now claims not to be."

Google appears to be well positioned for the foreseeable future, but it is worth remembering that few companies maintain their dominance. At one point, few thought the Big Three auto companies would ever falter—or the three television networks or AT&T, IBM, or AOL. For companies with histories of serious missteps—Apple, IBM—it was difficult to imagine that they'd rebound, until they did. To avoid the roller coaster, Google has to avoid two sets of obstacles, one external, the other internal.

THE EXTERNAL HURDLES START with Microsoft, but they don't end there. Because Google has been so audacious, it has "waked up the bears," colliding with various industries and companies. Alert to Google's growing dominance, Verizon in late 2008 chose Microsoft's search engine for its mobile phones. Newspapers and magazines now want Google to pay to link to their stories. Television and movies seek license fees from YouTube.

Telephone companies fear Google's Android. Advertising agencies seesaw back and forth between wariness and hostility. Cable and telephone broadband providers are angry about Google's call for an "open net." Rupert Murdoch is unhappy that Google is likely to end its lucrative advertising guarantee to his MySpace when the contract expires in 2010, as Time Warner was when Google announced in early 2009 that it would sell its 5 percent stake in AOL, cheapening the value of AOL and of Time Warner's stock. Microsoft needs no reminders that Google is their enemy and was reminded of this in July 2009 when Google announced—as Netscape, to Microsoft's chagrin and alarm, did a decade earlier—that it was retooling its browser to become an operating system for PCs, one without boot-up delays and that would be simpler and faster and cheaper than Windows. (Of course, Microsoft countered with a Web-based version of its Office software that is also free.) Overseas, Google is challenged. Its social network site, Orkut, has seen its market share slip in countries like India and Brazil, where it was once dominant. Even in search, there has been slippage; in Russia, a private start-up named Yandex has a market share approaching 50 percent, well ahead of Google. As with nations, there are few permanent allies. Friends like Apple are angry about Android, and although Jeff Bezos was an original Google investor (and declines to say if he still owns Google stock), Amazon is mounting a cloud-computing challenge as Google is mounting an electronic book challenge. "These companies air kiss each other, just as any Hollywood company does," observed Andrew Lack, the former president of NBC and the CEO of Sony Music, now the CEO of the multimedia division of Bloomberg LP. "So their level of sincerity is not much different than the traditional Hollywood. Usually we think of Hollywood and Washington, D.C., as company towns. Ironically, Silicon Valley is often right there with them."

Google knows that one day its cold war with Facebook could turn hot. By March 2009, Facebook had 200 million users, double the number it had when Sheryl Sandberg joined a year earlier. Sandberg projected that by the end of the year, Facebook would have 1,200 employees. Despite sneers that Facebook makes no money, Sandberg said if her company extracted the money it reinvests in its computerized infrastructure, "we've been profitable for seven quarters." (Of course, one can't extract these core business expense.) By the fall of 2009, she predicted that Facebook would take in more cash than it expends. Asked whether Facebook was a threat, Bill Campbell replied without hesitating, "Anybody that gets a widely accepted user platform is to be worried about. They could be the start page for people that use the Web." The Google model is based on getting users out of Google and to other sites, on maintaining the Internet as the primary platform. Facebook and other social networks seek to keep users on their sites, to become the hub of their online lives, to become their home.

Social networks might pose a threat to Google search. At the MIT Media Lab in the winter of 2009, a Ph.D. student named Kwan Lee was devising a mobile phone application for a social network search function. Lee began with the premise that "Ads on the side are not useful to me." Google search, he said, "is a pull model," in which the search program aggregates data and lets users decide what is useful. Lee thinks it is difficult for users to "pull" the data they want from the hundreds of thousands of links received in response to a single search query, much of which he considers spam. As a substitute, he is devising a "push" model with which friends who are part of a social network could push tips to friends, sharing what they purchased. It would also allow participants to ask questions of friends, who are likely to deliver more precise and trusted answers. "This makes search much more efficient," said Lee, fondling his iPhone in his space on the fourth floor of the Lab. "My goal is to reduce and eliminate spam," to allow "people to get recommendations from friends."

This could pose a threat to Google, for although it has a broader base of data, social networks like Facebook, Twitter, Ning, or Linkedin retain more in-depth information about individuals and their community of friends. A familiar brand name like Amazon could also pose a challenge. "What happens if people searching for a product go right to Amazon and not to Google?" asked an important Google adviser.

Google's founders are acutely aware that search is still fairly primitive. Type into your Google search box "Was Shakespeare real?" and in less than a second up pop 5,06,000 results. Because many books have been written exploring whether someone other than William Shakespeare penned his plays, one result would not be possible or even desirable. But 5 million? Page and Brin often say that their ideal is to have so much information about their users that Google can devise an algorithm that provides a single perfect answer.

Kwan Lee is not alone in thinking that Google is mistaken to treat search as an engineering problem. John Borthwick, who created one of the first city Web sites, sold it to AOL in 1997, and later became senior vice president of technology and alliances for Time Warner, thinks Google "lacks a social gene." (Borthwick has since founded and now runs Betaworks, which seeds money for social media.) Information, he said, "needs a social context. You need to incorporate the social graph [the connections among people] into search. Twitter becomes a platform for search. People put out Tweets—'I'm thinking about buying a camera. What does anyone think of this camera?'" It's the wisdom of crowds—your crowd of friends. "Google is just focused on CPU—central processing computers—and ignores the processing of the human brain." He believes this makes its search vulnerable. Google obviously has come to share this concern for a senior Google executive confirms that they tried—and failed—to acquire Twitter.

Search Engine Land's Danny Sullivan identifies another variation of this threat. "If I were Google I'd be worried about vertical searches," he said—searches that tap the knowledge of experts. Jason Calacanis, a Web entrepreneur, started a niche search engine, Mahalo.com. The problem with horizontal search, Calacanis said, is that it spews out too much information and assumes that the most linked sites are best. "The 'wisdom of crowds' is great to find trends," but there is such a "mob" of voices on the Web that search results produce too much useless information. He said he raised twenty million dollars to hire experts who produce targeted sets of no more than seven results—the seven best hotels in Paris, for instance. He hoped experts in various fields could produce answers to twenty-five thousand questions and computerize these. He vowed not to assign cookies to track a user's past searches, and said he'd be content in ten years if Mahalo had ten percent of all search traffic. He saw Google more as a partner than a competitor; the AdSense program generates a good deal of his site's income. The competition he worried about is from old media. "I would have been afraid if the

New York Times or Bloomberg took a bunch of editors to compete with us." Calacanis still can't understand why they didn't enter vertical search themselves. With experts in food, wine, movies, art, Iraq, finance—you name it—big newspapers might have been a search contender.

Of course, Calacanis himself might not be a contender. Perhaps a challenge will come from Wolfram Alpha, which was launched in May 2009 and does not search the Web or rely on experts but instead relies on databases to provide answers and offers additional links on the side of the search results. Unlike Google, these vertical search engines do not offer a universal search, which raises this question: how does a user anticipate which subjects are covered in the vertical search index? To date, with exceptions such as Expedia .com for travel, Monster.com for job searches, and HomeAway.com for vacation retreats, vertical searches have not thrived. And as Google moves toward better comprehension of the information users seek, it too will produce fewer and better-honed results. Google will have competition from Microsoft's renamed and reengineered search engine, Bing, launched in May 2009, which in July 2009 finally succeeded in merging with Yahoo search.

One could argue that the ultimate vertical search would be provided by Artificial Intelligence (AI), computers that could infer what users actually sought. This has always been an obsession of Google's founders, and they have recruited engineers who specialize in AI. The term is sometimes used synonymously with another, "the semantic Web," which has long been championed by Tim Berners-Lee. This vision appears to be a long way from becoming real. Craig Silverstein, Google employee number 1, said a thinking machine is probably "hundreds of years away." Marc Andreessen suggests that it is a pipe dream. "We are no closer to a computer that thinks like a person than we were fifty years ago," he said.

Sometimes lost in the excitement over the wonders of ever more relevant search is the potential social cost. In his provocative book *The Big Switch*, Nicholas Carr notes that Google's goal is to store 100 percent of each individual's data, what Google calls "transparent personalization." This would allow Google to "choose which information to show you," reducing inefficiencies. "A company run by mathematicians and engineers, Google

seems oblivious to the possible social costs of transparent personalization," Carr wrote. "They impose homogeneity on the Internet's wild het-
erogeneity. As the tools and algorithms become more sophisticated and
our online profiles more refined, the Internet will act increasingly as an
incredibly sensitive feedback loop, constantly playing back to us, in ampli-
fied form, our existing preferences." We will narrow our frames of reference, become more polarized in our views, gravitate toward those whose
opinions we share, and maybe be less willing to compromise because, he
said, the narrow information we receive will magnify our differences, making it harder to reach agreement. Carr also expressed concern that search
extracts another toll. "The common term 'surfing the Web' perfectly cap-
tures the essential superficiality of our relationship with the information
we find in such great quantities on the Internet. . . . The most revolutionary
consequence of the expansion of the Internet's power, scope, and usefulness may not be that computers will start to think like us but that we will
come to think like computers. Our consciousness will thin out, flatten, as
our minds are trained, link by link, to 'DO THIS with what you find HERE
and go THERE with the result.' The artificial intelligence we're creating
may turn out to be our own."

The fear was that Google and its online brethren shortened attention
spans and trivialized ideas by simplifying them. This was the thrust a quarter century ago of Neil Postman's influential book, *Amusing Ourselves to
Death*. He was writing of the public harm when television supplanted
print. I can't suppress a smile when I think how this communications
scholar, were he still alive, would react to the Internet, to the thousands
and sometimes millions of answers Google offers to a search question, or
to an online text-messaging tool like Twitter, with its insistence that no
communication be more than 140 characters.

Increasingly, teachers admonish their students that a Google search can
be too easy, allowing them to bypass books that broaden the context of
their thinking and surprise them with ideas their search words don't anticipate. Tara Brabazon, a professor of media studies at the University of
Brighton, in England, published a book, *The University of Google,* that

caught the attention of the press, in early 2008. Google, she told the *Times* of London the day before she was to deliver a lecture based on her work, "offers easy answers to difficult questions. But students do not know how to tell if they come from serious, refereed work or are merely composed of shallow ideas, superficial surfing and fleeting commitments." She does not let her first-year students use Google or Wikipedia as research tools because, she warned, "We need to teach our students the interpretive skills first before we teach them the technological skills." These social costs will matter to the company if they erode the trust Google has earned and if generations of college graduates and their instructors are dubious about Google's veracity or worth.

The other external threat to Google is government, a threat engineers have difficulty understanding; the Silicon Valley bubble can be as insular as the Beltway's. Google had fair warning when the Federal Trade Commission held up its DoubleClick acquisition, and when the Justice Department threatened antitrust charges if Google did not relinquish its advertising deal with Yahoo. And these challenges were under the antiregulatory administration of George W. Bush. There is, with merit, a common belief at Google that the administration of Barack Obama and the Democratic leadership in the House are more sympathetic to Valley companies and technology issues. Eric Schmidt was an important economic adviser to Obama, and other Google executives, like David Drummond, were early and fervent Obama supporters. But Google would forget at its peril that Democrats traditionally favor more regulation, not less; that Google has made some powerful frenemies that command attention in Washington; and that Google juggles nuclear issues—privacy, concentration of power, copyright—that could explode at any moment. In May 2009, the Obama administration's new antitrust chief, Christine A. Varney, announced that her department would more rigorously police tech firms like Google.

There are court threats and festering opposition to Google's Book Search settlement. By the spring of 2009, the settlement was separating Google from members of "the tribe," as Lawrence Lessig dubs them, who treat openness as a cause and crusade against those who advance their own narrow commercial interests and choke competition. The federal district court judge who must sign off on the agreement between Google and the publishers and the Authors Guild received amicus briefs from various groups asking him to address their antitrust and monopoly concerns. Under the terms of the settlement, Google was granted nearly exclusive rights to millions of "orphaned" books, or those books still under copyright but whose copyright holders are unknown. Because only Google would be granted the right to digitize these books and to sell them, the judge was petitioned to prevent a Google monopoly. Librarians expressed concern that Google would monitor reading habits and compile data. Some literary agents protested, as did Charles Nessen and a group of Harvard lawyers, that Google did not have the right to abrogate an orphaned copyright. And with Google effectively locking up the right to digitize all the books ever published, including orphaned books, the claim was that competitors would be shut out. Safeguards were required, they asserted, to ensure that Google would not one day jack up the prices it charges universities and others. The federal judge gave opponents until October 2009 to register their complaints. Seeking to head off growing concerns among libraries, in May 2009 Google reached an agreement with the University of Michigan to grant libraries a say in pricing decisions and to settle disagreements by arbitration, a model it hoped to extend to other libraries. Ominously, the Justice Department also opened an antitrust inquiry. Many who petitioned the court or lobbied Justice acknowledged that Google's effort to digitize books was salutary. Yet the din grew louder that Google was a mechanized steamroller.

And the U.S. government is not the only government Google must contend with. The European Union held up the DoubleClick merger, and may well object to Google's worldwide book deal that was made with American companies and authors. China censored their search engine and, in early 2009, blocked YouTube for a time from appearing before the world's largest Internet audience. As the Iranian government brutally suppressed street demonstrations in June 2009 not just with clubs but by jamming the Internet, the government of China had ordered PC makers to load filtering software on all machines sold after July 1. China claimed this would block pornography, but it would also grant the government a weapon to block political content it considered subversive. Not surprising, many governments are hostile to the idea of a free and open Web that Google advances, believing their national values—or the governing regime—are threatened. I soured on attending the World Economic Forum in Davos several years ago because I found too many panels there to be insufferably polite and boring—designed to bestow backslaps on corporate and government attendees. But what *is* mind stretching about Davos, and different from most conferences, is that attendees come from all over the world and bring with them different sets of values and assumptions about the meaning of words. I remember a panel in the late nineties moderated by Esther Dyson, an early champion of the Internet. She opened by extolling the democratic values—freedom, liberty, access to all information—advanced by the Web. The former foreign minister of Denmark chimed in with his agreement, emphasizing that the Web gave individuals more freedom. He and Dyson thought they were taking the unassailable moral high ground.

For the next several minutes, they sat slack-jawed as Singapore's ambassador to the United States challenged them. He said his government licensed Internet use with the idea that the Web must serve society, not the individual. "By licensing you are asking for responsible use," he said. An Egyptian diplomat educated in America chimed his agreement. He favored regulating "human dignity" situations, such as expressions that might be construed as "racist." He urged the adoption of international standards to prevent freedom of speech from being too free.

Astonished, Dyson and the former foreign minister challenged these ideas as threats to "liberal values."

"I am not a liberal," a member of the Iranian Parliament shot back, declaring that his government opposed the "pollution" of Western democratic values spread over the Web. "A nonliberal system does not equal intolerance," he said, explaining that his country favored "community" over "individual" values.

This exchange was a reminder that "common values" are not always common, and that Google, whose mission is to share and make the world's information accessible, will always have government bears to contend with.

THE THREATS FROM WITHIN GOOGLE are as significant as those from without. "What Google should fear most of all is hubris," said Yossi Vardi, the Israeli entrepreneur who funds start-ups and is a friend of Page's and Brin's. "If you are successful and young and everything plays in your direction, you feel you can do anything." When Marissa Mayer said that Googlers love to battle over ideas but "everyone" shares "a similar motivation to do good for the world," or when chief cultural officer Stacy Savides Sullivan said, "What separates us is that our founders care about users, not making money," they sincerely meant it. But history is littered with examples of people who believed too much in their own virtue and lost the humility that is a counterweight to hubris. Page and Brin, observed Stanford's Terry Winograd, "are utopians," believing deeply that "if people have better information they will live better lives. . . . They are technological optimists in the sense of saying, 'Let's produce this technology and things will work out.'" They don't always work out, and some of the clashes Google has had—with book publishers and the AP, or with ad agencies and governments—resulted from an inability to hear.

In the 1990s a coterie of math whizzes that included Nobel Prize winners Robert C. Merton and Myron S. Scholes crafted formulas they were certain would allow Long-Term Capital Management to consistently outperform the stock market; they failed spectacularly because their computer programs lacked common sense. This is the same mechanical thinking that often overlooks the needs of workers when designing assembly lines. In the same way, Google's engineers can get too wedded to their algorithms. As Google search has become more dominant, a chorus of complaints from media companies that the PageRank algorithm penalizes them has grown louder. By giving so much weight to the number of links a page received rather than the quality of the information reported, members of Google's Publisher's Advisory Council, which includes ESPN, the *Wall Street Journal,* Hearst, and the *New York Times,* complained that their links often appeared on page three or lower in the search results. Nat Ives of *Advertising Age* reported that the *Times* senior vice president, Martin Nisenholtz, told of doing a search for *Gaza* after the Israeli army launched an invasion to stop rocket attacks around New Year's 2009. "Google returned links," Ives reported, "to outdated BBC stories, Wikipedia entries, and even an anti-Semitic YouTube video well before coverage by the *Times,* which had an experienced reporter covering the war from inside Gaza itself." While it's true that judging "quality" in news is subjective, it's also true that Google's proclaimed desire to offer the best information often conflicts with algorithms that reflexively push to the top of the search results those sites with the most links. If such complaints received wide currency, they would sabotage the trust essential to Google's continued success.

Hubristically, Google engineers were convinced they could devise a system to successfully sell ads for YouTube. So far at least, they've failed. Why? They failed to comprehend the fear major advertisers have of placing their ads alongside potentially unfriendly user-generated content, and they failed to sufficiently anticipate that users would find ads intrusive. In early 2008, when Eric Schmidt envisioned employing a Google sales force of a thousand to sell ads for radio, Danny Sullivan was dubious. "They have no experience," he said, echoing Mel Karmazin's comments from his 2003 visit. "They may be able to cut costs, but a lot of people at Google don't understand that selling other ads is not like a search auction. They don't understand it is an art, not a science." In late 2008 and early 2009, a somewhat humbled Google canceled its print ads and its audio ads programs, and pared two hundred sales and marketing jobs.

Frantically, Google adopted a new approach to YouTube. With the site then on course to lose about five hundred million dollars in 2009, Schmidt transferred Salar Kamangar, who had crafted Google's first business plan and shepherded AdWords, to YouTube headquarters to work closely with its founders to design a monetization plan. And the management team at Google recognized that to attract advertising, YouTube could not rely on user-generated videos or three-minute clips from the networks. They needed long-form content, and in April 2009 made ad-sharing deals with the Universal Music Group, the world's largest music company, to create a music video channel on YouTube, and with several Hollywood studios and CBS to air movies and a library of TV shows. More ads appeared when Google accepted that YouTube needed more professional content, and its losses were shrinking.

Size is a concern for a company with more than twenty thousand employees. Venture capitalist Fred Wilson, a principal in Union Square Ventures, unhesitantly believes Google "is a great company." But he also believes: "They are a big company. Maybe they can't innovate anymore. It takes them meetings and processes to make decisions. Things don't get launched as quickly. They missed the whole video thing. YouTube beat them to it. They had to buy YouTube. They missed the whole social networking thing. Facebook beat them to that."

Losing focus is another danger for a company this large and wealthy. "My sense is that Google is like that fourteen-year-old who suddenly gets to wear grown-up clothing and maybe looks old enough to get a drink at a bar," said Strauss Zelnick, CEO of ZelnickMedia, which invests in and manages an array of media properties. "There's really nothing that doesn't look cool and interesting to a fourteen-year-old with an Amex card and no spending limit. Do you remember Michael Armstrong?" Zelnick recalled that Armstrong, the former CEO of AT&T, once boasted of spending a hundred billion dollars on acquisitions over four months. "I said, 'He's done.' No one does that well. *Focus*. Google has done a phenomenal job. Right now they can afford to, but at some point in time they are going to need to have a crisp vision of who they are and where they're going, and focus on that."

Although Mary Meeker believes Google is a great company, she offers another caution: the power and precariousness of a culture shaped by its founders. When founders stay involved in the enterprise—she cited Steve Jobs of Apple and Larry Ellison of Oracle—they often maintain the core values and mission of the business and bring something invaluable to the enterprise. But Jobs and Ellison lost focus, and watched their companies suffer. They also profoundly learned from their ordeals, while Page and Brin have yet to "experience nasty failure" and its concurrent ability to teach, as Al Gore also noted. And now with wives, and a son born to Brin in early 2009 and Page expecting his first child in the fall of 2009, and with incomprehensible wealth and two huge airplanes more conveniently at their disposal—Brin and Page persuaded NASA to waive its prohibition on private planes parking or using the nearby NASA facility—both young men are in the office less, jumping on their planes to take photographs in Africa, to explore the wilds of Alaska; Page likes to tool around in his Tesla electric car or fly his own helicopter and Brin to spend time building his own kite-powered sailboat. Will their attention wander from Google?

Today, Google appears impregnable. But a decade ago so did AOL, and so did the combination of AOL Time Warner. "There is nothing about their model that makes them invulnerable," Clayton Christensen, Harvard business historian and author of the seminal *The Innovators Dilemma,* told me. "Think IBM. They had a 70 percent market share of mainframe computers. Then the government decided to challenge them. Then the PC emerged." Seemingly overnight, computing moved from mainframes to PCs. For a long while, Microsoft seemed unstoppable, he said, only to be diverted by government intervention and the emergence of Linux and open-source software. "Lots of companies are successful and are applauded by the financial community," Christensen said. "Then their stock price stalls because they are no longer surprising investors with their growth. So they strive to grow but forget the principles that made them great—getting into the market quickly, not throwing money at the wrong thing. When you have so much money you become so patient that you wait too long. Again, look at Microsoft. No one can fault them for not investing in growth ideas. But none of these have grown up to be the next Windows." Maybe, he added, we are now beginning to "see this at Google." The company has poured money into YouTube and Android and cloud computing and the Chrome browser, but has yet "to figure out the business model for each."

Of course, these are the what-ifs. Today, and for the foreseeable future, few of Google's detractors would disagree with Fred Wilson, who said of Google, "There is no end in sight to the value they are creating." The value can be measured in rising profits and searches, but to quantify Google's success just in this fashion is to view the young company through a zoom lens rather than a wide-angle. The close-up misses how Google has transformed how we gather and use information, given us the equivalent of a personal digital assistant, made government and business and other institutions more transparent, helped people connect, served as a model service provider and employer, made the complex simple, and become an exemplar of the oft-stated but rarely followed maxim, "Trust your customer." Because it is *free,* Google will be difficult to assail.

No one can predict with certainty where Google and the digital wave is heading, when it will crest, or who it will flatten. If the public or its representatives come to believe Google plays favorites, aims to monopolize knowledge or its customers, invades their privacy, or arrogantly succumbs, in the words of Clayton Christensen, "to the falsehood that you can grow and grow because of network effects," then it will be more vulnerable. If Google maintains its deposit of public trust—continuing to put users first—and if it stays humble and moves with the swiftness of a fox, it will be difficult to catch.

Other companies have profoundly disrupted the business landscape. Think of the Ford automobile or the Intel chip. We can, however, be certain of this: Nowhere in the three billion daily searches it conducts, the two dozen or so petabytes (about twenty-four quadrillion bits) of data it stores, the more than twenty million books it plans to digitize, will we find another company that has swept so swiftly across the media horizon.

ACKNOWLEDGMENTS

This book was born two and one half years ago. I aspired to profile a company at the epicenter of the digital revolution, a company whose rise would also tell the story of how "new" media disrupted "old," and offer a glimpse into the future of media. Google was my chosen vehicle, but the company was reluctant to cooperate. Google's founders and many of its executives share a zeal to digitize books, but don't have much interest in reading them. They worried that cooperating on a book was an "inefficient" use of their time. I made the argument that my task was to understand and explain what they do and how they were changing the media world, and that they should look upon my project much as they look upon search. If my book was good, it would rise to the top of search results, becoming a common reference. After months of my kicking at the door, they opened it.

I could not have told this story without their cooperation. I made many weeklong visits to the Google campus in Mountain View, conducted a total of about 150 Google interviews, including 11 with CEO Eric Schmidt. I recorded each of these interviews; names and dates are contained in the endnotes. With the sole exception of one vice president, I interviewed everyone I asked to see, including Sergey Brin and Larry Page and Google directors, often more than once. With the blessing of his superiors, David Krane, who was one of Google's early hires, orchestrated and attended most interviews. He was a fountain of historical facts, and not once did he interrupt or intrude on an interview.

I was frequently asked by Google employees whether they would like this book. I always said that if I did my job there would be things that would displease them. No one at Google saw this book before publication. I am grateful to Google for its willingness to risk transparency. I am also grateful to about

150 individuals outside Google who granted interviews, many of them representatives of traditional media.

At Penguin Press, Ann Godoff has championed this project and been an irreplaceable partner on this as on previous books. Nick Trautwein lent his appreciable surgical skills to the editing of this book and stayed on top of everything. I am grateful to the rest of Ann's team, including her competent assistant, Lindsay Whalen; the marketing team assembled by Tracy Locke, especially the ever-industrious and cheerful Sarah Hutson; to copy editor Susan Johnson, who meticulously pored over every syllable; and to attorney Gary Mailman, who carefully vetted this book.

This book began at my journalistic home, *The New Yorker,* which published my initial 2007 magazine piece, "The Search Party." Editor David Remnick bestows on his writers the luxury of time, a keen editorial eye, and a sense that he is in the managerial dugout cheering. The editorial support writers receive at *The New Yorker,* from senior editors who read and comment on galleys to fact checkers who exhaustively exhume every sentence to copy editors who meticulously smooth prose—and from my longtime editor there, Jeffrey Frank—fills me with awe.

Lisa Chase gave a careful and close initial reading of the manuscript and reminded me what a gifted editor she is. Lawrence Lessig read the manuscript with the care he brings to legal briefs, and his comments were acute. Barry Harbaugh meticulously fact checked the manuscript. I wrestled for months to come up with a title. It took my friend Nora Ephron about thirty seconds to cut through my morass and suggest, "Googled." Another old friend, Milton Glaser, who designed the jacket of my first book, volunteered to design this jacket, and did so overnight. Kenneth Lerer offered valuable advice, as did his business associate, Jonah Peretti. I have received generous help from many other friends, including Tully Plesser, Susan Lyne, and John Eastman. My agent, Sloan Harris, has been a stalwart; you want him in your foxhole. Amanda Urban, as always, was my most demanding and provocative reader.

These are the folks who share credit; any blame is all mine.

Preface

Page

xi *YouTube, with ninety million unique visitors:* Nielsen VideoCensus, April 2009.

xi *"The Internet . . . makes information accessible":* author interview with Hal Varian, April 1, 2009.

xii *"Our goal is to change the world":* author one-on-one interview with Eric Schmidt at a forum sponsored by the *New Yorker* and the Newhouse School at Syracuse University, June 11, 2008.

xiii *Google could become a hundred-billion-dollar media company:* author interview with Eric Schmidt, September 12, 2007.

CHAPTER 1: Messing with the Magic

3 *With his suit and tie:* Karmazin Google meeting described in author interviews with Karmazin, May 13, 2008, and August 22, 2008; Nancy Peretsman, May 1, 2008; Eric Schmidt, April 16, 2008, and September 15, 2008; Sergey Brin, September 18, 2008; and Richard J. Bressler, September 26, 2008.

3 *Short and pugnacious:* Ken Auletta, "The Invisible Manager," *The New Yorker*, July 27, 1998.

4 *Google's private books revealed:* from August 2004 Google IPO registration with the Securities and Exchange Commission.

4 *Karmazin's destination:* description of 2400 Bayshore Parkway offices from visit by author, April 18, 2008; author interviews with David Krane, April 18, 2008, and with Marissa Mayer, September 18, 2008; and from Google video of headquarters, provided by Google.

6 *25.2 billion Web pages:* WorldWideWebSize.com, February 2, 2009.

7 *It was Google's ambition:* Schmidt and Page speech at Stanford on May 1, 2002, as seen on YouTube.

7 *several hundred million daily searches:* Schmidt and Page speech at Stanford on May 1, 2002, as seen on YouTube.

7 *the number of daily searches is now 3 billion:* internal Google documents.

7 *"our business is highly measurable":* author interview with Eric Schmidt, September 15, 2008.

8 *$3 million spent: Advertising Age,* September 11, 2008.

8 *$172 billion spent in the United States on advertising, and the additional $227 billion spent on marketing:* Zenith OptimediaReport, April 2009.

9 *Mayer . . . remembered the meeting vividly:* author interview with Marissa Mayer, September 18, 2008.

9 *"If Google makes":* author interview with Eric Schmidt, April 16, 2008.

9 *"the long tail":* Chris Anderson, the *Long Tail: Why the Future of Business Is Selling Less of More,* Hyperion, 2006.

10 *"aggregate content":* author interview with Larry Page, March 25, 2008.

10 *from a peak daily newspaper circulation:* Nicholas Carr, *Big Switch: Rewiring the World, From Edison to Google,* Norton; and The Project for Excellence in Journalism, "State of the News Media Report," March 2007.

10 *those networks . . . attract about 46 percent of viewers:* Nielsen data on the 2008–9 season, May 2009.

12 *"The innovator's dilemma":* Clayton M. Christensen, *Innovator's Dilemma,* Harvard Business School Press, 1997.

12 *"Your choices suck":* author interview with Mel Karmazin, May 13, 2008.

12 *"I will believe in the 500-channel world":* Sumner Redstone speech before the National Press Club, October 19, 1994.

13 *Vinod Khosla . . . once told:* "An Oral History of the Internet," *Vanity Fair,* July 2008.

13 *"a tsunami":* author interview with Craig Newmark, January 11, 2008.

14 *Nielsen reported:* The Nielsen Company, "Three Screen Report," May 2008.

14 *In 2008, more Americans:* press release from the Pew Research Center for People & the Press, December 23, 2008.

14 *the number one network television show:* Nielsen Media Research.

14 *an estimated 1.6 billion:* Universal McCann study, "Wave.3," March 2008, and John Markoff, the *New York Times,* August 30, 2008.

14 *newspapers, which traditionally claimed nearly a quarter:* JackMyers.com.

14 *lost 167,000 jobs: Advertising Age* report from the Bureau of Labor Statistics, February 18, 2008.

14 *two hundred billion dollars:* Myers Advertising and Marketing Investment Insights, annual advertising spending forecast, September 15, 2007.

14 *plunge below 20 percent:* McCann Erickson Worldwide chart of percentage of ad dollars by media, 1980-2007.

15 *it took telephones seventy-one years . . . just five years:* Progress & Freedom Foundation report, January 16, 2008, and "The Decade of Online Advertising," DoubleClick, April 2005.

15 *thirty-four technology stocks:* charts provided to the author by Yossi Vardi.

15 *1 million job applications:* author interview with Lazslo Bock, August 22, 2007.

15 *Its revenues . . . from advertising and other Google statistics:* Google's SEC filing for fiscal year ending December 31, 2007, Google Amendment No. 9 to Form S-1, filed with the SEC August 18, 2004, and Google 10-K filed with the SEC, December 31, 2008.

16 *daily advertising impressions:* Google Product Strategy Meeting attended by the author, April 16, 2008.

16 *Google's hundreds of millions of daily auctions:* reported in its Google 10-K SEC filing for the year ending December 31, 2007.

16 *index contained:* Google's third-quarter earnings report, October 16, 2008.

16 *billions of pages per day:* Google internal documents for March 2008, presented at an April 16, 2008, Google Product Strategy Meeting attended by the author.

16 *tens of billions:* May 2007 revenue report, the Interactive Advertising Bureau.

16 *YouTube . . . twenty-five million unique daily visitors; DoubleClick posted seventeen billion:* Eric Schmidt presentation to Google employees, April 28, 2008.

16 *Google's ad revenues in 2008:* "Media Spending 2006–2009 Estimates," JackMyers.com, January 29, 2008.

16 *"We began":* Google 10-K filed in 2008 for the period ending December 31, 2007.

16 *"We are in the advertising business":* author interview with Eric Schmidt, October 9, 2007.

17 *likens Google to . . . Andy Kaufman:* author interview with Marc Andreessen, May 5, 2007.

17 *"I sometimes feel":* author interview with Eric Schmidt, March 2, 2007.

17 *seventy million dollars:* Adam Lashinsky, "Where Does Google Go Next?" *Fortune,* May 26, 2008, and confirmed by Google.

18 *conveys a sense of freedom:* author interview with Krishna Bharat, September 12, 2007.

18 *Burning Man's ten stated principles:* Burning Man Web site.

18 *"Google is a cross":* author interview with Peter Norvig, August 21, 2007.

18 *She described the culture as "flat":* author interview with Stacy Savides Sullivan, August 21, 2007.

19 *the best U.S. company to work for: Fortune,* January 2008.

19 *salaries are modest:* SEC 14-A filing, March 24, 2009.

19 *stock option grants:* Google 10-K filed with the SEC for the fiscal year ending December 31, 2008.

19 *more applicants are accepted by Harvard . . . packet about each:* author interviews with Lazslo Bock, August 22, 2007, Leesa Gidaro, September 12, 2007, and David Drummond, March 25, 2008, and Google orientation for new employees, October 8, 2007, attended by author.

20 *consisted of 130 people:* author interview with David Krane, August 22, 2007.

20 *a total of eight hours of his time:* author interview with a senior executive at Google.

20 *a blog explaining why he left:* "Why Designer Doug Bowman Quit Google," Google Blogoscope, March 21, 2009.

20 *"knowledge workers":* author interview with Hal Varian, March 28, 2008.

20 *"In some ways":* author interview with Paul Buchheit, June 9, 2008.

21 *user experience matters most:* author interview with Matt Cutts, August 20, 2007.

21 *"church/state wall":* author interview with Larry Page, March 25, 2008.

21 *four thousand dollars a day:* Jason Calacanis blog from AdSense, July 28, 2008.

21 *one thousand employees have received this subsidy:* supplied to the author by Google.

22 *"moral force":* author interview with Eric Schmidt, June 11, 2008.

22 *"great values":* author interview with Al Gore, June 10, 2008.

23 *"How can you":* author interview with Eric Schmidt, September 12, 2007.

23 *Winograd . . . recounted a discussion at a TGIF:* author interview with Dr. Terry Winograd, September 16, 2008, confirmed by another Google executive.

CHAPTER 2: Starting in a Garage

27 *revenues that would reach . . . laptop PCs:* time line on Microsoft.com.

27 *I visited Gates:* author interview with Bill Gates, 1998, for my book *World War 3.0 Microsoft and Its Enemies,* Random House, 2001.

28 *"a reflexive belief":* author interview with John Battelle, March 20, 2008.

28 *"a penchant for pushing boundaries":* "The Story of Sergey Brin," *Moment,* February 2007.

28 *Accounts of Michael and Eugenia Brin's life in the Soviet Union and Sergey Brin's boyhood from:* author interview with Brin, September 18, 2008; *Google Story,* David A. Vise and Mark Malseed, Bantam Dell, 2005; Mark Malseed, "The Story of Sergey Brin," *Moment,* February 2007; and Guy Rolnik, "I've Been Very Lucky in My Life," Haaretz.com, May 24, 2008.

30 *"a nerd" . . . "pretty inspiring":* author interview with Brin, September 18, 2008, and Brin interview with the Academy of Achievement, a Museum of Living History, in Washington, D.C., October 28, 2000.

30 *he was non-practicing . . . "I was never comfortable with that":* Guy Rolnik, "I've Been Very Lucky in My Life," Haaretz.com, May 24, 2008.

30 *the couple stood in bathing suits:* Guy Rolnik, "I've Been Very Lucky in My Life," Haaretz, May 24, 2008.

30 *"What part of your success":* author interview with Sergey Brin, September 18, 2008.

31 *treated by faculty as a peer . . . maybe become a professor:* author interview with Brin, September 18, 2008.

31 *"he passed all his tests":* author interview with Craig Silverstein, September 17, 2007.

31 *"We were offended":* author interview with Sergey Brin, September 18, 2008.

32 *Larry was born:* e-mail exchange with Larry Page, April 24, 2009.

33 *Larry was inspired . . . by a biography of Nikola Tesla:* author interview with Page, March 25, 2008; John Battelle, *Search: Inside Story of How Google and Its Rivals Rewrote the Rules of Business,* Portfolio, 2005.

33 Page discusses childhood and Tesla in speech to the 2005 graduating class of engineers at the University of Michigan; http://disruptionmatters.com/2007/12/14/larry-pages-commencement-speech-at-the-2005-university-of-michigan/.

33 *"I knew I was going to build a company eventually":* Larry Page interview with the Academy of Achievement, a Museum of Living History, in Washington, D.C., October 28, 2000.

33 *his grandfather, an assembly-line worker:* author interview with Larry Page, March 25, 2008.

33 *"My dad actually said to me":* Larry Page speech to graduates at the engineering school of the University of Michigan, 2005.

33 Larry Page discusses his grandfather, parents, and college years as the commencement speaker at the University of Michigan graduation ceremonies, May 2, 2009, and available online.

34 *"I kept complaining":* Page in *Michigan Engineer*, Spring/Summer 2001.

34 *he was on the orientation team:* author interview with Sergey Brin, September 18, 2008.

35 *"I was thinking: what if we could download the whole Web":* Larry Page speech at University of Michigan graduation ceremonies, May 2, 2009 (available online).

35 *Larry downloaded:* John Battelle, *Search*, Portfolio, 2005.

35 *fifteen million people:* Mary Lu Carnevale, "The World-Wide Web," *Wall Street Journal*, November 15, 1993.

36 *memo to Bill Gates:* Nathan P. Myhrvold, "Impact of the Internet," November 15, 1994, gathered by the author for a May 12, 1997, profile of Myhrvold in *The New Yorker*.

36 *Myhrvold presciently warned:* Nathan P. Myhrvold, "No More Middleman: The Broad Impact of the Internet," November 27, 1995.

36 *Bill Gates galvanized his troops:* "The Internet Tidal Wave," May 25, 1995, and available via a Google search.

36 *"In this report":* Mary Meeker and Chris DePuy, *The Internet Report*, HarperBusiness, 1996.

37 *"He had a dial-up Web connection":* author interview with Mary Meeker, January 23, 2009.

37 *twenty-two billion dollars on wireless services:* Mark Landler, "An Aerial Assault on the Wired Nation," in the *New York Times*, February 26, 1996.

37 *he drew a distinction between incremental changes:* Nathan P. Myhrvold, "Upcoming Sea Changes," January 29, 1995.

37 *"how things work":* author interview with Terry Winograd, September 25, 2007.

37 *"the paradox of technology":* Donald A. Norman, *Design of Everyday Things*, Basic Books, 1988.

37 *an obsession of Larry's:* author interview with Larry Page, March 25, 2008.

38 *disdained games like golf:* author interview with Omid Kordestani, April 15, 2008.

38 *"two swords sharpening each other":* author interview with John Battelle, March 20, 2008.

38 *"they were not":* author interview with Terry Winograd, September 25, 2007.

38 *Page and Brin's breakthrough: Search,* John Battelle.

39 *"they didn't have this false respect":* author interview with Rajeev Motwani, October 12, 2007.

39 *snuck onto the loading dock:* author interview with Terry Winograd: September 16, 2008.

39 *"We wanted to finish school":* Page and Schmidt appearance at Stanford, May 1, 2002, available on YouTube.

40 *"You guys can always come back":* author interview with Larry Page, March 25, 2008; confirmed in a May 5, 2008 e-mail to the author from Jeffrey Ullman.

40 *They chose the name Google:* Sergey Brin interview with John Ince on PodVentureZone, January 2000.

40 *"two important features":* Page and Brin, "The Anatomy of a Large-Scale Hypertextual Web Search Engine"; a printed version, "The PageRank Citation Ranking: Bringing Order to the Web," was published January 29, 1998, and is available on the Web.

40 *"Brin and Page . . . are expressing a desire":* Nicholas Carr, *Big Switch: Rewiring the World, From Edison to Google,* W. W. Norton & Company, 2008.

41 *"They were . . . part of an engineering tribe":* author interview with Lawrence Lessig, March 30, 2009.

41 *"This is going to change the way":* author interview with Rajeev Motwani, October 12, 2007.

41 *"free of many of the old prejudices":* Nicholas Negroponte, *Being Digital,* Alfred A. Knopf, Inc., 1995.

42 *"Fortunately, I had taken up lock picking":* author interview with Sergey Brin, September 18, 2008.

42 They *"thought it was sleazy":* author interview with Rajeev Motwani, October 12, 2007.

43 *"I'll take stock":* author interview with Craig Silverstein, September 17, 2007.

43 Information about Google's early days in 1998 from author interviews with Ram Shriram, September 16, 2008, and June 12, 2008; Craig Silverstein, September 14, 2007, and September 17, 2007; Jeff Bezos, July 9, 2008; Sergey Brin, September 18, 2008; and Susan Wojcicki, September 10, 2007, and April 16, 2008.

45 *ten thousand search queries:* Google's "Google Milestones" chronology.

45 *Search really "does have a potential":* Karsten Lamm, *Stern,* January 1999.

CHAPTER 3: Buzz but Few Dollars (1999–2000)

46 *one million dollars received from its four initial investors:* Google's IPO document, August 2004.

46 *Google had indexed only about 10 percent . . . five hundred thousand daily:* author interview with Marissa Mayer, August 21, 2007.

47 *"a graduate-student Disneyland":* Michael Specter, "Search and Deploy: The Race to Build a Better Search Engine," *The New Yorker,* May 29, 2000.

47 *A green Ping-Pong table . . . " 'Do you speak?' ":* author interviews with Marissa Mayer, March 25, 2008, and November 4, 2008.

47 *five-million-dollar penthouse . . . in Palo Alto:* Julian Guthrie, "Googirl," *San Francisco Magazine,* March 2008, confirmed by a close colleague of hers.

48 *"we need a business plan":* author interview with Ram Shriram, September 16, 2008.

48 *"a binder on what other companies were doing":* author interview with Salar Kamangar, March 27, 2008.

48 *Kordestani was a perfect fit . . . "It was a very thoughtful process":* author interview with Omid Kordestani, April 15, 2008.

49 *Drummond remembers:* author interview with David Drummond, September 11, 2007.

50 *David Krane was working . . . "the Interlochen uniform":* author interview with David Krane, April 18, 2008.

51 *"Google wanted to create":* Ruth Kedar blog entry, January 15, 2008.

52 *Ron Conway . . . "more famous than I am!":* author interview with Ron Conway, March 25, 2008.

52 *Danny Sullivan . . . "science" of their search results:* author interviews with Danny Sullivan, August 27, 2007, and March 20, 2008.

53 *"had a purist view":* author interview with Ram Shiram, September 16, 2008.

53 *Barry Diller . . . "wildly self-possessed":* author interview with Barry Diller, March 3, 2009.

53 *the founders "were on a mission":* author interview with Susan Wojcicki, September 10, 2007.

54 *They set out to recruit:* author interview with Ram Shriram, September 16, 2008. Another account of the negotiations with Kleiner Perkins and Sequoia was provided by John Heilemann in *GQ*, March 2005.

54 *Doerr remembers the meeting vividly:* author interview with John Doerr, September 18, 2008.

54 *"devotion to their dream":* author interview with Michael Moritz, August 23, 2007.

55 *"The understanding when we invested":* author interview with Michael Moritz, August 23, 2007.

55 *"I think of him as Kobe Bryant":* author interview with Ram Shriram, June 12, 2008.

55 *They also held their first press conference:* Google home movie, June 7, 1999, shared with author by Google.

56 *"Big deal":* author interview with Sergey Brin, September 18, 2008.

56 *"We got overwhelmed with traffic":* author interview with Craig Silverstein, September 17, 2007.

56 *figure out how to block pornography searches:* author interview with Matt Cutts, August 20, 2007.

57 *called in a real estate agent:* author interview with Susan Wojcicki, April 16, 2008.

57 *"Chef Audition Week":* author interview with Marissa Mayer, March 25, 2008.

57 *"The fat found in fish":* interview with Charlie Ayers, Advancedengineeringbd .com, March 23, 2008.

57 *"I think they were a little bit perturbed":* author interview with Sergey Brin, October 10, 2007.

58 *The first place in the valley Al Gore visited . . . "It was hilarious!":* author interview with Al Gore, June 10, 2008.

58 *At around 4:30 . . . "Which prize?":* author attended this and all other Google TGIF's described.

59 *Doerr described Sergey:* author interview with John Doerr, September 18, 2008.

60 *game show: To Tell the Truth*, March 10, 2001, available on YouTube.

60 *"Larry can be a little raw":* author interview with Megan Smith, April 17, 2008.

60 *a fashionable cocktail party:* author attended party for 23andMe, September 9, 2008.

61 *7 million searches a day:* Google Web site.

61 *NASDAQ . . . fell 78 percent:* "How the Web Was Won," *Vanity Fair*, July 2008.

61 *"As in any successful venture":* author interview with Hal Varian, March 27, 2008.

61 *revenues would total $19.1 million:* Google August 2004 IPO filing with the SEC.

61 *"zero discussion":* author interview with Salar Kamangar, March 27, 2008.

61 *an encounter around this time with Page and Brin and Bill Gross:* John Battelle, *Search*, Portfolio, 2005.

62 *established Google as Yahoo's official search engine:* Randall Stross, *Planet Google: One Company's Audacious Plan to Organize Everything We Know*, Simon & Schuster, 2008; also Vise and Malseed and Battelle books.

62 *3.7 million shares:* Google's Form-1 Registration Statement from IPO filing, August 2004.

62 *"It was really about the quality of the search":* author interview with Danny Sullivan, March 20, 2008.

63 *moving too gingerly for Doerr and Moritz:* author interview with Doerr, September 18, 2008, and Moritz, August 23, 2007.

64 *"They thought everyone . . . was a clown":* author interview with Paul Buchheit, June 9, 2008.

64 *"they wanted a fellow intellectual":* author interview with Omid Kordestani, April 15, 2008.

64 *"they were not convinced":* author interview with Marissa Mayer, November 4, 2008.

64 *"They resisted hiring ordinary people":* author interview with Micheal Moritz, August 23, 2007.

64 *"All of us on the board":* author interviews with Ram Shriram, June 12, 2008, and September 16, 2008, and with Michael Moritz, August 23, 2007, and March 31, 2009.

65 *"It was chaos":* author interview with Tim Armstrong, February 28, 2008.

65 *The founders interviewed two computer scientists:* author interview with Marissa Mayer, November 4, 2008.

65 *indexed one billion Web pages:* Google Web site.

65 *$19 million . . . $14.6 million:* Google Form S-1, filed with the SEC on August 18, 2004.

CHAPTER 4: Prepping the Google Rocket (2001–2002)

66 *five billion songs:* Apple press release, June 2008.

66 *ten million entries:* Google search of Wikipedia.

67 *Don't settle:* Larry Page speech at Stanford University, May 1, 2002, available via a link on Page's Wikipedia page.

67 *"the real turning point":* author interview with Craig Silverstein, April 14, 2008.

67 *one senior engineer "had 130 direct reports":* author interview with Eric Schmidt, April 16, 2008.

67 *Doerr . . . thought his friend Eric Schmidt might be a perfect fit:* author interview with John Doerr, September 18, 2008.

67 *Brin had called Schmidt:* author interview with Eric Schmidt, April 16, 2008, and June 11, 2008.

68 *"They started going at it":* author interview with Eric Schmidt, October 9, 2007.

68 *Schmidt was born:* author interview with Eric Schmidt, June 11, 2008.

70 *Schmidt was paid a salary of $250,000:* Google's Form S-1 IPO Registration, August 18, 2004.

70 *The "three of them must agree":* author interview with Eric Schmidt, October 9, 2007.

70 *"Eric doesn't have a huge ego":* Stewart Alsop, quoted in *Search*, John Battelle.

70 *"I think it's inappropriate to comment":* author interview with Eric Schmidt, October 9, 2007.

70 *Instead of wearing:* author interview with Eric Schmidt, October 9, 2007.

71 *"They became office mates":* author interview with Rajeev Motwani, October 12, 2007.

71 *"He found a way":* author interview with Omid Kordestani, April 14, 2008.

71 *"had outgrown its usefulness":* author interview with Craig Silverstein, September 17, 2007.

71 *"Larry is shy . . . Sergey did all the talking":* author interview with Eric Schmidt, October 9, 2007.

72 *"In exchange for sitting down with me":* Search, John Battelle.

72 *Schmidt became Google's "catcher":* author interview with Eric Schmidt, October 9, 2007.

72 *"I don't know what a catcher does":* author interview with Sergey Brin, September 18, 2008.

72 *"He made us better understand":* author interview with Marissa Mayer, November 4, 2008.

73 *"I'll call you Monday morning":* author interview with Eric Schmidt, October 9, 2007.

73 *He kept Page and Brin "focused":* author interview with Paul Buchheit, June 9, 2008.

73 *Semel's arrival aroused the righteous anger:* Richard Siklos, "When Terry Met Jerry, Yahoo," *New York Times*, January 29, 2006.

73 *"Terry brought two things":* author interview with Bobby Kotick, August 17, 2008.

74 *"Semel did not know":* author interview with Ron Conway, March 25, 2008.

74 *"Help me with something" . . . "they did not want to sell":* author interview with Terry Semel, July 10, 2008; confirmed by author interview with Eric Schmidt, March 26, 2008.

75 *"Don't be evil":* author interviews with Paul Buchheit, June 9, 2008, and David Krane, November 3, 2008; *Search*, John Battelle.

75 *"Do you think Hitler thought he was evil?":* author interview with Andy Grove, August 20, 2007.

76 *"Most people who worked with me":* author interview with Eric Schmidt, June 11, 2008.

76 *"In all the years":* author interview with John Doerr, September 18, 2008.

76 *"He had a slow start":* author interview with Ram Shriram, September 16, 2008.

77 *a superb 2008 Fortune* **magazine piece:** Jennifer Reingold, *Fortune*, July 21, 2008.

77 *Doerr discusses Campbell:* author interview with John Doerr, September 18, 2008.

78 *a rare 2007 interview:* Lenny T. Mendonca and Kevin D. Sneader, "Coaching Innovation: An Interview with Intuit's Bill Campbell," *McKinsey Quarterly*, 2007.

78 *"Bill's contribution":* author interview with Michael Moritz, August 23, 2007.

78 *"were both impatient":* author interview with Ram Shriram, September 16, 2008.

79 *"I would sit with Larry":* author interview with Bill Campbell, March 26, 2008.

79 *"Sometimes when you are in a big and complex organization":* author interview with Bill Campbell, March 26, 2008.

79 *Likens Campbell to "a shrink" and "Bill took me under his wing":* author interview with Eric Schmidt, October 8, 2007.

79 *"he has the unique ability":* author interview with Larry Page, March 25, 2008.

79 *"especially high EQ":* author interviews with Sergey Brin, September 18, 2008, and March 26, 2008.

80 *"He's closer to us than the board":* author interview with David Krane, April 18, 2008.

80 *management "is a marathon":* author interview with Larry Page, March 25, 2008.

80 *"This is family for me . . . changing the world":* author interview with Bill Campbell, October 8, 2007.

81 *To better understand Bill Campbell Jr.:* author interview with Bill Campbell, March 26, 2008.

81 *"I really felt like I committed":* author interviews with Bill Campbell, June 11, 2008, September 16, 2008, and November 6, 2008, where he discusses his philosophy and biography.

83 *Although Jobs . . . Scully changed his mind:* Jennifer Reingold interview with John Scully in *Fortune*, July 21, 2008.

84 *"He's been incredibly important in the valley":* author interview with Marc Andreessen, September 15, 2008.

85 *one of Schmidt's initial targets . . . "all things take care of themselves":* author interviews with Sheryl Sandberg, September 10, 2007, and September 18, 2008.

87 *"Before Sheryl arrived":* author interview with Mary Meeker, January 23, 2009.

87 *Advertising . . . had not been viewed "as a priority":* author interview with Eric Schmidt, October 9, 2007.

87 *offered five million dollars:* author interview with Matt Cutts, August 20, 2007.

88 *"Google was really trying":* author interview with Benjamin A. Schachter, February 15, 2008.

88 *the effort at Sandberg was now working on:* author interview with Sheryl Sandberg, October 11, 2007.

88 *What Google was quietly exploring . . . monitor the results online:* author interviews with Salar Kamangar, March 27, 2008; Marissa Mayer, March 25, 2008; Susan Wojcicki, April 16, 2008; Hal Varian, March 27, 2008; and Sheryl Sandberg, September 18, 2008.

90 *Israeli entrepreneur Yossi Vardi:* author interview with Sergey Brin, September 18, 2008; Brin interview, Haaretz.com, June 2, 2008.

90 *"AdWords is brilliant":* author interview with Nathan Myhrvold, March 28, 2008.

91 *The effort was led and architected by Susan Wojcicki:* author interview with Susan Wojcicki, April 16, 2008.

91 *"basically turned the Web into a giant Google billboard":* Danny Sullivan, quoted by Jefferson Graham, "The House That Helped Build Google," *USA Today,* July 5, 2007.

91 *"He and an engineer" . . . "You see why I work with these people":* author interview with Eric Schmidt, September 12, 2007.

91 *a marketing budget of two hundred thousand dollars:* author interview with Susan Wojcicki, April 16, 2008.

92 *"probably was an accident":* Larry Page lecture at Stanford University, May 1, 2002.

92 *"It changed the way content providers think":* author interview with Susan Wojcicki, April 16, 2008.

92 *$7 million:* Google's Form S-1 filed with the SEC, August 18, 2004.

92 *"Now we could fund":* author interview with Urs Hölzle, September 10, 2007.

CHAPTER 5: Innocence or Arrogance? (2002–2003)

94 *"Google would be a defining company":* author interview with Eric Schmidt, September 17, 2007.

94 *"If we solve search":* Larry Page speech to Stanford University's 2002 class, available via a link on Page's Wikipedia page.

95 *"No one knew who Google was":* author interview with Lynda Clarizio, June 4, 2008.

95 *"I want us to bid to win":* author interview with Susan Wojcicki, April 16, 2008.

95 *"We could have gone bankrupt":* author interview with Sergey Brin, September 18, 2008.

95 *"Overture offered more money":* author interview with Robert Pittman, February 29, 2008.

95 *"Every time you did a search":* author interview with Nick Grouf, February 15, 2008.

95 *"affected how we thought":* author interview with Tim Armstrong, February 28, 2008.

95 *"What are you going to do":* author interview with Eric Schmidt, September 17, 2007.

96 *a "super librarian":* Larry Page speech at a press lunch prior to Google's annual shareholder meeting, attended by author, May 10, 2007.

96 *"We call up Al Gore":* author interview with Eric Schmidt, September 17, 2007.

96 *"I sampled college students":* author interview with Dan Clancy and Adam Smith, September 11, 2007.

96 *"If we had done that":* author interview with Sergey Brin, March 26, 2008.

97 *"We overlap a lot":* author interview with Sergey Brin, October 11, 2007.

97 *"He is also a principal proponent":* author interview with Laszlo Bock, March 24, 2008.

97 *"on the user end experience":* author interview with Bill Campbell, October 8, 2007.

97 *"brings more of an operational focus":* author interview with Craig Silverstein, September 17, 2007.

97 *"We're pretty lucky":* author interview with Sergey Brin, October 11, 2007.

97 *"What both bring":* author interview with Nick Fox, September 11, 2007.

98 *Brin was introduced . . . "She was a clear hire":* author interview with David Drummond, March 25, 2008, and with Sergey Brin, March 26, 2008.

98 *"Amid the surreal oddity of it":* e-mail exchange between the author and Alissa Lee, March 20, 2009.

98 *buying a Boeing 767:* author interview with John Doerr, September 18, 2008.

100 *"huge debate over Gmail":* author interview with Terry Winograd, September 25, 2007.

100 *"an unprecedented invasion says Electronic Privacy group":* ZDNet, May 4, 2004.

100 *"broaden horizons":* author interview with Krishna Bharat, September 12, 2007.

101 *"making copies and taking pieces":* author interview with Jim Kennedy, February 21, 2008.

101 *"there is nothing naïve about these guys":* author interview with the AP's Tom Curley, February 21, 2008.

102 *"This is a company":* author interview with Eric Schmidt, March 26, 2008.

102 *"Google is driven by engineers":* author interview with Gordon Crovitz, April 27, 2007.

102 *"Larry and Sergey didn't like management":* author interview with Eric Schmidt, April 16, 2008.

103 *"The biggest milestone":* author interview with John Doerr, September 18, 2008.

104 *Google's employee roster:* IPO filing, August 2004.

104 *Its new campus:* Google form 10-K, filed with the SEC for end of fiscal 2007.

CHAPTER 6: Google Goes Public (2004)

105 *To grow, Google needed to investment capital:* author interview with Eric Schmidt, October 8, 2007.

105 An excellent account of the process Google followed in devising its IPO can be found in Vise and Malseed's *Google Story.*

106 *"It seemed to me vaguely undemocratic":* author interview with John Doerr, September 18, 2008.

106 *"I didn't want to take a position":* author interview with Ram Shriram, September 16, 2008.

106 *consulting with Barry Diller:* author interview with Larry Page, March 25, 2008.

106 *"A Letter from the Founders":* contained in Google's S-1 Registration Statement with the SEC, August 2004.

107 *"We were concerned":* author interview with Larry Page, March 25, 2008.

107 *"Holy shit":* author interview with David Krane, November 4, 2008.

108 *"Will it break one hundred dollars?":* author interview with Marissa Mayer, November 4, 2008.

108 *The stock reached $108.31 . . . to its employees:* SEC Form S-1, August 2004.

109 *Even Bonnie Brown:* Stefanie Olsen, CNET News, January 23, 2008.

110 *"We began as a technology company":* Google IPO, SEC form 3-1, August 2004.

110 *two hundred million dollars in 2003:* author interview with Benjamin Schachter, February 15, 2008.

110 *"In a second":* author interview with Matt Cutts, March 26, 2008.

111 *"suggests that while Microsoft":* John Markoff, "Why Google Is Peering Out, at Microsoft," *New York Times,* May 3, 2004.

111 *"we believe that our user focus":* Google IPO, August 2004.

112 *"Being less experienced":* author interview with Larry Page, March 25, 2008.

112 *"A lot of it is common sense":* author interview with Sergey Brin, September 18, 2008.

112 *"They wanted to replicate the Stanford culture":* author interview with Ram Shriram, June 12, 2008.

112 *"They predicted things that did not make sense to me":* author interview with Urs Hölzle, September 10, 2007.

112 *"Their clear, coherent point of view":* author interview with Terry Winograd, September 25, 2007.

112 *"The number of times they made me change my opinion":* author interview with Rajeev Motwani, October 12, 2007.

113 *the construct framed by Eric Steven Raymond:* Eric Steven Raymond, "The Cathedral and the Bazaar," found at http:/www.catb.org/-esr/writings/cathedral-bazaar/.

113 *Page and Brin actually have more experience:* author interview with Eric Schmidt, September 12, 2007.

113 *"quintessential Montessori kids":* author interview with Marissa Mayer, August 21, 2007.

114 *"question everything":* Larry Page speech at University of Michigan, 2005.

114 *"There's kind of a strength in the duo":* author interview with Bill Campbell, October 8, 2007.

114 *"We agree eighty to ninety percent of the time":* author interview with Sergey Brin, March 26, 2008.

114 *"If we both feel the same way . . . we're probably right":* author interview with Larry Page, March 25, 2008.

114 *strength "to be different":* author interview with Susan Wojcicki, September 10, 2007.

114 *"having a mental sparring partner":* author interview with Jen Fitzpatrick, September 12, 2007.

114 *"Having the two of them being completely in sync":* author interview with Omid Kordestani, September 12, 2007.

114 *"to force a conversation":* author interview with Eric Schmidt, September 12, 2007.

115 *"Some companies would be worried":* author interview with Sheryl Sandberg, October 11, 2007.

115 *"people saw values we believed in":* author interview with Craig Newmark, January 11, 2008.

115 *the reason the troika "works is that whoever you go to":* author interview with Sheryl Sandberg, October 11, 2007.

116 *"Eric is the leader for the company":* author interview with Sergey Brin, October 11, 2007.

116 *"I can't imagine":* author interview with Bill Campbell, October 8, 2007.

116 *"A balanced appreciation":* author interview with Dan Rosensweig, February 27, 2008.

116 *"It borders on insulting":* author interview with Elliot Schrage, October 12, 2007.

116 *"catcher":* author interviews with Eric Schmidt, September 12, 2007, and October 9, 2007.

116 *At the press lunch:* post-Zeitgeist lunch attended by author, October 11, 2007.

117 *"the best business partner":* annual Google shareholder meeting attended by author, May 10, 2007.

117 *"Eric is the person who said":* author interview with Sheryl Sandberg, October 11, 2007.

117 *"I've become a huge cheerleader":* author interview with Michael Moritz, March 31, 2009.

118 *an incident at the 2005 World Economic Forum:* author interview with Andrew Lack, October 4, 2007.

118 *"no recollection of the specific incident":* e-mail from Arthur Sulzberger, Jr., April 29, 2009.

118 *"Schmidt confirmed Lack's account":* author interview with Eric Schmidt, April 1, 2009.

118 *"Here's the part you don't see":* author interview with Bill Campbell, April 1, 2009.

119 *"We're smart guys":* author interview with Terry Winograd, September 25, 2007.

120 *"privacy concerns":* Google IPO, August 2004.

CHAPTER 7: The New Evil Empire? (2004–2005)

122 *a faux documentary by two young journalists: EPIC 2014* available on YouTube.

122 *"evil empire":* author interview with Sheryl Sandberg, October 10, 2007.

122 *"Did not begin until Google went public":* author interview with Eric Schmidt, April 16, 2008.

122 *It took Microsoft fifteen years:* time line on Microsoft.com.

123 *"There's that same 'think big' attitude":* Steven Lurie, quoted in Gary Rivlin, "Relax, Bill Gates; It's Google's Turn as the Villain," *New York Times*, August 24, 2005.

123 *their "moon shot":* Jeffrey Toobin, "Google's Moon Shot," *The New Yorker*, April 18, 2007.

123 *"Google decides not to use that content":* Copies of Google library contracts with the University of Michigan and the University of California, 2006.

124 *"copyduty":* Kevin Kelly, "Scan This Book!" *New York Times Magazine*, May 14, 2006.

124 *"People don't buy books":* author interview with Sergey Brin, March 26, 2008.

125 *"Google went to libraries":* author interview with Richard Sarnoff, January 16, 2008.

125 *He mentioned "the huge risk":* author interview with Paul Aiken, February 14, 2008.

126 *"Fair use is as important a right as copyright infringement":* author interviews with David Drummond, September 11, 2007, and March 25, 2008.

126 *"finding a way to move forward":* author interview with John Hennessy, June 9, 2008.

127 *"If they had a copyright lawyer":* author interview with Tim Wu, September 20, 2007.

127 *"Our patents, trademarks, trade secrets":* Google IPO prospectus, 2004.

127 *"I think that's true":* author interview with Megan Smith, April 17, 2008.

128 *"We're a technology company":* author interview with David Eun, September 18, 2007.

128 *"It's probably both":* author interview with Paul Aitken, February 14, 2008.

128 *"The first thing he said was":* author interview with Mel Karmazin, May 13, 2008.

128 *That year, Yahoo generated profits of $1.1 billion:* Richard Siklos, "When Terry Met Jerry, Yahoo" *New York Times*, January 29. 2006.

129 *Google acquired fifteen smaller digital companies:* financial results for 2005 available on Google.com.

129 *The circulation of daily newspapers . . . fall more steeply:* Newspaper Association of America Web site.

129 *falling 20 percent on average:* Dick Edmonds, "A Bad Year for Newspaper Stocks—a Worse Year for the Gray Lady," *Poynter Online,* January 12, 2006.

130 *U.S. content and software companies lost:* Alan Cane, "Attacking the Pirates," *Financial Times,* February 28, 2007.

130 *About one billion songs per month:* Ethan Smith, "Sales of Music, Long in Decline, Plunge Sharply," *Wall Street Journal,* March 21, 2007.

130 *"I don't believe they have any incentive":* author interview with Sir Howard Stringer, February 8, 2008.

130 *three years earlier, in 2002:* National Cable and Telecommunications Association.

130 *The radio industry was also squeezed:* "Digitalization of the Media Industry: How Close to a Tipping Point?," The Kreisky Media Consultancy, May 6, 2006.

131 *concern about "market power":* author interview with Irwin Gotlieb, June 2, 2008.

131 *"In Google's 2004 annual report":* Annual 2004 report to shareholders from Larry Page and Sergey Brin, spring of 2005.

131 *the founders gave old-media executives more cause for concern:* annual letter to shareholders from Larry Page and Sergey Brin, 2004.

132 *"We told the pilots to head to London":* author interview with Sergey Brin, March 26, 2008.

132 *"he offered a number":* author interview with Jonathan Miller, February 12, 2008.

133 *Microsoft spurned the advice:* Robert A. Guth, "Microsoft Bid to Beat Google Builds on a History of Misses," *Wall Street Journal,* January 16, 2009.

133 *"thinking they had the deal done":* author interview with Tim Armstrong, February 28, 2008

133 *Google and AOL reached agreement:* Google and Time Warner AOL press release, December 20, 2005.

134 *"so fearful of Google":* Mylene Mangalindan and Robert A. Guth, "EBay Talks to

Microsoft, Yahoo About a Common Foe: Google," *Wall Street Journal*, April 21, 2006.

134   *"more like us than anyone":* Fred Vogelstein interview with Bill Gates, *Fortune*, April 18, 2005.

134   *If a user searched Tianamen Square:* Peter Bazalgette, *Guardian*, August 17, 2008.

134   *Four years later, at Google's annual shareholder meeting:* meeting on Google campus, May 8, 2008.

135   *comply with the government of Thailand:* Seth Mydans, "Agreeing to Block Some Videos, YouTube Returns to Thailand," *New York Times*, September 1, 2007.

135   *"There is no question":* Elliot Schrage testimony before the Committee on International Relations of the U.S. House of Representatives, February 15, 2006.

135   *"It took me awhile":* author interview with Eric Schmidt, April 1, 2009.

136   *"CNET was banished": Planet Google*, Randall Stross, September 2008.

137   *"Because it was last minute":* author interview with Sergey Brin, March 26, 2008.

137   The Washington Post *depicted the poor reception as a snub:* Arshad Mohammed and Sara Kehaulani, "Google is a Tourist in D.C., Brin Finds," *Washington Post*, June 7, 2006.

137   *"composed of ideological technologists":* author interview with Elliot Schrage, October 12, 2007.

138   *"One can make the argument":* author interview with Elliot Schrage, September 19, 2008.

138   *"in an important way, they are the same":* author interview with Lawrence Lessig, September 11, 2007.

CHAPTER 8: Chasing the Fox (2005–2006)

144   *sixteen million monthly visitors; that number would quadruple over the next fourteen months:* ComScore, *BusinessWeek,* November 5, 2007.

144   *"Sumner told Tom he did not want to get into a bidding war":* Julia Angwin, *Stealing Myspace: The Battle to Control the Most Popular Website in America*, Random House, 2009.

144   *"I think we have replaced MTV":* Tom Anderson in *Der Spiegel*, cited in Bill Wise, Search Insider, January 22, 2007, and Lotta Holmström in Grassroot Media, January 21, 2007.

145   *"I left":* author interview with Albie Hecht, January 15, 2008.

146   *2005 study of media usage:* "Generation M: Media in the Lives of 8-18 Year-Olds," A Kaiser Family Foundation Study, March 2005.

146   *A later study:* Forrester Research report chart on YouTube and Internet use, *Wall Street Journal*, November 19, 2008.

147   *Jason Hirschhorn was another Viacom refugee:* author interviews with Jason Hirschhorn, February 12 and 21, 2008, and e-mail exchanges, March 2009.

149   *Marc Andreessen has spent much of his life . . . an investor and board member:* author interviews with Marc Andreessen, May 9, 2007, and June 9, 2008.

150   *They named the site Ning:* author interview with Andreessen, March 30, 2009.

150   *"I wouldn't be sitting here without him":* author interview with Gina Bianchini, September 15, 2008.

150 *"You can talk about the economy":* author interview with Ben Horowitz, February 20, 2009.

152 *thirty-four million monthly viewers:* Nielsen/NetRatings, August 2006.

152 *"When we started":* author interview with Chad Hurley, September 11, 2007.

153 *"If that works":* author interview with Eric Schmidt, June 11, 2008.

153 *"Right now":* Steve Ballmer Q&A with the editors of *BusinessWeek,* October 11, 2006.

153 *thirteen of the twenty most popular videos:* Kevin J. Delaney and Matthew Karnitschnig, *Wall Street Journal,* February 21, 2007.

153 *"There are some issues with YouTube":* Redstone on Charlie Rose, quoted in the *New York Times,* October 10, 2006.

153 *"They can buy anything":* author interview with Irwin Gotlieb, June 2, 2008.

154 *"YouTube was an admission by Google":* author interview with Danny Sullivan, March 20, 2008.

154 *"They didn't value our content":* author interview with Jeff Zucker, April 25, 2008.

154 *"Every time we thought we came down":* author interview with Phillipe Daumann, May 1, 2007.

155 *"no revenue at the time":* author interviews with Eric Schmidt, October 8, 2007, and June 11, 2008.

155 *"give the majority of revenue to them":* Larry Page at a small press lunch attended by the author, May 10, 2007.

155 *"theft":* author interview with Phillipe Daumann, May 15, 2008.

155 *"it gets redistributed":* author interview with Jeff Bewkes, April 10, 2008.

156 *"I don't need somebody else to say":* author interview with Phillipe Daumann, May 15, 2008.

156 *willing to believe that Google "was well intentioned":* author interview with Jeff Bewkes, April 10, 2008.

156 *"You either find a way":* author interview with Albie Hecht, January 15, 2008.

157 *"Content is where people spend their time":* author interview with Herbert Allen III, January 24, 2007.

157 *"I figured that if things go well":* author interview with Robert Iger, May 17, 2007.

157 *"The first thing I did":* author interview with Robert Iger, May 17, 2007.

158 *$44 million in revenues in 2006:* "Spotlight on Television 2.0 Leaders: The Walt Disney Company," IP Media Monitor, October 2006.

159 *"the issue of the moment":* author interview with Steven Rattner, April 24, 2007.

159 *would spread CBS content:* author interviews with Les Moonves, June 12, 2007 and April 7, 2008.

159 *proposed agreement with Yahoo:* author interview with Jeff Fager, September 11, 2008.

161 *"I think Quincy is one of the most advanced thinkers":* author interview with David Eun, June 12, 2008.

161 *He cut it, though, for his first job:* author interviews with Quincy Smith, January 23, April 9, June 9, and June 24, 2008.

163 *CBS clips got twenty-nine million views:* CBS press release, November 21, 2006.

164 *"When you're a small company":* Eric Schmidt, quoted in "Google Gets Friendly," Jeremy Caplan, *Time,* October 1, 2006.

164 *"duplicate detection":* Google News announcement, August 31, 2007.

165 *The average daily circulation:* Audit Bureau of Circulation, October 2006.

165 *thirty-five minutes each day:* author interview with Martin Nisenholtz, September 18, 2008, citing Nielsen report, May 2008.

166 *Advertising in major newspapers:* the Newspaper Association of American and the *New York Times,* July 9, 2007.

166 *the AP's revenues grow annually at about 5 percent:* author interview with Tom Curley, February 21, 2008.

166 *Their conclusions, according to Jeremy Philips:* author interview with Jeremy Philips, May 18, 2007.

167 *At the end of 2006:* Letter from the Founders in Google's 2006 Annual Report, confirmed by Google's annual performance numbers and Quincy Smith testimonial, and available on Google.com.

168 *"I've never seen a company so loved on Wall Street":* author interview with Quincy Smith, January 23, 2008.

CHAPTER 9: War on Multiple Fronts (2007)

169 *"Once you get to a certain size":* author interview with Ivan Seidenberg on February 19, 2008.

169 *"We got frustrated":* author interview with Philipe Daumann, May 1, 2007.

170 *"The law basically said":* *Wired* interview, April 9, 2007.

170 *"a clip site":* author interview with Chad Hurley, September 11, 2007.

170 *"Everything Phillippe said was a lie":* Eric Schmidt tells author at the July 2008 Allen & Co conference in Sun Valley.

171 *"As a business, I think":* author interview with Ester Dyson, February 4, 2008.

171 *"If we're putting up programming for free":* author interview with Mel Karmazin, May 13, 1008.

171 *two websites it knew to be illegally downloading:* according to the February 12, 2007, *Wall Street Journal,* the two Web sites illegally downloading movies were EasyDownloadCenter.com and theDownloadPlace.com.

171 *publicly accused Google of a "cavalier" approach: Financial Times,* March 6, 2007.

171 *Facebook "doubles in size every six months":* author interview with Mark Zuckerberg, August 22, 2007.

173 **Remix: Making Art and Commerce Thrive in the Hybrid Economy:** Lawrence Lessig, Penguin Books, 2008.

174 *"They want to be the digital advertising network":* author interview with Herbert Allen III, January 24, 2007.

174 *gave Google "an opportunity to be the infrastructure backbone":* author interview with Wenda Harris Millard, April 26, 2007.

174 *"You can dive deep into that data":* Randall Rothenberg quoted in the *New York Times,* April 14, 2007.

174 *"track more than 100 metrics":* DoubleClick brochure, "Best Practices for Maximizing Web Advertising Effectiveness," September 19, 2007.

174 *twenty billion online ads each day:* author interview with David Rosenblatt, April 22, 2008.

175 *envisioned three advantages for Google:* author interview with Tim Armstrong, October 10, 2007.

176 *"We'd like to create one-stop shopping":* author interview with Richard Holden, August 20, 2007.

176 *"Instead of just selling remnant advertising":* author interview with David Rosenblatt, April 22, 2008.

176 *Irwin Gotlieb did see DoubleClick and its ad exchange as a potential disruptor:* author interview with Irwin Gotlieb, February 11, 2008.

177 *"In four decades in the advertising business":* author interviews with Irwin Gotlieb, February 11, 2008, May 21, 2008, June 2, 2008, September 26, 2008, and April 2009 e-mails.

179 *"In Hollywood, a screening room is a show-off room":* author interview with Michael Kassan, December 15, 2008.

180 *"take our client data":* author interview with Sir Martin Sorrell, February 18, 2008.

180 *The way it works:* author interview with Keval Desai, April 14, 2008.

181 *"It is absolutely our intention to be in every cable box":* author interview with Eileen Naughton, February 28, 2008.

182 *"Yes, he's right":* author interview with Terry Semel, July 9, 2008.

182 *conceded that "the roles will start shifting":* author interview with Smita Hashim, April 17, 2008.

182 *"to remind people why they love Google":* author interview with Andy Berendt, April 22, 2008.

183 *"If Google could introduce us":* author interview with Beth Comstock, May 2, 2007.

183 *"It raises issues":* Sir Martin Sorrell quoted in the *New York Post,* April 23, 2007.

183 *"worried about Google becoming large":* author interview with Tim Wu, September 20, 2007.

184 *"When I decide to go to the movies":* author interview with Eric Schmidt, October 8, 2007, and Schmidt interview in London, *Financial Times,* May 23, 2007.

184 *"I am really excited to tell you":* Google third quarter conference call, October 19, 2007

184 *two-day "Zeitgeist" conference:* author attended October 10, 2007.

185 *"the number one" privacy issue:* author interview with Sergey Brin, October 11, 2007.

CHAPTER 10: Waking the Government Bear

186 *public interest advocate, Jeffrey Chester:* author interviews with Jeff Chester, September 27, 2007, and October 15, 2007.

187 *"Why does Google need to collect all of this information?":* author interview with Marc Rotenberg, October 15, 2007.

187 *"behavioral targeting":* Arik Hesseldahl, "A Rich Vein for 'Reality Mining,'" *BusinessWeek,* May 5, 2008.

188 *Phorm:* Louis Story, "A Company Promises the Deepest Data Mining Yet," *New York Times,* March 20, 2008; BBC interview with Tim Berners-Lee posted on the Web by Richard Defendorf, March 17, 2008; and Nikki Talt and Tim Bradshaw,

"Brussels to Investigate Consumer Profiling by Online Advertisers," *Financial Times*, March 30, 2009.

189 *"If you're searching for an SUV":* author interview with Irwin Gotlieb, February 8, 2008.

189 *In its five-page Checkout privacy policy:* Google Checkout and Google privacy policies found on Google.com.

190 *"In 1984":* author interview with Lawrence Lessig, September 11, 2007.

190 *In its 2007 annual ranking:* press release from *Financial Times* and Millward Brown, April 23, 2007.

191 *"Privacy is one of those third rails":* author interview with Randall Rothenberg, January 10, 2008.

191 *"Unfortunately":* author interview with Eric Schmidt, October 9, 2007.

192 *"We think of the ad as content":* author interview with Jeff Huber, September 12, 2007.

192 *"There's nobody watching the store":* author interview with Jeff Chester, October 15, 2007.

193 *"We're working on expanding":* Eric Schmidt, October October, 19 2007.

193 *"opt-in":* author interview with Marc Rotenberg, October 15, 2007.

194 *"How many people yesterday":* author interview with Sergey Brin, October 11, 2007.

194 *"When you pay $1.6 billion":* author interview with Nick Grouf, May 15, 2008.

195 *"crumbled cookies":* Google announcement, July 16, 2007.

195 *"The product brand was very strong":* author interview with Alan Davidson, October 15, 2007.

195 *"they were almost alone":* author interview with Gigi Sohn, October 3, 2007.

196 *"We've been under the radar":* author interview with David Drummond, September 11, 2007.

196 *"No question that people here regularly discuss Microsoft's experience":* author interview with Elliot Schrage, October 12, 2007.

196 *"Microsoft is a bit of an unusual company":* author interview with Sergey and Brin, October 11, 2007.

196 *"In the end":* author interview with Beth Comstock, May 2, 2007.

197 *"I would say always":* author interview with Larry Page, March 25, 2008.

197 *Google had a great year in 2007:* January 31, 2008 Google press release found on Google.com.

197 *Twenty countries:* annual founders' letter, March 26, 2008.

197 *"We're an engineering company":* author interview with Sheryl Sandberg, October 7, 2007.

197 *"basic principles":* Eric Schmidt August 21, 2007 keynote address to the Progress and Freedom Foundation dinner available on YouTube.

198 *"That's probably correct":* author interview with Eric Schmidt, October 9, 2007.

198 *"Google if it were a person":* author interview with Tim Wu, September 20, 2007.

CHAPTER 11: Google Enters Adolescence (2007–2008)

199 *$868.6 million in stock in 2007:* Google 10-K filed with the SEC for the fiscal year ended December 31, 2007.

200 *"If you want to talk to Larry or Sergey":* author interview with Megan Smith, April 17, 2008.

200 *"Larry is going to take one side":* author interview with Tim Armstrong, February 28, 2008.

200 *Brin and Page were to meet with an engineering team:* GPS meeting, attended by author, October, 9, 2007. The ground rule was that any description of product discussed or engineer names had to be cleared with Google, which it was.

202 *"I'd make people describe things in English!":* author interview with Terry Semel, July 9, 2008.

203 *"I hope they try":* author interview with Sergey Brin, October 11, 2007.

203 *"self-imposed, bureaucratic response":* author interview with Larry Page, March 25, 2008.

203 *Page on Moore's law as management tool:* author interview with Larry Page, March 25, 2008.

204 *"a one-trick pony":* Steve Ballmer interview, *Financial Times*, June 20, 2008.

204 *"Google is extremely good with search":* author interview with Irwin Gotlieb, February 11, 2008.

204 *"'Where is the new pony?'":* author interview with Tad Smith, April 9, 2008.

204 *"I like the trick!":* author interview with Eric Schmidt, April 16, 2008.

204 *"a legitimate question":* author interview with Elliot Schrage, March 25, 2008.

204 *search advertising was slowing:* decline reported by ComScore from *BusinessWeek*, March 10, 2008.

205 *it had plunged 40 percent:* Google stock price from the *Wall Street Journal*, March 28, 2008.

205 *"Goodbye, Google":* Wendy Tanaka, Forbes.com, March 26, 2008.

205 *"more relevant":* author interview with Tim Armstrong, February 28, 2008.

205 *"The clicks are not what is relevant":* author interview with Hal Varian, March 27, 2008.

205 *"Google INC's GO-GO era":* Kevin J. Delaney, *Wall Street Journal,* April 18, 2008, and Miguel Helft, *New York Times,* April 18, 2008.

205 *Google hogged three quarters of all U.S. search:* search marketing firm Efficient Frontier, quoted in *BusinessWeek*, May 19, 2008.

205 *one of every three videos viewed online:* from ComScore as reported by the Jim Dalrymple, IDG News Service, March 17, 2008.

206 *The impact of this new medium:* author interview with Steve Grove of YouTube, April 15, 2008.

206 *"they'll never make money":* author interview with Irwin Gotlieb, June 2, 2008.

206 *"start working on monetizing it":* author interview with Eric Schmidt, March 26, 2008.

206 *"highest priority":* Eric Schmidt, CNBC interview, April 30, 2008.

207 *the iPhone delivered fifty times more search queries:* Google presentation by Deepak Anand, mobile marketing manager, May 2008.

207 *"As compared to the internet model":* Larry Page, October 10, 2007.

207 *Google's mobile quarterback was Andy Rubin:* author interview with Andy Rubin, March 24, 2008.

208 *"Since we think we have the most reliable network"*: author interview with Ivan Seidenberg, February 19, 2008.

210 *"they've provoked the bear"*: author interview with Ivan Seidenberg, February 19, 2008.

210 *At Apple board meetings*: author interview with Eric Schmidt, March 26, 2008.

210 *"We had the very good fortune"*: tape watched by author of All Hands staff meeting addressed by Eric Schmidt, April 28, 2008.

211 *"a planning process"*: author interview with Eric Schmidt, September 12, 2007.

211 *It was still talking to cable companies*: author interview with Eric Schmidt, April 16, 2008.

211 *if the cable companies could get together they would have "a Google-type ability"*: author interview with Jeff Bewkes, April 10, 2006.

212 *"The browser becomes the operating system"*: author interview with Christophe Bisciglia, September 19, 2008.

212 *YouTube was silenced for several hours on February 24, 2008*: Jane Spencer, "How a System Error in Pakistan Shut YouTube," *Wall Street Journal*, February 26, 2008.

213 *In its annual letter to shareholders*: annual Google founders' letter, March 26, 2008.

213 *They pledged to divert*: Dr. Larry Brilliant, 2.0 Conference attended by author in San Francisco, November 5, 2008.

214 *"Google gets more health questions"*: author interview with Dr. Roni Zieger, March 27, 2008.

214 *in a March 2008 speech*: Eric Schmidt speech, March 1, 2008.

214 Brin and Page declaration that Google's mission is to "Be good," and their pledge to gift Google Earth to relief organizations and to subsidize solar power from their joint appearance at the Sixth Annual Global Philanthropy Forum, April 11, 2007, and is available on YouTube.

214 *"If it were a person"*: founders' letter, December 31, 2004, Google annual report.

215 *"The story of Google today"*: author interview with Danny Sullivan, August 27, 2007.

215 *"Google's become a big company"*: author interview with Paul Buchheit, June 9, 2008.

215 *"Google did not invent YouTube"*: author interview with Scott Heiferman, January 25, 2008.

215 *Growing too big and losing focus*: author interview with Omid Kordestani, September 12, 2007.

215 *"For the last year my biggest worry"*: small press lunch with Eric Schmidt and founders attended by author after annual Google shareholder meeting, May 10, 2007.

216 *What to do about massage therapists*: author interview with Eric Schmidt, March 26, 2008.

216 *"from time to time"*: author interview with Larry Page, March 25, 2008.

218 *Schmidt defends management chaos*: author interview with Eric Schmidt, September 12, 2007.

219 *"a genius like Steve"*: author interview with Al Gore, June 10, 2008.

219 *"That can be stated as criticism":* author interview with Eric Schmidt, March 26, 2008.

219 *"Peanut Butter Manifesto":* Brad Garlinghouse memo to Yahoo executives, November 18, 2006, and available on the Web.

221 *"I am very disappointed in Eric Schmidt":* author interview with roger McNamee, April 27, 2008.

221 *"Google is in a great position":* author interview with Marc Andreessen, March 27, 2008.

221 *"Google is a precocious company":* author interview with Tim Wu, September 20, 2007.

222 *"I worry about complexity":* author interview with Sergey Brin, October 10, 2008.

222 *"I don't think I'm worried about advertising pressure":* author interview with Sergey Brin, March 26, 2008.

222 *"He had a vision":* author interview with Richard Sarnoff, January 16, 2008.

223 *three hundred million dollars in company stock:* Miguel Helft, *New York Times,* August 29, 2007.

223 *"Sheryl created AdWords":* author interview with Roger McNamee, April 27, 2008.

223 *Google offered her the CFO job:* author interview with Eric Schmidt, March 26, 2008.

223 *"Sheryl is a person who balances":* author interview with Elliot Schrage, March 25, 2008.

224 *Facebook had 123 million unique visitors:* Kevin Allison, *Financial Times,* June 23, 2008.

224 *half a billion dollars:* Microsoft/Viacom joint press release, December 19, 2007.

224 *"in a little shadow boxing":* author interview with Marc Andreessen, June 9, 2008.

225 *"Is Google's culture great":* Adam Lashinsky, "Google Is No. 1: Search and Enjoy," *Fortune,* January 29, 2007.

226 *"controlled chaos":* author interview with Ram Shriram, June 12, 2008.

226 *"I'd prefer 'less structured'":* author interview with Sergey Brin, March 26, 2008.

226 *"They had to go to another meeting":* author interview with Al Gore, June 10, 2008.

226 *"They had their own method":* author interview with Barry Diller, March 3, 2009.

227 *"There is a pattern in companies":* author interview with Larry Page, March 25, 2008.

CHAPTER 12: Is "Old" Media Drowning? (2008)

229 *On a sunny July afternoon:* the account of Iger, Chernin, and Mooves dialogue at Sun Valley from two eyewitnesses.

229 *"The era when I worked at ABC":* author interview with Michael Eisner, June 19, 2008.

229 *"If you read every piece":* author interview with Sir Howard Stringer, February 8, 2008.

229 *I asked then CEO Nobuyuki Idei:* author conversation with Nobuyuki Idei in 2004 in New York at which no notes were taken (thus no quote marks) but at which he knew he was speaking to a reporter who had interviewed him before.

230 *"It's fair":* author interview with Edgar Bronfman, Jr., July 5, 2007.

230 *15 million copies:* Jeffrey Cole keynote speech to the Monaco Media Forum, "State of the Mediasphere," November 12, 2008.

230 *3.7 million sales:* Nielsen Scan reports from chart in the *Wall Street Journal,* December 19, 2008.

230 *In 2007, worldwide digital music sales rose:* the International Federation of the Phonographic Industry, as reported in the *New York Times,* January 25, 2008.

230 *dive to $9 billion:* Forester Research report carried in the *Silicon Alley Insider,* February 20, 2008.

231 *"I never experienced any real restraints":* "Ripped from the Headlines: *Times* Editors Speak Out," *Los Angeles Times Magazine,* May 12, 2008.

231 *In 2007, newspaper advertising:* Richard Perez-Pena, *New York Times,* February 7, 2008.

231 *Business magazines:* author interview with John Huey, December 5, 2007.

232 *newspaper revenues in 2007 totaled sixty billion dollars:* author interview with Jim Kennedy, February 21, 2008.

232 *drop 87 percent:* newsroom job cuts reported regularly throughout 2008; Gannett stock drop from Reuters, April 17, 2009.

233 *"The cold our customers caught":* author interview with Thomas Glocer, June 5, 2008.

233 *"gets about 20 percent of our revenues":* author interview with Tom Curley, February 21, 2008.

233 *by 2008 Reuters had 2,600 reporters:* author interview with Thomas Glocer, June 5, 2008.

234 *lost 10 to 30 percent of their revenues:* Murdoch at annual All Things Digital Conference attended by author, May 27–28, 2008.

234 *only one of the top twenty-five newspapers to gain:* the Audit Bureau of Circulations six-month report on the circulation of 395 daily newspapers, April 27, 2009.

234 *"What really is going on":* author interview with Tad Smith, April 9, 2008.

234 *"There is a systematic change":* author interview with Eric Schmidt, March 26, 2008.

235 *"in so much better shape":* author interview with Paul Aiken, February 14, 2008.

235 *"has fallen dramatically":* "To Read or Not to Read: A Question of National Consequence," National Endowment for the Arts, November 19, 2007.

236 *revenues began a steady decline in 2006:* radio revenue declines reported by Jon Fine based on the Radio Advertising Bureau's data, *BusinessWeek,* March 10, 2008.

236 *$162.1 billion in 2008:* Group M, March 30, 2009.

237 *online advertising was soaring:* Interactive Advertising Bureau.

237 *"the long tail":* author interview with Nick Grouf, May 15, 2008.

238 *poor spent $180 per month on media services:* Annenberg Study from Jeffrey Cole

keynote speech to the Monaco Media Forum, November 12, 2008, and available on YouTube; and from author interview with Irwin Gotlieb, June 5, 2008.

238 *"We're not like a car":* author interview with Michael Lynton, April 6, 2008.

239 *When Robert Pittman cofounded MTV in 1981:* author interview with Robert Pittman, February 29, 2008.

240 *"at least two percentage points"*: author interview with Les Moonves, October 14, 2008.

240 *"as an advertising opportunity":* Brian Stelter, "In the Age of Tivo and Web Video, What Is Prime Time?" *New York Times,* May 12, 2008.

240 *Smith said CBS had about two hundred partners:* author interview with Quincy Smith, June 9, 2008.

240 *$600 million for CBS in 2008:* Ron Grover, "CBS's Moonves Has Big Plans for CNET," *BusinessWeek,* September 8, 2008.

241 *"If the story is really good":* author interview with Michael Eisner, June 19, 2008.

241 *"do a lot of snacking":* author interview with Jason Hirshhorn, February 12, 2008.

CHAPTER 13: Compete or Collaborate?

243 *"The economics around these digital properties":* Scott Kirsner, "NBCU Chief Addresses Harvard Business School," *Variety,* February 27, 2008.

243 *"not the right way to look at it":* author interview with David Rosenblatt, April 22, 2008.

243 *Microsoft, like Viacom, treated Google as an outright enemy:* "Inside Microsoft's War Against Google," *BusinessWeek,* May 19, 2008.

243 *There were reasons for Microsoft to pursue Yahoo:* a good account of the negotiations can be found in Matthew Karnitschnig and Robert A. Guth front page story in the *Wall Street Journal,* July 2, 2008.

244 *Ballmer and Yang met privately:* the annual D conference attended by author, May 27–30, 2008.

244 *Yahoo shareholders were bludgeoned:* Nick Wingfield and Jessica E. Vascellaro, "Ballmer Kills Hopes for Bid, Pummeling Yahoo Shares," *Wall Street Journal,* November 20, 2008.

244 *"sooner rather than later":* Nick Wingfield, "Ballmer Seeks Quick Yahoo Deal," *Wall Street Journal,* December 6, 2008.

245 *"The two biggest forces":* author interview with Roger McNamee, August 22, 2008.

245 *"unnerving":* Sergey Brin to Jordan Robertson of the AP, February 19, 2008.

245 *"If Microsoft wanted to do a business deal":* author interview with Eric Schmidt, April 16, 2008.

245 *"It gives them a tool":* author interview with Eric Schmidt, April 16, 2008.

245 *"the Yahoo business deal":* author interview with Eric Schmidt, September 15, 2008.

246 *They petitioned the Justice Department:* Susanne Vranica and Jessica E. Vascellaro, "Big Marketers Challenge Google-Yahoo Deal," *Wall Street Journal,* September 8, 2008.

246 *"If you look at our products":* press lunch briefing during Zeitgeist attended by author and Brin and Page, September 17, 2008.

247 *Brin stepped to a microphone:* Sergey Brin presentation to Google Zeitgeist conference, attended by author, September 17, 2008.

248 *The Justice Department did finally intervene:* "Yahoo-Google Deal Opposed," *Wall Street Journal,* September 16, 2008.

248 *"Microsoft":* author interview with Phillipe Daumann, May 15, 2008.

248 *"We're always better off":* author interview with Irwin Gotlieb, May 21, 2008.

248 *At Microsoft's annual two-day forum:* Microsoft's Advertising Leadership Forum, attended by author, May 19–21, 2008.

249 *"They've been saying it for a while":* author interview with Irwin Gotlieb, May 21, 2008.

249 *"maybe a genius idea":* author interview with Yusuf Mehdi, May 19, 2008.

250 *"If consumers perceive":* author interview with Sir Martin Sorrell, May 30, 2008.

250 *64.1 percent:* Nielsen Online, January 5, 2009.

250 *"All attempts by Microsoft":* author interview with Eric Schmidt, September 15, 2008.

250 *In WPP's annual report:* Sir Martin Sorrell letter to shareholders, WPP 2007 annual report, May 2008.

250 *"to develop the constructive side of our relationship":* account of Sir Martin Sorrell Cannes panel in Cannes, David Kaplan, *Ad Age,* June 20, 2008; and Eric Pfanner, *International Herald Tribune,* June 22, 2008.

250 *Google's 2008 national sales conference:* attended by author, June 11, 2008.

250 *"Because our customers must talk":* author interview with Eric Schmidt, September 15, 2008.

252 *"Google Version 2.0: The Calculating Predator":* Stephen E. Arnold, Infonortics Ltd., August 2007.

252 *The gruff Arnold, who responded to a phone call:* author interview with Stephen Arnold, March 17, 2008.

253 *"lean in":* author interview with David Calhoun, June 25, 2008.

254 *Mayer has one of the most important jobs:* author attended Marissa Mayer office hours and interviewed her afterward on September 18, 2008.

255 *"I think they're naïve":* author interview with Quincy Smith, June 9, 2008.

256 *"The CBS deal is one":* author interview with Eric Schmidt, September 15, 2008.

256 *To try to calm agency fears:* Brian Stelter, "Some Media Companies Choose to Profit from Pirated YouTube Clips," *New York Times,* August 16, 2008.

256 *"The audience is telling you what they like":* author interview with David Eun, June 12, 2008.

257 *in October 2008, it reached an accord with the U.S. publishing industry:* Google and the Association of American Publishers and the Authors Guild joint October 28, 2008, press release and joint conference call with the press on same date.

258 *"able to search the full text of almost 10 million books":* "Letter from the Founders," Google 2008 annual report, published in April 2009.

258 *"It's a new model for us":* author interview with David Drummond, November 5, 2008.

258 *"It is unfortunate":* Viacom statement reported by CNET, October 28, 2008.

259 *"There is a difference":* author interview with David Drummond, November 5, 2008.

259 *Google's "noncancelable guarantees":* Google 10-K filed with the SEC, December 31, 2008.

259 *"A lot has to do with how much they want":* author interview with David Drummond, November 5, 2008.

260 *dropped 17.7 percent:* Audit Bureau of Circulations report, April 27, 2009.

260 *plunged 11.5 percent:* Magazine Publishers of America, April 14, 2009.

260 *Drop in advertising and ad revenues for various media:* from Advertising and Marketing Investment Forecast, 2006–2010, Jack Myers Advertising and Marketing Investment Insights, March 10, 2009.

260 *"box office revenues rose by 2 percent":* from *Box Office Report,* January 20, 2009.

260 *Book sales:* Motoko Rich, "Declining Book Sales Cast Gloom at an Expo," *New York Times,* May 29, 2009.

260 *Would fall 8 percent:* Group M's semiannual report on ad spending, "This Year, Next Year," April 4, 2009.

260 *"fall by almost 7 percent":* Tim Bradshaw, "Global Ad Spending to Fall 7%, Publicis Unit Warns," *Financial Times,* April 14, 2009.

261 *In a December 2008 report:* Mary Meeker Morgan Stanley report, "Economy/Internet Trends," December 19, 2008.

CHAPTER 14: Happy Birthday (2008–2009)

262 *The first show was a new animation series:* Brooks Barnes, "Google and Creator of 'Family Guy' Strike a Deal," *New York Times,* June 30, 2008.

262 *There was Google AdPlanner: New York Times* and *Wall Street Journal,* June 4, 2008.

262 *There was the exchange of employees:* Ellen Byron, "A New Odd Couple: Google, P&G Swap Workers to Spur Innovation," *Wall Street Journal,* November 19, 2008.

263 *There was a new partnership with General Electric:* Michael Helft, "Idealists and Green Agenda: Environmental Investments Could Pay Off for Google," *New York Times,* October 28, 2008.

263 *Larry Page:* covered extensively in the press and blogosphere.

263 *"YouTube crossed the line":* author interview with David Calhoun, June 25, 2008.

263 *"does not feel safe":* author interview with Terry Semel, July 9, 2008.

263 *"hosts":* author interview with Eric Schmidt, September 15, 2008.

264 *"Knol is not a serious threat to Wikipedia":* Nate Anderson tech blog, January 19, 2009.

264 *A Google invented browser:* official Google Blog announces Chrome, September 1, 2008.

264 *"the defining technological shift of our generation":* Schmidt speech at annual shareholders meeting, May 8, 2008.

264 *"Everything we do is running on the Web platform"*: Larry Page and Sergey Brin at Chrome press conference from Kara Schwisher video blog on All Things D, and from Richard Waters, *Financial Times*, September 2, 2008.

264 *"the most important product"*: author interview with Eric Schmidt, September 15, 2008.

265 *Despite its importance to Schmidt:* Jessica E. Vascellaro and Robert A. Guth, "Google Tackles Microsoft in Launch of Browser," *Wall Street Journal*, September 2, 2008.

265 *"ten thousand iPhone applications:* reproduced in Mary Meeker's Morgan Stanley report, "Economy/Internet Trends," December 19, 2008.

265 *1.6 billion text messages:* Schmidt speaks at annual Google shareholders meeting, May 8, 2008 and viewed on Google.com.

265 *"Because his customers use so many more services"*: author interview with Ivan Seidenberg, October 30, 2008.

266 *"almost a third of all Google searches"*: Brin, "Letter from the Founders," Google 2008 annual report, April 2009.

266 *"I would love to argue"*: author interview with Eric Schmidt, September 15, 2008.

266 *"We're watching it"*: author interview with Ivan Seidenberg, October 30, 2008.

266 *"Privacy is a much noisier issue"*: author interview with Barry Diller, January 10, 2008.

267 *A March 2008 poll:* TRUSTe privacy survey from Stephanie Clifford, "Many See Privacy on Web as Big Issue, Survey Said," *New York Times*, March 16, 2009.

267 *Huxley more relevant than Orwell:* Neil Postman, *Amusing Ourselves to Death: Public Discourse in the Age of Show Business,* Viking Penguin, 1985.

268 *"It's a totally different kind of advertising"*: author interview with Irwin Gotlieb, February 11, 2008.

269 *the November 2008 Web 2.0 Summit:* attended by author, November 5–7, 2008.

269 *The gloom extended to Silicon Valley:* the recession's impact on the valley from a spate of reports, including: Ashlee Vance, "Tech Companies, Long Insulated, Now Feel Slump," *New York Times*, November 15, 2008; Richard Waters and Chris Nuttall, "Optimism Fades as Silicon Valley Suffers Job Losses," *Financial Times*, October 20, 2008; Daniel Lyons, "Down in the Valley," *Newsweek*, October 20, 2008.

271 *He wrote a blog in January 2009:* Michael Arrington, "Some Things Need to Change," TechCrunch.com, January 28, 2009.

271 *"travel" no longer a top search word:* Eric Schmidt, in a speech at Bloomberg headquarters in New York attended by the author, October 20, 2008.

271 *searches for "bankruptcy" had jumped 52 percent:* Jonathan Rosenberg at Google's first quarter earnings call on April 16, 2009.

271 *"most significant thing that happened at Google"*: author interview with Bill Campbell, November 6, 2008.

272 *"While Google's success is hard to dispute"*: author interview with Mary Meeker, January 23, 2009.

272 *"When everything runs well"*: author interview with Patrick Pichette, April 1, 2009.

272 *"Patrick is particularly good"*: Eric Schmidt interviewed by Mary Meeker March 3, 2009, at the Morgan Stanley conference in San Francisco.

272 *a bonus for 2008 of $1.2 million:* Form 8-K, filed with the SEC February 26, 2009.

273 *For the first time, Google was contracting:* Jessica E. Vascellaro and Scott Morrison, "Google Gears Down for Tougher Times," *Wall Street Journal*, December 3, 2008.

273 *"70 percent of newspapers":* Tim Armstrong at press briefing during Zeitgeist attended by author, September 17, 2008.

273 *from $1,425 per month to $2,500:* Joe Nocera, "On Day Care, Google Makes a Rare Fumble," *New York Times*, July 5, 2008.

274 *September 19, 2008, TGIF session:* attended by author.

274 *Google finances in 2008:* Google 10K filed with the SEC, December 31, 2008.

275 *"Display advertising":* author interview with Eric Schmidt, April 1, 2009.

275 *90 million views:* YouTube traffic from Nielsen Media Research, March 2009.

275 *"underwater":* Google 10-K filed with the SEC for the year ending December 31, 2008.

276 *"our safe landing":* author interview with Eric Schmidt, April 1, 2009.

276 *it experienced its first quarter-to-quarter revenue decline:* Google first quarter 2009 results released on April 16, 2009.

276 *"Because it is open source":* author interview with Eric Schmidt, April 1, 2009.

276 *"Although Schmidt disputed this":* Jessica E. Vascellaro, "Google CEO to Keep Seat on Apple Board," *Wall Street Journal*, May 8, 2009.

CHAPTER 15: Googled

282 *"part of people's lives":* Larry Page "The Playboy Interview" with Sergey Brin, *Playboy*, September 2004.

282 *"The Internet":* author interview with Hal Varian, April 1, 2009.

282 *"Fifteen to twenty years ago":* author interview with Michael Moritz, March 31, 2009.

283 *"It's very simple":* author interview with Sergey Brin, October 10, 2007.

283 *"a magic box":* author interview with Marc Andreessen, February 20, 2009.

284 *Google search often sends them 80 to 90 percent of their visitors:* Randall Stross, "Everybody Loves Google, Until It's Too Big," *New York Times*, February 22, 2009.

284 *"Is the company":* Nicholas G. Carr blog, The Google Enigma, January 27, 2008.

284 *Talgam, a renowned Israeli orchestra conductor:* September 18, 2008, presentation at Google Zeitgeist, attended by the author and available on YouTube.

285 *When Patrick Pichette:* author interview with Pichette, April 1, 2009.

285 *"the networked world":* Anne-Marie Slaughter, "America's Edge: Power in the Networked Century," *Foreign Affairs*, January/February, 2009.

286 *"Googly":* author interview with Laszlo Bock, March 24, 2008.

286 *"It's hard for me to know":* author interview with Larry Page, March 25, 2008.

286 *Marissa Mayer claimed that half of Google's products:* Marissa Mayer keynote speech March 15, 2008, to the SIGCSE, available online.

287 *The snickers:* David Pogue, "One Number to Ring Them All," *New York Times*, March 12, 2009.

288 *"the biggest company in history"*: Chris Anderson, *Free: The Future of a Radical Price,* Hyperion, 2009.

288 *Many Valley companies:* author interview with Bill Campbell, March 26, 2008.

288 *Stanford President:* author interview with John Hennessy, June 9, 2008.

288 *Page and Brin have acknowledged:* Adam Lashinsky, *Fortune,* January 29, 2007.

288 *Google has a pet dog policy:* Larry Page May 1, 2002 Stanford speech on YouTube.

288 *The e-commerce site Zappos:* Jeffrey M. O'Brien, "Zappos Knows How to Kick It," *Fortune,* February 2, 2009.

289 *"how does one make money"*: Kevin Kelly, "Better Than Free," Edge.org, February 6, 2008.

289 *"Google is not a conventional company"*: Google IPO filing, August 18, 2004.

290 *"Who would have thought"*: author interview with Steven Rattner, April 22, 2007.

290 *was again ranked:* "The World's 50 Most Admired Companies," *Fortune,* March 16, 2009.

290 *Gates on "creative capitalism"*: Robert A. Guth, "Bill Gates Issues Call for Kinder Capitalism," *Wall Street Journal,* January 24, 2008.

291 *"We believe the Internet"*: Yahoo press release, May 2, 2006.

291 *extols "nerd values"*: Craig Newmark commencement speech to UC Berkeley, May 13 2008; Jim Stengel quote from "Veteran Marketer Promotes a New Kind of Selling," *Wall Street Journal,* October 31, 2008. Account of Harvard Business School pledge in Leslie Wayne, "A Promise to Be Ethical in an Era of Temptation," *New York Times,* May 30, 2009.

292 *"My pause"*: author interview with Tom Glocer, June 5, 2008.

292 *"You can't wait"*: author interview with Peter Thiel, January 29, 2008.

293 *"When I landed"*: author interview with Michael Eisner, June 19, 2008.

293 *"feels incredibly exciting"*: author interview with Jeff Zucker, April 25, 2008.

294 *"All large media companies"*: author interview with Eric Schmidt, June 11, 2008.

295 *Sergey Brin told me that it is Google's willingness to "experiment"*: author interview with Sergey Brin, March 26, 2008.

295 *Google aims "to do everything"*: author interview with Marc Andreessen, March 27, 2008.

295 *"The French regarded"*: Clay Shirky, *Here Comes Everybody: The Power of Organizing Without Organizations,* The Penguin Press, 2008.

CHAPTER 16: Where Is the Wave Taking Old Media?

296 *"If we were having breakfast"*: author interview with Joe Schoendorf, May 10, 2007.

297 *I put America's Home Videos "*: author interview with Robert Iger, May 17, 2007.

297 **"Sometimes you have to guess"**: author interview with Bill Campbell, October 18, 2007.

297 *"The world is moving"*: author interview with Barry Diller, January 10, 2008.

297 *consumers "will happily go along"*: author interview with Irwin Gotlieb, June 2, 2008.

297 *Yossi Vardi, the Israeli entrepreneur:* author interview with Yossi Vardi, February 28, 2008.

298 *Free an "inevitability":* Chris Anderson, *Free: The Future of a Radical Price,* Hyperion, 2009.

298 *This is the answer:* Jeff Jarvis, *What Would Google Do?,* HarperCollins, 2009.

298 *"more than 1 billion clicks":* testimony of Marissa Mayer to hearing of the Senate Commerce Committee's Subcommittee on Communications, Technology, and the Internet, May 6, 2009.

298 *total U.S. ad spending:* Myers Advertising and Marketing Investment Insights.

299 *Newspaper ad revenues:* Zenith Optimedia, March 2009.

299 *"Even Wired Editor":* Chris Anderson, *Free: The Future of a Radical Price,* Hyperion, 2009.

299 *In a February 2009 Time cover story:* Walter Isaacson, "How to Save Newspapers," *Time,* February 16, 2009.

299 *The warning was given life:* Nat Ives, "Time Inc. Helps Out Future of 3-D," *Advertising Age,* March 13, 2009.

300 *page one of the Los Angeles Times* : Stephanie Clifford, "Front of Los Angeles Times Has an NBC 'Article,'" *New York Times,* April 10, 2009.

301 *"Wrestling had bigger audiences":* author interview with Robert Pittman, February 29, 2008.

301 *"I think people are getting":* author interview with Marc Andreessen, June 9, 2008.

301 *Each of the 40,000:* author interview with Scott Heiferman, January 25, 2008.

301 *"one quarter of CBS's":* author interview with Quincy Smith, September 16, 2008.

302 *The online dating service:* author interview with Barry Diller, March 3, 2009.

302 *Mary Meeker predicts:* author interview with Mary Meeker, January 23, 2009.

302 *By mid-2008 China:* "China's Internet Cafes Still Crucial to Online Game Growth," VentureBeat.com, August 17, 2008.

302 *"Piper Jaffray projected":* Matt Richtel and Bob Tedeschi in the *New York Times,* April 6, 2009.

302 *"we want to get credit card numbers":* author interview with MarcAndreessen, March 27, 2008.

302 *"the stealth device":* author interview with Ivan Seidenberg, October 30, 2008.

302 *"social network traffic":* author interview with Eric Schmidt, June 11, 2008.

303 *"We made one really big mistake":* author interview with Dr. John Hennessy, June 9, 2008.

303 *"A lot of people believe that":* author interview with Eric Schmidt, September 15, 2008.

303 *"my current view of the world":* author interview with Eric Schmidt, April 1, 2009.

303 *"newspaper ad dollars":* from the Web site of the Newspaper Association of America.

304 *Many students clamor:* e-mail exchange with Ernest Sotomayor, December 7, 2008.

304 *"many of our students":* e-mail exchange with Nicholas Lemann, September 4, 2008.

304 *"take the* **New York Times***":* financial data from Ken Auletta, "The Inheritance: Can Arthur Sulzberger, Jr., Save the *Times*—and Himself?," *New Yorker,* December 19, 2005.

305 *"the kinds of stories":* author interview with Larry Page, March 25, 2008.

305 *During the wrenching transition to print:* Clay Shirky blog, March 13, 2009.

306 *"Sell it!":* author interview with Marc Andreessen, June 9, 2008.

307 *more than a few papers "will disappear":* Rupert Murdoch speech at the D Conference attended by author, May 28, 2008.

307 *He wrote that newspapers:* Michael Hirschorn, "Get Me Rewrite!" *Atlantic Monthly,* December 2006.

309 *"Apple's iTunes":* author interview with Eric Schmidt, October 8, 2007.

309 *"for newspaper companies":* author interview with Andrew Lippman, February 10, 2009.

309 *"Can you put it behind a wall":* author interview with Marc Andreessen, February 20, 2009.

310 *Attorney General Eric Holder:* Randall Mikkelsen, "U.S. Law Chief Open to Antitrust Aid for Newspapers," Reuters, March 18, 2009.

310 *In 2009, three longtime media executives:* Richard Perez-Pena, "Plans for a Paid Online Media Service," *New York Times*, April 15, 2009.

310 *an online publication:* Jack Shafer, "Hello, Steve Brill, Get Me Rewrite," *Slate.com,* April 17, 2009.

310 *"I don't know how":* author interview with Larry Page, March 25, 2008.

311 *"We've been able":* author interview with Eric Schmidt, March 26, 2008.

311 *income from digital operations:*New York Times Co. financial disclosure for the year ending December 31, 2008.

311 *About half of the About Group's revenues:* two author e-mail exchanges with Arthur Sulzberger, Jr., April 29, 2009.

311 *"The official answer":* author interviews with Eric Schmidt, March 26, 2008 and April 1, 2009.

312 *"Our industry faces":* author e-mail exchange with Arthur Sulzberger, Jr., April 29, 2009.

313 *10 percent of these were downloaded:* author interview with Jeff Bezos, July 9, 2008. When I sought to update this number, Bezos's deputy, Craig Berman, reported in a May 2009 e-mail that it had grown to 35 percent.

313 *What gives publishers pause:* Motoko Rich, "Preparing to Sell E-Books, Google Takes on Amazon," *New York Times,* June 1, 2009.

313 *"Physical books":* Jeff Bezos interviewed at the D Conference attended by author, May 28, 2008, and interview with author, July 9, 2008.

314 *nightly audience has plunged:* nightly news audience decline from Richard Perez-Pena, *New York Times,* May 11, 2009.

314 *Jack Myers projects:* Myers Advertising and Marketing Investment Insights, March 10, 2009.

315 *Neilson reported in early 2009:* Nielsen report on fourth quarter 2008 television and Internet video cited in the *Wall Street Journal*, February 23, 2009.

315 *If four million:* Bobbie Kotick interviewed at D Conference attended by author, May 28, 2008.

315 *"To survive":* author interviews with Quincy Smith, January 23, 2008, and April 9, 2008, May 19 and 25, 2009, and with Les Moonves, July 8, 2009.

316 *The biggest box office:* Brian Stelter and Brad Stone, "Digital Pirates Winning Battle with Major Hollywood Studios," *New York Times*, February 5, 2009.

316 *Sergey Brin described going on a boat in Europe:* author interview with Sergey Brin, March 26, 2008.

317 *So they initiated efforts:* Sam Schechner and Vishesh Kumar, "Cable Firms Look to Offer TV Programs Online," *Wall Street Journal*, February 20, 2009, and interviews with senior television executives.

317 *Eric Schmidt saw a demonstration:* author interview with Eric Schmidt, April 1, 2009, and Sezmi.com.

318 *"We can go directly":* author interview with Ivan Seidenberg, October 30, 2008.

319 *Irwin Gotlieb also dismisses:* author interview with Irwin Gotlieb, February 9, 2009.

321 *"Do you feel bad":* author interview with Eric Schmidt, March 26, 2008.

CHAPTER 17: Where Is the Wave Taking Google?

322 *"When asked to describe the difference":* author interview with Eileen Naughton, February 28, 2008.

322 *"If you can solve search":* author interview with Larry Page available on YouTube, May 1, 2002.

323 *"we scale":* author interview with Sergey Brin, March 26, 2008.

323 *uploading eighty-six thousand full length movies:* "Letter from the Founders," Google 2008 annual report, April 2009.

323 *"Everything Google does":* Bala Lyer and Thomas H. Davenport, "Reverse Engineering Google's Innovation Machine," *Harvard Business Review*, April 2008.

324 *Its social network site:* author interviews with Google executives in Russia, Jason Bush, "Where Google Isn't Goliath," *BusinessWeek*, June 26, 2008.

324 *"These companies air kiss":* author interview with Andrew Lack, October 4, 2007.

324 *Facebook had 200 million users:* author interview with Sheryl Sandberg, March 30, 2009.

324 *"Anybody that gets":* author interview with Bill Campbell, October 8, 2007.

325 *Lee began with:* author interview with Kwan Lee, February 10, 2009.

325 *"lacks a social gene":* author interview with John Borthwick, April 28, 2008.

326 *"If I were Google":* author interview with Danny Sullivan, August 27, 2007.

326 *The problem with horizontal search:* author interview with Jason Calacanus, September 21, 2007.

327 *"the semantic web":* Katie Franklin, "Google May Be Displaced, Said World Wide Web Creator Tim Berners-Lee", *Daily Telegraph*, March 3, 2008.

327 *"hundreds of years away":* author interview with Craig Silverstein, September 17, 2007.

327 *"We are no closer":* author interview with Marc Andreessen, March 27, 2008.

327 *In his provocative book:* Nicholas Carr, *The Big Switch: Rewiring the World, from Edison to Google,* W. W. Norton & Company, 2008.

328 *"this was the thrust"*: Neil Postman, *Amusing Ourselves to Death: Public Discourse in the Age of Show Business*, Viking Penguin, 1985.

328 **Tara Brabazon, a professor:** accounts of Professor Brabazon address in both the *Economic Times* and the *Telegraph*, January 14, 2008.

329 Miguel Helft of the *New York Times* wrote a series of stories in April 2009 on challenges to Google's book settlement; amicus briefs were filed with U.S. District Court Judge Denny Chin on April 13 and 17, 2009.

330 Miguel Heft, "YouTube Blocked in China, Google Says," *New York Times*, March 25, 2009.

330 *"China ordered PC makers"*: "U.S. Makes Official Complaint to China over Internet Censorship," *Financial Times,* June 22, 2009.

331 *"What Google should fear"*: author interview with Yossi Vardi, February 28, 2008.

331 **When Marissa Mayer said:** author interview with Mayer, August 21, 2007.

331 *"What separates us"*: author interview with Stacey Savides Sullivan, August 21, 2007.

331 *"are utopians"*: author interview with Terry Winograd, September 25, 2007.

332 **In the 1990s:** an excellent exploration of long-term capital's demise is contained in Roger Lowenstein's *When Genuis Failed: The Rise and Fall of Long-Term Capital Management,* Random House, 2000.

332 *"'Google returned links"*: Nat Ives, "Media Giants Want to Top Google Results," *Advertising Age*, March 23, 2009.

333 **when Eric Schmidt envisioned:** Miguel Heft, "Google Ends Its Project for Selling Radio Ads," *New York Times*, February 13, 2009.

333 *"They have no experience"*: author interview with Danny Sullivan, March 20, 2008.

333 *"a great company"*: author interview with Fred Wilson, January 22, 2008.

333 *"Google is like that fourteen-year-old"*: author interview with Strauss Zelnick, January 9, 2008.

334 **Although Mary Meeker believes Google is a great company:** author interview with Mary Meeker, January 23, 2009.

334 *"There is nothing about their model"*: author interview with Clayton Christensen, April 17, 2009.

335 *"There is no end in sight"*: author interview with Fred Wilson, January 22, 2008.

335 *"to the falsehood that you can grow"*: author interview with Clayton Christensen, April 17, 2009.